PENGUIN ⊙ CLASSICS

IN THE SOUTH SEAS

ROBERT LOUIS STEVENSON was born in Edinburgh in 1850. The son of a prosperous civil engineer, he was expected to follow the family profession, but was allowed to study law at Edinburgh University. Stevenson reacted strongly against the Presbyterian respectability of the city's professional classes and this led to painful clashes with his parents. In his early twenties he became afflicted with a severe respiratory illness from which he was to suffer for the rest of his life; it was at this time that he determined to become a professional writer. The effects of the often harsh Scottish climate on his poor health forced him to spend long periods abroad. After a great deal of travelling he eventually settled in Samoa, where he died on 3 December 1894. At the time of his death Robert Louis Stevenson was working on his unfinished masterpiece, *Weir of Hermiston*.

Stevenson is most widely known for his fiction, notably *Dr Jekyll and Mr Hyde*, *Treasure Island* and *Kidnapped*, but he also wrote works of non-fiction. These include his descriptive and historical books on the South Seas area *In the South Seas* (1896) and *A Footnote to History* (1892), and *Father Damien* (1890), Stevenson's celebrated defence of a Belgian priest who devoted his life to the care of lepers.

NEIL RENNIE is a Reader in English at University College London and the author of *Far-Fetched Facts: The Literature of Travel and the Idea of the South Seas* (1995).

R. L. STEVENSON

IN THE SOUTH SEAS

Edited with an Introduction and Notes by
NEIL RENNIE

PENGUIN BOOKS

PENGUIN BOOKS

Published by the Penguin Group
Penguin Books Ltd, 27 Wrights Lane, London w8 5TZ, England
Penguin Putnam Inc., 375 Hudson Street, New York, New York 10014, USA
Penguin Books Australia Ltd, Ringwood, Victoria, Australia
Penguin Books Canada Ltd, 10 Alcorn Avenue, Toronto, Ontario, Canada M4V 3B2
Penguin Books (NZ) Ltd, Private Bag 102902, NSMC, Auckland, New Zealand

Penguin Books Ltd, Registered Offices: Harmondsworth, Middlesex, England

First published in book form 1896
Published in Penguin Classics 1998
3 5 7 9 10 8 6 4 2

Introduction and Notes Copyright © Neil Rennie, 1998
All rights reserved

The moral right of the editor has been asserted

Set in 10/12.5pt Monotype Baskerville
Typeset by Rowland Phototypesetting Ltd, Bury St Edmunds, Suffolk
Printed in England by Clays Ltd, St Ives plc

CONTENTS

IN THE SOUTH SEAS

PART I: THE MARQUESAS

ACKNOWLEDGEMENTS

Quotations from Stevenson's MS journals of the *Casco* and *Equator* voyages are by permission of the Huntington Library, San Marino, California, and quotations from Lloyd Osbourne's Diary for 1889 are by permission of the Beinecke Library, Yale University, New Haven, Connecticut. I would like to thank Ernest Mehew for allowing me to see the last two volumes of *The Letters of Robert Louis Stevenson* in proof, and for kindly informing me about the *Auckland Star* versions of Stevenson's South Sea Letters. I would also like to thank for their generous help: John and Winifred Rennie, Hugo Williams, Karl Miller, Philip Horne and Henry Woudhuysen.

Mr Stevenson smiled humorously. 'Treasure Island', he said,
'is not in the Pacific.'

(*Sydney Morning Herald*, 14 February 1890)

In the winter of 1887–8 Robert Louis Stevenson was at Saranac in
the Adirondack Mountains with his mother and his American wife,
Fanny, and stepson, Lloyd Osbourne. Lloyd had toothache, according
to Stevenson's mother's diary, 'and to amuse him Louis plans a yacht
trip, and they discuss all the arrangements even to where the piano is
to stand in the saloon'.[1] Stevenson, on his second visit to America,
was now the famous author of *Dr Jekyll and Mr Hyde*, as well as *Treasure
Island*, and among the editors who came to pay him court was Samuel
S. McClure, a pioneer of press syndication, who 'hears the yacht
mentioned', Mrs Stevenson recorded, 'and is most anxious to join in
the scheme'.[2] According to his *Autobiography*, McClure was reminded
of Stevenson's amusing travel books:

I thought at once of 'An Inland Voyage' and 'Travels with a Donkey,' and
told him that if he would write a series of articles describing his travels, I
would syndicate them for enough money to pay the expenses of his trip. I
think the South Seas must have been mentioned that evening, for I remember
that after I returned to New York I sent him a number of books about the
South Seas, including a South Pacific directory. The next time I went to
Saranac, we actually planned out the South Pacific cruise, talking about it
until late into the night.[3]

Stevenson had already, as a boy, discovered the South Seas in fiction. At the age of twelve he had written a first instalment of 'Creek Island, or Adventures in the South Seas', supposedly 'To be continued'.[4] A few years later, after church one Sunday in Edinburgh, Stevenson introduced himself to R. M. Ballantyne – 'Ballantyne the brave', as he was to call him in the verses prefacing *Treasure Island*.[5] The fifteen-year-old Stevenson declared himself an admirer of *The Coral Island*, which he had read twice, he told Ballantyne, and hoped to read twice more.[6]

Now these South Sea romances were to be transformed into Pacific reality. Lloyd Osbourne remembered how they wintered at Saranac with A. G. Findlay's *Directory for the Navigation of the South Pacific Ocean*:

Such was our reading, such the stuff our dreams were made of as the snow drove against our frozen windows; as the Arctic days closed in, gloomy and wild, and snow-shoes and buffalo coats were put by to steam in corners while we gathered round the lamp. Visions of palms while our ears were yet tingling from the snow we had rubbed on to save them from frost-bite; cascading streams in tropic Arcadies, with water as clear as crystal, while our own bedroom jugs upstairs were as solid as so much rock; undraped womanhood, bedecked with flowers, frisking in vales of Eden, while we were wooled to the neck like polar explorers, and dared not even thaw too quickly for fear of chilblains.[7]

At 5 a.m. on 28 June 1888 the chartered yacht *Casco* passed from San Francisco through the Golden Gate into the Pacific. Captain Otis had read *Treasure Island* but no further in Stevenson's works, as he informed the writer's mother.[8] 'What would you do if Mrs. Stevenson were to fall overboard?' her daughter-in-law asked Otis. 'Put it in the log!' he replied.[9] The *Casco*'s first stop was at Anaho Bay in the north of Nukuhiva, one of the Marquesas Islands, appropriated by the French in 1842. Stevenson was up on deck at 4, waiting for the island to emerge out of the dark on the morning of 20 July, and the *Casco* dropped anchor in the bay about noon.[10] He met the local chiefs and later the Catholic missionaries, who took him to the site of the supposed cannibal feasts of yesteryear and to the school where the boys were prepared for the future with prayers. He was keeping a journal which is more a draft of his travel book than a personal journal.

On 12 August the *Casco* sailed round the island, past the valley described in Herman Melville's *Typee* (1846), to the capital, Taiohae, 'another lovely bay' which reminded Stevenson's mother 'faintly of Rothesay, though without the lovely views outside'.[11] There they visited tattooed 'Queen' Vaekehu, grown slightly deaf, and Stevenson called on the French Resident, M. Delaruelle, who owned a copy of *Treasure Island* from which he hoped to learn English. Seeing Stevenson the next day in one of the shops, M. Delaruelle 'looked in and said: "Voyez-vous, je viens de faire la connaissance de Modestine"', which puzzled the *Casco*'s passengers until M. Delaruelle explained he had become acquainted with *Travels with a Donkey* (named Modestine).[12] Stevenson had much conversation with Stanislaus Moanatini, the adopted son of the Queen, and Fanny taught the Queen to roll cigarettes. Meanwhile the ship's Japanese cook was drunk ashore without leave and was placed in the Taiohae calaboose. A new cook was taken on, Ah Fu, a young Chinese man 'who had been marooned as a boy on [the nearby island of] Hiva Oa', according to Lloyd, 'and was much more of a Marquesan than he was anything else'.[13]

They sailed from Taiohae on 22 August, with the missionary Frère Michel Blanc aboard, and anchored at Tahauku, Hiva Oa, on 23 August. Stevenson, whose health was always precarious, had a headache, but the others visited Atuona, two miles away in the next bay, where Lloyd took photographs and Frère Michel arranged the amusing 'adoption' of Fanny, Lloyd and Margaret Stevenson by a Marquesan family. On Monday 27 August Stevenson rode up to the mountains with Frère Michel but caught a chill. A few days later, on 1 September, another yacht arrived, the *Nyanza*, with a Captain Dewar last encountered fifteen years previously on the French Riviera, and Stevenson caught a fresh chill at dinner on board.

Hoping a change would be good for him, they sailed from Hiva Oa on 4 September, and Stevenson wrote on the 6th to his old Edinburgh friend Charles Baxter: 'I shall have a fine book of travels, I feel sure; and will tell you more of the South Seas after very few months than any other writer has done – except Herman Melville perhaps, who is a howling cheese [i.e. an exemplar of smartness and cleverness]'.[14] After a difficult passage among the islands of the Paumotus (now called Tuamotus), they anchored at Fakarava on 9 September, their first experience of a coral atoll, a thin ring of low land with the ocean on the outside and a lagoon in the middle. They came ashore to be greeted by M. Donat-Rimarau, the half-French, half-Tahitian acting French Vice-Resident, and took a house with three rooms, verandahs front and back, and 'a copy of David Wilkie's "Village School" framed and hanging' in one of the bedrooms.[15] Here, after days spent bathing and collecting shells, in the moonlit evenings when, as Fanny recalled, 'the shadows that fell from the cocoanut leaves were so sharply defined that one involuntarily stepped over them', they sat on mattresses on the verandahs, listening to their regular visitor, M. Donat-Rimarau, and were 'entranced and thrilled by stories of Tahiti and the Paumotus, always of a supernatural character'.[16]

Stevenson had a cold, however, which worsened, and the *Casco* sailed for Tahiti, where there were doctors. The island was sighted at daybreak on 27 September, and Stevenson was taken ashore to a hotel at Papeete, the capital, where the doctor warned of the possibility of a fatal haemorrhage. Stevenson called for Captain Otis and calmly made arrangements for such a circumstance. His condition improved, however, and he moved with Fanny into a rented house, near the ruins of the prison where Melville had been confined in 1842. Meanwhile Lloyd and Stevenson's mother made a typewritten copy of his journal, which he had suspended.

They were unable to leave Papeete until 24 November, when Stevenson decided to visit Taravao on the south coast before sailing on to the islands of Huahine, Raiatea and Borabora in the Leeward Islands. He was ill again at Taravao, so Fanny arranged horses and a wagon and was able to take him to the village of Tautira, on the north-east coast, far from civilized Papeete. Here Stevenson was fed on raw fish in coconut milk by Princess Moe of the Tahitian royal family, and exchanged names with Ori a Ori, otherwise known as Teriitera, the subchief of the village. The *Casco* followed round the coast but Otis found the mainmast dangerously weakened by dry-rot.

While the *Casco* was refitted at Papeete, Stevenson and his family stayed on at Tautira with their Tahitian friends, whose unlimited hospitality moved Stevenson to tears. His health restored, he bathed regularly in the sea, worked on *The Master of Ballantrae*, visited the Anglo-Tahitian Chief Tati at Papara, and from Tati and his friends at Tautira 'got wonderful materials for my book, collected songs and legends on the spot', as he reported to his friend Sidney Colvin at the British Museum.[17]

Because of the delay, the excursion to the Leeward Islands was abandoned and on Christmas Day they sailed from Tautira for Honolulu, where they anchored on 24 January 1889. The *Casco* was met by Fanny's daughter Belle, and Belle's insolvent artist husband Joe Strong, and son Austin, aged eight, who accompanied the passengers from Tautira to a dinner eaten in the bewildering electric light of the Royal Hawaiian Hotel. Stevenson soon decided to send the *Casco* back to San Francisco and took a house near the beach at Waikiki, some four miles from Honolulu, though connected by telephone. There, to the sound of the surf, he resumed work on *The Master of Ballantrae*, running as a serial and requiring an ending, and was frequently interrupted by visits from Hawaiian society and in particular King Kalakaua, a prodigious drinker, who had read *Dr Jekyll and Mr Hyde* as well as *Treasure Island*.[18]

On 26 April, seeking new material for his travel book, Stevenson sailed as a passenger on a steamer to the main island of Hawaii, where he rode around the Kona Coast, delighted to be away for a week from the white society of Honolulu, 'among God's best – at least God's sweetest works – Polynesians'.[19] On 21 May he embarked again from Honolulu, for the leper colony on the island of Molokai, and Fanny wrote to Sidney Colvin, expressing her fears about the South Sea travel book:

Louis has the most enchanting material that any one ever had in the whole world for his book, and I am afraid he is going to spoil it all. He has taken into his Scotch Stevenson head, that a stern duty lies before him, and that his book must be a sort of scientific and historical impersonal thing, comparing the different languages (of which he knows nothing, really) and the different

peoples, . . . and the whole thing to be impersonal, leaving out all he knows
of the people themselves. And I believe there is no one living who has got so
near to them, or who understands them as he does. Think of a small treatise
on the Polynesian races being offered to people who are dying to hear about
Ori a Ori, the making of brothers with cannibals, the strange stories they told,
and the extraordinary adventures that befell us: – suppose Herman Melville
had given us his theories as to the Polynesian language and the probable good
or evil results of the missionary influence instead of *Omoo* and *Typee* . . .[20]

Fanny forgets that *Typee* and *Omoo* contained arguments about the
missionary influence as well as accounts of autobiographical adventures, but asks Colvin to write supporting her, 'otherwise Louis will
spend a great deal of time . . . actually *reading up* other people's books on
the Islands'.[21] Meanwhile Stevenson at the leper colony was ashamed of
his horror at the 'pantomime masks in poor human flesh'.[22] He heard
much, good and bad, about Father Damien, the Catholic priest who
had recently died of leprosy, a man he would later defend from
Protestant scorn, and he played croquet regularly with seven little
leper girls at the girls' boarding-home.

Stevenson was back at Waikiki at the beginning of June, where
preparations were being made for another South Sea cruise instead
of the voyage back to England. His mother would return to Scotland
to attend to an ailing sister, but Joe Strong was to come as photographer,
while Belle and Austin waited in Sydney. In a letter to Colvin, Stevenson
spoke of his plans for his travel book:

By the time I am done with this cruise I shall have the material for a very
singular book of travels: masses of strange stories and characters, cannibals,
pirates, ancient legends, old Polynesian poetry; never was so generous a
farrago.[23]

Whether this reflects Stevenson's own ideas or the influence of Fanny,
it does not sound so very different from Fanny's ideas about the
book. In any case, she informed Colvin (and Fanny Sitwell, Colvin's
companion and future wife) that 'Louis is coming round now to my
view of his book of travels'.[24]

On 24 June, the *Equator*, a trading ship, left Honolulu with Stevenson, Fanny, Lloyd, Joe Strong and Ah Fu aboard, seen off at the wharf by King Kalakaua and his royal band, playing 'Aloha 'Oe'.[25] The *Equator*'s captain, a young Scot in a Tam o' Shanter, dropped the Stevenson family off at the island of Butaritari in the Gilbert Islands (now the Republic of Kiribati) where a fortnight previously the High Chief had lifted a taboo on alcohol – to celebrate American Independence Day – and the islanders were still drunk. While Stevenson blames imported alcohol sold by foreign traders, Fanny writes of 'the entire island' being 'wildly drunk on "sour toddy" ', an indigenous nuisance.[26] Living in the house of a Hawaiian missionary, Stevenson managed to help negotiate a reimposition of the taboo. His family spent some weeks on the island, admired displays of Gilbertese dancing and reciprocated with a magic lantern show of Bible illustrations, inducing delight, faith and occasional mirth.

The *Equator* collected Stevenson and family and they sailed on 10 August and visited the island of Marakei in the central Gilberts, where Stevenson met some of the island traders and observed the politics of relations between missionaries, traders and islanders.[27] He took notes in his journal of the stories he was told about the traders and beach-combers, grisly tales of murder and gin, and was charmed by the domestic bliss of one murderer, who had ripped open the belly of another trader, and now doted on a New Hebridean wife and three little daughters in 'three sizes of Rob Roy Macgreggor frocks'.[28] From Marakei the *Equator* sailed to the island of Abaiang, and was headed for Nonouti and Tabiteuea in the southern Gilberts when the wind veered and the course was changed for Abemama, the island ruled by High Chief Tem Binoka, which they reached on 30 August. Tem Binoka had accommodation constructed – or, more accurately, transported – for them. As Lloyd recalled:

An Apemama house . . . is a sort of giant clothes basket . . . with a peaked roof, and standing on stilts about a yard high. With a dozen pairs of human legs under it, you can steer it to any spot you like . . . We started . . . with four such houses, forty-eight pairs of legs, and the King [Tem Binoka], Winchester in hand, firing in the direction – but over the head – of any one who seemed backward . . . Then a large shed came staggering in that was to serve as our dining-room; and a smaller shed by way of a kitchen.[29]

They spent several weeks in Equator Town, as they called it, where Stevenson and Lloyd worked, under an enormous mosquito-net, on *The Wrecker*, a novel inspired by a mysterious shipwreck they had heard about in Honolulu, and Stevenson took extensive notes on Tem Binoka for his travel book, writing to Colvin that 'Timpanok [Tem Binoka] is here the great attraction: all the rest is heat and tedium, and villainous dazzle, and yet more villainous mosquitoes'.[30] After some delay the *Equator* collected its passengers and they sailed from Abemama on 25 October and revisited Butaritari before leaving the Gilberts for the Samoan Islands. On board, Stevenson wrote to Colvin on 2 December, from the 'Schooner *Equator*, at sea 190 miles off Samoa':

My book is now practically modelled: if I can execute what is designed, there are few better books now extant on this globe; bar the epics, and the big tragedies, and histories, and the choice lyric poetics, and a novel or so – none. But it is not executed yet; and let not him that putteth on his armour, vaunt himself. At least, nobody has had such stuff; such wild stories, such beautiful scenes, such singular intimacies, such manners and traditions, so incredible a mixture of the beautiful and horrible, the savage and civilised. I will give you here some idea of the table of contents, which ought to make your mouth water. I propose to call the book – *The South Seas*; it is rather a large title, but not many people have seen more of them than I; perhaps no one: certainly no one capable of using the material.[31]

Part I was 'General. "Of schooners, islands, and maroons"' and was to contain the stories of smuggling, blackbirding (kidnapping islanders for labour) and maritime misdemeanours he had heard from Captain Reid of the *Equator* and others, and the stories of beachcomber characters and murders he had been told in the Gilberts. Part II was 'The Marquesas'; Part III, 'The Dangerous Archipelago', was to treat the Paumotus; and Part IV, 'Tahiti', was to contain sections on Tautira and the Tahitian songs and legends he had heard there and at Papara. Part V, 'The Eight Islands', would describe his experiences on the

Kona Coast and at Molokai. Part VI was 'The Gilberts', and Part VII 'Samoa which I have not yet reached'.[32] He thought he might briefly visit Fiji or Tonga, but wanted to be in England no later than June. 'I can hear the rattle of the hansom up Endell Street', he wrote, anticipating the journey to Colvin's residence at the British Museum.[33]

In December 1889 a missionary in the town of Apia on the Samoan island of Upolu encountered a tanned woman wearing a Gilbertese straw hat and carrying a mandolin, a thin man with a cigarette, and a younger man wearing dark glasses and carrying a concertina and a ukelele, a trio he took for 'a party of vaudeville artists *en route* to Australia or the States'.[34] Joe Strong is not included in this group portrait, perhaps because he had been ill, as well as disgraced by misbehaviour at Abemama and sacked from photographic duties.[35] He was sent on from Apia to join his wife and son in Sydney while Stevenson and his family lodged at first with H. J. Moors, a local trader, until Fanny, Lloyd and Ah Fu moved to accommodation a few miles out of Apia.[36] Stevenson stayed on 'in Apia for history's sake with Moors', taking notes from Moors and others for the Samoa part of the South Sea book, which he soon realized was growing into a separate work (later to be published as *A Footnote to History* (1892)).[37]

At some time in early January a fateful decision was taken – to buy some land (later named Vailima) near Apia, to build a house there, and to return to England only to make arrangements for permanent residence in the South Seas. Lloyd went on ahead to Sydney and Stevenson and Fanny followed in a German ship, the *Lübeck*, in February 1890. In a letter written on board, Stevenson described 'the fifty newspaper letters' for McClure as 'simply patches chosen from the travel volume (or volumes) as it gets written', and reported that 'The Big Travel Book' was 'Not begun, but all material ready'.[38] A reporter from the *Sydney Morning Herald* interviewed Stevenson at his hotel:

'I suppose', said our representative, 'that you will utilise your experience in the South Seas in your next work of fiction? By the by, did you visit Treasure Island?' Mr Stevenson smiled humorously. 'Treasure Island', he said, 'is not in the Pacific.'[39]

On 10 April a cable went from Sydney to Charles Baxter: 'Return Islands four months. Home September'.[40] Stevenson had fallen ill in Sydney and the cure was another voyage. Fanny had found a passage for Stevenson, herself and Lloyd (Ah Fu having disappeared to see his mother in China) on the steamer *Janet Nicoll*. She wrote explaining the delay to Colvin, and reporting on the South Sea book:

Of course this cruise will give additional interest to the book. I am very glad you spoke of the historical and scientific question. It has been rather heavy on my mind. If I were the public I shouldn't care a penny what Louis's theories were as to the formation of the islands, or their scientific history, or where the people came from originally – only what Louis's own experiences were. And no one has had such experiences. All the South Sea books speak, by hearsay only, of the terrible Tembinoka, but we threw ourselves into his arms, and went and lived with him for months, and learned to love him almost as much as we admired him.[41]

The *Janet Nicoll* sailed from Sydney on 11 April and, after calling at Auckland, Stevenson, Fanny and Lloyd landed on 30 April at Apia and the next day rode up to Vailima, where a little wooden house had 'been run up', which they could see from the deck as the *Janet Nicoll* steamed out of Apia harbour later on 1 May.[42] With frequent stops for copra at various islands, the *Janet Nicoll* sailed as far east as the pearl island of Penrhyn, which Stevenson later wrote up as one of the South Sea Letters for McClure, and then back through the Tokelau and Ellice Islands and north to the Gilberts again.[43] Tem Binoka was recovering from measles and 'looking older and thinner', according to Fanny's journal of the voyage.[44] The *Janet Nicoll* continued north into the Marshall Islands before returning back through the Gilberts, where Stevenson said farewell to Tem Binoka, this time for ever. They sailed through the New Hebrides without stopping and reached Noumea, capital of the French colony of New Caledonia, on 26 July. There Stevenson disembarked and made his only acquaintance with a Melanesian (rather than Polynesian or Micronesian) Pacific island, while Fanny and Lloyd continued in the *Janet Nicoll* to Sydney.

'In a wild cabin heated like the Babylonian furnace, four plies of blotting paper under my wet hand and the drops boiling from my brow', Stevenson had been working on his Samoan history and on his South Sea book during the *Janet Nicoll* cruise, rather than generating new material, and in a letter to McClure written before reaching New Caledonia he assured McClure that 'the letters are at last under weigh', and that those finished were to go to England to be printed, and would be sent to McClure in proof.[45] It was necessary to explain to McClure, however, 'that what you are to receive is not so much a certain number of letters, as a certain number of chapters in my book'.[46] Some of these fifteen chapters were better suited to the book than to be Letters, Stevenson thought, but McClure was to take for Letters as many chapters as he wished.

After a brief stay at Noumea, Stevenson rejoined his family at Sydney, from where he informed his friends that he would be returning to Samoa rather than to England. As he wrote to Henry James in August, with another Sydney cold:

I must tell you plainly – I *can't* tell Colvin – I do not think I shall come to England more than once, and then it'll be to die. Health I enjoy in the tropics; even here, which they call sub or semi-tropical, I come only to catch cold.[47]

He told the French writer Marcel Schwob that he was 'about waist-deep in my big book on the South Seas: *the* big book on the South Seas it ought to be, and shall'.[48] But in a letter to Colvin taking stock of the writing done on the *Janet Nicoll*, Stevenson's South Sea work, already conceived as taking two potential forms, as Letters and book, is divided yet again:

I have done well on that voyage; sixteen letters – at least, not that, but the draught of sixteen chapters of my book, from which thirteen or fourteen letters will be selected – go home to be set up.[49]

The book and the Letters which would be selected from it now become merely the 'draught' of the book, and the book itself, the ideal, final South Sea book, becomes another, finer, fatefully different thing.

Lloyd sailed for England to settle affairs there, and in September
Stevenson and Fanny sailed on the *Lübeck* for Apia – and Vailima,
where they inhabited the little wooden house while awaiting the
construction of the larger, proper house. To the sound of Fanny
organizing the livestock and the planting ('Paul, you take a spade to
do that . . . Here, you boy, . . . You no got work? You go find Simelē'),
Stevenson worked on the Paumotus material, revising the journal he
had written on the spot, and adding newly-heard stories of Samoan
ghosts to the Paumotuan and Tahitian stories he had heard from
Donat-Rimarau.[50]

The American historian Henry Adams visited Vailima at about this
time, and described his arrival in a letter home:

At last we came out on a clearing dotted with burned stumps exactly like a
clearing in our backwoods. In the middle stood a two-story Irish shanty with
steps outside to the upper floor, and a galvanized iron roof. A pervasive
atmosphere of dirt seemed to hang around it; and squalor like a railroad
navvy's board hut. As we reached the steps a figure came out that I cannot
do justice to. Imagine a man so thin and emaciated that he looked like a
bundle of sticks in a bag, with a head and eyes morbidly intelligent and restless.
He was costumed in very dirty striped cotton pyjamas, the baggy legs tucked
into coarse knit woollen stockings, one of which was bright brown in color,
the other a purplish dark tone. With him was a woman who retired for a
moment into the house to reappear a moment afterwards, probably in some
change of costume, but, as far as I could see, the change could have consisted
only in putting shoes on her bare feet. She wore the usual missionary nightgown
which was no cleaner than her husband's shirt and drawers, but she omitted
the stockings.[51]

Adams remarked of Stevenson's purchase of Vailima's four hundred
acres of 'mountain, and wholly impenetrable forest', that 'two hundred
acres would have been enough, and the balance might have been
profitably invested in soap'.[52] But he was impressed by the scope of
Stevenson's knowledge of the Pacific islands. 'He will tell his experiences in the form of Travels', Adams noted when Stevenson returned
the call a few weeks later, 'and I was rather surprised to find that his

range of study included pretty much everything: geology, sociology, laws, politics and ethnology'.[53] The South Sea book was still on the grand scale, apparently.

On 3 November, Stevenson reported on his progress to Colvin:

I have got in a better vein with the South Sea book, as I think you will see: I think these chapters will do for the volume without much change. Those that I did on the *Janet Nicoll*, under the most ungodly circumstances, I fear will want a lot of suppling and lightening; but I hope to have your remarks in a month or two upon that point.[54]

The difficulty, he told Colvin a few days later, was 'architectural', shaping and organizing the material so as to deliver information and at the same time keep the work moving, 'travelling':

Such a mass of stuff is to be handled if possible without repetition – so much foreign matter to be introduced, if possible with perspicuity – and as much as can be, a spirit of narrative to be preserved: you will find that come stronger as I proceed, and get the explanations worked through. Problems of style are (as yet) dirt under my feet: my problem is architectural-creative – to get this stuff jointed and moving. If I can do that, I will trouble you for style; anybody might write it, and it would be splendid: well-engineered, the masses right, the blooming thing travelling – twig?

This I wanted you to understand, for lots of the stuff sent home is, I imagine, rot – and slovenly rot – and some of it, pompous rot; and I want you to understand it's a *lay in*.[55]

The 'stuff sent home', the Marquesas chapters, was privately printed in London on 12 November to secure copyright, in a limited edition of twenty-two copies, entitled *The South Seas: A Record of Three Cruises*.[56] This was what McClure received for serialization. But the editors of the New York *Sun*, to whom McClure had contracted the Letters, protested, as McClure told Stevenson,

that the letters did not come as letters are supposed to come. They were not a correspondence from the South Seas, they were not dated and . . . in no way did the matter ... fulfil the definition of the word 'letter', as used in newspaper correspondence.[57]

McClure wrote later in his autobiography that the South Sea Letters 'were, on the whole, a disappointment to newspaper editors', for 'it was the moralist [in Stevenson] and not the romancer which his observations in the South Seas awoke in him, and the public found the moralist less interesting than the romancer'.[58] This was not *Treasure Island*.

Stevenson's literary friends in London were also displeased by *The South Seas*. 'There has been a good deal of disappointment among the few who have read the approaching *South Sea Letters*', Edmund Gosse informed a friend: 'The fact seems to be that it is very nice to *live* in Samoa, but not healthy to *write* there. Within a three-mile radius of Charing Cross is the literary atmosphere, I suspect.'[59] Even Henry James gently complained, in a letter to Stevenson of 12 January 1891:

I read with unrestrictive relish the first chapters of your prose volume (kindly vouchsafed me in the little copyright-catching red volume), and I loved 'em and blessed them quite. But I *did* make one restriction – I missed the *visible* in them – I mean as regards people, things, objects, faces, bodies, costumes, features, gestures, manners, the introductory, the *personal* painter-touch. It struck me that you either didn't feel – through some accident – your responsibility on this article quite enough; or, on some theory of your own, had declined it. No theory is kind to us that cheats us of *seeing*. However, no doubt we shall rub our eyes for satiety before we have done.[60]

On 6 January 1891, Stevenson took the regular steamer to Sydney, 'to get some more sea dirt on, the land-dirt having become monotonous', according to Henry Adams, in actual fact to meet Lloyd and Margaret Stevenson returning from England and Scotland.[61] In Stevenson's absence Fanny wrote to Colvin from Vailima about her 'desperate engagements with the man of genius over the South Sea book':

He has always had a weakness for teaching and preaching, so here was his chance. Instead of writing about his adventures in these wild islands, he would ventilate his own theories on the vexed questions of race and language. He wasted much precious time over grammars and dictionaries, with no results, for he was able to get an insight into hardly any native tongue. Then he must study the coral business. That, I believe, would have ruined the book but for my brutality.

She described returning to the shore after 'having some odd adventures and seeing many curious things' on an island visited by the *Janet Nicoll*, to find the man of genius

on the reef, halfway between the ship and shore, knee-deep in water, the tropical sun beating on his unprotected head, hammering at the reef with a big hatchet. His face was purple and his eyes injected with blood. 'Louis, you will die,' I cried, 'come away out of the sun quickly.' 'No,' he answered, 'I must get specimens from this extraordinary piece of coral . . .'. 'Louis,' I said, 'how ignorant you are! Why, that is only the common brain coral. Any schoolboy in San Francisco will give you specimens if you really want them.'[62]

Colvin's own criticisms of *The South Seas* were now arriving at Vailima, as Fanny wrote to inform Stevenson in Sydney:

One from Colvin with the Letters and his criticisms, all, I am pleased to see, the same as mine . . . Parts of it are very fine, but it loses immensely in not being a personal consecutive narrative. It gives too much the feeling that you had got your information second hand, and is only convincing in parts.[63]

In Sydney Stevenson took ill, as usual, and was looked after by his mother, while Lloyd went on ahead to Vailima. Meanwhile, in England and America the serialization of the South Sea Letters began, in the London *Black and White* and the New York *Sun*, with the Marquesas material from *The South Seas*. Responding to Colvin's criticisms on the steamer to Samoa in late February, Stevenson admitted his disappointment with the Marquesas material produced on the *Janet Nicoll*, but was optimistic about the Paumotus chapters, and hoped the Hawaiian material would be 'better yet'.[64] Life at Vailima was still too rough for Stevenson's mother, who took the steamer back to Sydney, while

Stevenson struggled on with the production of more Letters from his travel journal and notes, 'grinding along without a scrap of inspiration or a note of style', but consoling himself that the Letters would certainly be rewritten for the book: 'Unless I die, I shall find the time to make it good'.[65] A few days later he continued the same letter to Colvin from the Samoan island of Tutuila, having accepted an invitation from the American consul at Apia to come on an expedition, hoping 'to benefit by the change, and possibly get more stuff for Letters'.[66]

He returned, with a fever, to face the South Sea Letters and their difference from the South Sea book. 'One thing embarrasses me', he protested to Colvin:

No one ever seems to understand my attitude about that book; the stuff sent was never meant for other than a first state, I never meant it to appear as a book: knowing well that I have never had one hour of inspiration since it was begun, and have only beaten out my metal by brute force and patient repetition: I hoped some day to get 'a spate of style' and burnish it – fine mixed metaphor. I am now so sick that I intend, when the Letters are done and some more written that will be wanted, simply to make a book of it by the pruning knife.[67]

He mentioned some deep cuts to *The South Seas* Marquesas material, and some rewriting, and proposed

by similar drastic measures [to] make up a book of shreds and patches; which will not be what I had still hoped to make, but must have the value it has and be d—d to it. I cannot fight longer . . . [and] really five years were wanting, when I could have made a book; but I have a family, and – perhaps I could not make the book after all, and anyway, I'll never be allowed for Fanny has strong opinions and I prefer her peace of mind to my ideas.[68]

The difference between the book and the Letters is now a matter more of editing and cutting than of revising and rewriting. The book will be less than the Letters now, not more: the Letters edited, not the Letters revised.

Still toiling away at the Letters in May, with the story later called

'The Beach of Falesá' under way, Stevenson received adverse criticism of the Hawaiian material from Colvin, and responded by underlining, for emphasis, 'that *These Letters were never meant, and are not now meant, to be other than a quarry of materials from which the book may be drawn*'.[69] The main building at Vailima was finished by now and Margaret Stevenson came out again, after a brief stay in New Zealand, followed by Joe Strong, Belle and Austin from Sydney, while Stevenson still struggled on, working up his notes into Letters: 'A Letter usually takes me from a week to three days', he told Colvin, 'but I'm sometimes two days on a page'.[70] In June he was working on chapters of *The Wrecker*, his mystery thriller written with Lloyd Osbourne, as well as on more Letters, feeling the pressure of paying for Vailima. He thought the Gilbert Islands material, 'being the most interesting in matter and forming a compact whole', might be more successful.[71] He was thinking of writing another chapter as a 'Tail piece', on the re-encounter with Tem Binoka during the *Janet Nicoll* cruise.[72]

Later in the year Stevenson's correspondence to Colvin turns to his delight at 'The Beach of Falesá' and to Samoan politics, but in September he responded to Colvin's query about the missing Tahitian chapters, and his suggestion that, when Stevenson came to revise the South Sea Letters for the book, he might 'set right the places where you leave us puzzled as to the course, order and geography of your voyages':

One more word about the *South Seas* in answer to a question I observe I have forgotten to answer. The Tahiti part has never turned up, because it has never been written. As for telling you where I went or when, or anything about Honolulu, I would rather die; that is fair and plain. How can anybody care when or how I left Honolulu? This is (excuse me) childish. A man of upwards of forty cannot waste his time in communicating matter of that degree of indifference. The Letters, it appears, are tedious; by God, they would be more tedious still if I wasted my time upon such infantile and sucking-bottle details. If ever I put in any such detail, it is because it leads into something or serves as a transition. To tell it for its own sake, never![73]

Plainly he is hurt at the criticisms of the South Sea Letters and is asserting his contempt for the narrative of personal travels that Fanny and Colvin wanted from him. 'Let us forget this unfortunate affair', he concluded, while the serialization continued until the end of the year in New York and London, where *Black and White* found the Letters 'too monotonous', as Colvin reported, tucking them into corners, reducing the number and size of their artist's illustrations, and stopping at Hawaii, never even reaching the Gilberts.[74]

On 11 or 12 August 1894, however, with the Edinburgh Edition of his works in view, Stevenson responded enthusiastically to Colvin's suggestion of publishing 'picked passages from the unreprinted *Black and White* letters'.[75] 'I am strong for making a volume out of selections from the South Sea Letters', he replied:

I read over again the King of Apemama, and it is good in spite of your teeth, and a real curiosity, a thing that can never be seen again, now the group is annexed and Tembinoka dead.[76]

A few months later, Stevenson was dead himself, and the Edinburgh Edition of *In the South Seas* (1896) was posthumous. Colvin's Introduction explained that the South Sea Letters had not previously been published in book form because Stevenson had 'realised that the personal and the impersonal elements were not very successfully combined'.[77] Nevertheless, 'when the scheme of the Edinburgh Edition was maturing', Stevenson had 'desired that a selection should be made from them'.[78] The Hawaiian chapters 'did not come out at all to his own satisfaction', Colvin stated, 'and have accordingly been omitted'.[79] The Marquesas, Paumotus and Gilberts chapters were all included, however, and Colvin added that the writings about the Gilberts were 'the part of his work with which the author was himself best satisfied'.[80]

Such was the volume that resulted, posthumously, from Stevenson's travels in the South Seas. The fundamental problem from the beginning was that Stevenson wanted to transcend the personal travel narrative, and write an anthropological and historical work that would take in the whole South Seas. He wanted, not the story of his travels *In the South Seas*, but *The South Seas* themselves. The conception is in part hubristic – 'not many people have seen more of them than I' – and in part self-effacing: to leave out his best and most popular character – himself – and write about the islanders themselves. His friends and public wanted to read about Stevenson in the South Seas. As Gosse informed him, with at least some truth: 'Since Byron was in Greece, nothing has appealed to the ordinary literary man as so picturesque as that you should be in the South Seas'.[81] Certainly some of the South Sea material involves Stevenson personally, but some seems second-hand (most of 'The Story of a Plantation', for example), and Stevenson's family, a colourful supporting cast – Edinburgh mother in widow's cap, American wife in South Sea dress, bespectacled ukelele-playing stepson – is never properly introduced. We hear of a 'Mrs. Stevenson' in the Marquesas, a 'Mrs. Stevenson, senior' is mentioned a few pages later, and also a 'Mr. Osbourne', who may be one of the local traders.[82] The islanders themselves – 'your beloved blacks – or chocolates – confound them', as Colvin once remarked impatiently – were not, except as an exotic backdrop, of comparable interest to the general reader.[83] Autobiography was what was wanted, not anthropology.

For Stevenson to transcend his personal travels was also to abandon his main vehicle as a writer: narrative. Hence his terrible difficulties with the structure of his book, and his trouble to get it, as he said, 'travelling'. This aspiration to transcend his personal travels is evident in Stevenson's rewriting of his original journals. These were more like drafts of his travel writing than real journals, as appears clearly from his use of such formulations as 'difficult to describe in a work intended for the general reader', but in rewriting the journals for publication Stevenson was forming thematic and aesthetic patterns, sometimes incorporating material from later voyages and making grand inter-island comparisons, all at the expense of the consecutive narrative of events.[84] To Colvin's request for the mundane facts of Stevenson's itinerary, he responded disdainfully that 'all such information is given to one glance of an eye by a map with a little dotted line upon it'.[85] A little dotted line is no substitute, however, for a narrative that enables a reader to navigate vicariously in a sea of unfamiliar names and places.

As a consequence of Stevenson's disruption of his original daily journal entries, the narrative is particularly difficult to follow in the

Marquesas material, where his reorganization was most ambitious. A description of the *Casco*'s passengers' farewell to their first port of call, Anaho, closes the second chapter of *In the South Seas*, obscurely illustrating some general anthropological point, but preceding any account of their going ashore. One is reminded of Stevenson's scornful rejoinder to Colvin: 'To tell it for its own sake, never!' A description of the *Casco*'s voyage from Taiohae (on the island of Nukuhiva) to Tahauku (on the island of Hiva Oa) occurs in the course of a description of a local trip between two places on Nukuhiva (Anaho and Hatiheu) and is immediately followed by a description of the *Casco*'s arrival at Taiohae. Quite apart from the extravagant cross-references to places and islands visited subsequently, there is such rich confusion about the places and islands visited in the Marquesas that even the best of Stevenson's biographers – and the best informed about the Pacific islands – misplaces Stanislaus Moanatini on Hiva Oa rather than on Nukuhiva, where he belonged.[86]

The thematic patterns that replace the chronological narrative of travel make the events and characters at Anaho (on Nukuhiva) and Atuona (on Hiva Oa) seem repetitive and confusing. There are two chapters of expeditions to 'cannibal' places, 'A Cannibal High Place' and 'In a Cannibal Valley', both with missionary priests as guides, and there are two pairs of contrasted chiefs, traditional and colonial, in the chapters 'Chiefs and *Tapus*' and 'The Two Chiefs of Atuona'. But there is no discernible point in these doublings, this baffling symmetry, which is not made use of for development, or even contrast, despite one 'cannibal' place being 'high' and the other a 'valley', and one not seeming to be 'cannibal' at all.

The Marquesas and Paumotus are linked by the account of the *Casco*'s voyage between the two island groups, but the narrative lapses on arrival at the Paumotuan capital on Fakarava, where the chapter leaps ahead to take in all of Stevenson's stay there, and his experiences on two subsequent voyages, on the *Equator* and the *Janet Nicoll*. The chapter 'A House to Let in a Low Island' has some engaging narrative and amusing details of actual circumstances – the particular French lithograph incongruously hanging in the house, the early morning call for the cats at feeding time – so that the chapter preserves a sense of time and place. But the material in the following chapter on 'Traits and Sects in the Paumotus' is muddling and second-hand, deriving from a bewildering quantity and variety of more or less anonymous informants. A Scotsman on Tahiti, an unnamed Catholic Tahitian, a Mr Magee of Mangareva and a mysterious M. Wilmot are mentioned in a matter of two pages. Taiarapu in Tahiti turns up a few pages later, and then 'an eye-witness, Tasmanian born', who 'was present in a house on Makatea', which could be anywhere but is an island in the Paumotus Group.[87]

The narrative resumes with 'A Paumotuan Funeral', which Stevenson actually attended, but then is permanently lost in a succession of ghost stories, intended, perhaps, as a comparative study of Polynesian ideas of the afterlife, but forming a heap of sometimes second- or third-hand accounts taken from locations on all Stevenson's travels, even including his period at Vailima revising his journal and desperately composing Letters. 'I will give but a few instances at random', he writes, 'chiefly from my own doorstep in Upolu, during the past month (October 1890)'.[88] Stories from Tahiti are piled on stories from the Paumotus because Stevenson's principal source (the Catholic Tahitian) happened to be the half-Tahitian Donat-Rimarau, Vice-Resident at Fakarava. Stevenson's attempt to unify all his ghost material – and justify its enormous presence on a tiny atoll in the Paumotus – leaves the reader frustrated:

I try to deal with the whole matter here because of a particular quality in Paumotuan superstitions. It is true I heard them told by a man with a genius for such narrations. Close about our evening lamp, within sound of the island surf, we hung on his words, thrilling. The reader, in far other scenes, must listen close for the faint echo.[89]

In fairness it should be recognized that the theme marked by the chapters 'Death' and 'Depopulation' in the Marquesas is perhaps complemented by these ghost stories. Not that the theme of death in the South Seas ('et in Arcadia ego') was new. The Tahitian saying cited twice by Stevenson (once as a Marquesan saying) – 'The coral waxes, the palm grows, but man departs' – was actually invented by

Herman Melville.[90] Nor was the fascination with Polynesian ghosts original. The topic of ghosts preoccupied another previous South Sea writer, Pierre Loti, who also made use of Melville's Tahitian saying.[91] Tahitian ghosts were later the subject of one of Gauguin's best-known paintings, 'Manao Tupapau'.[92] Such ghosts and ghouls haunted the European *fin de siècle.*

The baggy chapter of 'Graveyard Stories' is by far the longest in the book, and abruptly ends the Paumotus part of *In the South Seas.* The next part, 'The Gilberts', in an attempt to bridge the gap in Stevenson's itinerary, opens with 'At Honolulu . . .'.[93] For all Stevenson's scorn for the humdrum data of travel ('How can anybody care when or why I left Honolulu?'), the reader is bewildered, surely, by the journey from ghosts to the Gilberts via Honolulu.

At this point, however, the travellers on the *Equator* voyage are introduced and the narrative reasserts itself, shaped by Stevenson's personal experiences at two firmly-established places, Butaritari and Abemama, each unified (and implicitly contrasted with the other) by the pervasive presence of its particular High Chief. The Butaritari section develops intriguingly, with the *Equator's* arrival and Stevenson's party's encounter with the stupefied and slumbering town. His portrait of the High Chief, lolling in front of the royal privy, on which 'two crossed rifles represented fasces', nicely balances the royal pomp and squalor:

He wore pyjamas which sorrowfully misbecame his bulk; his nose was hooked and cruel, his body overcome with sodden corpulence, his eye timorous and dull; he seemed at once oppressed with drowsiness and held awake by apprehension: a pepper rajah muddled with opium, and listening for the march of a Dutch army, looks perhaps not otherwise.[94]

This has been freshly written-up in revising what is already a fine piece of writing in the journal, from which an episode of cheap colonial comedy in the manner of Rider Haggard's *King Solomon's Mines* has rightly been removed:

the sovereign but twice condescended to smile, never to speak. The queen on the other hand will retain a lively impression of our visit; for when one of our party played the part of Commander Goode [i.e. Captain Good of *King Solomon's Mines*] and snapped his false teeth at her, she became deadly pale and was thenceforth unable to remove her eyes from the performer.[95]

A passage describing the falling of night around the family dining-table at Butaritari is atmospheric and brilliantly evocative of the various effects of light, and is not merely descriptive, but sets the scene for a missile which 'struck the table with a rattling smack and rebounded past my ear'.[96] The events of the restoration of the taboo and the ensuing festival give the Butaritari section a plot which derives directly from Stevenson's own experience. The rearrangement of the journal material enhances the narrative and the use of dates has point here (as it does not at Hiva Oa, for example) because the sequence of events has significance.

At Abemama, which provides the best of the four parts of the book, there is no longer an attempt to transcend the personal, to write *The South Seas* rather than *In the South Seas*. The cross-references to other islands in pursuit of comparison and generalization have been abandoned and replaced by an entertaining narrative and a powerful character around whom all the material naturally revolves: Tem Binoka, blue-spectacled and memorable, with his Winchester and his reiterated *raison d'état*, 'I think mo' betta'. His domineering presence is one of the main reasons why, as Stevenson said, the Gilberts material forms 'a compact whole', and his death and the annexation of the Gilberts by Britain are why, as Stevenson also recognized, this part of *In the South Seas* captures 'a real curiosity, a thing that can never be seen again'.[97]

Stevenson himself died a few months after writing those words, and even the colonial South Seas, the white men's islands, are now a phase of the past. *In the South Seas*, for all its imperfections, is a classic of Pacific travel, the work of the best British writer to see the South Seas. Although obsessed with soap, Henry Adams was impressed by Stevenson's achievement:

For months he has sailed about the islands in wretched trading schooners and stray steamers almost worse than sailing vessels, with such food as he could get, or lived on coral atolls eating bread-fruit and yams, all the time working hard with his pen, and of course always dirty, uncomfortable and poorly served, not to speak of being ill-clothed, which matters little in these parts. He has seen more of the islands than any literary or scientific man ever did before, and knows all he has seen.[98]

In his edition of Stevenson's *Letters*, Colvin mentioned that some of Stevenson's friends had found parts of the South Sea Letters 'impersonal and even tedious', but he added:

As a corrective of this opinion, I may perhaps mention here that there is a certain many-voyaged master-mariner as well as master-writer – no less a person than Mr. Joseph Conrad – who does not at all share it, and prefers *In the South Seas* to *Treasure Island*.[99]

Stevenson had travelled far from *Treasure Island*.

NOTES

1. Margaret Stevenson, 'Notes about Robert Louis Stevenson from his Mother's Diary', *The Works of Robert Louis Stevenson*, Vailima Edition, XXVI, *Miscellanea* (London, 1923), 353.

2. Ibid., 355.

3. S. S. McClure [and Willa Cather], *My Autobiography* (London, 1914), 191.

4. Robert Louis Stevenson, 'Creek Island, or Adventures in the South Seas', MS, quoted in Graham Balfour, *The Life of Robert Louis Stevenson* (London, 1901), I, 66.

5. R. L. Stevenson, 'To the Hesitating Purchaser', *Treasure Island* (London, 1883), [vi].

6. See Eric Quayle, *Ballantyne the Brave: A Victorian Writer and his Family* (London, 1967), 217. According to Quayle, who bases his account on Ballantyne family tradition, Stevenson met Ballantyne on 13 May 1866 and invited him to dinner that evening with his grandfather at Colinton. The Ballantyne family tradition derives from Ballantyne's wife, who was present at the meeting, but Stevenson's Colinton grandfather died in 1860, Stevenson himself was in Torquay on 13 May 1866, and he gives a different account of a meeting with Ballantyne in a fragment of autobiography dictated to Belle Strong at Vailima, first published as part of 'Memoirs of Himself', *Works*, Vailima Edition, XXVI (London, 1923), 226–7.

7. Lloyd Osbourne, *An Intimate Portrait of Robert Louis Stevenson* (New York, 1924), 83–4.

8. See Arthur Johnstone, *Recollections of Robert Louis Stevenson in the Pacific* (London, 1905), 24.

9. Margaret Stevenson, *From Saranac to the Marquesas and Beyond* (London, 1903), 67–8.

10. The correct date of 20 July is given in Stevenson's MS journal, 'Cruise of the *Casco*', Huntington Library, California. The date of 28 July in *In the South Seas* (1896) and all subsequent editions is incorrect.

11. Margaret Stevenson, *From Saranac*, 106.

12. Ibid., 112.

13. Lloyd Osbourne, *An Intimate Portrait*, 88.

14. Stevenson to Charles Baxter, *The Letters of Robert Louis Stevenson*, ed. Bradford A. Booth and Ernest Mehew (New Haven & London, 1994–5) (hereafter referred to as *Letters*), VI, 207.

15. Margaret Stevenson, *From Saranac*, 149.

16. Fanny Stevenson, 'Prefatory Note' to *Island Nights' Entertainments, The Works of Robert Louis Stevenson*, Vailima Edition, XV (London, 1922), 275–6.

17. Stevenson to Sidney Colvin, *Letters*, VI, 239.

18. See Isobel Field, *This Life I've Loved* (New York, 1937), 221.

19. Stevenson to Charles Baxter, *Letters*, VI, 295.

20. Fanny Stevenson to Sidney Colvin, *Letters*, VI, 303–4.

21. Ibid., 304.

22. Stevenson to Fanny Stevenson, *Letters*, VI, 306.

23. Stevenson to Sidney Colvin, *Letters*, VI, 312.

24. Fanny Stevenson to Sidney Colvin and Frances Sitwell, *Letters*, VI, 322.

25. See Thomas Murray MacCallum, *Adrift in the South Seas* (Los Angeles, California, 1934), 231.

26. Fanny Stevenson, *The Cruise of the 'Janet Nichol'* (London, 1915), 4.

27. Dates for the Gilberts voyage are sometimes derived from Lloyd Osbourne's Diary for 1889, MS, Beinecke Library, Yale.

28. Stevenson, Cruise of the *Equator*, MS, Huntington Library, California.

29. Lloyd Osbourne, *An Intimate Portrait*, 103–4.

30. Stevenson to Sidney Colvin, *Letters*, VI, 329.

31. Stevenson to Sidney Colvin, *Letters*, VI, 334–5.

32. Ibid., 335–6.

33. Ibid., 337.

34. W. E. Clarke, 'Robert Louis Stevenson in Samoa', *Yale Review*, 10 (January 1921), 275–6.

35. The exact nature of Joe's misbehaviour is unclear but it is referred to in the entries for 25 and 26 September in Lloyd's Diary for 1889, MS (Beinecke), and in Stevenson to Sidney Colvin, *Letters*, VI, 330.

36. H. J. Moors, *With Stevenson in Samoa* (London, 1910) is not entirely reliable.

37. Stevenson to Charles Baxter, *Letters*, VI, 345.

38. Stevenson to Edward Burlinghame, *Letters*, VI, 366.

39. *Sydney Morning Herald*, 14 February 1890, in R. C. Terry, ed., *Robert Louis Stevenson: Interviews and Recollections* (London, 1996), 153.

40. Cable to Charles Baxter, *Letters*, VI, 385.

41. Fanny Stevenson to Sidney Colvin, 'More Letters of Mrs. R. L. Stevenson', *Scribner's Magazine*, 75 (1924), 418.

42. Fanny Stevenson, *The Cruise of the 'Janet Nichol'*, 30.

43. See Stevenson, 'A Pearl Island: Penrhyn', reprinted from the New York *Sun* in *Works*, Vailima Edition, XXVI, 427–35, and Fanny's parallel account in *The Cruise of the 'Janet Nichol'*, 53ff.

44. Fanny Stevenson, *The Cruise of the 'Janet Nichol'*, 134–5.

45. Stevenson to Sidney Colvin, *Letters*, VI, 405; Stevenson (dictated to Lloyd) to S. S. McClure, *Letters*, VI, 394.

46. Ibid., 394–5.

47. Stevenson to Henry James, *Letters*, VI, 402.

48. Stevenson to Marcel Schwob, *Letters*, VI, 401.

49. Stevenson to Sidney Colvin, *Letters*, VI, 404.

50. Stevenson to Sidney Colvin, *Letters*, VII, 24. For some of the Vailima ghost stories in the 'Graveyard Stories' chapter of *In the South Seas*, see Fanny's diary, in *Our Samoan Adventure*, ed. Charles Neider (London, 1956), 39, 57.

51. Henry Adams to Elizabeth Cameron, *The Letters of Henry Adams*, ed. J. C. Levenson *et al.*, III (Cambridge, Mass., 1982), 296.

52. Henry Adams to John Hay, *The Letters of Henry Adams*, III, 303.

53. Henry Adams to Elizabeth Cameron, *The Letters of Henry Adams*, III, 329.

54. Stevenson to Sidney Colvin, *Letters*, VII, 21.

55. Ibid., 29.

56. See R. G. Swearingen, *The Prose Writings of Robert Louis Stevenson: A Guide* (London, 1980), 136–7.

57. S. S. McClure to Stevenson, quoted in Peter Lyon, *Success Story: The Life and Times of S. S. McClure* (New York, 1963), 106.

58. S. S. McClure, *My Autobiography*, 192.

59. Edmund Gosse to George A. Armour, in Evan Charteris, *The Life and Letters of Sir Edmund Gosse* (London, 1931), 225.

60. Henry James to Stevenson, in Henry James, *Henry James Letters*, ed. Leon Edel, III (London, 1980), 325.

61. Henry Adams to John Hay, *The Letters of Henry Adams*, III, 394.

62. Fanny Stevenson to Sidney Colvin, *Letters*, VII, 79. Stevenson's researches on the reef of Arorae in the Gilberts on 9 June 1890 are more briefly and comically described by Fanny in *The Cruise of the 'Janet Nichol'*, 112–14.

63. Fanny Stevenson to Stevenson, *Letters*, VII, 85, note 1.

64. Stevenson to Sidney Colvin, *Letters*, VII, 85.

65. Stevenson to Sidney Colvin, *Letters*, VII, 94.

66. Ibid., 97.

67. Stevenson to Sidney Colvin, *Letters*, VII, 101–2.

68. Ibid., 102.

69. Stevenson to Sidney Colvin, *Letters*, VII, 115.

70. Ibid., 117.

71. Stevenson to Sidney Colvin, *Letters*, VII, 135.

72. Ibid., 136.

73. Sidney Colvin to Stevenson, quoted in *Letters*, VII, 157, note 14; Stevenson to Sidney Colvin, *Letters*, VII, 157.

74. Ibid.; Sidney Colvin to Stevenson, quoted in *Letters*, VII, 157, note 14. See Stevenson, 'The South Seas: A Record of Three Cruises', *Black and White*, 6 February 1891 – 19 December 1891.

75. Sidney Colvin to Charles Baxter, copy by Baxter enclosed in Charles Baxter to Stevenson, in Stevenson, *R.L.S.: Stevenson's Letters to Charles Baxter*, ed. DeLancey Ferguson and Marshall Waingrow (New Haven & London, 1956), 346.

76. Stevenson to Sidney Colvin, *Letters*, VIII, 344.

77. Sidney Colvin, Editorial Note, *In the South Seas*, *The Works of Robert Louis Stevenson*, Edinburgh Edition, XX (Edinburgh, 1896), x.

78. Ibid.

79. Ibid.

80. Ibid.

81. Edmund Gosse to Stevenson, in *The Life and Letters of Sir Edmund Gosse*, 232–3.

82. Stevenson, *In the South Seas*, Part I, Chs III, XI, IV. In a letter to Colvin, Fanny wrote: 'That truly dreadful "Mrs Stevenson senior", which I thought had been changed, was left over from the time when he was fighting to keep his book impersonal' (Fanny Stevenson to Sidney Colvin, *Letters*, VII, 80).

83. Sidney Colvin to Stevenson, quoted in *Letters*, VIII, 279, note 1.

84. Stevenson, 'Cruise of the *Casco*', MS, Huntington Library, California.

85. Stevenson to Sidney Colvin, *Letters*, VII, 157.

86. See J. C. Furnas, *Voyage to Windward: The Life of Robert Louis Stevenson* (London, 1952), 276.

87. Stevenson, *In the South Seas*, Part II, Ch. IV.

88. Ibid., Part II, Ch. VI.

89. Ibid.

90. Ibid., Part I, Ch. I, and see Part I, Ch. IV, and Herman Melville, *Omoo: A Narrative of Adventures in the South Seas*, ed. H. Hayford *et al.* (Chicago, 1968), 192, and Neil Rennie, *Far-Fetched Facts: The Literature of Travel and the Idea of the South Seas* (Oxford, 1995), 203–4.

91. See [Pierre Loti], *Le Mariage de Loti – Rarahu* (Paris, 1880), [-1].

92. 'Manao Tupapau' ('tupapau' meaning 'spirit', or 'ghost'), painted in Tahiti in 1892, is in the Albright-Knox Art Gallery, Buffalo, NY.

93. Stevenson, *In the South Seas*, Part III, Ch. I.

94. Ibid.

95. Stevenson, Cruise of the *Equator*, MS, Huntington Library, California.

96. Stevenson, *In the South Seas*, Part III, Ch. V.

97. For a historical account of Tem Binoka, see H. E. Maude, 'Baiteke and Binoka of Abemama: arbiters of change in the Gilbert Islands', in J. W. Davidson and Deryck Scarr, eds, *Pacific Island Portraits* (Canberra, 1976).

98. Henry Adams to Elizabeth Cameron, *The Letters of Henry Adams*, III, 297.

99. Sidney Colvin, in *The Letters of Robert Louis Stevenson*, ed. Sidney Colvin (London, 1911), III, 262.

NOTE ON THE TEXT

This is a new edition of the work entitled *In the South Seas* (1896) which Sidney Colvin edited and selected from Stevenson's South Sea travel writings for the Edinburgh Edition of Stevenson's works. There are many MSS and proofs with MS corrections of the South Sea material at various stages of composition and revision in four libraries on two continents and several different published versions which would have to be examined and collated before it might be possible to establish exactly what sources Colvin drew on. I have examined Colvin's text in the light of Stevenson's original MS journals of his cruises in the *Casco* and *Equator* in 1888–9 (HM 2412, Huntington Library, San Marino, California) and the versions published in 1891–2 in *Black and White* (for the Marquesas and Paumotus material) and the *Auckland Star* (for the Gilbert Islands material, which was not included in *Black and White*). Because the 1896 edition may have incorporated revisions by Stevenson I have emended it only when it seemed obviously in error, and I have listed all substantive emendations in an appendix. In addition I have silently corrected some inconsistencies in the 1896 edition (in the use of italics for foreign words, for example) and unmuddled the names of characters in Victor Hugo's *Quatrevingt-treize*. *In the South Seas* has been reprinted for a century but this is the first critically emended edition.

FURTHER READING

BIBLIOGRAPHY

Roger G. Swearingen, *The Prose Writings of Robert Louis Stevenson: A Guide* (London, 1980).

LIFE AND LETTERS

Graham Balfour, *The Life of Robert Louis Stevenson* (2 vols; London, 1901).

J. C. Furnas, *Voyage to Windward: The Life of Robert Louis Stevenson* (London, 1952).

R. L. Stevenson, *The Letters of Robert Louis Stevenson*, ed. Bradford A. Booth and Ernest Mehew (8 vols; New Haven & London, 1994–5).

CRITICISM

Jeremy Treglown, Introduction, *In the South Seas*, ed. Jeremy Treglown (London, 1987).

Robert Irwin Hillier, *The South Seas Fiction of Robert Louis Stevenson* (New York, 1989).

Barry Menikoff, ' "These Problematic Shores": Robert Louis Stevenson in the South Seas', in *English Literature and the Wider World*, IV, *The Ends of the Earth*, ed. Simon Gatrell (London, 1992).

RELATED WRITINGS BY STEVENSON

In addition to the Marquesas, Paumotus and Gilbert Islands South Sea Letters included by Sidney Colvin in *In the South Seas* (1896), there were published, in newspapers and periodicals in different parts of the world and in differing versions during 1891–2, South Sea Letters about: the Kona Coast of Hawaii and Molokai, both visited while Stevenson was based at Waikiki in 1889; the island of Penrhyn (or Tongareva), visited on his *Janet Nicoll* voyage of 1890; the Samoan island of Tutuila, visited from his home at Vailima in 1891. Some of these South Sea Letters were reprinted and are accessible (in differing versions) in *In the South Seas*, *Works*, Swanston Edition, XVIII (London, 1912); *Miscellanea*, *Works*, Vailima Edition, XXVI (London, 1923); *In the South Seas*, *Works*, Tusitala Edition, XX (London, 1924); *Vailima Papers*, *Works*, Tusitala Edition, XXI (London, 1924); *Travels in Hawaii*, ed. A. Grove Day (Honolulu, 1973); and the Tutuila material was published in its original journal form in *Hitherto Unpublished Prose Writings* (Boston, 1921); in *Juvenilia, Moral Emblems, Fables and Other Papers*, *Works*, Vailima Edition, XXV (London, 1923); and in *Vailima Papers*, *Works*, Tusitala Edition, XXI (London, 1924). Three South Sea Letters have not been reprinted: the revised version of the Tutuila journal which appeared as two South Sea Letters, 'Tutuila: The American Harbour' in the *Auckland Star*, 30 January 1892, and 'Tutuila: The Cruise of the Schooner Nukunono' in the New York *Sun*, 13 December 1891, and the *Auckland Star*, 6 February 1892; and a second part of the Letter entitled 'The Kona Coast' (of which the first part was reprinted in Swanston, XVIII, Vailima, XXVI, and Tusitala, XX) which appeared in the *Auckland Star*, 8 August 1891.

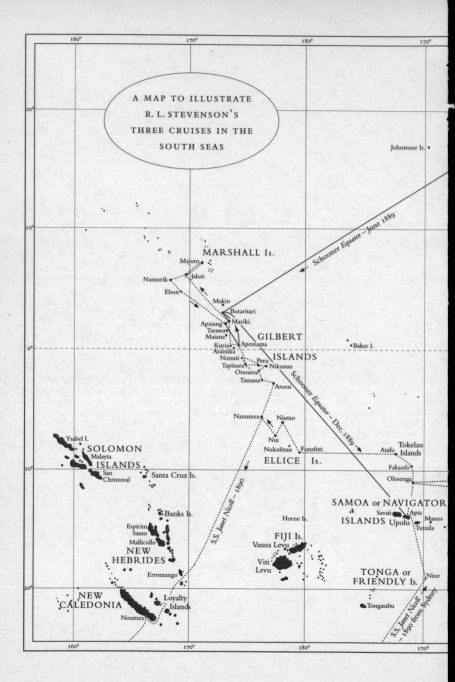

A MAP TO ILLUSTRATE
R. L. STEVENSON'S
THREE CRUISES IN THE
SOUTH SEAS

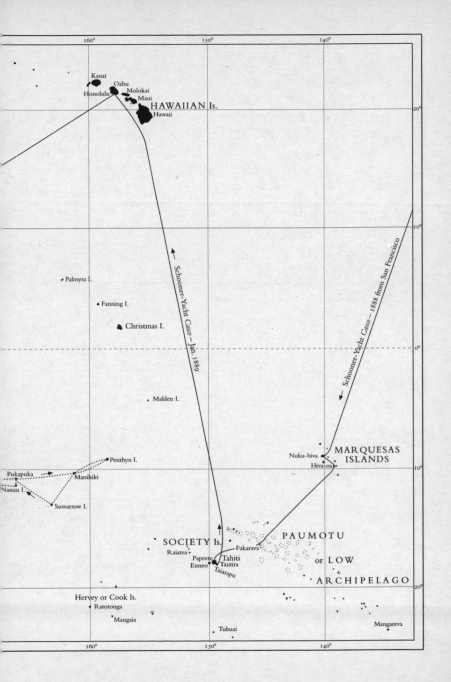

160° 150° 140°

Kauai
Oahu
Honolulu Molokai
Maui
HAWAIIAN Is.
Hawaii

20°

10°

Palmyra I.

Fanning I.

Christmas I.

Schooner-Yacht Casco – Jan. 1889

Schooner-Yacht Casco – 1888 from San Francisco

0°

Malden I.

MARQUESAS
ISLANDS
Nuku-hiva
Hiva-oa

Penrhyn I.

Pukapuka
Manihiki
Nassau I.
Suwarrow I.

10°

PAUMOTU

Fakarava
SOCIETY Is.
Raiatea
Papeete Tahiti
Eimeo Tautira
Taiarapu

or **LOW**

ARCHIPELAGO

20°

Hervey or Cook Is.
Rarotonga
Mangaia
Tubuai
Mangareva

160° 150° 140°

IN THE SOUTH SEAS

BEING AN ACCOUNT OF
EXPERIENCES AND OBSERVATIONS IN

THE MARQUESAS, PAUMOTUS
AND GILBERT ISLANDS

IN THE COURSE OF TWO CRUISES,
ON THE YACHT *CASCO* (1888) AND THE
SCHOONER *EQUATOR* (1889)

THE MARQUESAS

CHAPTER I

AN ISLAND LANDFALL

For nearly ten years my health had been declining; and for some while before I set forth upon my voyage, I believed I was come to the afterpiece of life, and had only the nurse and undertaker to expect. It was suggested that I should try the South Seas; and I was not unwilling to visit like a ghost, and be carried like a bale, among scenes that had attracted me in youth and health. I chartered accordingly Dr. Merrit's schooner yacht, the *Casco*, seventy-four tons register; sailed from San Francisco towards the end of June 1888, visited the eastern islands, and was left early the next year at Honolulu. Hence, lacking courage to return to my old life of the house and sick-room, I set forth to leeward in a trading schooner, the *Equator*, of a little over seventy tons, spent four months among the atolls (low coral islands) of the Gilbert group, and reached Samoa towards the close of '89. By that time gratitude and habit were beginning to attach me to the islands; I had gained a competency of strength; I had made friends; I had learned new interests; the time of my voyages had passed like days in fairyland; and I decided to remain. I began to prepare these pages at sea, on a third cruise, in the trading steamer *Janet Nicoll*. If more days are granted me, they shall be passed where I have found life most pleasant and man most interesting; the axes of my black boys are already clearing the foundations of my future house; and I must learn to address readers from the uttermost parts of the sea.

That I should thus have reversed the verdict of Lord Tennyson's hero[1] is less eccentric than appears. Few men who come to the islands leave them; they grow grey where they alighted; the palm shades and the trade-wind fans them till they die, perhaps cherishing to the last the fancy of a visit home, which is rarely made, more rarely enjoyed, and yet more rarely repeated. No part of the world exerts the same attractive power upon the visitor, and the task before me is to communicate to fireside travellers some sense of its seduction, and to describe the life, at sea and ashore, of many hundred thousand persons, some

5

of our own blood and language, all our contemporaries, and yet as remote in thought and habit as Rob Roy or Barbarossa,[2] the Apostles or the Caesars.

The first experience can never be repeated. The first love, the first sunrise, the first South Sea island, are memories apart and touched a virginity of sense. On the 20th of July 1888 the moon was an hour down by four in the morning. In the east a radiating centre of brightness told of the day; and beneath, on the skyline, the morning bank was already building, black as ink. We have all read of the swiftness of the day's coming and departure in low latitudes; it is a point on which the scientific and sentimental tourist are at one, and has inspired some tasteful poetry. The period certainly varies with the season; but here is one case exactly noted. Although the dawn was thus preparing by four, the sun was not up till six; and it was half-past five before we could distinguish our expected islands from the clouds on the horizon. Eight degrees south, and the day two hours a-coming. The interval was passed on deck in the silence of expectation, the customary thrill of landfall heightened by the strangeness of the shores that we were then approaching. Slowly they took shape in the attenuating darkness. Ua-huna, piling up to a truncated summit, appeared the first upon the starboard bow; almost abeam arose our destination, Nuka-hiva, whelmed in cloud; and betwixt and to the southward, the first rays of the sun displayed the needles of Ua-pu. These pricked about the line of the horizon; like the pinnacles of some ornate and monstrous church, they stood there, in the sparkling brightness of the morning, the fit sign-board of a world of wonders.

Not one soul aboard the *Casco* had set foot upon the islands, or knew, except by accident, one word of any of the island tongues; and it was with something perhaps of the same anxious pleasure as thrilled the bosom of discoverers that we drew near these problematic shores. The land heaved up in peaks and rising vales; it fell in cliffs and buttresses; its colour ran through fifty modulations in a scale of pearl and rose and olive; and it was crowned above by opalescent clouds. The suffusion of vague hues deceived the eye; the shadows of clouds were confounded with the articulations of the mountain; and the isle and its unsubstantial canopy rose and shimmered before us like a single mass. There was no beacon, no smoke of towns to be expected, no plying pilot. Somewhere, in that pale phantasmagoria of cliff and cloud, our haven lay concealed; and somewhere to the east of it – the only sea-mark given – a certain headland, known indifferently as Cape Adam and Eve, or Cape Jack and Jane, and distinguished by two colossal figures, the gross statuary of nature. These we were to find; for these we craned and stared, focussed glasses, and wrangled over charts; and the sun was overhead and the land close ahead before we found them. To a ship approaching, like the *Casco*, from the north, they proved indeed the least conspicuous features of a striking coast; the surf flying high above its base; strange, austere, and feathered mountains rising behind; and Jack and Jane, or Adam and Eve, impending like a pair of warts above the breakers.

Thence we bore away along shore. On our port beam we might hear the explosions of the surf; a few birds flew fishing under the prow; there was no other sound or mark of life, whether of man or beast, in all that quarter of the island. Winged by her own impetus and the dying breeze, the *Casco* skimmed under cliffs, opened out a cove, showed us a beach and some green trees, and flitted by again, bowing to the swell. The trees, from our distance, might have been hazel; the beach might have been in Europe; the mountain forms behind modelled in little from the Alps, and the forest which clustered on their ramparts a growth no more considerable than our Scottish heath. Again the cliff yawned, but now with a deeper entry; and the *Casco*, hauling her wind, began to slide into the bay of Anaho. The coco-palm, that giraffe of vegetables, so graceful, so ungainly, to the European eye so foreign, was to be seen crowding on the beach, and climbing and fringing the steep sides of mountains. Rude and bare hills embraced the inlet upon either hand; it was enclosed to the landward by a bulk of shattered mountains. In every crevice of that barrier the forest harboured, roosting and nesting there like birds about a ruin; and far above, it greened and roughened the razor edges of the summit.

Under the eastern shore, our schooner, now bereft of any breeze, continued to creep in: the smart creature, when once under way, appearing motive in herself. From close aboard arose the bleating of young lambs; a bird sang in the hillside; the scent of the land and of a hundred fruits or flowers flowed forth to meet us; and, presently, a house or two appeared, standing high upon the ankles of the hills, and one of these surrounded with what seemed a garden. These conspicuous habitations, that patch of culture, had we but known it, were a mark of the passage of whites; and we might have approached a hundred islands and not found their parallel. It was longer ere we spied the native village, standing (in the universal fashion) close upon a curve of beach, close under a grove of palms; the sea in front growling and whitening on a concave arc of reef. For the coco-tree and the island man are both lovers and neighbours of the surf. 'The coral waxes, the palm grows, but man departs,' says the sad Tahitian proverb;[3] but they are all three, so long as they endure, co-haunters of the beach. The mark of anchorage was a blow-hole in the rocks, near the south-easterly corner of the bay. Punctually to our use, the blow-hole spouted; the schooner turned upon her heel; the anchor plunged. It was a small sound, a great event; my soul went down with these moorings whence no windlass may extract nor any diver fish it up; and I, and some part of my ship's company, were from that hour the bondslaves of the isles of Vivien.[4]

Before yet the anchor plunged a canoe was already paddling from the hamlet. It contained two men: one white, one brown and tattooed across the face with bands of blue, both in immaculate white European clothes: the resident trader, Mr. Regler, and the native chief, Taipi-Kikino. 'Captain, is it permitted to come on board?' were the first words we heard among the islands. Canoe followed canoe till the ship swarmed with stalwart, six-foot men in every stage of undress; some in a shirt, some in a loin-cloth, one in a handkerchief imperfectly adjusted; some, and these the more considerable, tattooed from head to foot in awful patterns; some barbarous and knived; one, who sticks in my memory as something bestial, squatting on his hams in a canoe, sucking an orange and spitting it out again to alternate sides with ape-like vivacity – all talking, and we could not understand one word; all trying to trade with us who had no thought of trading, or offering us island curios at prices palpably absurd. There was no word of welcome; no show of civility; no hand extended save that of the chief and Mr. Regler. As we still continued to refuse the proffered articles, complaint ran high and rude; and one, the jester of the party, railed upon our meanness amid jeering laughter. Amongst other angry pleasantries – 'Here is a mighty fine ship,' said he, 'to have no money on board!' I own I was inspired with sensible repugnance; even with alarm. The ship was manifestly in their power; we had women on board; I knew nothing of my guests beyond the fact that they were cannibals; the Directory[5] (my only guide) was full of timid cautions; and as for the trader, whose presence might else have reassured me, were not whites in the Pacific the usual instigators and accomplices of native outrage? When he reads this confession, our kind friend, Mr. Regler, can afford to smile.

Later in the day, as I sat writing up my journal, the cabin was filled from end to end with Marquesans: three brown-skinned generations, squatted cross-legged upon the floor, and regarding me in silence with embarrassing eyes. The eyes of all Polynesians are large, luminous, and melting; they are like the eyes of animals and some Italians. A kind of despair came over me, to sit there helpless under all these staring orbs, and be thus blocked in a corner of my cabin by this speechless crowd: and a kind of rage to think they were beyond the reach of articulate communication, like furred animals, or folk born deaf, or the dwellers of some alien planet.

To cross the Channel is, for a boy of twelve, to change heavens; to cross the Atlantic, for a man of twenty-four, is hardly to modify his diet. But I was now escaped out of the shadow of the Roman empire, under whose toppling monuments we were all cradled, whose laws and letters are on every hand of us, constraining and preventing. I was now to see what men might be whose fathers had never studied Virgil, had never been conquered by Caesar, and never been ruled by the wisdom of Gaius or Papinian.[6] By the same step I had journeyed forth out of that comfortable zone of kindred languages, where the curse of Babel is so easy to be remedied; and my new fellow-creatures sat before me dumb like images. Methought, in my travels, all human relation was to be excluded; and when I returned home (for in those days I still projected my return) I should have but dipped into a picture-book without a text. Nay, and I even questioned if my travels should be much prolonged; perhaps they were destined to a speedy end; perhaps my subsequent friend, Kauanui, whom I remarked there, sitting silent with the rest, for a man of some authority, might leap from his hams with an ear-splitting signal, the ship be carried at a rush, and the ship's company butchered for the table.

There could be nothing more natural than these apprehensions, nor anything more groundless. In my experience of the islands, I had never again so menacing a reception; were I to meet with such to-day, I should be more alarmed and tenfold more surprised. The majority of Polynesians are easy folk to get in touch with, frank, fond of notice, greedy of the least affection, like amiable, fawning dogs; and even with the Marquesans, so recently and so imperfectly redeemed from a blood-boltered[7] barbarism, all were to become our intimates, and one, at least, was to mourn sincerely our departure.

CHAPTER II

MAKING FRIENDS

The impediment of tongues was one that I particularly over-estimated. The languages of Polynesia are easy to smatter, though hard to speak with elegance. And they are extremely similar, so that a person who has a tincture of one or two may risk, not without hope, an attempt upon the others.

And again, not only is Polynesian easy to smatter, but interpreters abound. Missionaries, traders, and broken white folk living on the bounty of the natives, are to be found in almost every isle and hamlet; and even where these are unserviceable, the natives themselves have often scraped up a little English, and in the French zone (though far less commonly) a little French-English, or an efficient pidgin, what is called to the westward 'Beach-la-Mar,'[1] comes easy to the Polynesian; it is now taught, besides, in the schools of Hawaii; and from the multiplicity of British ships, and the nearness of the States on the one hand and the colonies on the other, it may be called, and will almost certainly become, the tongue of the Pacific. I will instance a few examples. I met in Majuro a Marshall Island boy who spoke excellent

English; this he had learned in the German firm in Jaluit,[2] yet did not speak one word of German. I heard from a gendarme who had taught school in Rapa-iti[3] that while the children had the utmost difficulty or reluctance to learn French, they picked up English on the wayside, and as if by accident. On one of the most out-of-the-way atolls in the Carolines, my friend Mr. Benjamin Hird[4] was amazed to find the lads playing cricket on the beach and talking English; and it was in English that the crew of the *Janet Nicoll*,[5] a set of black boys from different Melanesian islands, communicated with other natives throughout the cruise, transmitted orders, and sometimes jested together on the fore-hatch. But what struck me perhaps most of all was a word I heard on the verandah of the Tribunal at Noumea.[6] A case had just been heard – a trial for infanticide against an ape-like native woman; and the audience were smoking cigarettes as they awaited the verdict. An anxious, amiable French lady, not far from tears, was eager for acquittal, and declared she would engage the prisoner to be her children's nurse. The bystanders exclaimed at the proposal; the woman was a savage, said they, and spoke no language. '*Mais, vous savez,*' objected the fair sentimentalist; '*ils apprennent si vite l'anglais!*'

But to be able to speak to people is not all. And in the first stage of my relations with natives I was helped by two things. To begin with, I was the showman of the *Casco*. She, her fine lines, tall spars, and snowy decks, the crimson fittings of the saloon, and the white, the gilt, and the repeating mirrors of the tiny cabin, brought us a hundred visitors. The men fathomed out her dimensions with their arms, as their fathers fathomed out the ships of Cook;[7] the women declared the cabins more lovely than a church; bouncing Junos were never weary of sitting in the chairs and contemplating in the glass their own bland images; and I have seen one lady strip up her dress, and, with cries of wonder and delight, rub herself bare-breeched upon the velvet cushions. Biscuit, jam, and syrup was the entertainment; and, as in European parlours, the photograph album went the round. This sober gallery, their everyday costumes and physiognomies, had become transformed, in three weeks' sailing, into things wonderful and rich and foreign; alien faces, barbaric dresses, they were now beheld and fingered, in the swerving cabin, with innocent excitement and surprise.

Her Majesty was often recognised, and I have seen French subjects kiss her photograph; Captain Speedy[8] – in an Abyssinian war-dress, supposed to be the uniform of the British army – met with much acceptance; and the effigies of Mr. Andrew Lang[9] were admired in the Marquesas. There is the place for him to go when he shall be weary of Middlesex and Homer.

It was perhaps yet more important that I had enjoyed in my youth some knowledge of our Scots folk of the Highlands and the Islands. Not much beyond a century has passed since these were in the same convulsive and transitionary state as the Marquesans of to-day. In both cases an alien authority enforced, the clans disarmed, the chiefs deposed, new customs introduced, and chiefly that fashion of regarding money as the means and object of existence. The commercial age, in each, succeeding at a bound to an age of war abroad and patriarchal communism at home. In one the cherished practice of tattooing, in the other a cherished costume, proscribed. In each a main luxury cut off: beef, driven under cloud of night from Lowland pastures, denied to the meat-loving Highlander; long-pig,[10] pirated from the next village, to the man-eating Kanaka.[11] The grumbling, the secret ferment, the fears and resentments, the alarms and sudden councils of Marquesan chiefs, reminded me continually of the days of Lovat and Struan.[12] Hospitality, tact, natural fine manners, and a touchy punctilio, are common to both races: common to both tongues the trick of dropping medial consonants. Here is a table of two widespread Polynesian words:–

	House.	*Love.**
Tahitian	FARE	AROHA
New Zealand	WHARE	
Samoan	FALE	TALOFA
Manihiki	FALE	ALOHA
Hawaiian	HALE	ALOHA
Marquesan	HA'E	KAOHA

* Where that word is used as a salutation I give that form.

The elision of medial consonants, so marked in these Marquesan instances, is no less common both in Gaelic and the Lowland Scots. Stranger still, that prevalent Polynesian sound, the so-called catch, written with an apostrophe, and often or always the gravestone of a perished consonant, is to be heard in Scotland to this day. When a Scot pronounces water, better, or bottle – *wa'er, be'er,* or *bo'le* – the sound is precisely that of the catch; and I think we may go beyond, and say, that if such a population could be isolated, and this mispronunciation should become the rule, it might prove the first stage of transition from *t* to *k*, which is the disease of Polynesian languages. The tendency of the Marquesans, however, is to urge against consonants, or at least on the very common letter *l*, a war of mere extermination. A hiatus is agreeable to any Polynesian ear; the ear even of the stranger soon grows used to these barbaric voids; but only in the Marquesan will you find such names as *Haaii* and *Paaaeua*, when each individual vowel must be separately uttered.

These points of similarity between a South Sea people and some of my own folk at home ran much in my head in the islands; and not only inclined me to view my fresh acquaintances with favour, but continually modified my judgment. A polite Englishman comes to-day to the Marquesans and is amazed to find the men tattooed; polite Italians came not long ago to England and found our fathers stained with woad; and when I paid the return visit as a little boy, I was highly diverted with the backwardness of Italy: so insecure, so much a matter of the day and hour, is the pre-eminence of race. It was so that I hit upon a means of communication which I recommend to travellers. When I desired any detail of savage custom, or of superstitious belief, I cast back in the story of my fathers, and fished for what I wanted with some trait of equal barbarism: Michael Scott,[13] Lord Derwentwater's[14] head, the second-sight,[15] the Water Kelpie,[16] – each of these I have found to be a killing bait; the black bull's head of Stirling procured me the legend of Rahero;[17] and what I knew of the Cluny Macphersons, or the Appin Stewarts,[18] enabled me to learn, and helped me to understand, about the Tevas[19] of Tahiti. The native was no longer ashamed, his sense of kinship grew warmer, and his lips were opened. It is this sense of kinship that the traveller must rouse and share; or he had better content himself with travels from the blue bed to the brown.[20] And the presence of one Cockney titterer will cause a whole party to walk in clouds of darkness.

The hamlet of Anaho stands on a margin of flat land between the west of the beach and the spring of the impending mountains. A grove of palms, perpetually ruffling its green fans, carpets it (as for a triumph) with fallen branches, and shades it like an arbour. A road runs from end to end of the covert among beds of flowers, the milliner's shop of the community; and here and there, in the grateful twilight, in an air filled with a diversity of scents, and still within hearing of the surf upon the reef, the native houses stand in scattered neighbourhood. The same word, as we have seen, represents in many tongues of Polynesia, with scarce a shade of difference, the abode of man. But although the word be the same, the structure itself continually varies; and the Marquesan, among the most backward and barbarous of islanders, is yet the most commodiously lodged. The grass huts of Hawaii, the birdcage houses of Tahiti, or the open shed, with the crazy Venetian blinds, of the polite Samoan – none of these can be compared with the Marquesan *paepae-hae*, or dwelling platform. The *paepae* is an oblong terrace built without cement of black volcanic stone, from twenty to fifty feet in length, raised from four to eight feet from the earth, and accessible by a broad stair. Along the back of this, and coming to about half its width, runs the open front of the house, like a covered gallery: the interior sometimes neat and almost elegant in its bareness, the sleeping space divided off by an endlong coaming, some bright raiment perhaps hanging from a nail, and a lamp and one of White's sewing-machines the only marks of civilisation. On the outside, at one end of the terrace, burns the cooking-fire under a shed; at the other there is perhaps a pen for pigs; the remainder is the evening lounge and *al fresco* banquet-hall of the inhabitants. To some houses water is brought down the mountain in bamboo pipes, perforated for the sake of sweetness. With the Highland comparison in my mind, I was struck to remember the sluttish mounds of turf and stone in which I have sat and been entertained in the Hebrides and the North Islands. Two things, I suppose, explain the contrast. In Scotland wood is rare, and with materials so rude as turf and stone the very hope of neatness is excluded. And in Scotland it is cold. Shelter and a hearth are needs so pressing that a man looks not beyond; he is out all day after a bare bellyful, and at night when he saith, 'Aha, it is warm!' he has not appetite for more. Or if for something else, then something higher; a fine school of poetry and song arose in these rough shelters, and an air like 'Lochaber no more' is an evidence of refinement more convincing, as well as more imperishable, than a palace.

To one such dwelling platform a considerable troop of relatives and dependants resort. In the hour of the dusk, when the fire blazes, and the scent of the cooked breadfruit fills the air, and perhaps the lamp glints already between the pillars of the house, you shall behold them silently assemble to this meal, men, women, and children; and the dogs and pigs frisk together up the terrace stairway, switching rival tails. The strangers from the ship were soon equally welcome: welcome to dip their fingers in the wooden dish, to drink cocoa-nuts, to share the circulating pipe, and to hear and hold high debate about the misdeeds of the French, the Panama Canal, or the geographical position of San Francisco and New Yo'ko. In a Highland hamlet, quite out of reach of any tourist, I have met the same plain and dignified hospitality.

I have mentioned two facts – the distasteful behaviour of our earliest visitors, and the case of the lady who rubbed herself upon the cushions – which would give a very false opinion of Marquesan manners. The great majority of Polynesians are excellently mannered; but the Marquesan stands apart, annoying and attractive, wild, shy, and refined. If you make him a present he affects to forget it, and it must be offered him again at his going: a pretty formality I have found nowhere else. A hint will get rid of any one or any number; they are so fiercely proud and modest; while many of the more lovable but blunter islanders crowd upon a stranger, and can be no more driven off than flies. A slight or an insult the Marquesan seems never to forget. I was one day talking by the wayside with my friend Hoka, when I perceived his eyes suddenly to flash and his stature to swell. A white horseman was coming down the mountain, and as he passed, and while he paused to exchange salutations with myself, Hoka was still staring and ruffling like a gamecock. It was a Corsican who had years before called him *cochon sauvage* – *coçon chauvage*, as Hoka mispronounced it. With people so nice and so touchy, it was scarce to be supposed that our company of greenhorns should not blunder into offences. Hoka, on one of his visits, fell suddenly in a brooding silence, and presently after left the ship with cold formality. When he took me back into favour, he adroitly and pointedly explained the nature of my offence: I had asked him to sell cocoa-nuts; and in Hoka's view articles of food were things that a gentleman should give, not sell; or at least that he should not sell to any friend. On another occasion I gave my boat's crew a luncheon of chocolate and biscuits. I had sinned, I could never learn how, against some point of observance; and though I was drily thanked, my offerings were left upon the beach. But our worst mistake was a slight we put on Toma, Hoka's adoptive father, and in his own eyes the rightful chief of Anaho. In the first place, we did not call upon him, as perhaps we should, in his fine new European house, the only one in the hamlet. In the second, when we came ashore upon a visit to his rival, Taipi-Kikino, it was Toma whom we saw standing at the head of the beach, a magnificent figure of a man, magnificently tattooed; and it was of Toma that we asked our question: 'Where is the chief?' 'What chief?' cried Toma, and turned his back on the blasphemers. Nor did he forgive us. Hoka came and went with us daily; but, alone I believe of all the countryside, neither Toma nor his wife set foot on board the *Casco*. The temptation resisted it is hard for a European to compute. The flying city of Laputa[21] moored for a fortnight in St. James's Park affords but a pale figure of the *Casco* anchored before Anaho; for the Londoner has still his change of pleasures, but the Marquesan passes to his grave through an unbroken uniformity of days.

On the afternoon before it was intended we should sail, a valedictory party came on board: nine of our particular friends equipped with gifts and dressed as for a festival. Hoka, the chief dancer and singer, the greatest dandy of Anaho, and one of the handsomest young fellows in the world – sullen, showy, dramatic, light as a feather and strong as an ox – it would have been hard, on that occasion, to recognise, as he sat there stooped and silent, his face heavy and grey. It was strange to see the lad so much affected; stranger still to recognise in his last gift one of the curios we had refused on the first day, and to know our friend, so gaily dressed, so plainly moved at our departure, for one of the half-naked crew that had besieged and insulted us on our arrival: strangest of all, perhaps, to find, in that carved handle of a fan, the last of those curiosities of the first day which had now all been given to us by their possessors – their chief merchandise, for which they had sought to ransom us as long as we were strangers, which they pressed on us for nothing as soon as we were friends. The last visit was not long protracted. One after another they shook hands and got down into their canoe; when Hoka turned his back immediately upon the ship, so that we saw his face no more. Taipi, on the other hand, remained standing and facing us with gracious valedictory gestures; and when Captain Otis[22] dipped the ensign, the whole party saluted with their hats. This was the farewell; the episode of our visit to Anaho was held concluded; and though the *Casco* remained nearly forty hours at her moorings, not one returned on board, and I am inclined to think they avoided appearing on the beach. This reserve and dignity is the finest trait of the Marquesan.

CHAPTER III

THE MAROON

Of the beauties of Anaho books might be written. I remember waking about three, to find the air temperate and scented. The long swell brimmed into the bay, and seemed to fill it full and then subside. Gently, deeply, and silently the *Casco* rolled; only at times a block piped like a bird. Oceanward, the heaven was bright with stars and the sea with their reflections. If I looked to that side, I might have sung with the Hawaiian poet:[1]

> *Ua maomao ka lani, ua kahaea luna,*
> *Ua pipi ka maka o ka hoku.*
> (The heavens were fair, they stretched above,
> Many were the eyes of the stars.)

And then I turned shoreward, and high squalls were overhead; the mountains loomed up black; and I could have fancied I had slipped ten thousand miles away and was anchored in a Highland loch; that when the day came, it would show pine, and heather, and green fern, and roofs of turf sending up the smoke of peats; and the alien speech that should next greet my ears must be Gaelic, not Kanaka.

And day, when it came, brought other sights and thoughts. I have watched the morning break in many quarters of the world; it has been certainly one of the chief joys of my existence, and the dawn that I saw with most emotion shone upon the bay of Anaho. The mountains abruptly overhang the port with every variety of surface and of inclination, lawn, and cliff, and forest. Not one of these but wore its proper tint of saffron, of sulphur, of the clove, and of the rose. The lustre was like that of satin; on the lighter hues there seemed to float an efflorescence; a solemn bloom appeared on the more dark. The light itself was the ordinary light of morning, colourless and clean; and on this ground of jewels, pencilled out the least detail of drawing. Meanwhile, around the hamlet, under the palms, where the blue shadow lingered, the red coals of cocoa husk and the light trails of smoke betrayed the awakening business of the day; along the beach men and women, lads and lasses, were returning from the bath in bright raiment, red and blue and green, such as we delighted to see in the coloured little pictures of our childhood; and presently the sun had cleared the eastern hill, and the glow of the day was over all.

The glow continued and increased, the business, for the main part, ceased before it had begun. Twice in the day there was a certain stir of shepherding along the seaward hills. At times a canoe went out to fish. At times a woman or two languidly filled a basket in the cotton patch. At times a pipe would sound out of the shadow of a house, ringing the changes on its three notes, with an effect like 'Que le jour me dure'[2] repeated endlessly. Or at times, across a corner of the bay, two natives might communicate in the Marquesan manner with conventional whistlings. All else was sleep and silence. The surf broke and shone around the shores; a species of black crane fished in the broken water; the black pigs were continually galloping by on some affair; but the people might never have awaked, or they might all be dead.

My favourite haunt was opposite the hamlet, where was a landing in a cove under a lianaed cliff. The beach was lined with palms and a tree called the *purao*,[3] something between the fig and mulberry in growth, and bearing a flower like a great yellow poppy with a maroon heart. In places rocks encroached upon the sand; the beach would be all submerged; and the surf would bubble warmly as high as to my knees, and play with cocoa-nut husks as our more homely ocean plays with wreck and wrack and bottles. As the reflux drew down, marvels of colour and design streamed between my feet; which I would grasp at, miss, or seize: now to find them what they promised, shells to grace a cabinet or be set in gold upon a lady's finger; now to catch only *maya*[4] of coloured sand, pounded fragments and pebbles, that, as soon as they were dry, became as dull and homely as the flints upon a garden path. I have toiled at this childish pleasure for hours in the strong sun, conscious of my incurable ignorance; but too keenly pleased to be ashamed. Meanwhile, the blackbird (or his tropical understudy) would be fluting in the thickets overhead.

A little further, in the turn of the bay, a streamlet trickled in the bottom of a den, thence spilling down a stair of rock into the sea. The draught of air drew down under the foliage in the very bottom of the den, which was a perfect arbour for coolness. In front it stood open on the blue bay and the *Casco* lying there under her awning and her cheerful colours. Overhead was a thatch of *purao*s, and over these again palms brandished their bright fans, as I have seen a conjurer make himself a halo out of naked swords. For in this spot, over a neck of low land at the foot of the mountains, the trade-wind streams into Anaho Bay in a flood of almost constant volume and velocity, and of a heavenly coolness.

It chanced one day that I was ashore in the cove with Mrs. Stevenson and the ship's cook.[5] Except for the *Casco* lying outside, and a crane or two, and the ever-busy wind and sea, the face of the world was of a prehistoric emptiness; life appeared to stand stockstill, and the sense of isolation was profound and refreshing. On a sudden, the trade-wind, coming in a gust over the isthmus, struck and scattered the fans of the palms above the den;[6] and, behold! in two of the tops there sat a native, motionless as an idol and watching us, you would have said, without a wink. The next moment the tree closed, and the glimpse was gone. This discovery of human presences latent overhead in a place where we had supposed ourselves alone, the immobility of our tree-top spies, and the thought that perhaps at all hours we were similarly supervised, struck us with a chill. Talk languished on the beach. As for the cook (whose conscience was not clear),[7] he never afterwards set foot on shore, and twice, when the *Casco* appeared to be driving on the rocks, it was amusing to observe that man's alacrity; death, he was persuaded, awaiting him upon the beach. It was more than a year later, in the Gilberts, that the explanation dawned upon myself. The natives were drawing palm-tree wine, a thing forbidden by law; and when the wind thus suddenly revealed them, they were doubtless more troubled than ourselves.

At the top of the den there dwelt an old, melancholy, grizzled man of the name of Tari (Charlie) Coffin. He was a native of Oahu, in the Sandwich Islands;[8] and had gone to sea in his youth in the American whalers; a circumstance to which he owed his name, his English, his down-east twang, and the misfortune of his innocent life. For one captain, sailing out of New Bedford, carried him to Nuka-hiva and marooned him there among the cannibals. The motive for this act was inconceivably small; poor Tari's wages, which were thus economised, would scarce have shook the credit of the New Bedford owners. And the act itself was simply murder. Tari's life must have hung in the beginning by a hair. In the grief and terror of that time, it is not unlikely he went mad, an infirmity to which he was still liable; or perhaps a child may have taken a fancy to him and ordained him to be spared. He escaped at least alive, married in the island, and when I knew him was a widower with a married son and a granddaughter. But the thought of Oahu haunted him; its praise was for ever on his lips; he beheld it, looking back, as a place of ceaseless feasting, song, and dance; and in his dreams I daresay he revisits it with joy. I wonder what he would think if he could be carried there indeed, and see the modern town of Honolulu brisk with traffic, and the palace with its guards, and the great hotel, and Mr. Berger's band with their uniforms and outlandish instruments; or what he would think to see the brown faces grown so few and the white so many; and his father's land sold for planting sugar, and his father's house quite perished, or perhaps the last of them struck leprous and immured between the surf and the cliffs on Molokai.[9] So simply, even in South Sea Islands, and so sadly, the changes come.

Tari was poor, and poorly lodged. His house was a wooden frame, run up by Europeans; it was indeed his official residence, for Tari was the shepherd of the promontory sheep. I can give a perfect inventory of its contents: three kegs, a tin biscuit-box, an iron saucepan, several cocoa-shell cups, a lantern, and three bottles, probably containing oil; while the clothes of the family and a few mats were thrown across the open rafters. Upon my first meeting with this exile he had conceived for me one of the baseless island friendships, had given me nuts to drink, and carried me up the den 'to see my house' – the only entertainment that he had to offer. He liked the 'Amelican,' he said, and the 'Inglisman,' but the 'Flessman' was his abhorrence; and he was careful to explain that if he had thought us 'Fless,' we should have had none of his nuts, and never a sight of his house. His distaste for the French I can partly understand, but not at all his toleration of the Anglo-Saxon. The next day he brought me a pig, and some days later one of our party going ashore found him in act to bring a second. We were still strange to the islands; we were pained by the poor man's generosity, which he could ill afford; and, by a natural enough but quite unpardonable blunder, we refused the pig. Had Tari been a Marquesan we should have seen him no more; being what he was, the most mild, long-suffering, melancholy man, he took a revenge a hundred times more painful. Scarce had the canoe with the nine villagers put off from their farewell before the *Casco* was boarded from the other side. It was Tari; coming thus late because he had no canoe of his own, and had found it hard to borrow one; coming thus solitary (as indeed we always saw him), because he was a stranger in the land, and the dreariest of company. The rest of my family basely fled from the encounter. I must receive our injured friend alone; and the interview must have lasted hard upon an hour, for he was loath to tear himself away. 'You go 'way. I see you no more – no, sir!' he lamented; and then looking about him with rueful admiration, 'This goodee ship – no, sir! – goodee ship!' he would exclaim: the 'no, sir,' thrown out sharply through the nose upon a rising inflection, an echo from New Bedford and the fallacious whaler. From these expressions of grief and praise he would return continually to the case of the rejected pig. 'I like give plesent all 'e same you,' he complained; 'only got pig: you no take him!' He was a poor man; he had no choice of gifts; he had only a pig, he repeated; and I had refused it. I have rarely been more wretched than to see him sitting there, so old, so grey, so poor, so hardly fortuned, of so rueful a countenance, and to appreciate, with growing keenness, the affront which I had so innocently dealt him; but it was one of those cases in which speech is vain.

Tari's son was smiling and inert; his daughter-in-law, a girl of sixteen, pretty, gentle, and grave, more intelligent than most Anaho women, and with a fair share of French; his grandchild, a mite of a creature at the breast. I went up the den one day when Tari was from home, and found the son making a cotton sack, and madame suckling mademoiselle. When I had sat down with them on the floor, the girl began to question me about England; which I tried to describe, piling the pan and the cocoa shells one upon another to represent the houses, and explaining, as best I was able, and by word and gesture, the over-population, the hunger, and the perpetual toil. *'Pas de cocotiers? pas de popoi?'*[10] she asked. I told her it was too cold, and went through an elaborate performance, shutting out draughts, and crouching over an imaginary fire, to make sure she understood. But she understood right well; remarked it must be bad for the health, and sat a while gravely reflecting on that picture of unwonted sorrows. I am sure it roused her pity, for it struck in her another thought always uppermost in the Marquesan bosom; and she began with a smiling sadness, and looking on me out of melancholy eyes, to lament the decease of her own people. *'Ici pas de Kanaques,'* said she; and taking the baby from her breast, she held it out to me with both her hands. *'Tenez* – a little baby like this; then dead. All the *Kanaques* die. Then no more.' The smile, and this instancing by the girl-mother of her own tiny flesh and blood, affected me strangely; they spoke of so tranquil a despair. Meanwhile the husband smilingly made his sack; and the unconscious babe struggled to reach a pot of raspberry jam, friendship's offering, which I had just brought up the den; and in a perspective of centuries

I saw their case as ours, death coming in like a tide, and the day already numbered when there should be no more Beretani, and no more of any race whatever, and (what oddly touched me) no more literary works and no more readers.

CHAPTER IV

DEATH

The thought of death, I have said, is uppermost in the mind of the Marquesan. It would be strange if it were otherwise. The race is perhaps the handsomest extant. Six feet is about the middle height of males; they are strongly muscled, free from fat, swift in action, graceful in repose; and the women, though fatter and duller, are still comely animals. To judge by the eye, there is no race more viable; and yet death reaps them with both hands. When Bishop Dordillon[1] first came to Tai-o-hae,[2] he reckoned the inhabitants at many thousands; he was but newly dead, and in the same bay Stanislao Moanatini[3] counted on his fingers eight residual natives. Or take the valley of Hapaa, known to readers of Herman Melville[4] under the grotesque misspelling of Hapar. There are but two writers who have touched the South Seas with any genius, both Americans: Melville and Charles Warren Stoddard;[5] and at the christening of the first and greatest, some influential fairy must have been neglected: 'He shall be able to see,' 'He shall be able to tell,' 'He shall be able to charm,' said the friendly godmothers; 'But he shall not be able to hear,' exclaimed the last. The tribe of Hapaa is said to have numbered some four hundred, when the smallpox came and reduced them by one-fourth. Six months later a woman developed tubercular consumption; the disease spread like a fire about the valley, and in less than a year two survivors, a man and a woman, fled from that new-created solitude. A similar Adam and Eve may some day wither among new races, the tragic residue of Britain. When I first heard this story the date staggered me; but I am now inclined to think it possible. Early in the year of my visit, for example, or late the year before, a first case of phthisis appeared in a household of seventeen persons, and by the month of August, when the tale was told me, one soul survived, and that was a boy who had been absent at his schooling. And depopulation works both ways, the doors of death being set wide open, and the door of birth almost closed. Thus, in the half-year ending July 1888 there were twelve deaths and but one birth in the district of the Hatiheu. Seven or eight more deaths were to be looked for in the ordinary course; and M. Aussel, the observant gendarme, knew of but one likely birth. At this rate it is no matter of surprise if the population in that part should have declined in forty years from six thousand to less than four hundred; which are, once more on the authority of M. Aussel, the estimated figures. And the rate of decline must have even accelerated towards the end.

A good way to appreciate the depopulation is to go by land from Anaho to Hatiheu on the adjacent bay. The road is good travelling, but cruelly steep. We seemed scarce to have passed the deserted house which stands highest in Anaho before we were looking dizzily down upon its roof; the *Casco* well out in the bay, and rolling for a wager, shrank visibly; and presently through the gap of Tari's isthmus, Uahuna was seen to hang cloudlike on the horizon. Over the summit, where the wind blew really chill, and whistled in the reed-like grass, and tossed the grassy fell of the pandanus, we stepped suddenly, as through a door, into the next vale and bay of Hatiheu. A bowl of mountains encloses it upon three sides. On the fourth this rampart has been bombarded into ruins, runs down to seaward in imminent and shattered crags, and presents the one practicable breach of the blue bay. The interior of this vessel is crowded with lovely and valuable trees, – orange, breadfruit, mummy-apple,[6] coco, the island chestnut, and for weeds, the pine and the banana. Four perennial streams water and keep it green; and along the dell, first of one, then of another, of these, the road, for a considerable distance, descends into this fortunate valley. The song of the waters and the familiar disarray of boulders gave us a strong sense of home, which the exotic foliage, the daft-like growth of the pandanus, the buttressed trunk of the banyan, the black pigs galloping in the bush, and the architecture of the native houses dissipated ere it could be enjoyed.

The houses on the Hatiheu side begin high up; higher yet, the more melancholy spectacle of empty *paepaes*. When a native habitation is deserted, the superstructure – pandanus thatch, wattle, unstable tropical timber – speedily rots, and is speedily scattered by the wind. Only the stones of the terrace endure; nor can any ruin, cairn, or standing stone, or vitrified fort present a more stern appearance of antiquity. We must have passed from six to eight of these now houseless platforms. On the main road of the island, where it crosses the valley of Taipi, Mr. Osbourne[7] tells me they are to be reckoned by the dozen; and as the roads have been made long posterior to their erection, perhaps to their desertion, and must simply be regarded as lines drawn at random through the bush, the forest on either hand must be equally filled with these survivals: the gravestones of whole families. Such ruins are *tapu*[8] in the strictest sense; no native must approach them; they have become outposts of the kingdom of the grave. It might appear a natural and pious custom in the hundreds who are left, the rearguard of perished thousands, that their feet should leave untrod these hearthstones of their fathers. I believe, in fact, the custom rests on different and more grim conceptions. But the house, the grave, and even the body of the dead, have been always particularly honoured by Marquesans. Until recently the corpse was sometimes kept in the family and daily oiled and sunned, until, by gradual and revolting stages, it dried into a kind of mummy. Offerings are still laid upon the grave. In Traitor's Bay, Mr. Osbourne saw a man buy a looking-glass to lay upon his son's. And the sentiment against the desecration of tombs, thoughtlessly ruffled in the laying down of the new roads, is a chief ingredient in the native hatred for the French.

The Marquesan beholds with dismay the approaching extinction of his race. The thought of death sits down with him to meat, and rises with him from his bed; he lives and breathes under a shadow of mortality awful to support; and he is so inured to the apprehension that he greets the reality with relief. He does not even seek to support a disappointment; at an affront, at a breach of one of his fleeting and communistic love-affairs, he seeks an instant refuge in the grave. Hanging is now the fashion. I heard[9] of three who had hanged themselves in the west end of Hiva-oa during the first half of 1888;

but though this be a common form of suicide in other parts of the South Seas, I cannot think it will continue popular in the Marquesas. Far more suitable to Marquesan sentiment is the old form of poisoning with the fruit of the *eva*,[10] which offers to the native suicide a cruel but deliberate death, and gives time for those decencies of the last hour, to which he attaches such remarkable importance. The coffin can thus be at hand, the pigs killed, the cry of the mourners sounding already through the house; and then it is, and not before, that the Marquesan is conscious of achievement, his life all rounded in, his robes (like Caesar's) adjusted for the final act. Praise not any man till he is dead, said the ancients; envy not any man till you hear the mourners, might be the Marquesan parody. The coffin, though of late introduction, strangely engages their attention. It is to the mature Marquesan what a watch is to the European schoolboy. For ten years Queen Vaekehu[11] had dunned the fathers; at last, but the other day, they let her have her will, gave her her coffin, and the woman's soul is at rest. I was told a droll instance of the force of this preoccupation. The Polynesians are subject to a disease seemingly rather of the will than of the body. I was told the Tahitians have a word for it, *erimatua*,[12] but cannot find it in my dictionary. A gendarme, M. Nouveau,[13] has seen men beginning to succumb to this insubstantial malady, has routed them from their houses, turned them on to do their trick upon the roads, and in two days has seen them cured. But this other remedy is more original: a Marquesan, dying of this discouragement – perhaps I should rather say this acquiescence – has been known, at the fulfilment of his crowning wish, on the mere sight of that desired hermitage, his coffin – to revive, recover, shake off the hand of death, and be restored for years to his occupations – carving *tiki*s (idols), let us say, or braiding old men's beards. From all this it may be conceived how easily they meet death when it approaches naturally. I heard one example, grim and picturesque. In the time of the small-pox in Hapaa, an old man was seized with the disease; he had no thought of recovery; had his grave dug by a wayside, and lived in it for near a fortnight, eating, drinking, and smoking with the passers-by, talking mostly of his end, and equally unconcerned for himself and careless of the friends whom he infected.

This proneness to suicide, and loose seat in life, is not peculiar to the Marquesan. What is peculiar is the wide-spread depression and acceptance of the national end. Pleasures are neglected, the dance languishes, the songs are forgotten. It is true that some, and perhaps too many, of them are proscribed; but many remain, if there were spirit to support or to revive them. At the last feast of the Bastille, Stanislao Moanatini shed tears when he beheld the inanimate performance of the dancers. When the people sang for us in Anaho, they must apologise for the smallness of their repertory. They were only young folk present, they said, and it was only the old that knew the songs. The whole body of Marquesan poetry and music was being suffered to die out with a single dispirited generation. The full import is apparent only to one acquainted with other Polynesian races; who knows how the Samoan coins a fresh song for every trifling incident, or who has heard (on Penrhyn,[14] for instance) a band of little stripling maids from eight to twelve keep up their minstrelsy for hours upon a stretch, one song following another without pause. In like manner, the Marquesan, never industrious, begins now to cease altogether from production. The exports of the group decline out of all proportion even with the death-rate of the islanders. 'The coral waxes, the palm grows, and man departs,' says the Marquesan; and he folds his hands. And surely this is nature. Fond as it may appear, we labour and refrain, not for the rewards of any single life, but with a timid eye upon the lives and memories of our successors; and where no one is to succeed, of his own family or his own tongue, I doubt whether Rothschilds would make money or Cato[15] practise virtue. It is natural, also, that a temporary stimulus should sometimes rouse the Marquesan from his lethargy. Over all the landward shore of Anaho cotton runs like a wild weed; man or woman, whoever comes to pick it, may earn a dollar in the day: yet when we arrived, the trader's store-house was entirely empty; and before we left it was near full. So long as the circus was there, so long as the *Casco* was yet anchored in the bay, it behoved every one to make his visit; and to this end every woman must have a new dress, and every man a shirt and trousers. Never before, in Mr. Regler's experience, had they displayed so much activity.

In their despondency there is an element of dread. The fear of ghosts and of the dark is very deeply written in the mind of the Polynesian; not least of the Marquesan. Poor Taipi, the chief of Anaho, was condemned to ride to Hatiheu on a moonless night. He borrowed a lantern, sat a long while nerving himself for the adventure, and when he at last departed, wrung the *Casco*s by the hand as for a final separation. Certain presences, called *vehinehae*, frequent and make terrible the nocturnal roadside; I was told by one they were like so much mist, and as the traveller walked into them dispersed and dissipated; another described them as being shaped like men and having eyes like cats; from none could I obtain the smallest clearness as to what they did, or wherefore they were dreaded. We may be sure at least they represent the dead; for the dead, in the minds of the islanders, are all-pervasive. 'When a native says that he is a man,' writes Dr. Codrington,[16] 'he means that he is a man and not a ghost; not that he is a man and not a beast. The intelligent agents of this world are to his mind the men who are alive, and the ghosts the men who are dead.' Dr. Codrington speaks of Melanesia; from what I have learned his words are equally true of the Polynesian. And yet more. Among cannibal Polynesians a dreadful suspicion rests generally on the dead; and the Marquesans, the greatest cannibals of all, are scarce likely to be free from similar beliefs. I hazard the guess that the *vehinehae* are the hungry spirits of the dead, continuing their life's business of the cannibal ambuscade, and lying everywhere unseen, and eager to devour the living. Another superstition I picked up through the troubled medium of Tari Coffin's English. The dead, he told me, came and danced by night around the *paepae* of their former family; the family were thereupon overcome by some emotion (but whether of pious sorrow or of fear I could not gather), and must 'make a feast,' of which fish, pig, and *popoi* were indispensable ingredients. So far this is clear enough. But here Tari went on to instance the new house of Toma and the house-warming feast which was just then in preparation as instances in point. Dare we indeed string them together, and add the case of the deserted ruin, as though the dead continually besieged the *paepae*s of the living: were kept at arm's-length, even from the first foundation, only by propitiatory feasts, and, so soon as the fire of life went out upon the hearth, swarmed back into possession of their ancient seat?

I speak by guess of these Marquesan superstitions. On the cannibal ghost I shall return elsewhere with certainty. And it is enough, for the present purpose, to remark that the men of the Marquesas, from whatever reason, fear and shrink from the presence of ghosts. Conceive how this must tell upon the nerves in islands where the number of the dead already so far exceeds that of the living, and the dead multiply and the living dwindle at so swift a rate. Conceive how the remnant huddles about the embers of the fire of life; even as old Red Indians, deserted on the march and in the snow, the kindly tribe all gone, the last flame expiring, and the night around populous with wolves.

CHAPTER V

DEPOPULATION

Over the whole extent of the South Seas, from one tropic to another, we find traces of a bygone state of over-population, when the resources of even a tropical soil were taxed, and even the improvident Polynesian trembled for the future. We may accept some of the ideas of Mr. Darwin's theory of coral islands,[1] and suppose a rise of the sea, or the subsidence of some former continental area, to have driven into the tops of the mountains multitudes of refugees. Or we may suppose, more soberly, a people of sea-rovers, emigrants from a crowded country, to strike upon and settle island after island, and as time went on to multiply exceedingly in their new seats. In either case the end must be the same; soon or late it must grow apparent that the crew are too numerous, and that famine is at hand. The Polynesians met this emergent danger with various expedients of activity and prevention. A way was found to preserve breadfruit by packing it in artificial pits; pits forty feet in depth and of proportionate bore are still to be seen, I am told, in the Marquesas; and yet even these were insufficient for the teeming people, and the annals of the past are gloomy with famine and cannibalism. Among the Hawaiians – a hardier people, in a more exacting climate – agriculture was carried far; the land was irrigated with canals; and the fish-ponds of Molokai prove the number and diligence of the old inhabitants. Meanwhile, over all the island world, abortion and infanticide prevailed. On coral atolls, where the danger was most plainly obvious, these were enforced by law and sanctioned by punishment. On Vaitupu, in the Ellices, only two children were allowed to a couple; on Nukufetau, but one. On the latter the punishment was by fine; and it is related that the fine was sometimes paid, and the child spared.

This is characteristic. For no people in the world are so fond or so long-suffering with children – children make the mirth and the adornment of their homes, serving them for playthings and for picture-galleries. 'Happy is the man that has his quiver full of them.'² The stray bastard is contended for by rival families; and the natural and the adopted children play and grow up together undistinguished. The spoiling, and I may almost say the deification, of the child, is nowhere carried so far as in the eastern islands; and furthest, according to my opportunities of observation, in the Paumotu group, the so-called Low or Dangerous Archipelago. I have seen a Paumotuan native turn from me with embarrassment and disaffection because I suggested that a brat would be the better for a beating. It is a daily matter in some eastern islands to see a child strike or even stone its mother, and the mother, so far from punishing, scarce ventures to resist. In some, when his child was born, a chief was superseded and resigned his name; as though, like a drone, he had then fulfilled the occasion of his being. And in some the lightest words of children had the weight of oracles. Only the other day, in the Marquesas, if a child conceived a distaste to any stranger, I am assured the stranger would be slain. And I shall have to tell in another place an instance of the opposite: how a child in Manihiki³ having taken a fancy to myself, her adoptive parents at once accepted the situation and loaded me with gifts.

With such sentiments the necessity for child-destruction would not fail to clash, and I believe we find the trace of divided feeling in the Tahitian brotherhood of Oro.⁴ At a certain date a new god was added to the Society-Island Olympus, or an old one refurbished and made popular. Oro was his name, and he may be compared with the Bacchus of the ancients. His zealots sailed from bay to bay, and from island to island; they were everywhere received with feasting; wore fine clothes;

sang, danced, acted; gave exhibitions of dexterity and strength: and were the artists, the acrobats, the bards, and the harlots of the group. Their life was public and epicurean; their initiation a mystery; and the highest in the land aspired to join the brotherhood. If a couple stood next in line to a high-chieftaincy, they were suffered, on grounds of policy, to spare one child; all other children, who had a father or a mother in the company of Oro, stood condemned from the moment of conception. A freemasonry, an agnostic sect, a company of artists, its members all under oath to spread unchastity, and all forbidden to leave offspring – I do not know how it may appear to others, but to me the design seems obvious. Famine menacing the islands, and the needful remedy repulsive, it was recommended to the native mind by these trappings of mystery, pleasure, and parade. This is the more probable, and the secret, serious purpose of the institution appears the more plainly, if it be true, that after a certain period of life, the obligation of the votary was changed; at first, bound to be profligate: afterwards, expected to be chaste.

Here, then, we have one side of the case. Man-eating among kindly men, child-murder among child-lovers, industry in a race the most idle, invention in a race the least progressive, this grim, pagan salvation-army of the brotherhood of Oro, the report of early voyagers, the wide-spread vestiges of former habitation, and the universal tradition of the islands, all point to the same fact of former crowding and alarm. And to-day we are face to face with the reverse. To-day in the Marquesas, in the Eight Islands of Hawaii, in Mangareva,[5] in Easter Island, we find the same race perishing like flies. Why this change? Or, grant that the coming of the whites, the change of habits, and the introduction of new maladies and vices, fully explain the depopulation, why is that depopulation not universal? The population of Tahiti, after a period of alarming decrease, has again become stationary. I hear of a similar result among some Maori tribes; in many of the Paumotus a slight increase is to be observed; and the Samoans are to-day as healthy and at least as fruitful as before the change. Grant that the Tahitians, the Maoris, and the Paumotuans have become inured to the new conditions; and what are we to make of the Samoans, who have never suffered?

Those who are acquainted only with a single group are apt to be ready with solutions. Thus I have heard the mortality of the Maoris attributed to their change of residence – from fortified hill-tops to the low, marshy vicinity of their plantations. How plausible! And yet the Marquesans are dying out in the same houses where their fathers multiplied. Or take opium. The Marquesas and Hawaii are the two groups the most infected with this vice; the population of the one is the most civilised, that of the other by far the most barbarous, of Polynesians; and they are two of those that perish the most rapidly. Here is a strong case against opium. But let us take unchastity, and we shall find the Marquesas and Hawaii figuring again upon another count. Thus, Samoans are the most chaste of Polynesians, and they are to this day entirely fertile; Marquesans are the most debauched: we have seen how they are perishing; Hawaiians are notoriously lax, and they begin to be dotted among deserts. So here is a case stronger still against unchastity; and here also we have a correction to apply. Whatever the virtues of the Tahitian, neither friend nor enemy dares call him chaste; and yet he seems to have outlived the time of danger. One last example: syphilis has been plausibly credited with much of the sterility. But the Samoans are, by all accounts, as fruitful as at first; by some accounts more so; and it is not seriously to be argued that the Samoans have escaped syphilis.

These examples show how dangerous it is to reason from any particular cause, or even from many in a single group. I have in my eye an able and amiable pamphlet by the Rev. S. E. Bishop: 'Why are the Hawaiians Dying Out?'[6] Any one interested in the subject ought to read this tract, which contains real information; and yet Mr. Bishop's views would have been changed by an acquaintance with other groups. Samoa is, for the moment, the main and the most instructive exception to the rule. The people are the most chaste and one of the most temperate of island peoples. They have never been tried and depressed with any grave pestilence. Their clothing has scarce been tampered with; at the simple and becoming tabard of the girls, Tartuffe,[7] in many another island, would have cried out; for the cool, healthy, and modest lava-lava or kilt, Tartuffe has managed in many another island to substitute stifling and inconvenient trousers.

Lastly, and perhaps chiefly, so far from their amusements having been curtailed, I think they have been, upon the whole, extended. The Polynesian falls easily into despondency: bereavement, disappointment, the fear of novel visitations, the decay or proscription of ancient pleasures, easily incline him to be sad; and sadness detaches him from life. The melancholy of the Hawaiian and the emptiness of his new life are striking; and the remark is yet more apposite to the Marquesas. In Samoa, on the other hand, perpetual song and dance, perpetual games, journeys, and pleasures, make an animated and a smiling picture of the island life. And the Samoans are to-day the gayest and the best entertained inhabitants of our planet. The importance of this can scarcely be exaggerated. In a climate and upon a soil where a livelihood can be had for the stooping, entertainment is a prime necessity. It is otherwise with us, where life presents us with a daily problem, and there is a serious interest, and some of the heat of conflict, in the mere continuing to be. So, in certain atolls, where there is no great gaiety, but man must bestir himself with some vigour for his daily bread, public health and the population are maintained; but in the lotos islands,[8] with the decay of pleasures, life itself decays. It is from this point of view that we may instance, among other causes of depression, the decay of war. We have been so long used in Europe to that dreary business of war on the great scale, trailing epidemics and leaving pestilential corpses in its train, that we have almost forgotten its original, the most healthful, if not the most humane, of all field sports – hedge-warfare. From this, as well as from the rest of his amusements and interests, the islander, upon a hundred islands, has been recently cut off. And to this, as well as to so many others, the Samoan still makes good a special title.

Upon the whole, the problem seems to me to stand thus:– Where there have been fewest changes, important or unimportant, salutary or hurtful, there the race survives. Where there have been most, important or unimportant, salutary or hurtful, there it perishes. Each change, however small, augments the sum of new conditions to which the race has to become inured. There may seem, *a priori*, no comparison between the change from 'sour toddy' to bad gin, and that from the island kilt to a pair of European trousers. Yet I am far from persuaded that the one is any more hurtful than the other; and the unaccustomed race will sometimes die of pin-pricks. We are here face to face with one of the difficulties of the missionary. In Polynesian islands he easily obtains pre-eminent authority; the king becomes his *mairedupalais*;[9] he can proscribe, he can command; and the temptation is ever towards too much. Thus (by all accounts) the Catholics in Mangareva, and thus (to my own knowledge) the Protestants in Hawaii, have rendered life in a more or less degree unliveable to their converts. And the mild, uncomplaining creatures (like children in a prison) yawn and await death. It is easy to blame the missionary. But it is his business to make changes. It is surely his business, for example, to prevent war; and yet I have instanced war itself as one of the elements of health. On the other hand, it were, perhaps, easy for the missionary to proceed more gently, and to regard every change as an affair of weight. I take the average missionary; I am sure I do him no more than justice when I suppose that he would hesitate to bombard a village, even in order to convert an archipelago. Experience begins to show us (at least in Polynesian islands) that change of habit is bloodier than a bombardment.

There is one point, ere I have done, where I may go to meet criticism. I have said nothing of faulty hygiene, bathing during fevers, mistaken treatment of children, native doctoring, or abortion – all causes frequently adduced. And I have said nothing of them because they are conditions common to both epochs, and even more efficient in the past than in the present. Was it not the same with unchastity, it may be asked? Was not the Polynesian always unchaste? Doubtless he was so always: doubtless he is more so since the coming of his remarkably chaste visitors from Europe. Take the Hawaiian account of Cook:[10] I have no doubt it is entirely fair. Take Krusenstern's candid, almost innocent, description of a Russian man-of-war at the Marquesas;[11] consider the disgraceful history of missions in Hawaii itself, where (in the war of lust) the American missionaries were once shelled by an English adventurer, and once raided and mishandled by the crew of an American warship; add the practice of whaling fleets to call at the Marquesas, and carry off a complement of women for the cruise; consider, besides, how the whites were at first regarded in the light of demigods, as appears plainly in the reception of Cook upon Hawaii; and again, in the story of the discovery of Tutuila, when the really decent women of Samoa prostituted themselves in public to the French;[12] and bear in mind how it was the custom of the adventurers, and we may almost say the business of the missionaries, to deride and infract even the most salutary *tapu*s. Here we see every engine of dissolution directed at once against a virtue never and nowhere very strong or popular; and the result, even in the most degraded islands, has been further degradation. Mr. Lawes, the missionary of Savage Island, told me[13] the standard of female chastity had declined there since the coming of the whites. In heathen time, if a girl gave birth to a bastard, her father or brother would dash the infant down the cliffs; and to-day the scandal would be small. Or take the Marquesas. Stanislao Moanatini told me that in his own recollection the young were strictly guarded; they were not suffered so much as to look upon one another in the street, but passed (so my informant put it) like dogs; and the other day the whole school-children of Nuka-hiva and Ua-pu escaped in a body to the woods, and lived there for a fortnight in promiscuous liberty. Readers of travels may perhaps exclaim at my authority, and declare themselves better informed. I should prefer the statement of an intelligent native like Stanislao (even if it stood alone, which it is far from doing) to the report of the most honest traveller. A ship of war comes to a haven, anchors, lands a party, receives and returns a visit, and the captain writes a chapter on the manners of the island. It is not considered what class is mostly seen. Yet we should not be pleased if a Lascar[14] foremast hand were to judge England by the ladies who parade Ratcliffe Highway,[15] and the gentlemen who share with them their hire. Stanislao's opinion of a decay of virtue even in these unvirtuous islands has been supported to me by others; his very example, the progress of dissolution amongst the young, is adduced by Mr. Bishop in Hawaii. And so far as Marquesans are concerned, we might have hazarded a guess of some decline in manners. I do not think that any race could ever have prospered or multiplied with such as now obtain; I am sure they would have been never at the pains to count paternal kinship. It is not possible to give details; suffice it that their manners appear to be imitated from

35

the dreams of ignorant and vicious children, and their debauches persevered in until energy, reason, and almost life itself are in abeyance.

CHAPTER VI

CHIEFS AND *TAPUS*

We used to admire exceedingly the bland and gallant manners of the chief called Taipi-Kikino. An elegant guest at table, skilled in the use of knife and fork, a brave figure when he shouldered a gun and started for the woods after wild chickens, always serviceable, always ingratiating and gay, I would sometimes wonder where he found his cheerfulness. He had enough to sober him, I thought, in his official budget. His expenses – for he was always seen attired in virgin white – must have by far exceeded his income of six dollars in the year, or say two shillings a month. And he was himself a man of no substance; his house the poorest in the village. It was currently supposed that his elder brother, Kauanui, must have helped him out. But how comes it that the elder brother should succeed to the family estate, and be a wealthy commoner, and the younger be a poor man, and yet rule as chief in Anaho? That the one should be wealthy and the other almost indigent is probably to be explained by some adoption; for comparatively few children are brought up in the house or succeed to the estates of their natural begetters. That the one should be chief instead of the other must be explained (in a very Irish fashion) on the ground that neither of them is a chief at all.

Since the return and the wars of the French,[1] many chiefs have been deposed, and many so-called chiefs appointed. We have seen, in the same house, one such upstart drinking in the company of two such extruded island Bourbons, men, whose word a few years ago was life and death, now sunk to be peasants like their neighbours. So when the French overthrew hereditary tyrants, dubbed the commons of the Marquesas free-born citizens of the republic, and endowed them with a vote for a *conseiller-général* at Tahiti, they probably conceived themselves upon the path to popularity; and so far from that, they were revolting public sentiment. The deposition of the chiefs was perhaps sometimes needful; the appointment of others may have been needful also; it was at least a delicate business. The Government of George II. exiled many Highland magnates. It never occurred to them to manufacture substitutes; and if the French have been more bold, we have yet to see with what success.

Our chief at Anaho was always called, he always called himself, Taipi-Kikino; and yet that was not his name, but only the wand of his false position. As soon as he was appointed chief, his name – which signified, if I remember exactly, 'Prince born among flowers' – fell in abeyance, and he was dubbed instead by the expressive byword, Taipi-Kikino – 'Highwater man-of-no-account' – or, Englishing more boldly, 'Beggar on horseback' – a witty and a wicked cut. A nickname in Polynesia destroys almost the memory of the original name. To-day, if we were Polynesians, Gladstone would be no more heard of. We should speak of and address our Nestor[2] as the Grand Old Man, and it is so that himself would sign his correspondence. Not the prevalence, then, but the significancy of the nickname is to be noted here. The new authority began with small prestige. Taipi has now been some time in office; from all I saw he seemed a person very fit. He is not the least unpopular, and yet his power is nothing. He is a chief to the French, and goes to breakfast with the Resident; but for any practical end of chieftaincy a rag doll were equally efficient.

We had been but three days in Anaho when we received the visit of the chief of Hatiheu, a man of weight and fame, late leader of a war upon the French, late prisoner in Tahiti, and the last eater of long-pig in Nuka-hiva. Not many years have elapsed since he was seen striding on the beach of Anaho, a dead man's arm across his shoulder. 'So does Kooamua to his enemies!' he roared to the passers-by, and took a bite from the raw flesh. And now behold this gentleman, very wisely replaced in office by the French, paying us a morning visit in European clothes. He was the man of the most character we had yet seen: his manners genial and decisive, his person tall, his face rugged, astute, formidable, and with a certain similarity to Mr. Gladstone's – only for the brownness of the skin, and the high-chief's tattooing, all one side and much of the other being of an even blue. Further acquaintance increased our opinion of his sense. He viewed the *Casco* in a manner then quite new to us, examining her lines and the running of the gear; to a piece of knitting on which one of the party was engaged, he must have devoted ten minutes' patient study; nor did he desist before he had divined the principles; and he was interested even to excitement by a type-writer, which he learned to work. When he departed he carried away with him a list of his family, with his own name printed by his own hand at the bottom. I should add that he was plainly much of a humorist, and not a little of a humbug. He told us, for instance, that he was a person of exact sobriety; such being the obligation of his high estate: the commons might be sots, but the chief could not stoop so low. And not many days after he was to be observed in a state of smiling and lop-sided imbecility, the *Casco* ribbon upside down on his dishonoured hat.

But his business that morning in Anaho is what concerns us here. The devil-fish, it seems, were growing scarce upon the reef; it was judged fit to interpose what we should call a close season; for that end, in Polynesia, a *tapu* (vulgarly spelt 'taboo') has to be declared, and who was to declare it? Taipi might; he ought; it was a chief part of his duty; but would any one regard the inhibition of a Beggar on Horseback? He might plant palm branches: it did not in the least follow that the spot was sacred. He might recite the spell: it was shrewdly supposed the spirits would not hearken. And so the old, legitimate cannibal must ride over the mountains to do it for him; and the respectable official in white clothes could but look on and envy. At about the same time, though in a different manner, Kooamua established a forest law. It was observed the coco-palms were suffering, for the plucking of green nuts impoverishes and at last endangers the tree. Now Kooamua could *tapu* the reef, which was public property, but he could not *tapu* other people's palms; and the expedient adopted was interesting. He *tapu*'d his own trees, and his example was imitated over all Hatiheu and Anaho. I fear Taipi might have *tapu*'d all that he possessed and found none to follow him. So much for the esteem in which the dignity of an appointed chief is held by others; a single circumstance will show what he thinks of it himself. I never met one, but he took an early opportunity to explain his situation. True, he was only an appointed chief when I beheld him; but somewhere else, perhaps upon some other isle, he was a chieftain by descent: upon which ground, he asked me (so to say it) to excuse his mushroom honours.

It will be observed with surprise that both these *tapu*s are for thoroughly sensible ends. With surprise, I say, because the nature of that institution is much misunderstood in Europe. It is taken usually in the sense of a meaningless or wanton prohibition, such as that which to-day prevents women in some countries from smoking, or yesterday prevented any one in Scotland from taking a walk on Sunday. The error is no less natural than it is unjust. The Polynesians have not been trained in the bracing, practical thought of ancient Rome; with them the idea of law has not been disengaged from that of morals or propriety; so that *tapu* has to cover the whole field, and implies indifferently that an act is criminal, immoral, against sound public policy, unbecoming or (as we say) 'not in good form.' Many *tapu*s were in consequence absurd enough, such as those which deleted words out of the language, and particularly those which related to women. *Tapu* encircled women upon all hands. Many things were forbidden to men; to women we may say that few were permitted. They must not sit on the *paepae*; they must not go up to it by the stair; they must not eat pork; they must not approach a boat; they must not cook at a fire which any male had kindled. The other day, after the roads were made, it was observed the women plunged along the margin through the bush, and when they came to a bridge waded through the water: roads and bridges were the work of men's hands, and *tapu* for the foot of women. Even a man's saddle, if the man be native, is a thing no self-respecting lady dares to use. Thus on the Anaho side of the island, only two white men, Mr. Regler and the gendarme, M. Aussel, possess saddles; and when a woman has a journey to make she must borrow from one or other. It will be noticed that these prohibitions tend, most of them, to an increased reserve between the sexes. Regard for female chastity is the usual excuse for these disabilities that men delight to lay upon their wives and mothers. Here the regard is absent; and behold the women still bound hand and foot with meaningless proprieties! The women themselves, who are survivors of the old regimen, admit that in those days life was not worth living.

And yet even then there were exceptions. There were female chiefs and (I am assured) priestesses besides; nice customs curtseyed to great dames, and in the most sacred enclosure of a High Place, Father Siméon Delmas[3] was shown a stone, and told it was the throne of some well-descended lady. How exactly parallel is this with European practice, when princesses were suffered to penetrate the strictest cloister, and women could rule over a land in which they were denied the control of their own children.

But the *tapu* is more often the instrument of wise and needful restrictions. We have seen it as the organ of paternal government. It serves besides to enforce, in the rare case of some one wishing to enforce them, rights of private property. Thus a man, weary of the coming and going of Marquesan visitors, *tapu's* his door; and to this day you may see the palm-branch signal, even as our great-grandfathers saw the peeled wand before a Highland inn.[4] Or take another case. Anaho is known as 'the country without *popoi*.' The word *popoi* serves in different islands to indicate the main food of the people: thus, in Hawaii, it implies a preparation of taro; in the Marquesas, of breadfruit. And a Marquesan does not readily conceive life possible without his favourite diet. A few years ago a drought killed the breadfruit trees and the bananas in the district of Anaho; and from this calamity, and the open-handed customs of the island, a singular state of things arose. Well-watered Hatiheu had escaped the drought; every householder of Anaho accordingly crossed the pass, chose some one in Hatiheu, 'gave him his name' – an onerous gift, but one not to be rejected – and from this improvised relative proceeded to draw his supplies, for all the world as though he had paid for them. Hence a continued traffic on the road. Some stalwart fellow, in a loin-cloth, and glistening with sweat, may be seen at all hours of the day, a stick across his bare shoulders, tripping nervously under a double burthen of green fruits. And on the far side of the gap a dozen stone posts on the wayside in the shadow of a grove mark the breathing-place of the *popoi*-carriers. A little back from the beach, and not half a mile from Anaho, I was the more amazed to find a cluster of well-doing breadfruits heavy with their harvest. 'Why do you not take these?' I asked. '*Tapu*,' said Hoka; and I thought to myself (after the manner of dull travellers) what children and fools these people were to toil over the mountain and despoil innocent neighbours when the staff of life was thus growing at their door. I was the more in error. In the general destruction these surviving trees were enough only for the family of the proprietor, and by the simple expedient of declaring a *tapu* he enforced his right.

The sanction of the *tapu* is superstitious; and the punishment of infraction either a wasting or a deadly sickness. A slow disease follows on the eating of *tapu* fish, and can only be cured with the bones of the same fish burned with the due mysteries. The cocoa-nut and breadfruit *tapu* works more swiftly. Suppose you have eaten *tapu* fruit at the evening meal, at night your sleep will be uneasy; in the morning, swelling and a dark discoloration will have attacked your neck, whence they spread upward to the face; and in two days, unless the cure be interjected, you must die. This cure is prepared from the rubbed leaves of the tree from which the patient stole; so that he cannot be saved without confessing to the *tuhuka*[5] the person whom he wronged. In the experience of my informant, almost no *tapu* had been put in use, except the two described: he had thus no opportunity to learn the nature and operation of the others; and, as the art of making them was jealously guarded amongst the old men, he believed the mystery would soon die out. I should add that he was no Marquesan, but a Chinaman, a resident in the group from boyhood, and a reverent believer in the spells which he described. White men, amongst whom Ah Fu[6] included himself, were exempt; but he had a tale of a Tahitian woman, who had come to the Marquesas, eaten *tapu* fish, and, although uninformed of her offence and danger, had been afflicted and cured exactly like a native.

Doubtless the belief is strong; doubtless, with this weakly and fanciful race, it is in many cases strong enough to kill; it should be strong indeed in those who *tapu* their trees secretly, so that they may detect a depredator by his sickness. Or, perhaps, we should understand the idea of the hidden *tapu* otherwise, as a politic device to spread uneasiness and extort confessions: so that, when a man is ailing, he shall ransack his brain for any possible offence, and send at once for any proprietor whose rights he has invaded. 'Had you hidden a *tapu*?' we may conceive him asking; and I cannot imagine the proprietor gainsaying it; and this is perhaps the strangest feature of the system – that it should be regarded from without with such a mental and implicit awe, and, when examined from within, should present so many apparent evidences of design.

We read in Dr. Campbell's *Poenamo*[7] of a New Zealand girl, who was foolishly told that she had eaten a *tapu* yam, and who instantly sickened, and died in the two days of simple terror. The period is the same as in the Marquesas; doubtless the symptoms were so too. How singular to consider that a superstition of such sway is possibly a manufactured article; and that, even if it were not originally invented, its details have plainly been arranged by the authorities of some Polynesian Scotland Yard. Fitly enough, the belief is to-day – and was probably always – far from universal. Hell at home is a strong deterrent with some; a passing thought with others; with others, again, a theme of public mockery, not always well assured; and so in the Marquesas with the *tapu*. Mr. Regler has seen the two extremes of scepticism and implicit fear. In the *tapu* grove he found one fellow stealing breadfruit, cheerful and impudent as a street arab; and it was only on a menace of exposure that he showed himself the least discountenanced. The other case was opposed in every point. Mr. Regler asked a native to accompany him upon a voyage; the man went gladly enough, but suddenly perceiving a dead *tapu* fish in the bottom of the boat, leaped back with a scream; nor could the promise of a dollar prevail upon him to advance.

The Marquesan, it will be observed, adheres to the old idea of the local circumscription of beliefs and duties. Not only are the white. exempt from consequences; but their transgressions seem to be viewed without horror. It was Mr. Regler who had killed the fish; yet the devout native was not shocked at Mr. Regler – only refused to join him in his boat. A white is a white: the servant (so to speak) of other and more liberal gods; and not to be blamed if he profit by his liberty. The Jews were perhaps the first to interrupt this ancient comity of faiths; and the Jewish virus is still strong in Christianity. All the world must respect our *tapu*s, or we gnash our teeth.

CHAPTER VII

HATIHEU

The bays of Anaho and Hatiheu are divided at their roots by the knife-edge of a single hill – the pass so often mentioned; but this isthmus expands to the seaward in a considerable peninsula: very bare and grassy; haunted by sheep and, at night and morning, by the piercing cries of the shepherds; wandered over by a few wild goats; and on its sea-front indented with long, clamorous caves, and faced with cliffs of the colour and ruinous outline of an old peat-stack. In one of these echoing and sunless gullies we saw, clustered like sea-birds on a splashing ledge, shrill as sea-birds in their salutation to the passing boat, a group of fisherwomen, stripped to their gaudy under-clothes. (The clash of the surf and the thin female voices echo in my memory.) We had that day a native crew and steersman, Kauanui; it was our first experience of Polynesian seamanship, which consists in hugging every point of land. There is no thought in this of saving time, for they will pull a long way in to skirt a point that is embayed. It seems that, as they can never get their houses near enough the surf upon the one side, so they can never get their boats near enough upon the other. The practice in bold water is not so dangerous as it looks – the reflex from the rocks sending the boat off. Near beaches with a heavy run of sea, I continue to think it very hazardous, and find the composure of the natives annoying to behold. We took unmingled pleasure, on the way out, to see so near at hand the beach and the wonderful colours of the surf. On the way back, when the sea had risen and was running strong against us, the fineness of the steersman's aim grew more embarrassing. As we came abreast of the sea-front, where the surf broke highest, Kauanui embraced the occasion to light his pipe, which then made the circuit of the boat – each man taking a whiff or two, and, ere he passed it on, filling his lungs and cheeks with smoke. Their faces were all puffed out like apples as we came abreast of the cliff foot, and the bursting surge fell back into the boat in showers. At the next point 'cocanetti' was the word, and the stroke borrowed my knife, and desisted from his labours to open nuts. These untimely indulgences may be compared to the tot of grog served out before a ship goes into action.

My purpose in this visit led me first to the boys' school, for Hatiheu is the university of the north islands. The hum of the lesson came out to meet us. Close by the door, where the draught blew coolest, sat the lay brother; around him, in a packed half-circle, some sixty high-coloured faces set with staring eyes; and in the background of the barn-like room benches were to be seen, and blackboards with sums on them in chalk. The brother rose to greet us, sensibly humble. Thirty years he had been there, he said, and fingered his white locks as a bashful child pulls out his pinafore. '*Et point de résultats, monsieur, presque pas de résultats.*' He pointed to the scholars: 'You see, sir, all the youth of Nuka-hiva and Ua-pu. Between the ages of six and fifteen this is all that remains; and it is but a few years since we had a hundred and twenty from Nuka-hiva alone. *Oui, monsieur, cela se dépérit.*' Prayers, and reading and writing, prayers again and arithmetic, and more prayers to conclude: such appeared to be the dreary nature of the course. For arithmetic all island people have a natural taste. In Hawaii they make good progress in mathematics. In one of the villages on Majuro,[1] and generally in the Marshall group, the whole population sit about the trader when he is weighing copra, and each on his own slate takes down the figures and computes the total. The trader, finding them so apt, introduced fractions, for which they had been taught no rule. At first they were quite gravelled, but ultimately, by sheer hard thinking, reasoned out the result, and came one after another to assure the trader he was right. Not many people in Europe could have done the like. The course at Hatiheu is therefore less dispiriting to Polynesians than a stranger might have guessed; and yet how bald it is at best! I asked the brother if he did not tell them stories, and he stared at me; if he did not teach them history, and he said, 'O yes, they had a little Scripture history – from the New Testament'; and repeated his lamentations over the lack of results. I had not the heart to put more questions; I could but say it must be very discouraging, and resist the impulse to add that it seemed also very natural. He looked up – 'My days are far spent,' he said; 'heaven awaits me.' May that heaven forgive me, but I was angry with the old man and his simple consolation. For think of his opportunity! The youth, from six to fifteen, are taken from their homes by Government, centralised at Hatiheu, where they are supported by a weekly tax of food; and, with the exception of one month in every year, surrendered wholly to the direction of the priests. Since the escapade already mentioned the holiday occurs at a different period for the girls and for the boys; so that a Marquesan brother and sister meet again, after their education is complete, a pair of strangers. It is a harsh law, and highly unpopular; but what a power it places in the hands of the instructors, and how languidly and dully is that power employed by the mission! Too much concern to make the natives pious, a design in which they all confess defeat, is, I suppose, the explanation of their miserable system. But they might see in the girls' school at Tai-o-hae, under the brisk, housewifely sisters, a different picture of efficiency, and a scene of neatness, airiness, and spirited and mirthful occupation that should shame them into cheerier methods. The sisters themselves lament their failure. They complain the annual holiday undoes the whole year's work; they complain particularly of the heartless indifference of the girls. Out of so many pretty and apparently affectionate pupils whom they have taught and reared, only two have ever returned to pay a visit of remembrance to their teachers. These, indeed, come regularly, but the rest, so soon as their school-days are over, disappear into the woods like captive insects. It is hard to imagine anything more discouraging; and yet I do not believe these ladies need despair. For a certain interval they keep the girls alive and innocently busy; and if it be at all possible to save the race, this would be the means. No such praise can be given to the boys' school at Hatiheu. The day is numbered already for them all; alike for the teacher and the scholars death is girt; he is afoot upon the march; and in the frequent interval they sit and yawn. But in life there seems a thread of purpose through the least significant; the drowsiest endeavour is not lost, and even the school at Hatiheu may be more useful than it seems.

Hatiheu is a place of some pretensions. The end of the bay towards Anaho may be called the civil compound, for it boasts the house of Kooamua, and close on the beach, under a great tree, that of the gendarme, M. Armand Aussel, with his garden, his pictures, his books, and his excellent table, to which strangers are made welcome. No more singular contrast is possible than between the gendarmerie and the priesthood, who are besides in smouldering opposition and full of mutual complaints. A priest's kitchen in the eastern islands is a depressing spot to see; and many, or most of them, make no attempt to keep a garden, sparsely subsisting on their rations. But you will never dine with a gendarme without smacking your lips; and M. Aussel's home-made sausage and the salad from his garden are unforgotten delicacies. Pierre Loti[2] may like to know that he is M. Aussel's favourite author, and that his books are read in the fit scenery of Hatiheu bay.

The other end is all religious. It is here that an overhanging and tip-tilted horn, a good sea-mark for Hatiheu, bursts naked from the verdure of the climbing forest, and breaks down shoreward in steep taluses[3] and cliffs. From the edge of one of the highest, perhaps seven hundred or a thousand feet above the beach, a Virgin looks insignificantly down, like a poor lost doll, forgotten there by a giant child. This laborious symbol of the Catholics is always strange to Protestants; we conceive with wonder that men should think it worth while to toil so many days, and clamber so much about the face of precipices, for an end that makes us smile; and yet I believe it was the wise Bishop Dordillon who chose the place, and I know that those who had a hand in the enterprise look back with pride upon its vanquished dangers. The boys' school is a recent importation; it was at first in Tai-o-hae, beside the girls'; and it was only of late, after their joint escapade, that the width of the island was interposed between the sexes. But Hatiheu must have been a place of missionary importance from before. About midway of the beach no less than three churches stand grouped in a patch of bananas, intermingled with some pine-apples. Two are of wood: the original church, now in disuse; and a second that, for some mysterious reason, has never been used. The new church is of stone, with twin towers, walls flangeing into buttresses, and sculptured front. The design itself is good, simple, and shapely; but the character is all in the detail, where the architect has bloomed into the sculptor. It is impossible to tell in words of the angels (although they are more like winged archbishops) that stand guard upon the door, of the cherubs in the corners, of the scapegoat gargoyles, or the quaint and spirited relief, where St. Michael (the artist's patron) makes short work of a protesting Lucifer. We were never weary of viewing the imagery, so innocent, sometimes so funny, and yet in the best sense – in the sense of inventive gusto and expression – so artistic. I know not whether it was more strange to find a building of such merit in a corner of a barbarous isle, or to see a building so antique still bright with novelty. The architect, a French lay brother, still alive and well, and meditating fresh foundations, must have surely drawn his descent from a master-builder in the age of the cathedrals; and it was in looking on the church of Hatiheu that I seemed to perceive the secret charm of mediaeval sculpture; that combination of the childish courage of the amateur, attempting all things, like the schoolboy on his slate, with the manly perseverance of the artist who does not know when he is conquered.

I had always afterwards a strong wish to meet the architect, Brother Michel;[4] and one day, when I was talking with the Resident in Tai-o-hae (the chief port of the island), there were shown in to us an old, worn, purblind, ascetic-looking priest, and a lay brother, a type of all that is most sound in France, with a broad, clever, honest, humorous countenance, an eye very large and bright, and a strong and healthy body inclining to obesity. But that his blouse was black and his face shaven clean, you might pick such a man to-day, toiling cheerfully in his own patch of vines, from half a dozen provinces of France; and yet he had always for me a haunting resemblance to an old kind friend of my boyhood, whom I name in case any of my readers should share with me that memory – Dr. Paul, of the West Kirk.[5] Almost at the first word I was sure it was my architect, and in a moment we were deep in a discussion of Hatiheu church. Brother Michel spoke always of his labours with a twinkle of humour, underlying which it was possible to spy a serious pride, and the change from one to another was often very human and diverting. '*Et vos gargouilles moyen-âge*,' cried I; '*comme elles sont originales!*' '*N'est-ce pas? Elles sont bien drôles!*' he said, smiling broadly; and the next moment, with a sudden gravity: '*Cependant il y en a une qui a une patte de cassé; il faut que je voie cela.*' I asked if he had any model – a point we much discussed. '*Non*,' said he simply; '*c'est une église idéale.*' The relievo[6] was his favourite performance, and very justly so. The angels at the door, he owned, he would like to destroy and replace. '*Ils n'ont pas de vie, ils manquent de vie. Vous devriez voir mon église à la Dominique;*[7] *j'ai là une Vierge qui est vraiment gentille.*' 'Ah,' I cried, 'they told me you had said you would never build another church, and I wrote in my journal I could not believe it.'[8] '*Oui, j'aimerais bien en faire une autre,*' he confessed, and smiled at the confession. An artist will understand how much I was attracted by this conversation. There is no bond so near as a community in that unaffected interest and slightly shamefaced pride which mark the intelligent man enamoured of an art. He sees the limitations of his aim, the defects of his practice; he smiles to be so employed upon the shores of death, yet sees in his own devotion something worthy. Artists, if they had the same sense of humour with the Augurs,[9] would smile like them on meeting, but the smile would not be scornful.

I had occasion to see much of this excellent man. He sailed with us from Tai-o-hae to Hiva-oa, a dead beat of ninety miles against a heavy sea. It was what is called a good passage, and a feather in the *Casco*'s cap; but among the most miserable forty hours that any one of us had ever passed. We were swung and tossed together all that time like shot in a stage thunder-box. The mate was thrown down and had his head cut open; the captain was sick on deck; the cook sick in the galley. Of all our party only two sat down to dinner. I was one. I own that I felt wretchedly; and I can only say of the other, who professed to feel quite well, that she fled at an early moment from the table. It was in these circumstances that we skirted the windward shore of that indescribable island of Ua-pu; viewing with dizzy eyes the coves, the capes, the breakers, the climbing forests, and the inaccessible stone needles that surmount the mountains. The place persists, in a dark corner of our memories, like a piece of the scenery of nightmares. The end of this distressful passage, where we were to land our passengers, was in a similar vein of roughness. The surf ran high on the beach at Taahauku; the boat broached-to and capsized; and all hands were submerged. Only the brother himself, who was well used to the experience, skipped ashore, by some miracle of agility, with scarce a sprinkling. Thenceforward, during our stay at Hiva-oa, he was our cicerone and patron; introducing us, taking us excursions, serving us in every way, and making himself daily more beloved.

Michel Blanc had been a carpenter by trade; had made money and retired, supposing his active days quite over; and it was only when he found idleness dangerous that he placed his capital and acquirements at the service of the mission. He became their carpenter, mason, architect, and engineer; added sculpture to his accomplishments, and was famous for his skill in gardening. He wore an enviable air of having found a port from life's contentions and lying there strongly anchored; went about his business with a jolly simplicity; complained of no lack of results — perhaps shyly thinking his own statuary result enough; and was altogether a pattern of the missionary layman.

CHAPTER VIII

THE PORT OF ENTRY

The port – the mart, the civil and religious capital of these rude islands – is called Tai-o-hae, and lies strung along the beach of a precipitous green bay in Nuka-hiva. It was midwinter when we came thither, and the weather was sultry, boisterous, and inconstant. Now the wind blew squally from the land down gaps of splintered precipice; now, between the sentinel islets of the entry, it came in gusts from seaward. Heavy and dark clouds impended on the summits; the rain roared and ceased; the scuppers of the mountain gushed; and the next day we would see the sides of the amphitheatre bearded with white falls.[1] Along the beach the town shows a thin file of houses, mostly white, and all ensconced in the foliage of an avenue of green *puraos*; a pier gives access from the sea across the belt of breakers; to the eastward there stands, on a projecting bushy hill, the old fort which is now the calaboose, or prison; eastward still, alone in a garden, the Residency flies the colours of France. Just off Calaboose Hill, the tiny Government schooner rides almost permanently at anchor, marks eight bells in the morning (there or thereabout) with the unfurling of her flag, and salutes the setting sun with the report of a musket.

Here dwell together, and share the comforts of a club (which may be enumerated as a billiard-board, absinthe, a map of the world on Mercator's projection, and one of the most agreeable verandahs in the tropics), a handful of whites of varying nationality, mostly French officials, German and Scottish merchant clerks, and the agents of the opium monopoly. There are besides three tavern-keepers, the shrewd Scot[2] who runs the cotton gin-mill,[3] two white ladies, and a sprinkling of people 'on the beach' – a South Sea expression for which there is no exact equivalent. It is a pleasant society, and a hospitable. But one man, who was often to be seen seated on the logs at the pier-head, merits a word for the singularity of his history and appearance. Long ago, it seems, he fell in love with a native lady, a High Chiefess in Ua-pu. She, on being approached, declared she could never marry a man who was untattooed; it looked so naked; whereupon, with some greatness of soul, our hero put himself in the hands of the *tuhuka*s,[4] and, with still greater, persevered until the process was complete. He had certainly to bear a great expense, for the *tuhuka* will not work without reward; and certainly exquisite pain. Kooamua, high chief as he was, and one of the old school, was only part tattooed; he could not, he told us with lively pantomime, endure the torture to an end. Our enamoured countryman was more resolved; he was tattooed from head to foot in the most approved methods of the art; and at last presented himself before his mistress a new man. The fickle fair one could never behold him from that day except with laughter. For my part, I could never see the man without a kind of admiration; of him it might be said, if ever of any, that he had loved not wisely, but too well.[5]

The Residency stands by itself, Calaboose Hill screening it from the fringe of town along the further bay. The house is commodious, with wide verandahs; all day it stands open, back and front, and the trade blows copiously over its bare floors. On a week-day the garden offers a scene of most untropical animation, half a dozen convicts toiling there cheerfully with spade and barrow, and touching hats and smiling to the visitor like old attached family servants. On Sunday these are gone, and nothing to be seen but dogs of all ranks and sizes peacefully slumbering in the shady grounds; for the dogs of Tai-o-hae are very courtly-minded, and make the seat of Government their promenade and place of siesta. In front and beyond, a strip of green down loses itself in a low wood of many species of acacia; and deep in the wood a ruinous wall encloses the cemetery of the Europeans. English and Scottish sleep there, and Scandinavians, and French *maîtres de manœuvres* and *maîtres ouvriers*: mingling alien dust. Back in the woods perhaps, the blackbird, or (as they call him there) the island nightingale, will be singing home strains; and the ceaseless requiem of the surf hangs on the ear. I have never seen a resting-place more quiet; but it was a long thought how far these sleepers had all travelled, and from what diverse homes they had set forth, to lie here in the end together.

On the summit of its promontory hill, the calaboose stands all day with doors and window-shutters open to the trade. On my first visit a dog was the only guardian visible. He, indeed, rose with an attitude so menacing that I was glad to lay hands on an old barrel-hoop; and I think the weapon must have been familiar, for the champion instantly retreated, and as I wandered round the court and through the building, I could see him, with a couple of companions, humbly dodging me about the corners. The prisoners' dormitory was a spacious, airy room, devoid of any furniture; its whitewashed walls covered with inscriptions in Marquesan and rude drawings: one of the pier, not badly done; one of a murder; several of French soldiers in uniform. There was one legend in French: '*Je n'est* (sic) '*pas le sou.*' From this noontide quietude it must not be supposed the prison was untenanted; the calaboose at Tai-o-hae does a good business. But some of its occupants were gardening at the Residency, and the rest were probably at work upon the streets, as free as our scavengers at home, although not so industrious. On the approach of evening they would be called in like children from play; and the harbour-master (who is also the jailer) would go through the form of locking them up until six the next morning. Should a prisoner have any call in town, whether of pleasure or affairs, he has but to unhook the window-shutter; and if he is back again, and the shutter decently replaced, by the hour of call on the morrow, he may have met the harbour-master in the avenue, and there will be no complaint, far less any punishment. But this is not all.

The charming French Resident, M. Delaruelle, carried me one day to the calaboose on an official visit. In the green court, a very ragged gentleman, his legs deformed with the island elephantiasis,[6] saluted us smiling. 'One of our political prisoners – an insurgent from Raiatea,'[7] said the Resident; and then to the jailer: 'I thought I had ordered him a new pair of trousers.' Meanwhile no other convict was to be seen – '*Eh bien*,' said the Resident, '*où sont vos prisonniers?*' '*Monsieur le Résident,*' replied the jailer, saluting with soldierly formality, '*comme c'est jour de fête, je les ai laissé aller à la chasse.*' They were all upon the mountains hunting goats! Presently we came to the quarters of the women, likewise deserted – '*Où sont vos bonnes femmes?*' asked the Resident; and the jailer cheerfully responded: '*Je crois, Monsieur le Résident, qu'elles sont allées quelquepart faire une visite.*' It had been the design of M. Delaruelle, who was much in love with the whimsicalities of his small realm, to elicit something comical; but not even he expected anything so perfect as the last. To complete the picture of convict life in Tai-o-hae, it remains to be added that these criminals draw a salary as regularly as the President of the Republic. Ten sous a day is their hire. Thus they have money, food, shelter, clothing, and, I was about to write, their liberty. The French are certainly a good-natured people, and make easy masters. They are besides inclined to view the Marquesans with an eye of humorous indulgence. 'They are dying, poor devils!' said M. Delaruelle: 'the main thing is to let them die in peace.' And it was not only well said, but I believe expressed the general thought. Yet there is another element to be considered; for these convicts are not merely useful, they are almost essential to the French existence. With a people incurably idle, dispirited by what can only be called endemic pestilence, and inflamed with ill-feeling against their new masters, crime and convict labour are a godsend to the Government.

Theft is practically the sole crime. Originally petty pilferers, the men of Tai-o-hae now begin to force locks and attack strong-boxes. Hundreds of dollars have been taken at a time; though, with that redeeming moderation so common in Polynesian theft, the Marquesan burglar will always take a part and leave a part, sharing (so to speak) with the proprietor. If it be Chilian coin – the island currency – he will escape; if the sum is in gold, French silver, or bank-notes, the police wait until the money begins to come in circulation, and then easily pick out their man. And now comes the shameful part. In plain English, the prisoner is tortured until he confesses and (if that be possible) restores the money. To keep him alone, day and night, in the black hole, is to inflict on the Marquesan torture inexpressible. Even his robberies are carried on in the plain daylight, under the open sky, with the stimulus of enterprise, and the countenance of an accomplice; his terror of the dark is still insurmountable; conceive, then, what he endures in his solitary dungeon; conceive how he longs to confess, become a full-fledged convict, and be allowed to sleep beside his comrades. While we were in Tai-o-hae a thief was under prevention. He had entered a house about eight in the morning, forced a trunk, and stolen eleven hundred francs; and now, under the horrors of darkness, solitude, and a bedevilled cannibal imagination, he was reluctantly confessing and giving up his spoil. From one cache, which he had already pointed out, three hundred francs had been recovered, and it was expected that he would presently disgorge the rest. This would be ugly enough if it were all; but I am bound to say, because it is a matter the French should set at rest, that worse is continually hinted. I heard that one man was kept six days with his arms bound backward round a barrel; and it is the universal report that every gendarme in the South Seas is equipped with something in the nature of a thumbscrew. I do not know this. I never had the face to ask any of the gendarmes – pleasant, intelligent, and kindly fellows – with whom I have been intimate, and whose hospitality I have enjoyed; and perhaps the tale reposes (as I hope it does) on a misconstruction of that ingenious cat's-cradle with which the French agent of police so readily secures a prisoner. But whether physical or moral, torture is certainly employed; and by a barbarous injustice, the state of accusation (in which a man may very well be innocently placed) is positively painful; the state of conviction (in which all are supposed guilty) is comparatively free, and positively pleasant. Perhaps worse still, – not only the accused, but sometimes his wife, his mistress, or his friend, is subjected to the same hardships. I was admiring, in the *tapu* system, the ingenuity of native methods of detection; there is not much to admire in those of the French, and to lock up a timid child in a dark room, and, if he prove obstinate, lock up his sister in the next, is neither novel nor humane.

The main occasion of these thefts is the new vice of opium-eating. 'Here nobody ever works, and all eat opium,' said a gendarme; and Ah Fu knew a woman who ate a dollar's worth in a day. The successful thief will give a handful of money to each of his friends, a dress to a woman, pass an evening in one of the taverns of Tai-o-hae, during which he treats all comers, produce a big lump of opium, and retire to the bush to eat and sleep it off. A trader, who did not sell opium,[8] confessed to me that he was at his wit's end. 'I do not sell it, but others do,' said he. 'The natives only work to buy it; if they walk over to me to sell their cotton, they have just to walk over to some one else to buy their opium with my money. And why should they be at the bother of two walks? There is no use talking,' he added – 'opium is the currency of this country.'

The man under prevention during my stay at Tai-o-hae lost patience while the Chinese opium-seller was being examined in his presence. 'Of course he sold me opium!' he broke out; 'all the Chinese here sell opium. It was only to buy opium that I stole; it is only to buy opium that anybody steals. And what you ought to do is to let no opium come here, and no Chinamen.' This is precisely what is done in Samoa by a native Government; but the French have bound their own hands, and for forty thousand francs sold native subjects to crime and death. This horrid traffic may be said to have sprung up by accident. It was Captain Hart[9] who had the misfortune to be the means of beginning it, at a time when his plantations flourished in the Marquesas, and he found a difficulty in keeping Chinese coolies. To-day the plantations are practically deserted and the Chinese gone; but in the meanwhile the natives have learned the vice, the patent brings in a round sum, and the needy Government at Papeete[10] shut their eyes and open their pockets. Of course, the patentee is supposed to sell to Chinamen alone; equally of course, no one could afford to pay forty thousand francs for the privilege of supplying a scattered handful of Chinese; and every one knows the truth, and all are ashamed of it. French officials shake their heads when opium is mentioned; and the agents of the farmer blush for their employment. Those that live in glass houses should not

throw stones; as a subject of the British crown, I am an unwilling
shareholder in the largest opium business under heaven. But the British
case is highly complicated; it implies the livelihood of millions; and
must be reformed, when it can be reformed at all, with prudence.
This French business, on the other hand, is a nostrum[11] and a mere
excrescence. No native industry was to be encouraged: the poison is
solemnly imported. No native habit was to be considered: the vice
has been gratuitously introduced. And no creature profits, save the
Government at Papeete – the not very enviable gentlemen who pay
them, and the Chinese underlings who do the dirty work.

CHAPTER IX

THE HOUSE OF TEMOANA

The history of the Marquesas is, of late years, much confused by the
coming and going of the French. At least twice they have seized the
archipelago, at least once deserted it;[1] and in the meanwhile the natives
pursued almost without interruption their desultory cannibal wars.
Through these events and changing dynasties, a single considerable
figure may be seen to move: that of the high chief, a king, Temoana.[2]
Odds and ends of his history came to my ears: how he was at first a
convert of the Protestant mission; how he was kidnapped or exiled
from his native land, served as cook aboard a whaler, and was shown,
for small charge, in English seaports; how he returned at last to the
Marquesas, fell under the strong and benign influence of the late
bishop, extended his influence in the group, was for a while joint ruler
with the prelate, and died at last the chief supporter of Catholicism
and the French. His widow remains in receipt of two pounds a month
from the French Government. Queen she is usually called, but in the
official almanac she figures as '*Madame Vaekehu, Grande Chefesse.*' His
son (natural or adoptive, I know not which), Stanislao Moanatini,
chief of Akaui, serves in Tai-o-hae as a kind of Minister of Public
Works; and the daughter of Stanislao is High Chiefess of the southern
island of Tauata. These, then, are the greatest folk of the archipelago;

we thought them also the most estimable. This is the rule in Polynesia, with few exceptions; the higher the family, the better the man – better in sense, better in manners, and usually taller and stronger in body. A stranger advances blindfold. He scrapes acquaintance as he can. Save the tattoo in the Marquesas, nothing indicates the difference of rank; and yet almost invariably we found, after we had made them, that our friends were persons of station. I have said 'usually taller and stronger.' I might have been more absolute, – over all Polynesia, and a part of Micronesia, the rule holds good; the great ones of the isle, and even of the village, are greater of bone and muscle, and often heavier of flesh, than any commoner. The usual explanation – that the high-born child is more industriously shampooed,[3] is probably the true one. In New Caledonia, at least, where the difference does not exist or has never been remarked, the practice of shampooing seems to be itself unknown. Doctors would be well employed in a study of the point.

Vaekehu lives at the other end of the town from the Residency, beyond the buildings of the mission. Her house is on the European plan: a table in the midst of the chief room; photographs and religious pictures on the wall. It commands to either hand a charming vista: through the front door, a peep of green lawn, scurrying pigs, the pendent fans of the coco-palm and the splendour of the bursting surf: through the back, mounting forest glades and coronals of precipice. Here, in the strong thorough-draught, Her Majesty received us in a simple gown of print, and with no mark of royalty but the exquisite finish of her tattooed mittens, the elaboration of her manners, and the gentle falsetto in which all the highly refined among Marquesan ladies (and Vaekehu above all others) delight to sing their language. An adopted daughter interpreted, while we gave the news, and rehearsed by name our friends of Anaho. As we talked, we could see, through the landward door, another lady of the household at her toilet under the green trees; who presently, when her hair was arranged, and her hat wreathed with flowers, appeared upon the back verandah with gracious salutations.

Vaekehu is very deaf; '*merci*' is her only word of French; and I do not know that she seemed clever. An exquisite, kind refinement, with a shade of quietism, gathered perhaps from the nuns, was what chiefly struck us. Or rather, upon that first occasion, we were conscious of a sense as of district-visiting on our part, and reduced evangelical gentility on the part of our hostess. The other impression followed after she was more at ease, and came with Stanislao and his little girl to dine on board the *Casco*. She had dressed for the occasion: wore white, which very well became her strong brown face; and sat among us, eating or smoking her cigarette, quite cut off from all society, or only now and then included through the intermediary of her son. It was a position that might have been ridiculous, and she made it ornamental; making believe to hear and to be entertained; her face, whenever she met our eyes, lighting with the smile of good society; her contributions to the talk, when she made any, and that was seldom, always compli- mentary and pleasing. No attention was paid to the child, for instance, but what she remarked and thanked us for. Her parting with each, when she came to leave, was gracious and pretty, as had been every step of her behaviour. When Mrs. Stevenson held out her hand to say good-bye, Vaekehu took it, held it, and a moment smiled upon her; dropped it, and then, as upon a kindly afterthought, and with a sort of warmth of condescension, held out both hands and kissed my wife upon both cheeks. Given the same relation of years and of rank, the thing would have been so done on the boards of the Comédie- Française;[4] just so might Madame Brohan have warmed and condes- cended to Madame Broisat in the *Marquis de Villemer*.[5] It was my part to accompany our guests ashore: when I kissed the little girl good-bye at the pier steps, Vaekehu gave a cry of gratification, reached down her hand into the boat, took mine, and pressed it with that flattering softness which seems the coquetry of the old lady in every quarter of the earth. The next moment she had taken Stanislao's arm, and they moved off along the pier in the moonlight, leaving me bewildered. This was a queen of cannibals; she was tattooed from hand to foot, and perhaps the greatest masterpiece of that art now extant, so that a while ago, before she was grown prim, her leg was one of the sights of Tai-o-hae;[6] she had been passed from chief to chief; she had been fought for and taken in war; perhaps, being so great a lady, she had sat on the high place, and throned it there, alone of her sex, while the drums were going twenty strong and the priests carried up the bloodstained baskets of long-pig. And now behold her, out of that past of violence and sickening feasts, step forth, in her age, a quiet, smooth, elaborate old lady, such as you might find at home (mittened also, but not often so well-mannered) in a score of country houses. Only Vaekehu's mittens were of dye, not of silk; and they had been paid for, not in money, but the cooked flesh of men. It came in my mind with a clap, what she could think of it herself, and whether at heart, perhaps, she might not regret and aspire after the barbarous and stirring past.[7] But when I asked Stanislao – 'Ah!' said he, 'she is content; she is religious, she passes all her days with the sisters.'

Stanislao (Stanislaos, with the final consonant evaded after the Polynesian habit) was sent by Bishop Dordillon to South America, and there educated by the fathers. His French is fluent, his talk sensible and spirited, and in his capacity of ganger-in-chief,[8] he is of excellent service to the French. With the prestige of his name and family, and with the stick when needful, he keeps the natives working and the roads passable. Without Stanislao and the convicts, I am in doubt what would become of the present regimen in Nuka-hiva; whether the highways might not be suffered to close up, the pier to wash away, and the Residency to fall piecemeal about the ears of impotent officials. And yet though the hereditary favourer, and one of the chief props of French authority, he has always an eye upon the past. He showed me where the old public place had stood, still to be traced by random piles of stone; told me how great and fine it was, and surrounded on all sides by populous houses, whence, at the beating of the drums, the folk crowded to make holiday. The drum-beat of the Polynesian has a strange and gloomy stimulation for the nerves of all. White persons feel it – at these precipitate sounds their hearts beat faster; and, according to old residents, its effect on the natives was extreme. Bishop Dordillon might entreat; Temoana himself command and threaten; at the note of the drum wild instincts triumphed. And now it might beat upon these ruins, and who should assemble? The houses are down, the people dead, their lineage extinct; and the sweepings and fugitives of distant bays and islands encamp upon their graves. The decline of the dance Stanislao especially laments. '*Chaque pays a ses coutumes,*' said he; but in the report of any gendarme, perhaps corruptly eager to increase the number of *délits* and the instruments of his own power, custom after custom is placed on the expurgatorial index. '*Tenez, une danse qui n'est pas permise,*' said Stanislao: '*je ne sais pas pourquoi, elle est très jolie, elle va comme çà,*' and sticking his umbrella upright in the road, he sketched the steps and gestures. All his criticisms of the present, all his regrets for the past, struck me as temperate and sensible. The short term of office of the Resident he thought the chief defect of the administration; that officer having scarce begun to be efficient ere he was recalled. I thought I gathered, too, that he regarded with some fear the coming change from a naval to a civil governor. I am sure at least that I regard it so myself; for the civil servants of France have never appeared to any foreigner as at all the flower of their country, while her naval officers may challenge competition with the world. In all his talk, Stanislao was particular to speak of his own country as a land of savages; and when he stated an opinion of his own, it was with some apologetic preface, alleging that he was 'a savage who had travelled.' There was a deal, in this elaborate modesty, of honest pride. Yet there was something in the precaution that saddened me; and I could not but fear he was only forestalling a taunt that he had heard too often.

I recall with interest two interviews with Stanislao. The first was a certain afternoon of tropic rain, which we passed together in the verandah of the club; talking at times with heightened voices as the showers redoubled overhead, passing at times into the billiard-room, to consult, in the dim, cloudy daylight, that map of the world which forms its chief adornment. He was naturally ignorant of English history, so that I had much of news to communicate. The story of Gordon[9] I told him in full, and many episodes of the Indian Mutiny,[10] Lucknow, the second battle of Cawnpore, the relief of Arrah, the death of poor Spottiswoode,[11] and Sir Hugh Rose's[12] hotspur, midland campaign. He was intent to hear; his brown face, strongly marked with small-pox, kindled and changed with each vicissitude. His eyes glowed with the reflected light of battle; his questions were many and intelligent, and it was chiefly these that sent us so often to the map. But it is of our parting that I keep the strongest sense. We were to sail on the morrow, and the night had fallen, dark, gusty, and rainy, when we stumbled up the hill to bid farewell to Stanislao. He had already loaded us with gifts; but more were waiting. We sat about the table over cigars and green cocoa-nuts; claps of wind blew through the house and extinguished the lamp, which was always instantly relighted with a single match; and these recurrent intervals of darkness were felt as a relief. For there was something painful and embarrassing in the kindness of that separation. '*Ah, vous devriez rester ici, mon cher ami!*' cried Stanislao. '*Vous êtes les gens qu'il faut pour les Kanaques; vous êtes doux, vous et votre famille; vous seriez obéis dans toutes les îles.*' We had been civil; not always that, my conscience told me, and never anything beyond; and all this to-do is a measure, not of our considerateness, but of the want of it in others. The rest of the evening, on to Vaekehu's and back as far as to the pier, Stanislao walked with my arm and sheltered me with his umbrella; and after the boat had put off, we could still distinguish, in the murky darkness, his gestures of farewell. His words, if there were any, were drowned by the rain and the loud surf.

I have mentioned presents, a vexed question in the South Seas; and one which well illustrates the common, ignorant habit of regarding races in a lump. In many quarters the Polynesian gives only to receive. I have visited islands where the population mobbed me for all the world like dogs after the waggon of cat's-meat; and where the frequent proposition, 'You my pleni (friend),' or (with more of pathos) 'You all 'e same my father,' must be received with hearty laughter and a shout. And perhaps everywhere, among the greedy and rapacious, a gift is regarded as a sprat to catch a whale. It is the habit to give gifts and to receive returns, and such characters, complying with the custom, will look to it nearly that they do not lose. But for persons of a different stamp the statement must be reversed. The shabby Polynesian is anxious till he has received the return gift; the generous is uneasy until he has made it. The first is disappointed if you have not given more than he; the second is miserable if he thinks he has given less than you. This is my experience; if it clash with that of others, I pity their fortune, and praise mine: the circumstance cannot change what I have seen, nor lessen what I have received. And indeed I find that those who oppose me often argue from a ground of singular presumptions;

comparing Polynesians with an ideal person, compact of generosity and gratitude, whom I never had the pleasure of encountering; and forgetting that what is almost poverty to us is wealth almost unthinkable to them. I will give one instance: I chanced to speak with consideration of these gifts of Stanislao's with a certain clever man, a great hater and contemner of Kanakas. 'Well! what were they?' he cried. 'A pack of old men's beards. Trash!' And the same gentleman, some half an hour later, being upon a different train of thought, dwelt at length on the esteem in which the Marquesans held that sort of property, how they preferred it to all others except land, and what fancy prices it would fetch. Using his own figures, I computed that, in this commodity alone, the gifts of Vaekehu and Stanislao represented between two and three hundred dollars; and the queen's official salary is of two hundred and forty in the year.

But generosity on the one hand, and conspicuous meanness on the other, are in the South Seas, as at home, the exception. It is neither with any hope of gain, nor with any lively wish to please, that the ordinary Polynesian chooses and presents his gifts. A plain social duty lies before him, which he performs correctly, but without the least enthusiasm. And we shall best understand his attitude of mind, if we examine our own to the cognate absurdity of marriage presents. There we give without any special thought of a return; yet if the circumstance arise, and the return be withheld, we shall judge ourselves insulted. We give them usually without affection, and almost never with a genuine desire to please; and our gift is rather a mark of our own status than a measure of our love to the recipients. So in a great measure and with the common run of the Polynesians: their gifts are formal; they imply no more than social recognition; and they are made and reciprocated, as we pay and return our morning visits. And the practice of marking and measuring events and sentiments by presents is universal in the island world. A gift plays with them the part of stamp and seal; and has entered profoundly into the mind of islanders. Peace and war, marriage, adoption and naturalisation, are celebrated or declared by the acceptance or the refusal of gifts; and it is as natural for the islander to bring a gift as for us to carry a card-case.

CHAPTER X

A PORTRAIT AND A STORY

I have had occasion several times to name the late bishop, Father Dordillon, 'Monseigneur,' as he is still almost universally called, Vicar-Apostolic of the Marquesas and Bishop of Cambysopolis *in partibus*. Everywhere in the islands, among all classes and races, this fine, old, kindly, cheerful fellow is remembered with affection and respect. His influence with the natives was paramount. They reckoned him the highest of men – higher than an admiral; brought him their money to keep; took his advice upon their purchases; nor would they plant trees upon their own land till they had the approval of the father of the islands. During the time of the French exodus[1] he singly represented Europe, living in the Residency, and ruling by the hand of Temoana. The first roads were made under his auspices and by his persuasion. The old road between Hatiheu and Anaho was got under way from either side on the ground that it would be pleasant for an evening promenade, and brought to completion by working on the rivalry of the two villages. The priest would boast in Hatiheu of the progress made in Anaho, and he would tell the folk of Anaho, 'If you don't take care, your neighbours will be over the hill before you are at the top.' It could not be so done to-day; it could then; death, opium, and depopulation had not gone so far; and the people of Hatiheu, I was told, still vied with each other in fine attire, and used to go out by families, in the cool of the evening, boat-sailing and racing in the bay. There seems some truth at least in the common view, that this joint reign of Temoana and the bishop was the last and brief golden age of the Marquesas. But the civil power returned, the mission was packed out of the Residency at twenty-four hours' notice, new methods supervened, and the golden age (whatever it quite was) came to an end. It is the strongest proof of Father Dordillon's prestige that it survived, seemingly without loss, this hasty deposition.

His method with the natives was extremely mild. Among these barbarous children he still played the part of the smiling father; and he was careful to observe, in all indifferent matters, the Marquesan etiquette. Thus, in the singular system of artificial kinship, the bishop had been adopted by Vaekehu as a grandson; Mrs. Fisher, of Hatiheu,[2] as a daughter. From that day, Monseigneur never addressed the young lady except as his mother, and closed his letters with the formalities of a dutiful son. With Europeans he could be strict, even to the extent of harshness. He made no distinction against heretics, with whom he was on friendly terms; but the rules of his own Church he would see observed; and once at least he had a white man clapped in jail for the desecration of a saint's day. But even this rigour, so intolerable to laymen, so irritating to Protestants, could not shake his popularity. We shall best conceive him by examples nearer home; we may all have known some divine of the old school in Scotland, a literal Sabbatarian, a stickler for the letter of the law, who was yet in private modest, innocent, genial, and mirthful. Much such a man, it seems, was Father Dordillon. And his popularity bore a test yet stronger. He had the name, and probably deserved it, of a shrewd man in business and one that made the mission pay. Nothing so much stirs up resentment as the inmixture in commerce of religious bodies; but even rival traders spoke well of Monseigneur.

His character is best portrayed in the story of the days of his decline. A time came when, from the failure of sight, he must desist from his literary labours: his Marquesan hymns, grammars, and dictionaries; his scientific papers, lives of saints, and devotional poetry. He cast about for a new interest: pitched on gardening, and was to be seen all day, with spade and waterpot, in his childlike eagerness, actually running between the borders. Another step of decay, and he must leave his garden also. Instantly a new occupation was devised, and he sat in the mission cutting paper flowers and wreaths. His diocese was not great enough for his activity; the churches of the Marquesas were papered with his handiwork, and still he must be making more. 'Ah,' said he, smiling, 'when I am dead what a fine time you will have clearing out my trash!' He had been dead about six months; but I was pleased to see some of his trophies still exposed, and looked upon them with a smile: the tribute (if I have read his cheerful character aright) which he would have preferred to any useless tears. Disease continued progressively to disable him; he who had clambered so stalwartly over the rude rocks of the Marquesas, bringing peace to warfaring clans, was for some time carried in a chair between the mission and the church, and at last confined to bed, impotent with dropsy, and tormented with bed-sores and sciatica. Here he lay two months without complaint; and on the 11th January 1888, in the seventy-ninth year of his life, and the thirty-fourth of his labours in the Marquesas, passed away.

Those who have a taste for hearing missions, Protestant or Catholic, decried, must seek their pleasure elsewhere than in my pages. Whether Catholic or Protestant, with all their gross blots, with all their deficiency of candour, of humour, and of common sense, the missionaries are the best and the most useful whites in the Pacific. This is a subject which will follow us throughout; but there is one part of it that may conveniently be treated here. The married and the celibate missionary, each has his particular advantage and defect. The married missionary, taking him at the best, may offer to the native what he is much in want of – a higher picture of domestic life; but the woman at his elbow tends to keep him in touch with Europe and out of touch with Polynesia, and to perpetuate, and even to ingrain, parochial decencies far best forgotten. The mind of the female missionary tends, for instance, to be continually busied about dress. She can be taught with extreme difficulty to think any costume decent but that to which she grew accustomed on Clapham Common; and to gratify this prejudice, the native is put to useless expense, his mind is tainted with the morbidities of Europe, and his health is set in danger. The celibate missionary, on the other hand, and whether at best or worst, falls readily into native ways of life; to which he adds too commonly what is either a mark of celibate man at large, or an inheritance from mediaeval saints – I mean slovenly habits and an unclean person. There are, of course, degrees in this; and the sister (of course, and all honour to her) is as fresh as a lady at a ball. For the diet there is nothing to be said – it must amaze and shock the Polynesian – but for the adoption of native habits there is much. '*Chaque pays a ses coutumes,*' said Stanislao; these it is the missionary's delicate task to modify; and the more he can do so from within, and from a native standpoint, the better he will do his work; and here I think the Catholics have sometimes the advantage; in the Vicariate of Dordillon, I am sure they had it. I have heard the bishop blamed for his indulgence to the natives, and above all because he did not rage with sufficient energy against cannibalism. It was a part of his policy to live among the natives like an elder brother; to follow where he could; to lead where it was necessary; never to drive; and to encourage the growth of new habits, instead of violently rooting up the old. And it might be better, in the long-run, if this policy were always followed.

It might be supposed that native missionaries would prove more indulgent, but the reverse is found to be the case. The new broom sweeps clean; and the white missionary of to-day is often embarrassed by the bigotry of his native coadjutor. What else should we expect? On some islands, sorcery, polygamy, human sacrifice, and tobacco-smoking have been prohibited, the dress of the native has been modified, and himself warned in strong terms against rival sects of Christianity; all by the same man, at the same period of time, and with the like authority. By what criterion is the convert to distinguish the essential from the unessential? He swallows the nostrum[3] whole; there has been no play of mind, no instruction, and, except for some brute utility in the prohibitions, no advance. To call things by their proper names, this is teaching superstition. It is unfortunate to use the word; so few people have read history, and so many have dipped into little atheistic manuals, that the majority will rush to a conclusion, and suppose the labour lost. And far from that: These semi-spontaneous superstitions, varying with the sect of the original evangelist and the customs of the island, are found in practice to be highly fructifying; and in particular those who have learned and who go forth again to teach them offer an example to the world. The best specimen of the Christian hero that I ever met was one of these native missionaries.[4] He had saved two lives at the risk of his own; like Nathan,[5] he had bearded a tyrant in his hour of blood; when a whole white population fled, he alone stood to his duty; and his behaviour under domestic sorrow with which the public has no concern filled the beholder with sympathy and admiration. A poor little smiling laborious man he looked; and you would have thought he had nothing in him but that of which indeed he had too much – facile good-nature.

It chances that the only rivals of Monseigneur and his mission in the Marquesas were certain of these brown-skinned evangelists, natives from Hawaii. I know not what they thought of Father Dordillon: they are the only class I did not question; but I suspect the prelate to have regarded them askance, for he was eminently human. During my stay at Tai-o-hae, the time of the yearly holiday came round at the girls' school; and a whole fleet of whale-boats came from Ua-pu to take the daughters of that island home. On board of these was Kauwealoha,[6] one of the pastors, a fine, rugged old gentleman, of that leonine type so common in Hawaii. He paid me a visit in the *Casco*, and there entertained me with a tale of one of his colleagues, Kekela,[7] a missionary in the great cannibal isle of Hiva-oa. It appears that shortly after a kidnapping visit from a Peruvian slaver, the boats of an American whaler put into a bay upon that island, were attacked, and made their escape with difficulty, leaving their mate, a Mr. Whalon,[8] in the hands of the natives. The captive, with his arms bound behind his back, was cast into a house; and the chief announced the capture to Kekela. And here I begin to follow the version of Kauwealoha; it is a good specimen of Kanaka English; and the reader is to conceive it delivered with violent emphasis and speaking pantomime.

' "I got 'Melican mate," the chief he say. "What you go do 'Melican mate?" Kekela he say. "I go make fire, I go kill, I go eat him," he say; "you come to-mollow eat piece." "I no *want* eat 'Melican mate!" Kekela he say; "why you want?" "This bad shippee, this slave shippee," the chief he say. "One time a shippee he come from Pelu, he take away plenty Kanaka, he take away my son. 'Melican mate he bad man. I go eat him; you eat piece." "I no *want* eat 'Melican mate!" Kekela he say; and he *cly* – all night he cly! To-mollow Kekela he get up, he put on blackee coat, he go see chief; he see Missa Whela, him hand tie' like this. (*Pantomime.*) Kekela he cly. He say chief:– "Chief, you like things of mine? you like whale-boat?" "Yes," he say. "You like file-a'm?" (fire-arms). "Yes," he say. "You like blackee coat?" "Yes," he say. Kekela he take Missa Whela by he shoul'a' (shoulder), he take him light out house; he give chief he whale-boat, he file-a'm, he blackee coat. He take Missa Whela he house, make him sit down with he wife and chil'en. Missa Whela all-the-same pelison (prison);

he wife, he chil'en in Amelica; he cly – O, he cly. Kekela he solly. One day Kekela he see ship. (*Pantomime.*) He say Missa Whela, "Tha' Whala?" Missa Whela he say, "Yes." Kanaka they begin go down beach. Kekela he get eleven Kanaka, get oa' (oars), get evely thing. He say Missa Whela, "Now you go quick." They jump in whale-boat. "Now you low!" Kekela he say: "you low quick, quick!" (*Violent pantomime, and a change indicating that the narrator has left the boat and returned to the beach.*) All the Kanaka they say, "How! 'Melican mate he go away?" – jump in boat; low afta. (*Violent pantomime and change again to boat.*) Kekela he say, "Low quick!"'

Here I think Kauwealoha's pantomime had confused me; I have no more of his *ipsissima verba*;[9] and can but add, in my own less spirited manner, that the ship was reached, Mr. Whalon taken aboard, and Kekela returned to his charge among the cannibals. But how unjust it is to repeat the stumblings of a foreigner in a language only partly acquired! A thoughtless reader might conceive Kauwealoha and his colleague to be a species of amicable baboon; but I have here the antidote. In return for his act of gallant charity, Kekela was presented by the American Government with a sum of money, and by President Lincoln personally with a gold watch. From his letter of thanks, written in his own tongue, I give the following extract. I do not envy the man who can read it without emotion.

When I saw one of your countrymen, a citizen of your great nation, ill-treated, and about to be baked and eaten, as a pig is eaten, I ran to save him, full of pity and grief at the evil deed of these benighted people. I gave my boat for the stranger's life. This boat came from James Hunnewell, a gift of friendship. It became the ransom of this countryman of yours, that he might not be eaten by the savages who knew not Jehovah. This was Mr. Whalon, and the date, Jan. 14, 1864.

As to this friendly deed of mine in saving Mr. Whalon, its seed came from your great land, and was brought by certain of your countrymen, who had received the love of God. It was planted in Hawaii, and I brought it to plant in this land and in these dark regions, that they might receive the root of all that is good and true, which is *love*.

1. Love to Jehovah.

2. Love to self.

3. Love to our neighbour.

If a man have a sufficiency of these three, he is good and holy, like his God, Jehovah, in his triune character (Father, Son, and Holy Ghost), one-three, three-one. If he have two and wants one, it is not well; and if he have one and wants two, this, indeed, is not well; but if he cherishes all three, then is he holy, indeed, after the manner of the Bible.

This is a great thing for your great nation to boast of, before all the nations of the earth. From your great land a most precious seed was brought to the land of darkness. It was planted here, not by means of guns and men-of-war and threatenings. It was planted by means of the ignorant, the neglected, the despised. Such was the introduction of the word of the Almighty God into this group of Nuuhiwa. Great is my debt to Americans, who have taught me all things pertaining to this life and to that which is to come.

How shall I repay your great kindness to me? Thus David asked of Jehovah, and thus I ask of you, the President of the United States. This is my only payment – that which I have received of the Lord, love – (aloha).

CHAPTER XI

LONG-PIG — A CANNIBAL HIGH PLACE

Nothing more strongly arouses our disgust than cannibalism, nothing so surely unmortars a society; nothing, we might plausibly argue, will so harden and degrade the minds of those that practise it. And yet we ourselves make much the same appearance in the eyes of the Buddhist and the vegetarian. We consume the carcases of creatures of like appetites, passions, and organs with ourselves; we feed on babes, though not our own; and the slaughter-house resounds daily with screams of pain and fear. We distinguish, indeed; but the unwillingness of many nations to eat the dog, an animal with whom we live on terms of the next intimacy, shows how precariously the distinction is grounded. The pig is the main element of animal food among the islands; and I had many occasions, my mind being quickened by my cannibal surroundings, to observe his character and the manner of his death. Many islanders live with their pigs as we do with our dogs; both crowd around the hearth with equal freedom; and the island pig is a fellow of activity, enterprise, and sense. He husks his own cocoa-nuts, and (I am told) rolls them into the sun to burst; he is the terror of the shepherd. Mrs. Stevenson, senior,[1] has seen one fleeing to the woods with a lamb in his mouth; and I saw another come rapidly (and erroneously) to the conclusion that the *Casco* was going down, and swim through the flush water to the rail in search of an escape. It was told us in childhood that pigs cannot swim; I have known one to leap overboard, swim five hundred yards to shore, and return to the house of his original owner. I was once, at Tautira,[2] a pig-master on a considerable scale; at first, in my pen, the utmost good feeling prevailed; a little sow with a belly-ache came and appealed to us for help in the manner of a child; and there was one shapely black boar, whom we called Catholicus, for he was a particular present from the Catholics of the village, and who early displayed the marks of courage and friendliness; no other animal, whether dog or pig, was suffered to approach him at his food, and for human beings he showed a full measure of that toadying fondness, so common in the lower animals, and possibly their chief title to the name. One day, on visiting my piggery, I was amazed to see Catholicus draw back from my approach with cries of terror; and if I was amazed at the change, I was truly embarrassed when I learnt its reason. One of the pigs had been that morning killed; Catholicus had seen the murder, he had discovered he was dwelling in the shambles, and from that time his confidence and his delight in life were ended. We still reserved him a long while, but he could not endure the sight of any two-legged creature, nor could we, under the circumstances, encounter his eye without confusion. I have assisted besides, by the ear, at the act of butchery itself; the victim's cries of pain I think I could have borne, but the execution was mismanaged, and his expression of terror was contagious: that small heart moved to the same tune with ours. Upon such 'dread foundations'[3] the life of the European reposes, and yet the European is among the less cruel of races. The paraphernalia of murder, the preparatory brutalities of his existence, are all hid away; an extreme sensibility reigns upon the surface; and ladies will faint at the recital of one tithe of what they daily expect of their butchers. Some will be even crying out upon me in their hearts for the coarseness of this paragraph. And so with the island cannibals. They were not cruel; apart from this custom, they are a race of the most kindly; rightly speaking, to eat a man's flesh after he is dead is far less hateful than to oppress him whilst he lives;[4] and even the victims of their appetite were gently used in life and suddenly and painlessly despatched at last. In island circles of refinement it was doubtless thought bad taste to expatiate on what was ugly in the practice.

Cannibalism is traced from end to end of the Pacific, from the Marquesas to New Guinea, from New Zealand to Hawaii, here in the lively haunt of its exercise, there by scanty but significant survivals. Hawaii is the most doubtful. We find cannibalism chronicled in Hawaii, only in the history of a single war, where it seems to have been thought exceptional, as in the case of mountain outlaws, such as fell by the hand of Theseus.[5] In Tahiti, a single circumstance survived, but that appears conclusive. In historic times, when human oblation was made in the *marae*,[6] the eyes of the victim were formally offered to the chief: a delicacy to the leading guest. All Melanesia[7] appears tainted. In Micronesia,[8] in the Marshalls,[9] with which my acquaintance is no more than that of a tourist, I could find no trace at all; and even in the Gilbert zone[10] I long looked and asked in vain. I was told tales indeed of men who had been eaten in a famine; but these were nothing to my purpose, for the same thing is done under the same stress by all kindreds and generations of men. At last, in some manuscript notes of Dr. Turner's,[11] which I was allowed to consult at Malua,[12] I came on one damning evidence: on the island of Onoatoa[13] the punishment for theft was to be killed and eaten. How shall we account for the universality of the practice over so vast an area, among people of such varying civilisation, and, with whatever intermixture, of such different blood? What circumstance is common to them all, but that they lived on islands destitute, or very nearly so, of animal food? I can never find it in my appetite that man was meant to live on vegetables only. When our stores ran low among the islands, I grew to weary for the recurrent day when economy allowed us to open another tin of miserable mutton. And in at least one ocean language, a particular word denotes that a man is 'hungry for fish,' having reached that stage when vegetables can no longer satisfy, and his soul, like those of the Hebrews in the desert, begins to lust after flesh-pots. Add to this the evidences of overpopulation and imminent famine already adduced, and I think we see some ground of indulgence for the island cannibal.

It is right to look at both sides of any question; but I am far from making the apology of this worse than bestial vice. The higher Polynesian races, such as the Tahitians, Hawaiians, and Samoans, had one and all outgrown, and some of them had in part forgot, the practice, before Cook or Bougainville[11] had shown a top-sail in their waters. It lingered only in some low islands where life was difficult to maintain, and among inveterate savages like the New-Zealanders or the Marquesans. The Marquesans intertwined man-eating with the whole texture of their lives; long-pig was in a sense their currency and sacrament; it formed the hire of the artist, illustrated public events, and was the occasion and attraction of a feast. To-day they are paying the penalty of this bloody commixture. The civil power, in its crusade against man-eating, has had to examine one after another all Marquesan arts and pleasures, has found them one after another tainted with a cannibal element, and one after another has placed them on the proscript list. Their art of tattooing stood by itself, the execution exquisite, the designs most beautiful and intricate; nothing more handsomely sets off a handsome man; it may cost some pain in the beginning, but I doubt if it be near so painful in the long-run, and I am sure it is far more becoming than the ignoble European practice of tight-lacing among women. And now it has been found needful to forbid the art. Their songs and dances were numerous (and the law has had to abolish them by the dozen). They now face empty-handed the tedium of their uneventful days; and who shall pity them? The least rigorous will say that they were justly served.

Death alone could not satisfy Marquesan vengeance: the flesh must be eaten. The chief who seized Mr. Whalon preferred to eat him; and he thought he had justified the wish when he explained it was a vengeance. Two or three years ago, the people of a valley seized and slew a wretch who had offended them. His offence, it is to be supposed, was dire; they could not bear to leave their vengeance incomplete, and, under the eyes of the French, they did not dare to hold a public festival. The body was accordingly divided; and every man retired to his own house to consummate the rite in secret, carrying his proportion of the dreadful meat in a Swedish match-box. The barbarous substance of the drama and the European properties employed offer a seizing contrast to the imagination. Yet more striking is another incident of the very year when I was there myself, 1888. In the spring, a man and woman skulked about the school-house in Hiva-oa till they found a particular child alone. Him they approached with honeyed words and carneying[15] manners – 'You are So-and-so, son of So-and-so?' they asked; and caressed and beguiled him deeper in the woods. Some instinct woke in the child's bosom, or some look betrayed the horrid purpose of his deceivers. He sought to break from them; he screamed; and they, casting off the mask, seized him the more strongly and began to run. His cries were heard; his schoolmates, playing not far off, came running to the rescue; and the sinister couple fled and vanished in the woods. They were never identified; no prosecution followed; but it was currently supposed they had some grudge against the boy's father, and designed to eat him in revenge. All over the islands, as at home among our own ancestors, it will be observed that the avenger takes no particular heed to strike an individual. A family, a class, a village, a whole valley or island, a whole race of mankind, share equally the guilt of any member. So, in the above story, the son was to pay the penalty for his father; so Mr. Whalon, the mate of an American whaler, was to bleed and be eaten for the misdeeds of a Peruvian slaver. I am reminded of an incident in Jaluit in the Marshall group, which was told me by an eye-witness, and which I tell here again for the strangeness of the scene. Two men had awakened the animosity of the Jaluit chiefs; and it was their wives who were selected to be punished. A single native served as executioner. Early in the morning, in the face of a large concourse of spectators, he waded out upon the reef between his victims. These neither complained nor resisted; accompanied their destroyer patiently; stooped down, when they had waded deep enough, at his command; and he (laying one hand upon the shoulders of each) held them under water till they drowned. Doubtless, although my

72

informant did not tell me so, their families would be lamenting aloud upon the beach.

It was from Hatiheu that I paid my first visit to a cannibal high place.

The day was sultry and clouded. Drenching tropical showers succeeded bursts of sweltering sunshine. The green pathway of the road wound steeply upward. As we went, our little schoolboy guide a little ahead of us, Father Siméon had his portfolio in his hand, and named the trees for me, and read aloud from his notes the abstract of their virtues. Presently the road, mounting, showed us the vale of Hatiheu on a larger scale; and the priest, with occasional reference to our guide, pointed out the boundaries and told me the names of the larger tribes that lived at perpetual war in the old days: one on the north-east, one along the beach, one behind upon the mountain. With a survivor of this latter clan Father Siméon had spoken; until the pacification he had never been to the sea's edge, nor, if I remember exactly, eaten of sea-fish. Each in its own district, the septs lived cantoned and beleaguered. One step without the boundaries was to affront death. If famine came, the men must out to the woods to gather chestnuts and small fruits; even as to this day, if the parents are backward in their weekly doles, school must be broken up and the scholars sent foraging. But in the old days, when there was trouble in one clan, there would be activity in all its neighbours; the woods would be laid full of ambushes; and he who went after vegetables for himself might remain to be a joint for his hereditary foes. Nor was the pointed occasion needful. A dozen different natural signs and social junctures called this people to the war-path and the cannibal hunt. Let one of chiefly rank have finished his tattooing, the wife of one be near upon her time, two of the debouching streams have deviated nearer on the beach of Hatiheu, a certain bird have been heard to sing, a certain ominous formation of cloud observed above the northern sea; and instantly the arms were oiled, and the man-hunters swarmed into the wood to lay their fratricidal ambuscades. It appears besides that occasionally, perhaps in famine, the priest would shut himself in his house, where he lay for a stated period like a person dead. When he came forth it was to run for three days through the territory of the clan, naked and starving, and to sleep at night alone in the high place. It was now the turn of the others to keep the house, for to encounter the priest upon his rounds was death. On the eve of the fourth day the time of the running was over; the priest returned to his roof, the laymen came forth, and in the morning the number of the victims was announced. I have this tale of the priest on one authority[16] – I think a good one, – but I set it down with diffidence. The particulars are so striking that, had they been true, I almost think I must have heard them oftener referred to. Upon one point there seems to be no question: that the feast was sometimes furnished from within the clan. In times of scarcity, all who were not protected by their family connections – in the Highland expression, all the commons of the clan – had cause to tremble. It was vain to resist, it was useless to flee. They were begirt upon all hands by cannibals; and the oven was ready to smoke for them abroad in the country of their foes, or at home in the valley of their fathers.

At a certain corner of the road our scholar-guide struck off to his left into the twilight of the forest. We were now on one of the ancient native roads, plunged in a high vault of wood, and clambering, it seemed, at random over boulders and dead trees; but the lad wound in and out and up and down without a check, for these paths are to the natives as marked as the king's highway is to us; insomuch that, in the days of the man-hunt, it was their labour rather to block and deface than to improve them. In the crypt of the wood the air was clammy and hot and cold; overhead, upon the leaves, the tropical rain uproariously poured, but only here and there, as through holes in a leaky roof, a single drop would fall, and make a spot upon my mackintosh. Presently the huge trunk of a banyan hove in sight, standing upon what seemed the ruins of an ancient fort; and our guide, halting and holding forth his arm, announced that we had reached the *paepae tapu*.

Paepae signifies a floor or platform such as a native house is built on; and even such a *paepae* – a *paepae-hae* – may be called a *paepae tapu* in a lesser sense when it is deserted and becomes the haunt of spirits; but the public high place, such as I was now treading, was a thing on a great scale. As far as my eyes could pierce through the dark undergrowth, the floor of the forest was all paved. Three tiers of terrace ran on the slope of the hill; in front, a crumbling parapet contained the main arena; and the pavement of that was pierced and parcelled out with several wells and small enclosures. No trace remained of any superstructure, and the scheme of the amphitheatre was difficult to seize. I visited another in Hiva-oa, smaller but more perfect, where it was easy to follow rows of benches, and to distinguish isolated seats of honour for eminent persons; and where, on the upper platform, a single joist of the temple or dead-house still remained, its uprights richly carved. In the old days the high place was sedulously tended. No tree except the sacred banyan was suffered to encroach upon its grades, no dead leaf to rot upon the pavement. The stones were smoothly set, and I am told they were kept bright with oil. On all sides the guardians lay encamped in their subsidiary huts to watch and cleanse it. No other foot of man was suffered to draw near; only the priest, in the days of his running, came there to sleep – perhaps to dream of his ungodly errand; but, in the time of the feast, the clan trooped to the high place in a body, and each had his appointed seat. There were places for the chiefs, the drummers, the dancers, the women, and the priests. The drums – perhaps twenty strong, and some of them twelve feet high – continuously throbbed in time. In time the singers kept up their long-drawn, lugubrious, ululating song; in time, too, the dancers, tricked out in singular finery, stepped, leaped, swayed, and gesticulated – their plumed fingers fluttering in the air like butterflies. The sense of time, in all these ocean races, is extremely perfect; and I conceive in such a festival that almost every sound and movement fell in one. So much the more unanimously must have grown the agitation of the feasters; so much the more wild must have been the scene to any European who could have beheld them there, in the strong sun and the strong shadow of the banyan, rubbed with saffron to throw in a more high relief the arabesque of the tattoo; the women bleached by days of confinement to a complexion almost European; the chiefs crowned with silver plumes of old men's beards and girt with kirtles of the hair of dead women. All manner of island food was meanwhile spread for the women and the commons; and, for those who were privileged to eat of it, there were carried up to the dead-house the baskets of long-pig. It is told that the feasts were long kept up; the people came from them brutishly exhausted with debauchery, and the chiefs heavy with their beastly food. There are certain sentiments which we call emphatically human – denying the honour of that name to those who lack them. In such feasts – particularly where the victim had been slain at home, and men banqueted on the poor clay of a comrade with whom they had played in infancy, or a woman whose favours they had shared – the whole body of these sentiments is outraged. To consider it too closely is to understand, if not to excuse, these fervours of self-righteous old ship-captains, who would man their guns, and open fire in passing, on a cannibal island.

And yet it was strange. There, upon the spot, as I stood under the high, dripping vault of the forest, with the young priest on the one hand, in his kilted gown, and the bright-eyed Marquesan schoolboy on the other, the whole business appeared infinitely distant, and, fallen in the cold perspective and dry light of history. The bearing of the priest, perhaps, affected me. He smiled; he jested with the boy, the heir both of these feasters and their meat; he clapped his hands, and gave me a stave of one of the old, ill-omened choruses. Centuries might have come and gone since this slimy theatre was last in operation; and I beheld the place with no more emotion than I might have felt in visiting Stonehenge. In Hiva-oa, as I began to appreciate that the thing was still living and latent about my footsteps, and that it was still within the bounds of possibility that I might hear the cry of the trapped victims, my historic attitude entirely failed, and I was sensible of some repugnance for the natives. But here, too, the priests maintained their jocular attitude: rallying the cannibals as upon an eccentricity rather absurd than horrible; seeking, I should say, to shame them from the practice by good-natured ridicule, as we shame a child from stealing sugar. We may here recognise the temperate and sagacious mind of Bishop Dordillon.

CHAPTER XII

THE STORY OF A PLANTATION

Taahauku, on the south-westerly coast of the island of Hiva-oa –
Tahuku, say the slovenly whites – may be called the port of Atuona.
It is a narrow and small anchorage, set between low cliffy points, and
opening above upon a woody valley: a little French fort, now disused
and deserted, overhangs the valley and the inlet. Atuona itself, at the
head of the next bay, is framed in a theatre of mountains, which
dominate the more immediate settling of Taahauku and give the
salient character of the scene. They are reckoned at no higher than
four thousand feet; but Tahiti with eight thousand, and Hawaii with
fifteen, can offer no such picture of abrupt, melancholy alps. In the
morning, when the sun falls directly on their front, they stand like a
vast wall: green to the summit, if by any chance the summit should
be clear – watercourses here and there delineated on their face, as
narrow as cracks. Towards afternoon, the light falls more obliquely,
and the sculpture of the range comes in relief, huge gorges sinking
into shadow, huge, tortuous buttresses standing edged with sun. At all
hours of the day they strike the eye with some new beauty, and the
mind with the same menacing gloom.

The mountains, dividing and deflecting the endless airy deluge of
the Trade, are doubtless answerable for the climate. A strong draught
of the wind blew day and night over the anchorage. Day and night
the same fantastic and attenuated clouds fled across the heavens, the
same dusky cap of rain and vapour fell and rose on the mountain.
The land-breezes came very strong and chill, and the sea, like the air,
was in perpetual bustle. The swell crowded into the narrow anchorage
like sheep into a fold; broke all along both sides, high on the one, low
on the other; kept a certain blowhole sounding and smoking like a
cannon; and spent itself at last upon the beach.

On the side away from Atuona, the sheltering promontory was a
nursery of coco-trees. Some were mere infants, none had attained to
any size, none had yet begun to shoot skyward with that whip-like

shaft of the mature palm. In the young trees the colour alters with the age and growth. Now all is of a grass-like hue, infinitely dainty; next the rib grows golden, the fronds remaining green as ferns; and then, as the trunk continues to mount and to assume its final hue of grey, the fans put on manlier and more decided depths of verdure, stand out dark upon the distance, glisten against the sun, and flash like silver fountains in the assault of the wind. In this young wood of Taahauku, all these hues and combinations were exampled and repeated by the score. The trees grew pleasantly spaced upon a hilly sward, here and there interspersed with a rack for drying copra, or a tumble-down hut for storing it. Every here and there the stroller had a glimpse of the *Casco* tossing in the narrow anchorage below; and beyond he had ever before him the dark amphitheatre of the Atuona mountains and the cliffy bluff that closes it to seaward. The trade-wind moving in the fans made a ceaseless noise of summer rain; and from time to time, with the sound of a sudden and distant drum-beat, the surf would burst in a sea-cave.

At the upper end of the inlet, its low, cliffy lining sinks, at both sides, into a beach. A copra warehouse stands in the shadow of the shoreside trees, flitted about for ever by a clan of dwarfish swallows; and a line of rails on a high wooden staging bends back into the mouth of the valley. Walking on this, the new-landed traveller becomes aware of a broad fresh-water lagoon (one arm of which he crosses), and beyond, of a grove of noble palms, sheltering the house of the trader, Mr. Keane. Overhead, the cocos join in a continuous and lofty roof; blackbirds are heard lustily singing; the island cock springs his jubilant rattle and airs his golden plumage; cow-bells sound far and near in the grove; and when you sit in the broad verandah, lulled by this symphony, you may say to yourself, if you are able: 'Better fifty years of Europe . . .'[1] Farther on, the floor of the valley is flat and green, and dotted here and there with stripling coco palms. Through the midst, with many changes of music, the river trots and brawls; and along its course, where we should look for willows, *purao*s grow in clusters, and make shadowy pools after an angler's heart. A vale more rich and peaceful, sweeter air, a sweeter voice of rural sounds, I have found nowhere. One circumstance alone might strike the experienced:

here is a convenient beach, deep soil, good water, and yet nowhere any *paepae*s, nowhere any trace of island habitation.

It is but a few years since this valley was a place choked with jungle, the debatable land and battle-ground of cannibals. Two clans laid claim to it – neither could substantiate the claim, and the roads lay desert, or were only visited by men in arms. It is for this very reason that it wears now so smiling an appearance: cleared, planted, built upon, supplied with railways, boat-houses, and bath-houses. For, being no man's land, it was the more readily ceded to a stranger. The stranger was Captain John Hart: Ima Hati, 'Broken-arm,' the natives call him, because when he first visited the islands his arm was in a sling. Captain Hart, a man of English birth but an American subject, had conceived the idea of cotton culture in the Marquesas during the American War,[2] and was at first rewarded with success. His plantation at Anaho was highly productive; island cotton fetched a high price, and the natives used to debate which was the stronger power, Ima Hati or the French: deciding in favour of the captain, because, though the French had the most ships, he had the more money.

He marked Taahauku for a suitable site, acquired it, and offered the superintendence to Mr. Robert Stewart, a Fifeshire man, already some time in the islands, who had just been ruined by a war on Tauata. Mr. Stewart was somewhat averse to the adventure, having some acquaintance with Atuona and its notorious chieftain, Moipu. He had once landed there, he told me, about dusk, and found the remains of a man and woman partly eaten. On his starting and sickening at the sight, one of Moipu's young men picked up a human foot, and provocatively staring at the stranger, grinned and nibbled at the heel. None need be surprised if Mr. Stewart fled incontinently to the bush, lay there all night in a great horror of mind, and got off to sea again by daylight on the morrow. 'It was always a bad place, Atuona,' commented Mr. Stewart, in his homely Fifeshire voice. In spite of this dire introduction, he accepted the captain's offer, was landed at Taahauku with three Chinamen, and proceeded to clear the jungle.

War was pursued at that time, almost without interval, between the men of Atuona and the men of Haamau; and one day, from the opposite sides of the valley, battle – or I should rather say the noise of battle – raged all the afternoon: the shots and insults of the opposing clans passing from hill to hill over the heads of Mr. Stewart and his Chinamen. There was no genuine fighting; it was like a bicker of schoolboys, only some fool had given the children guns. One man died of his exertions in running, the only casualty. With night the shots and insults ceased; the men of Haamau withdrew; and victory, on some occult principle, was scored to Moipu. Perhaps, in consequence, there came a day when Moipu made a feast, and a party from Haamau came under safe-conduct to eat of it. These passed early by Taahauku, and some of Moipu's young men were there to be a guard of honour. They were not long gone before there came down from Haamau, a man, his wife, and a girl of twelve, their daughter, bringing fungus. Several Atuona lads were hanging round the store; but the day being one of truce none apprehended danger. The fungus was weighed and paid for; the man of Haamau proposed he should have his axe ground in the bargain; and Mr. Stewart demurring at the trouble, some of the Atuona lads offered to grind it for him, and set it on the wheel. While the axe was grinding, a friendly native whispered Mr. Stewart to have a care of himself, for there was trouble in hand; and, all at once, the man of Haamau was seized, and his head and arm stricken from his body, the head at one sweep of his own newly sharpened axe. In the first alert, the girl escaped among the cotton; and Mr. Stewart, having thrust the wife into the house and locked her in from the outside, supposed the affair was over. But the business had not passed without noise, and it reached the ears of an older girl who had loitered by the way, and who now came hastily down the valley, crying as she came for her father. Her, too, they seized and beheaded; I know not what they had done with the axe, it was a blunt knife that served their butcherly turn upon the girl; and the blood spurted in fountains and painted them from head to foot. Thus horrible from crime, the party returned to Atuona, carrying the heads to Moipu. It may be fancied how the feast broke up; but it is notable that the guests were honourably suffered to retire. These passed back through Taahauku in extreme disorder; a little after the valley began to be over-run with shouting and triumphing braves; and a letter of warning coming at the same time to Mr. Stewart, he and his Chinamen took refuge with the Protestant missionary in Atuona. That night the store was gutted, and the bodies cast in a pit and covered with leaves. Three days later the schooner had come in; and things appearing quieter, Mr. Stewart and the captain landed in Taahauku to compute the damage and to view the grave, which was already indicated by the stench. While they were so employed, a party of Moipu's young men, decked with red flannel to indicate martial sentiments, came over the hills from Atuona, dug up the bodies, washed them in the river, and carried them away on sticks. That night the feast began.

Those who knew Mr. Stewart before this experience declare the man to be quite altered. He stuck, however, to his post; and somewhat later, when the plantation was already well established, and gave employment to sixty Chinamen and seventy natives, he found himself once more in dangerous times. The men of Haamau, it was reported, had sworn to plunder and erase the settlement; letters came continually from the Hawaiian missionary, who acted as intelligence department; and for six weeks Mr. Stewart and three other whites slept in the cotton-house at night in a rampart of bales, and (what was their best defence) ostentatiously practised rifle-shooting by day upon the beach. Natives were often there to watch them; the practice was excellent; and the assault was never delivered – if it ever was intended, which I doubt, for the natives are more famous for false rumours than for deeds of energy. I was told the late French war[3] was a case in point; the tribes on the beach accusing those in the mountains of designs which they had never the hardihood to entertain. And the same testimony to their backwardness in open battle reached me from all sides. Captain Hart once landed after an engagement in a certain bay; one man had his hand hurt, an old woman and two children had been slain; and the captain improved the occasion by poulticing the hand, and taunting both sides upon so wretched an affair. It is true these wars were often merely formal – comparable with duels to the first blood. Captain Hart visited a bay where such a war was being carried on between two brothers, one of whom had been thought wanting in civility to the guests of the other. About one-half of the population served day about upon alternate sides, so as to be well with each when the inevitable peace should follow. The forts of the belligerents were over against each other, and close by. Pigs were cooking. Well-oiled braves, with well-oiled muskets, strutted on the *paepae* or sat down to feast. No business, however needful, could be done, and all thoughts were supposed to be centred in this mockery of war. A few days later, by a regrettable accident, a man was killed; it was felt at once the thing had gone too far, and the quarrel was instantly patched up. But the more serious wars were prosecuted in a similar spirit; a gift of pigs and a feast made their inevitable end; the killing of a single man was a great victory, and the murder of defenceless solitaries counted a heroic deed.

The foot of the cliffs, about all these islands, is the place of fishing. Between Taahauku and Atuona we saw men, but chiefly women, some nearly naked, some in thin white or crimson dresses, perched in little surf-beat promontories – the brown precipice overhanging them, and the convolvulus overhanging that, as if to cut them off the more completely from assistance. There they would angle much of the morning; and as fast as they caught any fish, eat them, raw and living, where they stood. It was such helpless ones that the warriors from the opposite island of Tauata slew, and carried home and ate, and were thereupon accounted mighty men of valour. Of one such exploit I can give the account of an eye-witness. 'Portuguese Joe,' Mr. Keane's cook, was once pulling an oar in an Atuona boat, when they spied a stranger in a canoe with some fish and a piece of *tapa*.[4] The Atuona men cried upon him to draw near and have a smoke. He complied, because, I suppose, he had no choice; but he knew, poor devil, what he was coming to, and (as Joe said) 'he didn't seem to care about the smoke.' A few questions followed, as to where he came from, and what was his business. These he must needs answer, as he must needs draw at the unwelcome pipe, his heart the while drying in his bosom. And then, of a sudden, a big fellow in Joe's boat leaned over, plucked the stranger from his canoe, struck him with a knife in the neck – inward and downward, as Joe showed in pantomime more expressive than his words – and held him under water, like a fowl, until his struggles ceased. Whereupon the long-pig was hauled on board, the boat's head turned about for Atuona, and these Marquesan braves pulled home rejoicing. Moipu was on the beach and rejoiced with them on their arrival. Poor Joe toiled at his oar that day with a white face, yet he had no fear for himself. 'They were very good to me – gave me plenty grub: never wished to eat white man,' said he.

If the most horrible experience was Mr. Stewart's, it was Captain Hart himself who ran the nearest danger. He had bought a piece of land from Timau, chief of a neighbouring bay, and put some Chinese there to work. Visiting the station with one of the Godeffroys,[5] he found his Chinamen trooping to the beach in terror; Timau had driven them out, seized their effects, and was in war attire with his young men. A boat was despatched to Taahauku for reinforcement; as they awaited her return, they could see, from the deck of the schooner, Timau and his young men dancing the war-dance on a hill-top till past twelve at night; and so soon as the boat came (bringing three gendarmes, armed with chassepots,[6] two white men from Taa-hauku station, and some native warriors) the party set out to seize the chief before he should awake. Day was not come, and it was a very bright moonlight morning, when they reached the hill-top where (in a house of palm-leaves) Timau was sleeping off his debauch. The assailants were fully exposed, the interior of the hut quite dark; the position far from sound. The gendarmes knelt with their pieces ready, and Captain Hart advanced alone. As he drew near the door he heard the snap of a gun cocking from within, and in sheer self-defence – there being no other escape – sprang into the house and grappled Timau. 'Timau, come with me!' he cried. But Timau – a great fellow, his eyes blood-red with the abuse of *kava*,[7] six foot three in stature – cast him on one side; and the captain, instantly expecting to be either shot or brained, discharged his pistol in the dark. When they carried Timau out at the door into the moonlight, he was already dead, and, upon this unlooked-for termination of their sally, the whites appeared to have lost all conduct, and retreated to the boats, fired upon by the natives as they went. Captain Hart, who almost rivals Bishop Dordillon in popularity, shared with him the policy of extreme indulgence to the natives, regarding them as children, making light of their defects, and constantly in favour of mild measures. The death of Timau has thus somewhat weighed upon his mind; the more so, as the chieftain's musket was found in the house unloaded. To a less delicate conscience the matter will seem light. If a drunken savage elects to cock a fire-arm, a gentleman advancing towards him in the open cannot wait to make sure if it be charged.

I have touched on the captain's popularity. It is one of the things that most strikes a stranger in the Marquesas. He comes instantly on two names, both new to him, both locally famous, both mentioned by all with affection and respect – the bishop's and the captain's. It gave me a strong desire to meet with the survivor,[8] which was subsequently gratified – to the enrichment of these pages. Long after that again, in the Place Dolorous – Molokai[9] – I came once more on the traces of that affectionate popularity. There was a blind white leper there, an old sailor – 'an old tough,' he called himself – who had long sailed among the eastern islands. Him I used to visit, and, being fresh from the scenes of his activity, gave him the news. This (in the true island style) was largely a chronicle of wrecks; and it chanced I mentioned the case of one not very successful captain, and how he had lost a vessel for Mr. Hart; thereupon the blind leper broke forth in lamentation. 'Did he lose a ship of John Hart's?' he cried; 'poor John Hart! Well, I'm sorry it was Hart's,' with needless force of epithet, which I neglect to reproduce.

Perhaps, if Captain Hart's affairs had continued to prosper, his popularity might have been different. Success wins glory, but it kills affection, which misfortune fosters. And the misfortune which overtook the captain's enterprise was truly singular. He was at the top of his career. Ile Masse[10] belonged to him, given by the French as an indemnity for the robberies at Taahauku. But the Ile Masse was only suitable for cattle; and his two chief stations were Anaho, in Nuka-hiva, facing the north-east, and Taahauku in Hiva-oa, some hundred miles to the southward, and facing the south-west. Both these were on the same day swept by a tidal wave, which was not felt in any other bay or island of the group. The south coast of Hiva-oa was bestrewn with building timber and camphor-wood chests, containing goods; which, on the promise of a reasonable salvage, the natives very honestly brought back, the chests apparently not opened, and some of the wood after it had been built into their houses. But the recovery of such jetsam could not affect the result. It was impossible the captain should withstand this partiality of fortune; and with his fall the prosperity of the Marquesas ended. Anaho is truly extinct, Taahauku but a shadow of itself; nor has any new plantation arisen in their stead.

CHAPTER XIII

CHARACTERS

There was a certain traffic in our anchorage at Atuona; different indeed from the dead inertia and quiescence of the sister island, Nuka-hiva. Sails were seen steering from its mouth; now it would be a whale-boat manned with native rowdies, and heavy with copra for sale; now perhaps a single canoe come after commodities to buy. The anchorage was besides frequented by fishers; not only the lone females perched in niches of the cliff, but whole parties, who would sometimes camp and build a fire upon the beach, and sometimes lie in their canoes in the midst of the haven and jump by turns in the water; which they would cast eight or nine feet high, to drive, as we supposed, the fish into their nets. The goods the purchasers came to buy were sometimes quaint. I remarked one outrigger returning with a single ham swung from a pole in the stern. And one day there came into Mr. Keane's store a charming lad, excellently mannered, speaking French correctly though with a babyish accent; very handsome too, and much of a dandy, as was shown not only in his shining raiment, but by the nature of his purchases. These were five ship-biscuits, a bottle of scent, and two balls of washing blue. He was from Tauata, whither he returned the same night in an outrigger, daring the deep with these young-ladyish treasures. The gross of the native passengers were more ill-favoured: tall, powerful fellows, well tattooed, and with disquieting manners. Something coarse and jeering distinguished them, and I was often reminded of the slums of some great city. One night, as dusk was falling, a whale-boat put in on that part of the beach where I chanced to be alone. Six or seven ruffianly fellows scrambled out; all had enough English to give me 'good-bye,' which was the ordinary salutation; or 'good-morning,' which they seemed to regard as an intensitive; jests followed, they surrounded me with harsh laughter and rude looks, and I was glad to move away. I had not yet encountered Mr. Stewart, or I should have been reminded of his first landing at Atuona and the humorist who nibbled at the heel. But their neighbourhood depressed me; and I felt, if I had been there a castaway and out of reach of help, my heart would have been sick.

Nor was the traffic altogether native. While we lay in the anchorage there befell a strange coincidence. A schooner was observed at sea and aiming to enter. We knew all the schooners in the group, but this appeared larger than any; she was rigged, besides, after the English manner; and, coming to an anchor some way outside the *Casco*, showed at last the blue ensign. There were at that time, according to rumour, no fewer than four yachts in the Pacific; but it was strange that any two of them should thus lie side by side in that outlandish inlet: stranger still that in the owner of the *Nyanza*, Captain Dewar,[1] I should find a man of the same country and the same county with myself, and one whom I had seen walking as a boy on the shores of the Alpes Maritimes.

We had besides a white visitor from shore, who came and departed in a crowded whale-boat manned by natives; having read of yachts in the Sunday papers, and being fired with the desire to see one. Captain Chase, they called him, an old whaler-man, thickset and white-bearded, with a strong Indiana drawl; years old in the country, a good backer in battle, and one of those dead shots whose practice at the target struck terror in the braves of Haamau. Captain Chase dwelt farther east in a bay called Hanamate, with a Mr. McCallum; or rather they had dwelt together once, and were now amicably separated. The captain is to be found near one end of the bay, in a wreck of a house, and waited on by a Chinese. At the point of the opposing corner another habitation stands on a tall *paepae*. The surf runs there exceeding heavy, seas of seven and eight feet high bursting under the walls of the house, which is thus continually filled with their clamour, and rendered fit only for solitary, or at least for silent, inmates. Here it is that Mr. McCallum, with a Shakespeare and a Burns, enjoys the society of the breakers. His name and his Burns testify to Scottish blood; but he is an American born, somewhere far east; followed the trade of a ship-carpenter; and was long employed, the captain of a hundred Indians, breaking up wrecks about Cape Flattery.[2] Many of the whites who are to be found scattered in the South Seas represent the more artistic portion of their class; and not only enjoy the poetry of that new life, but came there on purpose to enjoy it. I have been shipmates with a man, no longer young, who sailed upon that voyage, his first time to sea, for the mere love of Samoa; and it was a few letters in a newspaper that sent him on that pilgrimage. Mr. McCallum was another instance of the same. He had read of the South Seas; loved to read of them; and let their image fasten in his heart: till at length he could refrain no longer – must set forth, a new Rudel,[3] for that unseen homeland – and has now dwelt for years in Hiva-oa, and will lay his bones there in the end with full content; having no desire to behold again the places of his boyhood, only, perhaps – once, before he dies – the rude and wintry landscape of Cape Flattery. Yet he is an active man, full of schemes; has bought land of the natives; has planted five thousand coco palms; has a desert island in his eye, which he desires to lease, and a schooner in the stocks, which he has laid and built himself, and even hopes to finish. Mr. McCallum and I did not meet, but, like gallant troubadours, corresponded in verse. I hope he will not consider it a breach of copyright if I give here a specimen of his muse. He and Bishop Dordillon are the two European bards of the Marquesas.

> Sail, ho! Ahoy! *Casco*,
>   First among the pleasure fleet
>   That came around to greet
> These isles from San Francisco.
>
> And first, too; only one
>   Among the literary men
>   That this way has ever been –
> Welcome, then, to Stevenson.

Please not offended be
At this little notice
Of the *Casco*, Captain Otis,
With the novelist's family.

Avoir une voyage magnifical
Is our wish sincere,
That you'll have from here
Allant sur la Grande Pacifical.

But our chief visitor was one Mapiao, a great *tuhuka* – which seems to mean priest, wizard, tattooer, practiser of any art, or, in a word, esoteric person – and a man famed for his eloquence on public occasions and witty talk in private. His first appearance was typical of the man. He came down clamorous to the eastern landing, where the surf was running very high; scorned all our signals to go round the bay; carried his point, was brought aboard at some hazard to our skiff, and set down in one corner of the cockpit to his appointed task. He had been hired, as one cunning in the art, to make my old men's beards into a wreath: what a wreath for Celia's arbour![4] His own beard (which he carried, for greater safety, in a sailor's knot) was not merely the adornment of his age, but a substantial piece of property. One hundred dollars was the estimated value; and as Brother Michel never knew a native to deposit a greater sum with Bishop Dordillon, our friend was a rich man in virtue of his chin. He had something of an East Indian cast, but taller and stronger: his nose hooked, his face narrow, his forehead very high, the whole elaborately tattooed. I may say I have never entertained a guest so trying. In the least particular he must be waited on; he would not go to the scuttle-butt[5] for water; he would not even reach to get the glass, it must be given him in his hand; if aid were denied him, he would fold his arms, bow his head, and go without: only the work would suffer. Early the first forenoon he called aloud for biscuit and salmon; biscuit and ham were brought; he looked on them inscrutably, and signed they should be set aside. A number of considerations crowded on my mind; how the sort of work on which he was engaged was probably *tapu* in a high degree;

should by rights, perhaps, be transacted on a *tapu* platform which no female might approach; and it was possible that fish might be the essential diet. Some salted fish I therefore brought him, and along with that a glass of rum: at sight of which Mapiao displayed extraordinary animation, pointed to the zenith, made a long speech in which I picked up *umati* – the word for the sun – and signed to me once more to place these dainties out of reach. At last I had understood, and every day the programme was the same. At an early period of the morning his dinner must be set forth on the roof of the house and at a proper distance, full in view but just out of reach; and not until the fit hour, which was the point of noon, would the artificer partake. This solemnity was the cause of an absurd misadventure. He was seated plaiting, as usual, at the beards, his dinner arrayed on the roof, and not far off a glass of water standing. It appears he desired to drink; was of course far too great a gentleman to rise and get the water for himself; and spying Mrs. Stevenson, imperiously signed to her to hand it. The signal was misunderstood; Mrs. Stevenson was, by this time, prepared for any eccentricity on the part of our guest; and instead of passing him the water, flung his dinner overboard. I must do Mapiao justice: all laughed, but his laughter rang the loudest.

These troubles of service were at worst occasional; the embarrass-ment of the man's talk incessant. He was plainly a practised conver-sationalist; the nicety of his inflections, the elegance of his gestures, and the fine play of his expression, told us that. We, meanwhile, sat like aliens in a playhouse; we could see the actors were upon some material business and performing well, but the plot of the drama remained undiscoverable. Names of places, the name of Captain Hart, occasional disconnected words, tantalised without enlightening us; and the less we understood, the more gallantly, the more copiously, and with still the more explanatory gestures, Mapiao returned to the assault. We could see his vanity was on the rack; being come to a place where that fine jewel of his conversational talent could earn him no respect; and he had times of despair when he desisted from the endeavour, and instants of irritation when he regarded us with uncon-cealed contempt. Yet for me, as the practitioner of some kindred mystery to his own, he manifested to the last a measure of respect. As we sat under the awning, in opposite corners of the cockpit, he braiding hairs from dead men's chins, I forming runes upon a sheet of folio paper, he would nod across to me as one *tuhuka* to another, or, crossing the cockpit, study for a while my shapeless scrawl and encourage me with a heartfelt '*mitai!* – good!' So might a deaf painter sympathise far off with a musician, as the slave and master of some uncomprehended and yet kindred art. A silly trade, he doubtless considered it; but a man must make allowance for barbarians – *chaque pays a ses coutumes* – and he felt the principle was there.

The time came at last when his labours, which resembled those rather of Penelope[6] than Hercules,[7] could be no more spun out, and nothing remained but to pay him and say farewell. After a long, learned argument in Marquesan, I gathered that his mind was set on fish-hooks; with three of which, and a brace of dollars, I thought he was not ill rewarded for passing his forenoons in our cockpit, eating, drinking, delivering his opinions, and pressing the ship's company into his menial service. For all that, he was a man of so high a bearing, and so like an uncle of my own who should have gone mad and got tattooed, that I applied to him, when we were both on shore, to know if he were satisfied. '*Mitai ehipe?*' I asked. And he, with rich unction, offering at the same time his hand – '*Mitai ehipe, mitai kaekae; kaoha nui!*' – or, to translate freely: 'The ship is good, the victuals are up to the mark, and we part in friendship.' Which testimonial uttered, he set off along the beach with his head bowed and the air of one deeply injured.

I saw him go, on my side, with relief. It would be more interesting to learn how our relation seemed to Mapiao. His exigence, we may suppose, was merely loyal. He had been hired by the ignorant to do a piece of work; and he was bound that he would do it the right way. Countless obstacles, continual ignorant ridicule, availed not to dissuade him. He had his dinner laid out; watched it, as was fit, the while he worked; ate it at the fit hour; was in all things served and waited on; and could take his hire in the end with a clear conscience, telling himself the mystery was performed duly, the beards rightfully braided, and we (in spite of ourselves) correctly served. His view of our stupidity, even he, the mighty talker, must have lacked language to express. He never interfered with my *tuhuka* work; civilly praised it, idle as it seemed; civilly supposed that I was competent in my own mystery: such being the attitude of the intelligent and the polite. And we, on the other hand – who had yet the most to gain or lose, since the product was to be ours – who had professed our disability by the very act of hiring him to do it – were never weary of impeding his own more important labours, and sometimes lacked the sense and the civility to refrain from laughter.

CHAPTER XIV

IN A CANNIBAL VALLEY

The road from Taahauku to Atuona skirted the north-westerly side of the anchorage, somewhat high up, edged, and sometimes shaded, by the splendid flowers of the *flamboyant*[1] – its English name I do not know. At the turn of the land, Atuona came in view: a long beach, a heavy and loud breach of surf, a shore-side village scattered among trees, and the guttered mountains drawing near on both sides above a narrow and rich ravine. Its infamous repute perhaps affected me; but I thought it the loveliest, and by far the most ominous and gloomy, spot on earth. Beautiful it surely was; and even more salubrious. The healthfulness of the whole group is amazing; that of Atuona almost in the nature of a miracle. In Atuona, a village planted in a shore-side marsh, the houses standing everywhere intermingled with the pools of a taro-garden, we find every condition of tropical danger and discomfort; and yet there are not even mosquitoes – not even the hateful day-fly of Nuka-hiva – and fever, and its concomitant, the island *fe'efe'e*,[2] are unknown.

This is the chief station of the French on the man-eating isle of Hiva-oa. The sergeant of gendarmerie enjoys the style of the vice-resident, and hoists the French colours over a quite extensive compound. A Chinaman, a waif from the plantation, keeps a restaurant in the rear quarters of the village; and the mission is well represented by the sisters' school and Brother Michel's church. Father

Orens,[3] a wonderful octogenarian, his frame scarce bowed, the fire of his eye undimmed, has lived, and trembled, and suffered in this place since 1843. Again and again, when Moipu had made coco-brandy, he has been driven from his house into the woods. 'A mouse that dwelt in a cat's ear' had a more easy resting-place; and yet I have never seen a man that bore less mark of years. He must show us the church, still decorated with the bishop's artless ornaments of paper – the last work of industrious old hands, and the last earthly amusement of a man that was much of a hero. In the sacristy we must see his sacred vessels, and, in particular, a vestment which was a *'vraie curiosité,'* because it had been given by a gendarme. To the Protestant there is always something embarrassing in the eagerness with which grown and holy men regard these trifles; but it was touching and pretty to see Orens, his aged eyes shining in his head, display his sacred treasures.

August 26. – The vale behind the village, narrowing swiftly to a mere ravine, was choked with profitable trees. A river gushed in the midst. Overhead, the tall coco-palms made a primary covering; above that, from one wall of the mountain to another, the ravine was roofed with cloud; so that we moved below, amid teeming vegetation, in a covered house of heat. On either hand, at every hundred yards, instead of the houseless, disembowelling *paepae*s of Nuka-hiva, populous houses turned out their inhabitants to cry *'Kaoha!'* to the passers-by. The road, too, was busy: strings of girls, fair and foul, as in less favoured countries; men bearing breadfruit; the sisters, with a little guard of pupils; a fellow bestriding a horse – passed and greeted us continually; and now it was a Chinaman who came to the gate of his flower-yard, and gave us 'Good-day' in excellent English; and a little farther on it would be some natives who set us down by the wayside, made us a feast of mummy-apple, and entertained us as we ate with drumming on a tin case. With all this fine plenty of men and fruit, death is at work here also. The population, according to the highest estimate, does not exceed six hundred in the whole vale of Atuona; and yet, when I once chanced to put the question, Brother Michel counted up ten whom he knew to be sick beyond recovery. It was here, too, that I could at last gratify my curiosity with the sight of a native house in the very article of dissolution. It had fallen flat along the *paepae*, its poles sprawling ungainly; the rains and the mites contended against it; what remained seemed sound enough, but much was gone already; and it was easy to see how the insects consumed the walls as if they had been bread, and the air and the rain ate into them like vitriol.

A little ahead of us, a young gentleman, very well tattooed, and dressed in a pair of white trousers and a flannel shirt, had been marching unconcernedly. Of a sudden, without apparent cause, he turned back, took us in possession, and led us undissuadably along a by-path to the river's edge. There, in a nook of the most attractive amenity, he bade us to sit down: the stream splashing at our elbow, a shock of nondescript greenery enshrining us from above; and thither, after a brief absence, he brought us a cocoa-nut, a lump of sandal-wood, and a stick he had begun to carve: the nut for present refreshment, the sandal-wood for a precious gift, and the stick – in the simplicity of his vanity – to harvest premature praise. Only one section was yet carved, although the whole was pencil-marked in lengths; and when I proposed to buy it, Poni (for that was the artist's name) recoiled in horror. But I was not to be moved, and simply refused restitution, for I had long wondered why a people who displayed, in their tattooing, so great a gift of arabesque invention, should display it nowhere else. Here, at last, I had found something of the same talent in another medium; and I held the incompleteness, in these days of world-wide brummagem,[4] for a happy mark of authenticity. Neither my reasons nor my purpose had I the means of making clear to Poni; I could only hold on to the stick, and bid the artist follow me to the gendarmerie, where I should find interpreters and money; but we gave him, in the meanwhile, a boat-call in return for his sandal-wood. As he came behind us down the vale he sounded upon this continually. And continually, from the wayside houses, there poured forth little groups of girls in crimson, or of men in white. And to these must Poni pass the news of who the strangers were, of what they had been doing, of why it was that Poni had a boat-whistle; and of why he was now being haled to the vice-residency, uncertain whether to be punished or rewarded, uncertain whether he had lost a stick or made a bargain, but hopeful on the whole, and in the meanwhile highly consoled by the boat-whistle. Whereupon he would tear himself away from this particular group of inquirers, and once more we would hear the shrill call in our wake.

August 27. – I made a more extended circuit in the vale with Brother Michel. We were mounted on a pair of sober nags, suitable to these rude paths; the weather was exquisite, and the company in which I found myself no less agreeable than the scenes through which I passed. We mounted at first by a steep grade along the summit of one of those twisted spurs that, from a distance, mark out provinces of sun and shade upon the mountain-side. The ground fell away on either hand with an extreme declivity. From either hand, out of profound ravines, mounted the song of falling water and the smoke of household fires. Here and there the hills of foliage would divide, and our eye would plunge down upon one of these deep-nested habitations. And still, high in front, arose the precipitous barrier of the mountain, greened over where it seemed that scarce a harebell could find root, barred with the zigzags of a human road where it seemed that not a goat could scramble. And in truth, for all the labour that it cost, the road is regarded even by the Marquesans as impassable; they will not risk a horse on that ascent; and those who lie to the westward come and go in their canoes. I never knew a hill to lose so little on a near approach: a consequence, I must suppose, of its surprising steepness. When we turned about, I was amazed to behold so deep a view behind, and so high a shoulder of blue sea, crowned by the whale-like island of Motane. And yet the wall of mountain had not visibly dwindled, and I could even have fancied, as I raised my eyes to measure it, that it loomed higher than before.

We struck now into covert paths, crossed and heard more near at hand the bickering of the streams, and tasted the coolness of those recesses where the houses stood. The birds sang about us as we descended. All along our path my guide was being hailed by voices: '*Mikaël – Kaoha, Mikaël!*' From the doorstep, from the cotton-patch, or out of the deep grove of island-chestnuts, these friendly cries arose, and were cheerily answered as we passed. In a sharp angle of a glen, on a rushing brook and under fathoms of cool foliage, we struck a house upon a well-built *paepae*, the fire brightly burning under the *popoi*-shed against the evening meal; and here the cries became a chorus, and the house folk, running out, obliged us to dismount and breathe. It seemed a numerous family: we saw eight at least; and one of these honoured me with a particular attention. This was the mother, a woman naked to the waist, of an aged countenance, but with hair still copious and black, and breasts still erect and youthful. On our arrival I could see she remarked me, but instead of offering any greeting, disappeared at once into the bush. Thence she returned with two crimson flowers. 'Good-bye!' was her salutation, uttered not without coquetry; and as she said it she pressed the flowers into my hand – 'Good-bye! I speak Inglis.' It was from a whaler-man, who (she informed me) was 'a plenty good chap,' that she had learned my language; and I could not but think how handsome she must have been in these times of her youth, and could not but guess that some memories of the dandy whaler-man prompted her attentions to myself. Nor could I refrain from wondering what had befallen her lover; in the rain and mire of what sea-ports he had tramped since then; in what close and garish drinking-dens had found his pleasure; and in the ward of what infirmary dreamed his last of the Marquesas. But she, the more fortunate, lived on in her green island. The talk, in this lost house upon the mountains, ran chiefly upon Mapiao and his visits to the *Casco*: the news of which had probably gone abroad by then to all the island, so that there was no *paepae* in Hiva-oa where they did not make the subject of excited comment.

Not much beyond we came upon a high place in the foot of the ravine. Two roads divided it, and met in the midst. Save for this intersection the amphitheatre was strangely perfect, and had a certain ruder air of things Roman. Depths of foliage and the bulk of the mountain kept it in a grateful shadow. On the benches several young folk sat clustered or apart. One of these, a girl perhaps fourteen years of age, buxom and comely, caught the eye of Brother Michel. Why was she not at school? – she was done with school now. What was she doing here? – she lived here now. Why so? – no answer but a deepening blush. There was no severity in Brother Michel's manner; the girl's own confusion told her story. '*Elle a honte*,' was the missionary's comment, as we rode away. Near by in the stream, a grown girl was bathing naked in a goyle[5] between two stepping-stones; and it amused me to see with what alacrity and real alarm she bounded on her many-coloured under-clothes. Even in these daughters of cannibals shame was eloquent.

It is in Hiva-oa, owing to the inveterate cannibalism of the natives, that local beliefs have been most rudely trodden underfoot. It was here that three religious chiefs were set under a bridge, and the women of the valley made to defile over their heads upon the roadway: the poor, dishonoured fellows sitting there (all observers agree) with streaming tears. Not only was one road driven across the high place, but two roads intersected in its midst. There is no reason to suppose that the last was done of purpose, and perhaps it was impossible entirely to avoid the numerous sacred places of the islands. But these things are not done without result. I have spoken already of the regard of Marquesans for the dead, making (as it does) so strange a contrast with their unconcern for death. Early on this day's ride, for instance, we encountered a petty chief, who inquired (of course) where we were going, and suggested by way of amendment: 'Why do you not rather show him the cemetery?' I saw it; it was but newly opened, the third within eight years. They are great builders here in Hiva-oa; I saw in my ride *paepae*s that no European dry-stone mason could have equalled, the black volcanic stones were laid so justly, the corners were so precise, the levels so true; but the retaining-wall of the new graveyard stood apart, and seemed to be a work of love. The sentiment of honour for the dead is therefore not extinct. And yet observe the consequence of violently countering men's opinions. Of the four prisoners in Atuona gaol, three were of course thieves; the fourth was there for sacrilege. He had levelled up a piece of the graveyard – to give a feast upon, as he informed the court – and declared he had no thought of doing wrong. Why should he? He had been forced at the point of the bayonet to destroy the sacred places of his own piety; when he had recoiled from the task, he had been jeered at for a superstitious fool. And now it is supposed he will respect our European superstitions as by second nature.

CHAPTER XV

THE TWO CHIEFS OF ATUONA

It had chanced (as the *Casco* beat through the Bordelais Straits for Taahauku) she approached on one board very near the land in the opposite isle of Tauata, where houses were to be seen in a grove of tall coco-palms. Brother Michel pointed out the spot. 'I am at home now,' said he. 'I believe I have a large share in these cocoa-nuts; and in that house madame my mother lives with her two husbands!' 'With two husbands?' somebody inquired. '*C'est ma honte*,' replied the brother dryly.

A word in passing on the two husbands. I conceive the brother to have expressed himself loosely. It seems common enough to find a native lady with two consorts; but these are not two husbands. The first is still the husband; the wife continues to be referred to by his name; and the position of the coadjutor, or *pikio*, although quite regular, appears undoubtedly subordinate. We had opportunities to observe one household of the sort. The *pikio* was recognised; appeared openly along with the husband when the lady was thought to be insulted, and the pair made common cause like brothers. At home the inequality was more apparent. The husband sat to receive and entertain visitors; the *pikio* was running the while to fetch cocoa-nuts like a hired servant, and I remarked he was sent on these errands in preference even to the son. Plainly we have here no second husband; plainly we have the tolerated lover. Only, in the Marquesas, instead of carrying his lady's fan and mantle, he must turn his hand to do the husband's housework.

The sight of Brother Michel's family estate led the conversation for some while upon the method and consequence of artificial kinship. Our curiosity became extremely whetted; the brother offered to have the whole of us adopted, and some two days later we became accordingly the children of Paaaeua, appointed chief of Atuona. I was unable to be present at the ceremony, which was primitively simple. The two Mrs. Stevensons and Mr. Osbourne, along with Paaaeua, his wife, and an adopted child of theirs, son of a shipwrecked Austrian, sat down to an excellent island meal, of which the principal and the only necessary dish was pig. A concourse watched them through the apertures of the house; but none, not even Brother Michel, might partake; for the meal was sacramental, and either creative or declaratory of the new relationship. In Tahiti things are not so strictly ordered; when Ori and I 'made brothers,'[1] both our families sat with us at table, yet only he and I, who had eaten with intention, were supposed to be affected by the ceremony. For the adoption of an infant I believe no formality to be required; the child is handed over by the natural parents, and grows up to inherit the estates of the adoptive. Presents are doubtless exchanged, as at all junctures of island life, social or international; but I never heard of any banquet – the child's presence at the daily board perhaps sufficing. We may find the rationale in the ancient Arabian idea that a common diet makes a common blood, with its derivative axiom that 'he is the father who gives the child its morning draught.' In the Marquesan practice, the sense would thus be evanescent; from the Tahitian, a mere survival, it will have entirely fled. An interesting parallel will probably occur to many of my readers.

What is the nature of the obligation assumed at such a festival? It will vary with the characters of those engaged, and with the circumstances of the case. Thus it would be absurd to take too seriously our adoption at Atuona. On the part of Paaaeua it was an affair of social ambition; when he agreed to receive us in his family the man had not so much as seen us, and knew only that we were inestimably rich and travelled in a floating palace. We, upon our side, ate of his baked meats with no true *animus affiliandi*,[2] but moved by the single sentiment of curiosity. The affair was formal, and a matter of parade, as when in Europe sovereigns call each other cousin. Yet, had we stayed at Atuona, Paaaeua would have held himself bound to establish us upon his land, and to set apart young men for our service, and trees for our support. I have mentioned the Austrian. He sailed in one of two sister ships, which left the Clyde in coal; both rounded the Horn, and both, at several hundred miles of distance, though close on the same point of time, took fire at sea on the Pacific. One was destroyed; the derelict iron frame of the second, after long, aimless cruising, was at length recovered, refitted, and hails to-day from San Francisco. A boat's crew from one of these disasters reached, after great hardships, the isle of Hiva-oa. Some of these men vowed they would never again confront the chances of the sea; but alone of them all the Austrian has been exactly true to his engagement, remains where he landed, and designs to die where he has lived. Now, with such a man, falling and taking root among islanders, the processes described may be compared to a gardener's graft. He passes bodily into the native stock; ceases wholly to be alien; has entered the commune of the blood, shares the prosperity and consideration of his new family, and is expected to impart with the same generosity the fruits of his European skill and knowledge. It is this implied engagement that so frequently offends the ingrafted white. To snatch an immediate advantage – to get (let us say) a station for his store – he will play upon the native custom and become a son or a brother for the day, promising himself to cast down the ladder by which he shall have ascended, and repudiate the kinship so soon as it shall grow burdensome. And he finds there are two parties to the bargain. Perhaps his Polynesian relative is simple, and conceived the blood-bond literally; perhaps he is shrewd, and himself entered the covenant with a view to gain. And either way the store is ravaged, the house littered with lazy natives; and the richer the man grows, the more numerous, the more idle, and the more affectionate he finds his native relatives. Most men thus circumstanced contrive to buy or brutally manage to enforce their independence; but many vegetate without hope, strangled by parasites.

We had no cause to blush with Brother Michel. Our new parents were kind, gentle, well-mannered, and generous in gifts; the wife was a most motherly woman, the husband a man who stood justly high with his employers. Enough has been said to show why Moipu should be deposed; and in Paaaeua the French had found a reputable substitute. He went always scrupulously dressed, and looked the picture of propriety, like a dark, handsome, stupid, and probably religious young man hot from a European funeral. In character he seemed the ideal of what is known as the good citizen. He wore gravity like an ornament. None could more nicely represent the desired character as an appointed chief, the outpost of civilisation and reform. And yet, were the French to go and native manners to revive, fancy beholds him crowned with old men's beards and crowding with the first to a man-eating festival. But I must not seem to be unjust to Paaaeua. His respectability went deeper than the skin; his sense of the becoming sometimes nerved him for unexpected rigours.

One evening Captain Otis and Mr. Osbourne were on shore in the village.[3] All was agog; dancing had begun; it was plain it was to be a night of festival, and our adventurers were overjoyed at their good fortune. A strong fall of rain drove them for shelter to the house of Paaaeua, where they were made welcome, wiled into a chamber, and shut in. Presently the rain took off, the fun was to begin in earnest, and the young bloods of Atuona came round the house and called to my fellow-travellers through the interstices of the wall. Late into the night the calls were continued and resumed, and sometimes mingled with taunts; late into the night the prisoners, tantalised by the noises of the festival, renewed their efforts to escape. But all was vain; right across the door lay that god-fearing householder, Paaaeua, feigning sleep; and my friends had to forgo their junketing. In this incident, so delightfully European, we thought we could detect three strands of sentiment. In the first place, Paaaeua had a charge of souls: these were young men, and he judged it right to withhold them from the primrose path. Secondly, he was a public character, and it was not fitting that his guests should countenance a festival of which he disapproved. So might some strict clergyman at home address a worldly visitor: 'Go to the theatre if you like, but, by your leave, not from my house!' Thirdly, Paaaeua was a man jealous and with some cause (as shall be shown) for jealousy; and the feasters were the satellites of his immediate rival, Moipu.

For the adoption had caused much excitement in the village; it made the strangers popular. Paaaeua, in his difficult posture of appointed chief, drew strength and dignity from their alliance, and only Moipu and his followers were malcontent. For some reason nobody (except myself) appears to dislike Moipu. Captain Hart, who has been robbed and threatened by him; Father Orens, whom he has fired at, and repeatedly driven to the woods; my own family, and even the French officials – all seemed smitten with an irrepressible affection for the man. His fall had been made soft; his son, upon his death, was to succeed Paaaeua in the chieftaincy; and he lived, at the time of our visit, in the shoreward part of the village in a good house, and with a strong following of young men, his late braves and pot-hunters. In this society, the coming of the *Casco*, the adoption, the return feast on board, and the presents exchanged between the whites and their new parents, were doubtless eagerly and bitterly canvassed. It was felt that a few years ago the honours would have gone elsewhere. In this unwonted business, in this reception of some hitherto undreamed-of and outlandish potentate – some Prester John[4] or old Assaracus[5] – a few years back it would have been the part of Moipu to play the hero and the host, and his young men would have accompanied and adorned the various celebrations as the acknowledged leaders of society. And now, by a malign vicissitude of fortune, Moipu must sit in his house quite unobserved; and his young men could but look in at the door the while their rivals feasted. Perhaps M. Grévy[6] felt a touch of bitterness towards his successor when he beheld him figure on the broad stage of the centenary of eighty-nine; the visit of the *Casco* which Moipu had missed by so few years was a more unusual occasion in Atuona than a centenary in France; and the dethroned chief determined to reassert himself in the public eye.

Mr. Osbourne had gone into Atuona photographing; the population of the village had gathered together for the occasion on the place before the church, and Paaaeua, highly delighted with this new appearance of his family, played the master of ceremonies. The church had been taken, with its jolly architect before the door; the nuns with their pupils; sundry damsels in the ancient and singularly unbecoming robes of *tapa*; and Father Orens in the midst of a group of his parishioners. I know not what else was in hand, when the photographer became aware of a sensation in the crowd, and, looking around, beheld a very noble figure of a man appear upon the margin of a thicket and stroll nonchalantly near. The nonchalance was visibly affected; it was plain he came there to arouse attention, and his success was instant. He was introduced; he was civil, he was obliging, he was always ineffably superior and certain of himself; a well-graced actor. It was presently suggested that he should appear in his war costume; he gracefully consented; and returned in that strange, inappropriate, and ill-omened array (which very well became his handsome person) to strut in a circle of admirers, and be thenceforth the centre of photography. Thus had Moipu effected his introduction, as by accident, to the white strangers, made it a favour to display his finery, and reduced his rival to a secondary *rôle* on the theatre of the disputed village. Paaaeua felt the blow; and, with a spirit which we never dreamed he could possess, asserted his priority. It was found impossible that day to get a photograph of Moipu alone; for whenever he stood up before the camera his successor placed himself unbidden by his side, and gently but firmly held to his position. The portraits of the pair, Jacob and Esau,[7] standing shoulder to shoulder, one in his careful European dress, one in his barbaric trappings, figure the past and present of their island. A graveyard with its humble crosses would be the aptest symbol of the future.

We are all impressed with the belief that Moipu had planned his campaign from the beginning to the end. It is certain that he lost no time in pushing his advantage. Mr. Osbourne was inveigled to his house; various gifts were fished out of an old sea-chest; Father Orens was called into service as interpreter, and Moipu formally proposed to 'make brothers' with Mata-Galahi – Glass-Eyes, – the not very euphonious name under which Mr. Osbourne passed in the Marquesas. The feast of brotherhood took place on board the *Casco*. Paaaeua had arrived with his family, like a plain man; and his presents, which had been numerous, had followed one another, at intervals through several days. Moipu, as if to mark at every point the opposition, came with a certain feudal pomp, attended by retainers bearing gifts of all descriptions, from plumes of old men's beard to little, pious, Catholic engravings.

I had met the man before this in the village, and detested him on sight; there was something indescribably raffish in his looks and ways that raised my gorge; and when man-eating was referred to, and he laughed a low, cruel laugh, part boastful, part bashful, like one reminded of some dashing peccadillo, my repugnance was mingled with nausea. This is no very human attitude, nor one at all becoming in a traveller. And, seen more privately, the man improved. Something negroid in character and face was still displeasing; but his ugly mouth became attractive when he smiled, his figure and bearing were certainly noble, and his eyes superb. In his appreciation of jams and pickles, in his delight in the reverberating mirrors of the dining cabin, and consequent endless repetition of Moipus and Mata-Galahis, he showed himself engagingly a child. And yet I am not sure; and what seemed childishness may have been rather courtly art. His manners struck me as beyond the mark; they were refined and caressing to the point of grossness, and when I think of the serene absent-mindedness with which he first strolled in upon our party, and then recall him running on hands and knees along the cabin sofas, pawing the velvet, dipping into the beds, and bleating commendatory '*mitais*' with exaggerated emphasis, like some enormous over-mannered ape, I feel the more sure that both must have been calculated. And I sometimes wonder next, if Moipu were quite alone in this polite duplicity, and ask myself whether the *Casco* were quite so much admired in the Marquesas as our visitors desired us to suppose.

I will complete this sketch of an incurable cannibal grandee with two incongruous traits. His favourite morsel was the human hand, of which he speaks to-day with an ill-favoured lustfulness. And when he said good-bye to Mrs. Stevenson, holding her hand, viewing her with tearful eyes, and chanting his farewell improvisation in the falsetto of Marquesan high society, he wrote upon her mind a sentimental impression which I try in vain to share.

PART II

THE PAUMOTUS

THE DANGEROUS ARCHIPELAGO —
ATOLLS AT A DISTANCE

In the early morning of 4th September a whale-boat manned by natives dragged us down the green lane of the anchorage and round the spouting promontory. On the shore level it was a hot, breathless, and yet crystal morning; but high overhead the hills of Atuona were all cowled in cloud, and the ocean-river of the trades streamed without pause. As we crawled from under the immediate shelter of the land, we reached at last the limit of their influence. The wind fell upon our sails in puffs, which strengthened and grew more continuous; presently the *Casco* heeled down to her day's work; the whale-boat, quite outstripped, clung for a noisy moment to her quarter; the stipulated bread, rum, and tobacco were passed in; a moment more and the boat was in our wake, and our late pilots were cheering our departure.

This was the more inspiriting as we were bound for scenes so different, and though on a brief voyage, yet for a new province of creation. That wide field of ocean, called loosely the South Seas, extends from tropic to tropic, and from perhaps 120 degrees W. to 150 degrees E., a parallelogram of one hundred degrees by forty-seven, where degrees are the most spacious. Much of it lies vacant, much is closely sown with isles, and the isles are of two sorts. No distinction is so continually dwelt upon in South Sea talk as that between the 'low' and the 'high' island, and there is none more broadly marked in nature. The Himalayas are not more different from the Sahara. On the one hand, and chiefly in groups of from eight to a dozen, volcanic islands rise above the sea; few reach an altitude of less than 4000 feet; one exceeds 13,000; their tops are often obscured in cloud, they are all clothed with various forests, all abound in food, and are all remarkable for picturesque and solemn scenery. On the other hand, we have the atoll; a thing of problematic origin and history, the reputed creature of an insect apparently unidentified;[1] rudely annular in shape; enclosing a lagoon; rarely extending beyond a quarter of a mile at its chief width; often rising at its highest point to less than the stature of a man – man himself, the rat and the land crab, its chief inhabitants; not more variously supplied with plants; and offering to the eye, even when perfect, only a ring of glittering beach and verdant foliage, enclosing and enclosed by the blue sea.

In no quarter are the atolls so thickly congregated, in none are they so varied in size from the greatest to the least, and in none is navigation so beset with perils, as in that archipelago that we were now to thread. The huge system of the trades is, for some reason, quite confounded by this multiplicity of reefs; the wind intermits, squalls are frequent from the west and south-west, hurricanes are known. The currents are, besides, inextricably intermixed; dead reckoning becomes a farce; the charts are not to be trusted; and such is the number and similarity of these islands that, even when you have picked one up, you may be none the wiser. The reputation of the place is consequently infamous; insurance offices exclude it from their field, and it was not without misgiving that my captain risked the *Casco* in such waters. I believe, indeed, it is almost understood that yachts are to avoid this baffling archipelago; and it required all my instances[2] – and all Mr. Otis's private taste for adventure – to deflect our course across its midst.

For a few days we sailed with a steady trade, and a steady westerly current setting us to leeward; and toward sundown of the seventh it was supposed we should have sighted Takaroa, one of Cook's so-called King George Islands. The sun set; yet a while longer the old moon – semi-brilliant herself, and with a silver belly, which was her successor – sailed among gathering clouds; she, too, deserted us; stars of every degree of sheen, and clouds of every variety of form disputed the sub-lustrous night; and still we gazed in vain for Takaroa. The mate[3] stood on the bowsprit, his tall grey figure slashing up and down against the stars, and still

nihil astra praeter

Vidit et undas.[4]

The rest of us were grouped at the port anchor davit, staring with no less assiduity, but with far less hope on the obscure horizon. Islands we beheld in plenty, but they were of 'such stuff as dreams are made on,'[5] and vanished at a wink, only to appear in other places; and by and by not only islands, but refulgent and revolving lights began to stud the darkness; light-houses of the mind or of the wearied optic nerve, solemnly shining and winking as we passed. At length the mate himself despaired, scrambled on board again from his unrestful perch, and announced that we had missed our destination. He was the only man of practice in these waters, our sole pilot, shipped for that end at Tai-o-hae. If he declared we had missed Takaroa, it was not for us to quarrel with the fact, but, if we could, to explain it. We had certainly run down our southing. Our canted wake upon the sea and our somewhat drunken-looking course upon the chart both testified with no less certainty to an impetuous westward current. We had no choice but to conclude we were again set down to leeward; and the best we could do was to bring the *Casco* to the wind, keep a good watch, and expect morning.

I slept that night, as was then my somewhat dangerous practice, on deck upon the cockpit bench. A stir at last awoke me, to see all the eastern heaven dyed with faint orange, the binnacle lamp already dulled against the brightness of the day, and the steersman leaning eagerly across the wheel. 'There it is, sir!' he cried, and pointed in the very eyeball of the dawn. For a while I could see nothing but the bluish ruins of the morning bank, which lay far along the horizon, like melting icebergs. Then the sun rose, pierced a gap in these *débris* of vapours, and displayed an inconsiderable islet, flat as a plate upon the sea, and spiked with palms of disproportioned altitude.

So far, so good. Here was certainly an atoll; and we were certainly got among the archipelago. But which? And where? The isle was too small for either Takaroa or Takapoto: in all our neighbourhood, indeed, there was none so inconsiderable, save only Tikei; and Tikei, one of Roggewein's[6] so-called Pernicious Islands, seemed beside the question. At that rate, instead of drifting to the west, we must have fetched up thirty miles to windward. And how about the current? It had been setting us down, by observation, all these days: by the deflection of our wake, it should be setting us down that moment. When had it stopped? When had it begun again? and what kind of torrent was that which had swept us eastward in the interval? To these questions, so typical of navigation in that range of isles, I have no answer. Such were at least the facts; Tikei our island turned out to be; and it was our first experience of the dangerous archipelago, to make our landfall thirty miles out.

The sight of Tikei, thrown direct against the splendour of the morning, robbed of all its colour, and deformed with disproportioned trees like bristles on a broom, had scarce prepared us to be much in love with atolls. Later the same day we saw under more fit conditions the island of Taiaro. 'Lost in the Sea' is possibly the meaning of the name. And it was so we saw it; lost in blue sea and sky: a ring of white beach, green underwood, and tossing palms, gem-like in colour; of a fairy, of a heavenly prettiness. The surf ran all around it, white as snow, and broke at one point, far to seaward, on what seems an uncharted reef. There was no smoke, no sign of man; indeed, the isle is not inhabited, only visited at intervals. And yet a trader (Mr. Narii Salmon[7]) was watching from the shore and wondering at the unexpected ship. I have spent since then long months upon low islands; I know the tedium of their undistinguished days; I know the burden of their diet. With whatever envy we may have looked from the deck on these green coverts, it was with a tenfold greater that Mr. Salmon and his comrades saw us steer, in our trim ship, to seaward.

The night fell lovely in the extreme. After the moon went down, the heaven was a thing to wonder at for stars. And as I lay in the cockpit and looked upon the steersman I was haunted by Emerson's verses:[8]

> And the lone seaman all the night
> Sails astonished among stars.

By this glittering and imperfect brightness, about four bells in the first watch we made our third atoll, Raraka. The low line of the isle lay straight along the sky; so that I was at first reminded of a tow-path, and we seemed to be mounting some engineered and navigable stream. Presently a red star appeared, about the height and brightness of a danger signal, and with that my simile was changed; we seemed rather to skirt the embankment of a railway, and the eye began to look instinctively for the telegraph-posts, and the ear to expect the coming of a train. Here and there, but rarely, faint tree-tops broke the level. And the sound of the surf accompanied us, now in a drowsy monotone, now with a menacing swing.

The isle lay nearly east and west, barring our advance on Fakarava. We must, therefore, hug the coast until we gained the western end, where, through a passage eight miles wide, we might sail southward between Raraka and the next isle, Kauehi. We had the wind free, a lightish air; but clouds of an inky blackness were beginning to arise, and at times it lightened – without thunder. Something, I know not what, continually set us up upon the island. We lay more and more to the nor'ard; and you would have thought the shore copied our manoeuvre and outsailed us. Once and twice Raraka headed us again – again, in the sea fashion, the quite innocent steersman was abused – and again the *Casco* kept away. Had I been called on, with no more light than that of our experience, to draw the configuration of that island, I should have shown a series of bow-window promontories, each overlapping the other to the nor'ard, and the trend of the land from the south-east to the north-west, and behold, on the chart it lay near east and west in a straight line.

We had but just repeated our manoeuvre and kept away – for not more than five minutes the railway embankment had been lost to view and the surf to hearing – when I was aware of land again, not only on the weather bow, but dead ahead. I played the part of the judicious landsman, holding my peace till the last moment; and presently my mariners perceived it for themselves.

'Land ahead!' said the steersman.

'By God, it's Kauehi!' cried the mate.

And so it was. And with that I began to be sorry for cartographers. We were scarce doing three and a half; and they asked me to believe that (in five minutes) we had dropped an island, passed eight miles of open water, and run almost high and dry upon the next. But my captain was more sorry for himself to be afloat in such a labyrinth; laid the *Casco* to, with the log line up and down, and sat on the stern rail and watched it till the morning. He had had enough of night in the Paumotus.

By daylight on the 9th we began to skirt Kauehi, and had now an opportunity to see near at hand the geography of atolls. Here and there, where it was high, the farther side loomed up; here and there the near side dipped entirely and showed a broad path of water into the lagoon; here and there both sides were equally abased, and we could look right through the discontinuous ring to the sea horizon on the south. Conceive, on a vast scale, the submerged hoop of the duck-hunter, trimmed with green rushes to conceal his head – water within, water without – you have the image of the perfect atoll. Conceive one that has been partly plucked of its rush fringe; you have the atoll of Kauehi. And for either shore of it at closer quarters, conceive the line of some old Roman highway traversing a wet morass, and here sunk out of view and there re-arising, crowned with a green tuft of thicket; only instead of the stagnant waters of a marsh, the live ocean now boiled against, now buried the frail barrier. Last night's impression in the dark was thus confirmed by day, and not corrected. We sailed indeed by a mere causeway in the sea, of nature's handiwork, yet of no greater magnitude than many of the works of man.

The isle was uninhabited; it was all green brush and white sand, set in transcendently blue water; even the coco-palms were rare, though some of these completed the bright harmony of colour by hanging out a fan of golden yellow. For long there was no sign of life beyond the vegetable, and no sound but the continuous grumble of the surf. In silence and desertion these fair shores slipped past, and were submerged and rose again with clumps of thicket from the sea. And then a bird or two appeared, hovering and crying; swiftly these became more numerous, and presently, looking ahead, we were aware of a vast effervescence of winged life. In this place the annular isle was mostly under water, carrying here and there on its submerged line a wooded islet. Over one of these the birds hung and flew with an incredible density like that of gnats or hiving bees; the mass flashed white and black, and heaved and quivered, and the screaming of the creatures rose over the voice of the surf in a shrill clattering whirr. As you descend some inland valley a not dissimilar sound announces the nearness of a mill and pouring river. Some stragglers, as I said, came to meet our approach; a few still hung about the ship as we departed.

The crying died away, the last pair of wings was left behind, and once more the low shores of Kauehi streamed past our eyes in silence like a picture. I supposed at the time that the birds lived, like ants or citizens, concentred where we saw them. I have been told since (I know not if correctly) that the whole isle, or much of it, is similarly peopled; and that the effervescence at a single spot would be the mark of a boat's crew of egg-hunters from one of the neighbouring inhabited atolls. So that here at Kauehi, as the day before at Taiaro, the *Casco* sailed by under the fire of unsuspected eyes. And one thing is surely true, that even on these ribbons of land an army might lie hid and no passing mariner divine its presence.

CHAPTER II

FAKARAVA: AN ATOLL AT HAND

By a little before noon we were running down the coast of our destination, Fakarava: the air very light, the sea near smooth; though still we were accompanied by a continuous murmur from the beach, like the sound of a distant train. The isle is of a huge longitude, the enclosed lagoon thirty miles by ten or twelve, and the coral tow-path, which they call the land, some eighty or ninety miles by (possibly) one furlong. That part by which we sailed was all raised; the underwood excellently green, the topping wood of coco-palms continuous – a mark, if I had known it, of man's intervention. For once more, and once more unconsciously, we were within hail of fellow-creatures, and that vacant beach was but a pistol-shot from the capital city of the archipelago. But the life of an atoll, unless it be enclosed, passes wholly on the shores of the lagoon; it is there the villages are seated, there the canoes ply and are drawn up; and the beach of the ocean is a place accursed and deserted, the fit scene only for wizardry and shipwreck, and in the native belief a haunting ground of murderous spectres.

By and by we might perceive a breach in the low barrier; the woods ceased; a glittering point ran into the sea, tipped with an emerald shoal, the mark of entrance. As we drew near we met a little run of sea – the private sea of the lagoon having there its origin and end, and here, in the jaws of the gateway, trying vain conclusions with the more majestic heave of the Pacific. The *Casco* scarce avowed a shock; but there are times and circumstances when these harbour mouths of inland basins vomit floods, deflecting, burying, and dismasting ships. For, conceive a lagoon perfectly sealed but in the one point, and that of merely navigable width; conceive the tide and wind to have heaped for hours together in that coral fold a superfluity of waters, and the tide to change and the wind fall – the open sluice of some great reservoirs at home will give an image of the unstemmable effluxion.

We were scarce well headed for the pass before all heads were craned over the rail. For the water, shoaling under our board, became changed in a moment to surprising hues of blue and grey; and in its transparency the coral branched and blossomed, and the fish[1] of the inland sea cruised visibly below us, stained and striped, and even beaked like parrots. I have paid in my time to view many curiosities; never one so curious as that first sight over the ship's rail in the lagoon of Fakarava. But let not the reader be deceived with hope. I have since entered, I suppose, some dozen atolls in different parts of the Pacific, and the experience has never been repeated. That exquisite hue and transparency of submarine day, and these shoals of rainbow fish, have not enraptured me again.

Before we could raise our eyes from that engaging spectacle the schooner had slipped betwixt the pier-heads of the reef, and was already quite committed to the sea within. The containing shores are so little erected, and the lagoon itself is so great, that, for the more part, it seemed to extend without a check to the horizon. Here and there, indeed, where the reef carried an islet, like a signet-ring upon a finger, there would be a pencilling of palms; here and there, the green wall of wood ran solid for a length of miles; and on the port hand, under the highest grove of trees, a few houses sparkled white – Rotoava, the metropolitan settlement of the Paumotus. Hither we beat in three tacks, and came to an anchor close in shore, in the first smooth water since we had left San Francisco, five fathoms deep, where a man might look overboard all day at the vanishing cable, the coral patches, and the many-coloured fish.

Fakarava was chosen to be the seat of Government from nautical considerations only. It is eccentrically situate; the productions, even for a low island, poor; the population neither many nor – for Low Islanders – industrious. But the lagoon has two good passages, one to leeward, one to windward, so that in all states of the wind it can be left and entered, and this advantage, for a government of scattered islands, was decisive. A pier of coral, landing-stairs, a harbour light upon a staff and pillar, and two spacious Government bungalows in a handsome fence, give to the northern end of Rotoava a great air of consequence. This is confirmed on the one hand by an empty prison, on the other by a gendarmerie pasted over with hand-bills in Tahitian, land-law notices from Papeete, and republican sentiments from Paris, signed (a little after date) 'Jules Grévy, *Perihidente*.' Quite at the far end a belfried Catholic chapel concludes the town; and between, on a smooth floor of white coral sand and under the breezy canopy of coco-palms, the houses of the natives stand irregularly scattered, now close on the lagoon for the sake of the breeze, now back under the palms for love of shadow.

Not a soul was to be seen. But for the thunder of the surf on the far side, it seemed you might have heard a pin drop anywhere about that capital city. There was something thrilling in the unexpected silence, something yet more so in the unexpected sound. Here before us a sea reached to the horizon, rippling like an inland mere; and behold! close at our back another sea assaulted with assiduous fury the reverse of the position. At night the lantern was run up and lit a vacant pier. We landed and walked long. In one house lights were seen and voices heard, where the population (I was told) sat playing cards. A little beyond, from deep in the darkness of the palm grove, we saw the glow and smelt the aromatic odour of a coal of cocoa-nut husk, a relic of the evening kitchen. Crickets sang; some shrill thing whistled in a tuft of weeds; and the mosquito hummed and stung. There was no other trace that night of man, bird, or insect in the isle. The moon, now three days old, and as yet but a silver crescent on a still visible sphere, shone through the palm canopy with vigorous and scattered lights. The alleys where we walked were smoothed and weeded like a boulevard; here and there were plants set out; here and there dusky cottages clustered in the shadow, some with verandahs. A public garden by night, a rich and fashionable watering-place in a by-season, offer sights and vistas not dissimilar. And still, on the one side, stretched the lapping mere, and from the other the deep sea still growled in the night. But it was most of all on board, in the dead hours, when I had been better sleeping, that the spell of Fakarava seized and held me. The moon was down. The harbour lantern and two of the greater planets drew vari-coloured wakes on the lagoon. From shore the cheerful watch-cry of cocks rang out at intervals above the organ-point of surf. And the thought of this depopulated capital, this protracted thread of annular island with its crest of coco-palms and fringe of breakers, and that tranquil inland sea that stretched before me till it touched the stars, ran in my head for hours with delight.

So long as I stayed upon that isle these thoughts were constant. I lay down to sleep, and woke again with an unblunted sense of my surroundings. I was never weary of calling up the image of that narrow causeway, on which I had my dwelling, lying coiled like a serpent, tail to mouth, in the outrageous ocean, and I was never weary of passing – a mere quarter-deck parade – from the one side to the other, from the shady, habitable shores of the lagoon to the blinding desert and uproarious breakers of the opposite beach. The sense of insecurity in such a thread of residence is more than fanciful. Hurricanes and tidal waves overlap these humble obstacles; Oceanus[2] remembers his strength, and, where houses stood and palms flourished, shakes his white beard again over the barren coral. Fakarava itself has suffered; the trees immediately beyond my house were all of recent replantation; and Anaa[3] is only now recovered from a heavier stroke. I knew one who was then dwelling in the isle. He told me that he and two ship captains walked to the sea beach. There for a while they viewed the on-coming breakers, till one of the captains clapped suddenly his hand before his eyes and cried aloud that he could endure no longer to behold them. This was in the afternoon; in the dark hours of the night the sea burst upon the island like a flood; the settlement was razed, all but the church and presbytery; and, when day returned, the survivors saw themselves clinging in an abattis[4] of uprooted coco-palms and ruined houses.

Danger is but a small consideration. But men are more nicely sensible of a discomfort; and the atoll is a discomfortable home. There are some, and these probably ancient, where a deep soil has formed and the most valuable fruit-trees prosper. I have walked in one, with equal admiration and surprise, through a forest of huge breadfruits, eating bananas and stumbling among taro as I went.[5] This was in the atoll of Namorik in the Marshall group, and stands alone in my experience. To give the opposite extreme, which is yet far more near the average, I will describe the soil and productions of Fakarava. The surface of that narrow strip is for the more part of broken coral limestone, like volcanic clinkers, and excruciating to the naked foot; in some atolls, I believe, not in Fakarava, it gives a fine metallic ring when struck. Here and there you come upon a bank of sand, exceeding fine and white, and these parts are the least productive. The plants (such as they are) spring from and love the broken coral, whence they grow with that wonderful verdancy that makes the beauty of the atoll from the sea. The coco-palm in particular luxuriates in that stern *solum*,[6] striking down his roots to the brackish, percolated water, and bearing his green head in the wind with every evidence of health and pleasure. And yet even the coco-palm must be helped in infancy with some extraneous nutriment, and through much of the low archipelago there is planted with each nut a piece of ship's biscuit and a rusty nail. The pandanus comes next in importance, being also a food tree; and he, too, does bravely. A green bush called *miki* runs everywhere; occasionally a *purao* is seen; and there are several useless weeds. According to M. Cuzent,[7] the whole number of plants on an atoll such as Fakarava will scarce exceed, even if it reaches to, one score. Not a blade of grass appears; not a grain of humus, save when a sack or two has been imported to make the semblance of a garden; such gardens as bloom in cities on the window-sill. Insect life is sometimes dense; a cloud of mosquitoes, and, what is far worse, a plague of flies blackening our food, have sometimes driven us from a meal on Apemama;[8] and even in Fakarava the mosquitoes were a pest. The land crab may be seen scuttling to his hole, and at night the rats besiege the houses and the artificial gardens. The crab is good eating; possibly so is the rat; I have not tried. Pandanus fruit is made, in the

Gilberts, into an agreeable sweetmeat, such as a man may trifle with at the end of a long dinner; for a substantial meal I have no use for it. The rest of the food-supply, in a destitute atoll such as Fakarava, can be summed up in the favourite jest of the archipelago – cocoa-nut beefsteak. Cocoa-nut green, cocoa-nut ripe, cocoa-nut germinated; cocoa-nut to eat and cocoa-nut to drink; cocoa-nut raw and cooked, cocoa-nut hot and cold – such is the bill of fare. And some of the entrées are no doubt delicious. The germinated nut, cooked in the shell and eaten with a spoon, forms a good pudding; cocoa-nut milk – the expressed juice of a ripe nut, not the water of a green one – goes well in coffee, and is a valuable adjunct in cookery through the South Seas; and cocoa-nut salad, if you be a millionaire, and can afford to eat the value of a field of corn for your dessert, is a dish to be remembered with affection. But when all is done there is a sameness, and the Israelites of the low islands murmur at their manna.

The reader may think I have forgot the sea. The two beaches do certainly abound in life, and they are strangely different. In the lagoon the water shallows slowly on a bottom of fine slimy sand, dotted with clumps of growing coral. Then comes a strip of tidal beach on which the ripples lap. In the coral clumps the great holy-water clam (*Tridacna*) grows plentifully; a little deeper lie the beds of the pearl-oyster and sail the resplendent fish that charmed us at our entrance; and these are all more or less vigorously coloured. But the other shells are white like lime, or faintly tinted with a little pink, the palest possible display; many of them dead besides, and badly rolled. On the ocean side, on the mounds of the steep beach, over all the width of the reef right out to where the surf is bursting, in every cranny, under every scattered fragment of the coral, an incredible plenty of marine life displays the most wonderful variety and brilliancy of hues. The reef itself has no passage of colour but is imitated by some shell. Purple and red and white, and green and yellow, pied and striped and clouded, the living shells wear in every combination the livery of the dead reef – if the reef be dead – so that the eye is continually baffled and the collector continually deceived. I have taken shells for stones and stones for shells, the one as often as the other. A prevailing character of the coral is to be dotted with small spots of red, and it is wonderful how many varieties of shell have adopted the same fashion and donned the disguise of the red spot. A shell I had found in plenty in the Marquesas I found here also unchanged in all things else, but there were the red spots. A lively little crab wore the same marking. The case of the hermit or soldier crab was more conclusive, being the result of conscious choice. This nasty little wrecker, scavenger, and squatter has learned the value of a spotted house; so it be of the right colour he will choose the smallest shard, tuck himself in a mere corner of a broken whorl, and go about the world half naked; but I never found him in this imperfect armour unless it was marked with the red spot.

Some two hundred yards distant is the beach of the lagoon. Collect the shells from each, set them side by side, and you would suppose they came from different hemispheres; the one so pale, the other so brilliant; the one prevalently white, the other of a score of hues, and infected with the scarlet spot like a disease. This seems the more strange, since the hermit crabs pass and repass the island, and I have met them by the Residency well, which is about central, journeying either way. Without doubt many of the shells in the lagoon are dead. But why are they dead? Without doubt the living shells have a very different background set for imitation. But why are these so different? We are only on the threshold of the mysteries.

Either beach, I have said, abounds with life. On the sea-side and in certain atolls this profusion of vitality is even shocking: the rock under foot is mined with it. I have broken off – notably in Funafuti and Arorai[9] – great lumps of ancient weathered rock that rang under my blows like iron, and the fracture has been full of pendent worms as long as my hand, as thick as a child's finger, of a slightly pinkish white, and set as close as three or even four to the square inch. Even in the lagoon, where certain shell-fish seem to sicken, others (it is notorious) prosper exceedingly and make the riches of these islands. Fish, too, abound; the lagoon is a closed fish-pond, such as might rejoice the fancy of an abbot; sharks swarm there, and chiefly round the passages, to feast upon this plenty, and you would suppose that man had only to prepare his angle. Alas! it is not so. Of those painted fish that came in hordes about the entering *Casco*, some bore poisonous spines, and others were poisonous if eaten. The stranger must refrain, or take his chance of painful and dangerous sickness. The native, on his own isle, is a safe guide; transplant him to the next, and he is helpless as yourself. For it is a question both of time and place. A fish caught in a lagoon may be deadly; the same fish caught the same day at sea, and only a few hundred yards without the passage, will be wholesome eating: in a neighbouring isle perhaps the case will be reversed; and perhaps a fortnight later you shall be able to eat of them indifferently from within and from without. According to the natives, these bewildering vicissitudes are ruled by the movement of the heavenly bodies. The beautiful planet Venus plays a great part in all island tales and customs; and among other functions, some of them more awful, she regulates the season of good fish. With Venus in one phase, as we had her, certain fish were poisonous in the lagoon: with Venus in another, the same fish was harmless and a valued article of diet. White men explain these changes by the phases of the coral.

It adds a last touch of horror to the thought of this precarious annular gangway in the sea, that even what there is of it is not of honest rock, but organic, part alive, part putrescent; even the clean sea and the bright fish about it poisoned, the most stubborn boulder burrowed in by worms, the lightest dust venomous as an apothecary's drugs.

CHAPTER III

A HOUSE TO LET IN A LOW ISLAND

Never populous, it was yet by a chapter of accidents that I found the island so deserted that no sound of human life diversified the hours; that we walked in that trim public garden of a town, among closed houses, without even a lodging-bill in a window to prove some tenancy in the back quarters; and, when we visited the Government bungalow, that Mr. Donat,[1] acting Vice-Resident, greeted us alone, and entertained us with cocoa-nut punches in the Sessions Hall and seat of judgment of that widespread archipelago, our glasses standing arrayed with summonses and census returns. The unpopularity of a late Vice-

Resident had begun the movement of exodus, his native employés resigning court appointments and retiring each to his own coco-patch in the remoter districts of the isle. Upon the back of that, the Governor in Papeete[2] issued a decree: All land in the Paumotus must be defined and registered by a certain date. Now, the folk of the archipelago are half nomadic; a man can scarce be said to belong to a particular atoll; he belongs to several, perhaps holds a stake and counts cousinship in half a score; and the inhabitants of Rotoava in particular, man, woman, and child, and from the gendarme to the Mormon prophet and the schoolmaster, owned – I was going to say land – owned at least coral blocks and growing coco-palms in some adjacent isle. Thither – from the gendarme to the babe in arms, the pastor followed by his flock, the schoolmaster carrying along with him his scholars, and the scholars with their books and slates – they had taken ship some two days previous to our arrival, and were all now engaged disputing boundaries. Fancy overhears the shrillness of their disputation mingle with the surf and scatter sea-fowl. It was admirable to observe the completeness of their flight, like that of hibernating birds; nothing left but empty houses, like old nests to be reoccupied in spring; and even the harmless necessary dominie[3] borne with them in their transmigration. Fifty odd set out, and only seven, I was informed, remained. But when I made a feast on board the *Casco*, more than seven, and nearer seven times seven, appeared to be my guests. Whence they appeared, how they were summoned, whither they vanished when the feast was eaten, I have no guess. In view of Low Island tales, and that awful frequentation which makes men avoid the seaward beaches of an atoll, some two score of those that ate with us may have returned, for the occasion, from the kingdom of the dead.

It was this solitude that put it in our minds to hire a house, and become, for the time being, in-dwellers of the isle – a practice I have ever since, when it was possible, adhered to. Mr. Donat placed us, with that intent, under the convoy of one Taniera Mahinui, who combined the incongruous characters of catechist and convict. The reader may smile, but I affirm he was well qualified for either part. For that of convict, first of all, by a good substantial felony, such as in all lands casts the perpetrator in chains and dungeons. Taniera was a man of birth – the chief a while ago, as he loved to tell, of a district in Anaa of 800 souls. In an evil hour it occurred to the authorities in Papeete to charge the chiefs with the collection of the taxes. It is a question if much were collected; it is certain that nothing was handed on; and Taniera, who had distinguished himself by a visit to Papeete and some high living in restaurants, was chosen for the scapegoat. The reader must understand that not Taniera but the authorities in Papeete were first in fault. The charge imposed was disproportioned. I have not yet heard of any Polynesian capable of such a burden; honest and upright Hawaiians – one in particular, who was admired even by the whites as an inflexible magistrate – have stumbled in the narrow path of the trustee. And Taniera, when the pinch came, scorned to denounce accomplices; others had shared the spoil, he bore the penalty alone. He was condemned in five years. The period, when I had the pleasure of his friendship, was not yet expired; he still drew prison rations, the sole and not unwelcome reminder of his chains, and, I believe, looked forward to the date of his enfranchisement with mere alarm. For he had no sense of shame in the position; complained of nothing but the defective table of his place of exile; regretted nothing but the fowls and eggs and fish of his own more favoured island. And as for his parishioners, they did not think one hair the less of him. A schoolboy, mulcted in ten thousand lines of Greek and dwelling sequestered in the dormitories, enjoys unabated consideration from his fellows. So with Taniera: a marked man, not a dishonoured; having fallen under the lash of the unthinkable gods; a Job, perhaps, or say a Taniera in the den of lions. Songs are likely made and sung about this saintly Robin Hood. On the other hand, he was even highly qualified for his office in the Church; being by nature a grave, considerate, and kindly man; his face rugged and serious, his smile bright; the master of several trades, a builder both of boats and houses; endowed with a fine pulpit voice; endowed besides with such a gift of eloquence that at the grave of the late chief of Fakarava he set all the assistants weeping. I never met a man of a mind more ecclesiastical; he loved to dispute and to inform himself of doctrine and the history of sects; and when I showed him the cuts in a volume of Chambers's *Encyclopaedia* – except for one of an ape – reserved his whole enthusiasm for cardinals' hats, censers, candlesticks, and cathedrals. Methought when he looked upon the cardinal's hat a voice said low in his ear: 'Your foot is on the ladder.'

Under the guidance of Taniera we were soon installed in what I believe to have been the best-appointed private house in Fakarava. It stood just beyond the church in an oblong patch of cultivation. More than three hundred sacks of soil were imported from Tahiti for the Residency garden; and this must shortly be renewed, for the earth blows away, sinks in crevices of the coral, and is sought for at last in vain. I know not how much earth had gone to the garden of my villa; some at least, for an alley of prosperous bananas ran to the gate, and over the rest of the enclosure, which was covered with the usual clinker-like fragments of smashed coral, not only coco-palms and *mikis* but also fig-trees flourished, all of a delicious greenness. Of course there was no blade of grass. In front a picket fence divided us from the white road, the palm-fringed margin of the lagoon, and the lagoon itself, reflecting clouds by day and stars by night. At the back, a bulwark of uncemented coral enclosed us from the narrow belt of bush and the nigh ocean beach where the seas thundered, the roar and wash of them still humming in the chambers of the house.

This itself was of one story, verandahed front and back. It contained three rooms, three sewing-machines, three sea-chests, chairs, tables, a pair of beds, a cradle, a double-barrelled gun, a pair of enlarged coloured photographs, a pair of coloured prints after Wilkie[4] and Mulready,[5] and a French lithograph with the legend: '*Le brigade du Général Lepasset brûlant son drapeau devant Metz.*'[6] Under the stilts of the house a stove was rusting, till we drew it forth and put it in commission. Not far off was the burrow in the coral whence we supplied ourselves with brackish water. There was live stock, besides, on the estate – cocks and hens and a brace of ill-regulated cats, whom Taniera came every morning with the sun to feed on grated cocoa-nut. His voice was our regular réveillé, ringing pleasantly about the garden: 'Pooty–pooty–poo–poo–poo!'

Far as we were from the public offices, the nearness of the chapel made our situation what is called eligible in advertisements, and gave us a side look on some native life. Every morning, as soon as he had fed the fowls, Taniera set the bell agoing in the small belfry; and the faithful, who were not very numerous, gathered to prayers. I was once present: it was the Lord's day, and seven females and eight males composed the congregation. A woman played precentor,[7] starting with a longish note; the catechist joined in upon the second bar; and then the faithful in a body. Some had printed hymn-books which they followed; some of the rest filled up with 'eh—eh—eh,' the Paumotuan fol-de-rol. After the hymn, we had an antiphonal prayer or two; and then Taniera rose from the front bench, where he had been sitting in his catechist's robes, passed within the altar-rails, opened his Tahitian Bible, and began to preach from notes. I understood one word – the name of God; but the preacher managed his voice with taste, used rare and expressive gestures, and made a strong impression of sincerity. The plain service, the vernacular Bible, the hymn-tunes mostly on an English pattern – 'God save the Queen,' I was informed, a special favourite, – all, save some paper flowers upon the altar, seemed not merely but austerely Protestant. It is thus the Catholics have met their low island proselytes half-way.

Taniera had the keys of our house; it was with him I made my bargain, if that could be called a bargain in which all was remitted to my generosity; it was he who fed the cats and poultry, he who came to call and pick a meal with us like an acknowledged friend; and we long fondly supposed he was our landlord. This belief was not to bear the test of experience; and, as my chapter has to relate, no certainty succeeded it.

We passed some days of airless quiet and great heat; shell-gatherers were warned from the ocean beach, where sunstroke waited them from ten till four; the highest palm hung motionless, there was no voice audible but that of the sea on the far side. At last, about four of a certain afternoon, long cats-paws flawed the face of the lagoon; and presently in the tree-tops there awoke the grateful bustle of the trades, and all the houses and alleys of the island were fanned out. To more than one enchanted ship, that had lain long becalmed in view of the green shore, the wind brought deliverance; and by day-light on the morrow a schooner and two cutters lay moored in the port of Rotoava. Not only in the outer sea, but in the lagoon itself, a certain traffic woke with the reviving breeze; and among the rest one François, a half-blood, set sail with the first light in his own half-decked cutter. He had held before a court appointment; being, I believe, the Residency sweeper-out. Trouble arising with the unpopular Vice-Resident, he had thrown his honours down, and fled to the far parts of the atoll to plant cabbages – or at least coco-palms. Thence he was now driven by such need as even a Cincinnatus[8] must acknowledge, and fared for the capital city, the seat of his late functions, to exchange half a ton of copra for necessary flour. And here, for a while, the story leaves to tell of his voyaging.

It must tell, instead, of our house, where, toward seven at night, the catechist came suddenly in with his pleased air of being welcome; armed besides with a considerable bunch of keys. These he proceeded to try on the sea-chests, drawing each in turn from its place against the wall. Heads of strangers appeared in the doorway and volunteered suggestions. All in vain. Either they were the wrong keys or the wrong boxes, or the wrong man was trying them. For a little Taniera fumed and fretted; then had recourse to the more summary method of the hatchet; one of the chests was broken open, and an armful of clothing, male and female, baled out and handed to the strangers on the verandah.

These were François, his wife, and their child. About eight A.M., in the midst of the lagoon, their cutter had capsized in jibbing. They got her righted, and though she was still full of water put the child on board. The mainsail had been carried away, but the jib still drew her sluggishly along, and François and the woman swam astern and worked the rudder with their hands. The cold was cruel; the fatigue, as time went on, became excessive; and in that preserve of sharks, fear hunted them. Again and again, François, the half-breed, would have desisted and gone down; but the woman, whole blood of an amphibious race, still supported him with cheerful words. I am reminded of a woman of Hawaii who swam with her husband, I dare not say how many miles, in a high sea, and came ashore at last with his dead body in her arms. It was about five in the evening, after nine hours' swimming, that François and his wife reached land at Rotoava. The gallant fight was won, and instantly the more childish side of native character appears. They had supped, and told and retold their story, dripping as they came; the flesh of the woman, whom Mrs. Stevenson helped to shift,[9] was cold as stone; and François, having changed to a dry cotton shirt and trousers, passed the remainder of the evening on my floor and between open doorways, in a thorough-draught. Yet François, the son of a French father, speaks excellent French himself and seems intelligent.

It was our first idea that the catechist, true to his evangelical vocation, was clothing the naked from his superfluity. Then it came out that François was but dealing with his own. The clothes were his, so was the chest, so was the house. François was in fact the landlord. Yet you observe he had hung back on the verandah while Taniera tried his 'prentice hand upon the locks; and even now, when his true character appeared, the only use he made of the estate was to leave the clothes of his family drying on the fence. Taniera was still the friend of the house, still fed the poultry, still came about us on his daily visits, François, during the remainder of his stay, holding bashfully aloof. And there was stranger matter. Since François had lost the whole load of his cutter, the half ton of copra, an axe, bowls, knives, and clothes – since he had in a manner to begin the world again, and his necessary flour was not yet bought or paid for – I proposed to advance him what he needed on the rent. To my enduring amazement he refused, and the reason he gave – if that can be called a reason which but darkens counsel – was that Taniera was his friend. His friend, you observe; not his creditor. I inquired into that, and was assured that Taniera, an exile in a strange isle, might possibly be in debt himself, but certainly was no man's creditor.

Very early one morning we were awakened by a bustling presence in the yard, and found our camp had been surprised by a tall, lean, old native lady, dressed in what were obviously widow's weeds. You could see at a glance she was a notable woman, a housewife, sternly practical, alive with energy, and with fine possibilities of temper. Indeed there was nothing native about her but the skin; and the type abounds, and is everywhere respected, nearer home. It did us good to see her scour the grounds, examining the plants and chickens; watering, feeding, trimming them; taking angry, purpose-like possession. When she neared the house our sympathy abated; when she came to the broken chest I wished I were elsewhere. We had scarce a word in common; but her whole lean body spoke for her with indignant eloquence. 'My chest!' it cried, with a stress on the possessive. 'My chest – broken open! This is a fine state of things!' I hastened to lay the blame where it belonged – on François and his wife – and found I had made things worse instead of better. She repeated the names at first with incredulity, then with despair. A while she seemed stunned, next fell to disembowelling the box, piling the goods on the floor, and visibly computing the extent of François's ravages; and presently after she was observed in high speech with Tanicra, who seemed to hang an ear like one reproved.

Here, then, by all known marks, should be my landlady at last; here was every character of the proprietor fully developed. Should I not approach her on the still depending question of my rent? I carried the point to an adviser. 'Nonsense!' he cried. 'That's the old woman, the mother. It doesn't belong to her. I believe that's the man the house belongs to,' and he pointed to one of the coloured photographs on the wall. On this I gave up all desire of understanding; and when the time came for me to leave, in the judgment-hall of the archipelago, and with the awful countenance of the acting Governor, I duly paid my rent to Taniera. He was satisfied, and so was I. But what had he to do with it? Mr. Donat, acting magistrate and a man of kindred blood, could throw no light upon the mystery; a plain private person, with a taste for letters, cannot be expected to do more.

CHAPTER IV

TRAITS AND SECTS IN THE PAUMOTUS

The most careless reader must have remarked a change of air since the Marquesas. The house, crowded with effects, the bustling housewife counting her possessions, the serious, indoctrinated island pastor, the long fight for life in the lagoon: here are traits of a new world. I read in a pamphlet (I will not give the author's name)[1] that the Marquesan especially resembles the Paumotuan. I should take the two races, though so near in neighbourhood, to be extremes of Polynesian diversity. The Marquesan is certainly the most beautiful of human races, and one of the tallest – the Paumotuan averaging a good inch shorter, and not even handsome; the Marquesan open-handed, inert, insensible to religion, childishly self-indulgent – the Paumotuan greedy, hardy, enterprising, a religious disputant, and with a trace of the ascetic character.

Yet a few years ago, and the people of the archipelago were crafty savages. Their isles might be called sirens'[2] isles, not merely from the attraction they exerted on the passing mariner, but from the perils that awaited him on shore. Even to this day, in certain outlying islands, danger lingers; and the civilised Paumotuan dreads to land and hesitates to accost his backward brother. But, except in these, to-day the peril is a memory. When our generation were yet in the cradle and playroom it was still a living fact. Between 1830 and 1840, Hao, for instance, was a place of the most dangerous approach, where ships were seized and crews kidnapped. As late as 1856, the schooner *Sarah Ann* sailed from Papeete and was seen no more. She had women on board, and children, the captain's wife, a nursemaid, a baby, and the two young sons of a Captain Steven on their way to the mainland for schooling. All were supposed to have perished in a squall. A year later, the captain of the *Julia*, coasting along the island variously called Bligh, Lagoon, and Tematangi, saw armed natives follow the course of his schooner, clad in many-coloured stuffs. Suspicion was at once aroused; the mother of the lost children was profuse of money; and one expedition having found the place deserted, and returned content with firing a few shots, she raised and herself accompanied another. None appeared to greet or to oppose them; they roamed a while among abandoned huts and empty thickets; then formed two parties and set forth to beat, from end to end, the pandanus jungle of the island. One man remained alone by the landing-place – Teina, a chief of Anaa, leader of the armed natives who made the strength of the expedition. Now that his comrades were departed this way and that, on their laborious exploration, the silence fell profound; and this silence was the ruin of the islanders. A sound of stones rattling caught the ear of Teina. He looked, thinking to perceive a crab, and saw instead the brown hand of a human being issue from a fissure in the ground. A shout recalled the search parties and announced their doom to the buried caitiffs. In the cave below, sixteen were found crouching among human bones and singular and horrid curiosities. One was a head of golden hair, supposed to be a relic of the captain's wife; another was half of the body of a European child, sun-dried and stuck upon a stick, doubtless with some design of wizardry.

The Paumotuan is eager to be rich. He saves, grudges, buries money, fears not work. For a dollar each, two natives passed the hours of daylight cleaning our ship's copper. It was strange to see them so indefatigable and so much at ease in the water – working at times with their pipes lighted, the smoker at times submerged and only the glowing bowl above the surface; it was stranger still to think they were next congeners[3] to the incapable Marquesan. But the Paumotuan not only saves, grudges, and works, he steals besides; or, to be more precise, he swindles. He will never deny a debt, he only flees his creditor. He is always keen for an advance; so soon as he has fingered it he disappears. He knows your ship; so soon as it nears one island, he is off to another. You may think you know his name; he has already changed it. Pursuit in that infinity of isles were fruitless. The result can be given in a nutshell. It has been actually proposed in a Government report to secure debts by taking a photograph of the debtor; and the other day in Papeete credits on the Paumotus to the amount of sixteen thousand pounds were sold for less than forty – *quatre cent mille francs pour moins de mille francs*. Even so, the purchase was thought hazardous; and only the man who made it and who had special opportunities could have dared to give so much.

The Paumotuan is sincerely attached to those of his own blood and household. A touching affection sometimes unites wife and husband. Their children, while they[4] are alive, completely rule them; after they[5] are dead, their bones or their mummies are often jealously[6] preserved and carried from atoll to atoll in the wanderings of the family. I was told there were many houses in Fakarava with the mummy of a child locked in a sea-chest; after I heard it, I would glance a little jealously[7] at those by my own bed; in that cupboard, also, it was possible there was a tiny skeleton.

The race seems in a fair way to survive. From fifteen islands, whose rolls I had occasion to consult, I found a proportion of 59 births to 47 deaths for 1887. Dropping three out of the fifteen, there remained for the other twelve the comfortable ratio of 50 births to 32 deaths. Long habits of hardship and activity doubtless explain the contrast with Marquesan figures. But the Paumotuan displays, besides, a certain concern for health and the rudiments of a sanitary discipline. Public talk with these free-spoken people plays the part of the Contagious Diseases Act; incomers to fresh islands anxiously inquire if all be well; and syphilis, when contracted, is successfully treated with indigenous herbs. Like their neighbours of Tahiti, from whom they have perhaps imbibed the error, they regard leprosy with comparative indifference, elephantiasis with disproportionate fear. But, unlike indeed to the Tahitian, their alarm puts on the guise of self-defence. Any one stricken with this painful and ugly malady is confined to the ends of villages, denied the use of paths and highways, and condemned to transport himself between his house and coco-patch by water only, his very footprint being held infectious. *Fe'efe'e*, being a creature of marshes and the sequel of malarial fever, is not original in atolls. On the single isle of Makatea, where the lagoon is now a marsh, the disease has made a home. Many suffer: they are excluded (if Mr. Wilmot[8] be right) from much of the comfort of society; and it is believed they take a secret vengeance. The dejections of the sick are considered highly poisonous. Early in the morning, it is narrated, aged and malicious persons creep into the sleeping village, and stealthily make water at the doors of the houses of young men. Thus they propagate disease; thus they breathe on and obliterate comeliness and health, the objects of their envy. Whether horrid fact or more abominable legend, it equally depicts that something bitter and energetic which distinguishes Paumotuan man.

The archipelago is divided between two main religions, Catholic and Mormon. They front each other proudly with a false air of permanence; yet are but shapes, their membership in a perpetual flux. The Mormon attends mass with devotion; the Catholic sits attentive at a Mormon sermon, and to-morrow each may have transferred allegiance. One man had been a pillar of the Church of Rome for fifteen years; his wife dying, he decided that must be a poor religion that could not save a man his wife, and turned Mormon. According to one informant, Catholicism was the more fashionable in health, but on the approach of sickness it was judged prudent to secede. As a Mormon, there were five chances out of six you might recover; as a Catholic, your hopes were small; and this opinion is perhaps founded on the comfortable rite of unction.

We all know what Catholics are, whether in the Paumotus or at home. But the Paumotuan Mormon seemed a phenomenon apart. He marries but the one wife, uses the Protestant Bible, observes Protestant forms of worship, forbids the use of liquor and tobacco, practises adult baptism by immersion, and after every public sin, rechristens the backslider. I advised with Mahinui, whom I found well informed in the history of the American Mormons, and he declared against the least connection. '*Pour moi*,' said he, with a fine charity, '*les Mormons ici un petit Catholiques*.' Some months later I had an opportunity to consult an orthodox fellow-countryman,[9] an old dissenting Highlander, long settled in Tahiti, but still breathing of the heather of Tiree.[10] 'Why do they call themselves Mormons?' I asked. 'My dear, and that is my question!' he exclaimed. 'For by all that I can hear of their doctrine, I have nothing to say against it, and their life, it is above reproach.' And for all that, Mormons they are, but of the earlier sowing: the so-called Josephites, the followers of Joseph Smith, the opponents of Brigham Young.[11]

Grant, then, the Mormons to be Mormons. Fresh points at once arise: What are the Israelites? and what the Kanitus? For a long while back the sect had been divided into Mormons proper and so-called Israelites, I never could hear why. A few years since there came a visiting missionary of the name of Williams, who made an excellent collection, and retired, leaving fresh disruption imminent. Something irregular (as I was told) in his way of 'opening the service' had raised partisans and enemies; the church was once more rent asunder; and a new sect, the Kanitu, issued from the division. Since then Kanitus and Israelites, like the Cameronians and the United Presbyterians,[12] have made common cause; and the ecclesiastical history of the Paumotus is, for the moment, uneventful. There will be more doing before

long, and these isles bid fair to be the Scotland of the South. Two
things I could never learn. The nature of the innovations of the Rev.
Mr. Williams none would tell me, and of the meaning of the name
Kanitu none had a guess. It was not Tahitian, it was not Marquesan;
it formed no part of that ancient speech of the Paumotus, now passing
swiftly into obsolescence. One man, a priest, God bless him! said it
was the Latin for a little dog. I have found it since as the name of a
god in New Guinea; it must be a bolder man than I who should hint
at a connection. Here, then, is a singular thing: a brand-new sect,
arising by popular acclamation, and a nonsense word invented for its
name.

The design of mystery seems obvious, and according to a very
intelligent observer, Mr. Magee of Mangareva, this element of the
mysterious is a chief attraction of the Mormon Church. It enjoys some
of the status of Freemasonry at home, and there is for the convert
some of the exhilaration of adventure. Other attractions are certainly
conjoined. Perpetual rebaptism, leading to a succession of baptismal
feasts, is found, both from the social and the spiritual side, a pleasing
feature. More important is the fact that all the faithful enjoy office;
perhaps more important still, the strictness of the discipline. 'The veto
on liquor,' said Mr. Magee, 'brings them plenty members.' There is
no doubt these islanders are fond of drink, and no doubt they refrain
from the indulgence; a bout on a feast-day, for instance, may be
followed by a week or a month of rigorous sobriety. Mr. Wilmot
attributes this to Paumotuan frugality and the love of hoarding; it goes
far deeper. I have mentioned that I made a feast on board the *Casco*.
To wash down ship's bread and jam, each guest was given the choice
of rum or syrup, and out of the whole number only one man voted –
in a defiant tone, and amid shouts of mirth – for 'Trum'! This was in
public. I had the meanness to repeat the experiment, whenever I had
a chance, within the four walls of my house; and three at least, who
had refused at the festival, greedily drank rum behind a door. But
there were others thoroughly consistent. I said the virtues of the race
were bourgeois and puritan; and how bourgeois is this! how puritanic!
how Scottish! and how Yankee! – the temptation, the resistance, the
public hypocritical conformity, the Pharisees,[13] the Holy Willies,[14] and

the true disciples. With such a people the popularity of an ascetic Church appears legitimate; in these strict rules, in this perpetual supervision, the weak find their advantage, the strong a certain pleasure; and the doctrine of rebaptism, a clean bill and a fresh start, will comfort many staggering professors.

There is yet another sect, or what is called a sect – no doubt improperly – that of the Whistlers. Duncan Cameron, so clear in favour of the Mormons, was no less loud in condemnation of the Whistlers. Yet I do not know; I still fancy there is some connection, perhaps fortuitous, probably disavowed. Here at least are some doings in the house of an Israelite clergyman (or prophet) in the island of Anaa, of which I am equally sure that Duncan would disclaim and the Whistlers hail them for an imitation of their own. My informant,[15] a Tahitian and a Catholic, occupied one part of the house; the prophet and his family lived in the other. Night after night the Mormons, in the one end, held their evening sacrifice of song; night after night, in the other, the wife of the Tahitian lay awake and listened to their singing with amazement. At length she could contain herself no longer, woke her husband, and asked him what he heard. 'I hear several persons singing hymns,' said he. 'Yes,' she returned, 'but listen again! Do you not hear something supernatural?' His attention thus directed, he was aware of a strange buzzing voice – and yet he declared it was beautiful – which justly accompanied the singers. The next day he made inquiries. 'It is a spirit,' said the prophet, with entire simplicity, 'which has lately made a practice of joining us at family worship.' It did not appear the thing was visible, and, like other spirits raised nearer home in these degenerate days, it was rudely ignorant, at first could only buzz, and had only learned of late to bear a part correctly in the music.

The performances of the Whistlers are more business-like. Their meetings are held publicly with open doors, all being 'cordially invited to attend.' The faithful sit about the room – according to one informant, singing hymns; according to another, now singing and now whistling; the leader, the wizard – let me rather say, the medium – sits in the midst, enveloped in a sheet and silent; and presently, from just above his head, or sometimes from the midst of the roof, an aerial whistling proceeds, appalling to the inexperienced. This, it appears, is the language of the dead; its purport is taken down progressively by one of the expert, writing, I was told, 'as fast as a telegraph operator'; and the communications are at last made public. They are of the baldest triviality; a schooner is perhaps announced, some idle gossip reported of a neighbour, or if the spirit shall have been called to consultation on a case of sickness, a remedy may be suggested. One of these, immersion in scalding water, not long ago proved fatal to the patient. The whole business is very dreary, very silly, and very European; it has none of the picturesque qualities of similar conjurations in New Zealand; it seems to possess no kernel of possible sense, like some that I shall describe among the Gilbert islanders. Yet I was told that many hardy, intelligent natives were inveterate whistlers. 'Like Mahinui?' I asked, willing to have a standard; and I was told 'Yes.' Why should I wonder? Men more enlightened than my convict-catechist sit down at home to follies equally sterile and dull.

The medium is sometimes female. It was a woman, for instance, who introduced these practices on the north coast of Taiarapu,[16] to the scandal of her own connections, her brother-in-law in particular declaring she was drunk. But what shocked Tahiti might seem fit enough in the Paumotus, the more so as certain women there possess, by the gift of nature, singular and useful powers. They say they are honest, well-intentioned ladies, some of them embarrassed by their weird inheritance. And indeed the trouble caused by this endowment is so great, and the protection afforded so infinitesimally small, that I hesitate whether to call it a gift or a hereditary curse. You may rob this lady's coco-patch, steal her canoes, burn down her house, and slay her family scatheless; but one thing you must not do: you must not lay a hand upon her sleeping-mat, or your belly will swell, and you can only be cured by the lady or her husband. Here is the report of an eye-witness, Tasmanian born,[17] educated, a man who has made money – certainly no fool. In 1886 he was present in a house on Makatea,[18] where two lads began to skylark on the mats, and were (I think) ejected. Instantly after, their bellies began to swell; pains took hold on them; all manner of island remedies were exhibited in vain, and rubbing only magnified their sufferings. The man of the house was called, explained the nature of the visitation, and prepared the cure. A cocoa-nut was husked, filled with herbs, and with all the ceremonies of a launch, and the utterance of spells in the Paumotuan language, committed to the sea. From that moment the pains began to grow more easy and the swelling to subside. The reader may stare. I can assure him, if he moved much among old residents of the archipelago, he would be driven to admit one thing of two – either that there is something in the swollen bellies or nothing in the evidence of man.

I have not met these gifted ladies; but I had an experience of my own, for I have played, for one night only, the part of the whistling spirit. It had been blowing wearily all day, but with the fall of night the wind abated, and the moon, which was then full, rolled in a clear sky. We went southward down the island on the side of the lagoon, walking through long-drawn forest aisles of palm, and on a floor of snowy sand. No life was abroad, nor sound of life; till in a clear part of the isle we spied the embers of a fire, and not far off, in a dark house, heard natives talking softly. To sit without a light, even in company, and under cover, is for a Paumotuan a somewhat hazardous extreme. The whole scene – the strong moonlight and crude shadows on the sand, the scattered coals, the sound of the low voices from the house, and the lap of the lagoon along the beach – put me (I know not how) on thoughts of superstition. I was barefoot, I observed my steps were noiseless, and drawing near to the dark house, but keeping well in shadow, began to whistle. 'The Heaving of the Lead'[19] was my air – no very tragic piece. With the first note the conversation and all movement ceased; silence accompanied me while I continued; and when I passed that way on my return, I found the lamp was lighted in the house, but the tongues were still mute. All night, as I now think, the wretches shivered and were silent. For indeed, I had no guess at the time at the nature and magnitude of the terrors I inflicted, or with what grisly images the notes of that old song had peopled the dark house.

CHAPTER V

A PAUMOTUAN FUNERAL

No, I had no guess of these men's terrors. Yet I had received ere that a hint, if I had understood; and the occasion was a funeral.

A little apart in the main avenue of Rotoava, in a low hut of leaves that opened on a small enclosure, like a pigsty on a pen, an old man dwelt solitary with his aged wife. Perhaps they were too old to migrate with the others; perhaps they were too poor, and had no possessions to dispute. At least they had remained behind; and it thus befell that they were invited to my feast. I daresay it was quite a piece of politics in the pigsty whether to come or not to come, and the husband long swithered between curiosity and age, till curiosity conquered, and they came, and in the midst of that last merry-making death tapped him on the shoulder. For some days, when the sky was bright and the wind cool, his mat would be spread in the main highway of the village, and he was to be seen lying there inert, a mere handful of man, his wife inertly seated by his head. They seemed to have outgrown alike our needs and faculties; they neither spoke nor listened; they suffered us to pass without a glance; the wife did not fan, she seemed not to attend upon her husband, and the two poor antiques sat juxtaposed under the high canopy of palms, the human tragedy reduced to its bare elements, a sight beyond pathos, stirring a thrill of curiosity. And yet there was one touch of the pathetic haunted me: that so much youth and expectation should have run in these starved veins, and the man should have squandered all his lees of life on a pleasure party.

On the morning of 17th September the sufferer died, and, time pressing, he was buried the same day at four. The cemetery lies to seaward behind Government House; broken coral, like so much road-metal, forms the surface; a few wooden crosses, a few inconsider-able upright stones, designate graves; a mortared wall, high enough to lean on, rings it about; a clustering shrub surrounds it with pale leaves. Here was the grave dug that morning, doubtless by uneasy diggers, to the sound of the nigh sea and the cries of sea-birds;

meanwhile the dead man waited in his house, and the widow and another aged woman leaned on the fence before the door, no speech upon their lips, no speculation in their eyes.

Sharp at the hour the procession was in march, the coffin wrapped in white and carried by four bearers; mourners behind – not many, for not many remained in Rotoava, and not many in black, for these were poor; the men in straw hats, white coats, and blue trousers or the gorgeous parti-coloured *pariu*, the Tahitian kilt; the women, with a few exceptions, brightly habited. Far in the rear came the widow, painfully carrying the dead man's mat; a creature aged beyond humanity, to the likeness of some missing link.

The dead man had been a Mormon; but the Mormon clergyman was gone with the rest to wrangle over boundaries in the adjacent isle, and a layman took his office. Standing at the head of the open grave, in a white coat and blue *pariu*, his Tahitian Bible in his hand and one eye bound with a red handkerchief, he read solemnly that chapter in Job[1] which has been read and heard over the bones of so many of our fathers, and with a good voice offered up two prayers. The wind and the surf bore a burthen. By the cemetery gate a mother in crimson suckled an infant rolled in blue. In the midst the widow sat upon the ground and polished one of the coffin-stretchers with a piece of coral; a little later she had turned her back to the grave and was playing with a leaf. Did she understand? God knows. The officiant paused a moment, stooped, and gathered and threw reverently on the coffin a handful of rattling coral. Dust to dust: but the grains of this dust were gross like cherries, and the true dust that was to follow sat near by, still cohering (as by miracle) in the tragic semblance of a female ape.

So far, Mormon or not, it was a Christian funeral. The well-known passage had been read from Job, the prayers had been rehearsed, the grave was filled, the mourners straggled homeward. With a little coarser grain of covering earth, a little nearer outcry of the sea, a stronger glare of sunlight on the rude enclosure, and some incongruous colours of attire, the well-remembered form had been observed.

By rights it should have been otherwise. The mat should have been buried with its owner; but, the family being poor, it was thriftily reserved for a fresh service. The widow should have flung herself upon the grave and raised the voice of official grief, the neighbours have chimed in, and the narrow isle rung for a space with lamentation. But the widow was old; perhaps she had forgotten, perhaps never understood, and she played like a child with leaves and coffin-stretchers. In all ways my guest was buried with maimed rites. Strange to think that his last conscious pleasure was the *Casco* and my feast; strange to think that he had limped there, an old child, looking for some new good. And the good thing, rest, had been allotted him.

But though the widow had neglected much, there was one part she must not utterly neglect. She came away with the dispersing funeral; but the dead man's mat was left behind upon the grave, and I learned that by set of sun she must return to sleep there. This vigil is imperative. From sundown till the rising of the morning star the Paumotuan must hold his watch above the ashes of his kindred. Many friends, if the dead have been a man of mark, will keep the watchers company; they will be well supplied with coverings against the weather; I believe they bring food, and the rite is persevered in for two weeks. Our poor survivor, if, indeed, she properly survived, had little to cover, and few to sit with her; on the night of the funeral a strong squall chased her from her place of watch; for days the weather held uncertain and outrageous; and ere seven nights were up she had desisted, and returned to sleep in her low roof. That she should be at the pains of returning for so short a visit to a solitary house, that this borderer of the grave should fear a little wind and a wet blanket, filled me at the time with musings. I could not say she was indifferent; she was so far beyond me in experience that the court of my criticism waived jurisdiction; but I forged excuses, telling myself she had perhaps little to lament, perhaps suffered much, perhaps understood nothing. And lo! in the whole affair there was no question whether of tenderness or piety, and the sturdy return of this old remnant was a mark either of uncommon sense or of uncommon fortitude.

Yet one thing had occurred that partly set me on the trail. I have said the funeral passed much as at home. But when all was over, when we were trooping in decent silence from the graveyard gate and down the path to the settlement, a sudden inbreak of a different spirit startled and perhaps dismayed us. Two people walked not far apart in our procession: my friend Mr. Donat – Donat-Rimarau. 'Donat the much-handed' – acting Vice-Resident, present ruler of the archipelago, by far the man of chief importance on the scene, but known besides for one of an unshakable good temper; and a certain comely, strapping young Paumotuan woman, the comeliest on the isle, not (let us hope) the bravest or the most polite. Of a sudden, ere yet the grave silence of the funeral was broken, she made a leap at the Resident, with pointed finger, shrieked a few words, and fell back again with a laughter, not a natural mirth. 'What did she say to you?' I asked. 'She did not speak to *me*,' said Donat, a shade perturbed; 'she spoke to the ghost of the dead man.' And the purport of her speech was this: 'See there! Donat will be a fine feast for you to-night.'

'M. Donat called it a jest,' I wrote at the time in my diary.[2] 'It seemed to me more in the nature of a terrified conjuration, as though she would divert the ghost's attention from herself. A cannibal race may well have cannibal phantoms.' The guesses of the traveller appear foredoomed to be erroneous; yet in these I was precisely right. The woman had stood by in terror at the funeral, being then in a dread spot, the graveyard. She looked on in terror to the coming night, with that ogre, a new spirit, loosed upon the isle. And the words she had cried in Donat's face were indeed a terrified conjuration, basely to shield herself, basely to dedicate another in her stead. One thing is to be said in her excuse. Doubtless she partly chose Donat because he was a man of great good-nature, but partly, too, because he was a man of the half-caste. For I believe all natives regard white blood as a kind of talisman against the powers of hell. In no other way can they explain the unpunished recklessness of Europeans.

CHAPTER VI

GRAVEYARD STORIES

With my superstitious friend, the islander, I fear I am not wholly frank, often leading the way with stories of my own, and being always a grave and sometimes an excited hearer. But the deceit is scarce mortal, since I am as pleased to hear as he to tell, as pleased with the story as he with the belief; and besides, it is entirely needful. For it is scarce possible to exaggerate the extent and empire of his superstitions; they mould his life, they colour his thinking; and when he does not speak to me of ghosts, and gods, and devils, he is playing the dissembler and talking only with his lips. With thoughts so different, one must indulge the other; and I would rather that I should indulge his superstition than he my incredulity. Of one thing, besides, I may be sure: Let me indulge it as I please, I shall not hear the whole; for he is already on his guard with me, and the amount of the lore is boundless.

I will give but a few instances at random, chiefly from my own doorstep in Upolu,[1] during the past month (October 1890). One of my workmen was sent the other day to the banana patch, there to dig; this is a hollow of the mountain, buried in woods, out of all sight and cry of mankind; and long before dusk Lafaele was back again beside the cook-house with embarrassed looks; he dared not longer stay alone, he was afraid of 'spilits in the bush.'[2] It seems these are the souls of the unburied dead, haunting where they fell, and wearing woodland shapes of pig, or bird, or insect; the bush is full of them, they seem to eat nothing, slay solitary wanderers apparently in spite, and at times, in human form, go down to villages and consort with the inhabitants undetected. So much I learned a day or so after, walking in the bush with a very intelligent youth, a native. It was a little before noon; a grey day and squally; and perhaps I had spoken lightly. A dark squall burst on the side of the mountain; the woods shook and cried; the dead leaves rose from the ground in clouds, like butterflies; and my companion came suddenly to a full stop. He was afraid, he said, of the trees falling; but as soon as I had changed the subject of our talk he proceeded with alacrity. A day or two before a messenger came up the mountain from Apia with a letter; I was in the bush, he must await my return, then wait till I had answered: and before I was done his voice sounded shrill with terror of the coming night and the long forest road. These are the commons. Take the chiefs. There has been a great coming and going of signs and omens in our group. One river ran down blood; red eels were captured in another; an unknown fish was thrown upon the coast, an ominous word found written on its scales. So far we might be reading in a monkish chronicle; now we come on a fresh note, at once modern and Polynesian. The gods of Upolu and Savaii, our two chief islands, contended recently at cricket. Since then they are at war.[3] Sounds of battle are heard to roll along the coast. A woman saw a man swim from the high seas and plunge direct into the bush; he was no man of that neighbourhood; and it was known he was one of the gods, speeding to a council. Most perspicuous of all, a missionary on Savaii, who is also a medical man, was disturbed late in the night by knocking; it was no hour for the dispensary, but at length he woke his servant and sent him to inquire; the servant, looking from a window, beheld crowds of persons, all with grievous wounds, lopped limbs, broken heads, and bleeding bullet-holes; but when the door was opened all had disappeared. They were gods from the field of battle. Now these reports have certainly significance;[4] it is not hard to trace them to political grumblers or to read in them a threat of coming trouble; from that merely human side I found them ominous myself. But it was the spiritual side of their significance that was discussed in secret council by my rulers. I shall best depict this mingled habit of the Polynesian mind by two connected instances. I once lived in a village, the name of which I do not mean to tell.[5] The chief and his sister were persons perfectly intelligent: gentlefolk, apt of speech. The sister was very religious, a great church-goer, one that used to reprove me if I stayed away; I found afterwards that she privately worshipped a shark. The chief himself was somewhat of a freethinker; at the least, a latitudinarian:[6] he was a man, besides, filled with European knowledge and accomplishments; of an impassive, ironical habit; and I should as soon have expected superstition in Mr. Herbert Spencer.[7] Hear the sequel. I had discovered by unmistakable signs that they buried too shallow in the village graveyard, and I took my friend, as the responsible authority, to task. 'There is something wrong about your graveyard,' said I, 'which you must attend to, or it may have very bad results.' 'Something wrong? What is it?' he asked, with an emotion that surprised me. 'If you care to go along there any evening about nine o'clock you can see for yourself,' said I. He stepped backward. 'A ghost!' he cried.

In short, in the whole field of the South Seas, there is not one to blame another. Half blood and whole, pious and debauched, intelligent and dull, all men believe in ghosts, all men combine with their recent Christianity fear of and a lingering faith in the old island deities. So, in Europe, the gods of Olympus slowly dwindled into village bogies; so to-day, the theological Highlander sneaks from under the eye of the Free Church divine to lay an offering by a sacred well.

I try to deal with the whole matter here because of a particular quality in Paumotuan superstitions. It is true I heard them told by a man with a genius for such narrations.[8] Close about our evening lamp, within sound of the island surf, we hung on his words, thrilling. The reader, in far other scenes, must listen close for the faint echo.

This bundle of weird stories sprang from the burial and the woman's selfish conjuration. I was dissatisfied with what I heard, harped upon questions, and struck at last this vein of metal. It is from sundown to about four in the morning that the kinsfolk camp upon the grave; and these are the hours of the spirits' wanderings. At any time of the night – it may be earlier, it may be later – a sound is to be heard below, which is the noise of his liberation; at four sharp, another and a louder marks the instant of the re-imprisonment; between-whiles, he goes his malignant rounds. 'Did you ever see an evil spirit?' was once asked of a Paumotuan. 'Once.' 'Under what form?' 'It was in the form of a crane.' 'And how did you know that crane to be a spirit?' was asked. 'I will tell you,' he answered; and this was the purport of his inconclusive narrative. His father had been dead nearly a fortnight; others had wearied of the watch; and as the sun was setting, he found himself by the grave alone. It was not yet dark, rather the hour of the afterglow, when he was aware of a snow-white crane upon the coral mound; presently more cranes came, some white, some black; then the cranes vanished, and he saw in their place a white cat, to which there was silently joined a great company of cats of every hue conceivable; then these also disappeared, and he was left astonished.

This was an anodyne appearance. Take instead the experience of Rua-a-mariterangi on the isle of Katiu.[9] He had a need for some pandanus, and crossed the isle to the sea-beach, where it chiefly flourishes. The day was still, and Rua was surprised to hear a crashing sound among the thickets, and then the fall of a considerable tree. Here must be some one building a canoe; and he entered the margin of the wood to find and pass the time of day with this chance neighbour. The crashing sounded more at hand; and then he was aware of something drawing swiftly near among the tree-tops. It swung by its heels downward, like an ape, so that its hands were free for murder; it depended safely by the slightest twigs; the speed of its coming was incredible; and soon Rua recognised it for a corpse, horrible with age, its bowels hanging as it came. Prayer was the weapon of Christian in the Valley of the Shadow,[10] and it is to prayer that Rua-a-mariterangi attributes his escape. No merely human expedition had availed.

This demon was plainly from the grave; yet you will observe he was abroad by day. And inconsistent as it may seem with the hours of the night watch and the many references to the rising of the morning star, it is no singular exception. I could never find a case of another who had seen this ghost, diurnal and arboreal in its habits; but others have heard the fall of the tree, which seems the signal of its coming. Mr. Donat was once pearling on the uninhabited isle of Haraiki.[11] It was a day without a breath of wind, such as alternate in the archipelago with days of contumelious breezes. The divers were in the midst of the lagoon upon their employment; the cook, a boy of ten, was over his pots in the camp. Thus were all souls accounted for except a single native who accompanied Donat into the woods in quest of sea-fowls' eggs. In a moment, out of the stillness, came the sound of the fall of a great tree. Donat would have passed on to find the cause. 'No,' cried his companion, 'that was no tree. It was something *not right*. Let us go back to camp.' Next Sunday the divers were turned on, all that part of the isle was thoroughly examined, and sure enough no tree had fallen. A little later Mr. Donat saw one of his divers flee from a similar sound, in similar unaffected panic, on the same isle. But neither would explain, and it was not till afterwards, when he met with Rua, that he learned the occasion of their terrors.

But whether by day or night, the purpose of the dead in these abhorred activities is still the same. In Samoa, my informant had no idea of the food of the bush spirits; no such ambiguity would exist in the mind of a Paumotuan. In that hungry archipelago, living and dead must alike toil for nutriment; and the race having been cannibal in the past, the spirits are so still. When the living ate the dead, horrified nocturnal imagination drew the shocking inference that the dead might eat the living. Doubtless they slay men, doubtless even mutilate them, in mere malice. Marquesan spirits sometimes tear out the eyes of travellers; but even that may be more practical than appears, for the eye is a cannibal dainty. And certainly the root-idea of the dead, at least in the far eastern islands, is to prowl for food. It was as a dainty morsel for a meal that the woman denounced Donat at the funeral. There are spirits besides who prey in particular not on the bodies but on the souls of the dead. The point is clearly made in a Tahitian story. A child fell sick, grew swiftly worse, and at last showed signs of death. The mother hastened to the house of a sorcerer, who lived hard by. 'You are yet in time,' said he; 'a spirit has just run past my door carrying the soul of your child wrapped in the leaf of a *purao*; but I have a spirit stronger and swifter who will run him down ere he has time to eat it.' Wrapped in a leaf: like other things edible and corruptible.

Or take an experience of Mr. Donat's on the island of Anaa. It was a night of a high wind, with violent squalls; his child was very sick, and the father, though he had gone to bed, lay wakeful, hearkening to the gale. All at once a fowl was violently dashed on the house wall. Supposing he had forgot to put it in shelter with the rest, Donat arose, found the bird (a cock) lying on the verandah, and put it in the hen-house, the door of which he securely fastened. Fifteen minutes later the business was repeated, only this time, as it was being dashed against the wall, the bird crew. Again Donat replaced it, examining the hen-house thoroughly and finding it quite perfect; as he was so engaged the wind puffed out his light, and he must grope back to the door a good deal shaken. Yet a third time the bird was dashed upon the wall; a third time Donat set it, now near dead, beside its mates; and he was scarce returned before there came a rush, like that of a furious strong man, against the door, and a whistle as loud as that of a railway engine rang about the house. The sceptical reader may here detect the finger of the tempest; but the women gave up all for lost and clustered on the beds lamenting. Nothing followed, and I must suppose the gale somewhat abated, for presently after a chief came visiting. He was a bold man to be abroad so late, but doubtless carried a bright lantern. And he was certainly a man of counsel, for as soon as he heard the details of these disturbances he was in a position to explain their nature. 'Your child,' said he, 'must certainly die. This is the evil spirit of our island who lies in wait to eat the spirits of the newly dead.' And then he went on to expatiate on the strangeness of the spirit's conduct. He was not usually, he explained, so open of assault, but sat silent on the house-top waiting, in the guise of a bird, while within the people tended the dying and bewailed the dead, and had no thought of peril. But when the day came and the doors were opened and men began to go abroad, blood-stains on the wall betrayed the tragedy.

This is the quality I admire in Paumotuan legend. In Tahiti the spirit-eater is said to assume a vesture which has much more of pomp, but how much less of horror. It has been seen by all sorts and conditions, native and foreign; only the last insist it is a meteor. My authority[12] was not so sure. He was riding with his wife about two in the morning; both were near asleep, and the horses not much better. It was a brilliant and still night, and the road wound over a mountain, near by a deserted *marae* (old Tahitian temple). All at once the appearance passed above them: a form of light; the head round and greenish; the body long, red, and with a focus of yet redder brilliancy about the midst. A buzzing hoot accompanied its passage; it flew direct out of one *marae*, and direct for another down the mountain side. And this, as my informant argued, is suggestive. For why should a mere meteor frequent the altars of abominable gods? The horses, I should say, were equally dismayed with their riders. Now I am not dismayed at all – not even agreeably. Give me rather the bird upon the house-top and the morning blood-gouts on the wall.

But the dead are not exclusive in their diet. They carry with them to the grave, in particular, the Polynesian taste for fish, and enter at times with the living into a partnership in fishery. Rua-a-mariterangi is again my authority;[13] I feel it diminishes the credit of the fact, but how it builds up the image of this inveterate ghost-seer! He belongs to the miserably poor island of Taenga,[14] yet his father's house was always well supplied. As Rua grew up he was called at last to go a-fishing with this fortunate parent. They rowed into the lagoon at dusk, to an unlikely place, and the boy lay down in the stern, and the father began vainly to cast his line over the bows. It is to be supposed that Rua slept; and when he awoke there was the figure of another beside his father, and his father was pulling in the fish hand over hand. 'Who is that man, father?' Rua asked. 'It is none of your business,' said the father; and Rua supposed the stranger had swum off to them from shore. Night after night they fared into the lagoon, often to the most unlikely places; night after night the stranger would suddenly be seen on board, and as suddenly be missed; and morning after morning the canoe returned laden with fish. 'My father is a very lucky man,' thought Rua. At last, one fine day, there came first one boat party and then another, who must be entertained; father and son put off later than usual into the lagoon; and before the canoe was landed it was four o'clock, and the morning star was close on the horizon. Then the stranger appeared seized with some distress; turned about, showing for the first time his face, which was that of one long dead, with shining eyes; stared into the east, set the tips of his fingers to his mouth like one a-cold, uttered a strange, shuddering sound between a whistle and a moan – a thing to freeze the blood; and, the day-star just rising from the sea, he suddenly was not. Then Rua understood why his father prospered, why his fishes rotted early in the day, and why some were always carried to the cemetery and laid upon the graves. My informant[15] is a man not certainly averse to superstition, but he keeps his head, and takes a certain superior interest, which I may be allowed to call scientific. The last point reminding him of some parallel practice in Tahiti, he asked Rua if the fish were left, or carried home again after a formal dedication. It appears old Mariterangi practised both methods; sometimes treating his shadowy partner to a mere oblation, sometimes honestly leaving his fish to rot upon the grave.

It is plain we have in Europe stories of a similar complexion; and the Polynesian *varua ino* or *aitu o le vao* is clearly the near kinsman of the Transylvanian vampire. Here is a tale in which the kinship appears broadly marked. On the atoll of Penrhyn,[16] then still partly savage, a certain chief[17] was long the salutary terror of the natives. He died, he was buried; and his late neighbours had scarce tasted the delights of licence ere his ghost appeared about the village. Fear seized upon all; a council was held of the chief men and sorcerers; and with the approval of the Rarotongan[18] missionary, who was as frightened as the rest, and in the presence of several whites – my friend Mr. Ben Hird being one – the grave was opened, deepened until water came, and the body re-interred face down. The still recent staking of suicides in England and the decapitation of vampires in the east of Europe form close parallels.

So in Samoa only the spirits of the unburied awake fear. During the late war[19] many fell in the bush, their bodies, sometimes headless, were brought back by native pastors and interred; but this (I know not why) was insufficient, and the spirit still lingered on the theatre of death. When peace returned a singular scene was enacted in many places, and chiefly round the high gorges of Lotoanuu, where the struggle was long centred and the loss had been severe. Kinswomen of the dead came carrying a mat or sheet and guided by survivors of the fight. The place of death was earnestly sought out; the sheet was spread upon the ground; and the women, moved with pious anxiety, sat about and watched it. If any living thing alighted it was twice brushed away; upon the third coming it was known to be the spirit of the dead, was folded in, carried home and buried beside the body; and the *aitu* rested. The rite was practised beyond doubt in simple piety; the repose of the soul was its object: its motive, reverent affection. The present king[20] disowns indeed all knowledge of a dangerous *aitu*; he declares the souls of the unburied were only wanderers in limbo, lacking an entrance to the proper country of the dead, unhappy, nowise hurtful. And this severely classic opinion doubtless represents the views of the enlightened. But the flight of my Lafaele marks the grosser terrors of the ignorant.

This belief in the exorcising efficacy of funeral rites perhaps explains a fact, otherwise amazing, that no Polynesian seems at all to share our European horror of human bones and mummies. Of the first they made their cherished ornaments; they preserved them in houses or in mortuary caves; and the watchers of royal sepulchres dwelt with their children among the bones of generations. The mummy, even in the making, was as little feared. In the Marquesas, on the extreme coast, it was made by the household with continual unction and exposure to the sun; in the Carolines,[21] upon the farthest west, it is still cured in the smoke of the family hearth. Head-hunting, besides, still lives around my doorstep in Samoa. And not ten years ago, in the Gilberts, the widow must disinter, cleanse, polish, and thenceforth carry about her, by day and night, the head of her dead husband. In all these cases we may suppose the process, whether of cleansing or drying, to have fully exorcised the *aitu*.

But the Paumotuan belief is more obscure. Here the man is duly buried, and he has to be watched. He is duly watched, and the spirit goes abroad in spite of watches. Indeed, it is not the purpose of the vigils to prevent these wanderings; only to mollify by polite attention the inveterate malignity of the dead. Neglect (it is supposed) may irritate and thus invite his visits, and the aged and weakly sometimes balance risks and stay at home. Observe, it is the dead man's kindred and next friends who thus deprecate his fury with nocturnal watchings. Even the placatory vigil is held perilous, except in company, and a boy was pointed out to me in Rotoava, because he had watched alone by his own father. Not the ties of the dead, nor yet their proved character, affect the issue. A late Resident, who died in Fakarava of sunstroke, was beloved in life and is still remembered with affection; none the less his spirit went about the island clothed with terrors, and the neighbourhood of Government House was still avoided after dark. We may sum up the cheerful doctrine thus: All men become vampires, and the vampire spares none. And here we come face to face with a tempting inconsistency. For the whistling spirits are notoriously clannish; I understood them to wait upon and to enlighten kinsfolk only, and that the medium was always of the race of the communicating spirit. Here, then, we have the bonds of the family, on the one hand, severed at the hour of death; on the other, helpfully persisting.

The child's soul in the Tahitian tale was wrapped in leaves. It is the spirits of the newly dead that are the dainty. When they are slain, the house is stained with blood. Rua's dead fisherman was decomposed; so – and horribly – was his arboreal demon. The spirit, then, is a thing material; and it is by the material ensigns of corruption that he is distinguished from the living man. This opinion is widespread, adds a gross terror to the more ugly Polynesian tales, and sometimes defaces the more engaging with a painful and incongruous touch. I will give two examples sufficiently wide apart, one from Tahiti, one from Samoa.

And first from Tahiti. A man[22] went to visit the husband of his sister, then some time dead. In her life the sister had been dainty in the island fashion, and went always adorned with a coronet of flowers. In the midst of the night the brother awoke and was aware of a heavenly fragrance going to and fro in the dark house. The lamp I must suppose to have burned out; no Tahitian would have lain down without one lighted. A while he lay wondering and delighted; then called upon the rest. 'Do none of you smell flowers?' he asked. 'O,' said his brother-in-law, 'we are used to that here.' The next morning these two men went walking, and the widower confessed that his dead wife came about the house continually, and that he had even seen her. She was shaped and dressed and crowned with flowers as in her lifetime; only she moved a few inches above the earth with a very easy progress, and flitted dry-shod above the surface of the river. And now comes my point: It was always in a back view that she appeared; and these brothers-in-law, debating the affair, agreed that this was to conceal the inroads of corruption.

Now for the Samoan story. I owe it to the kindness of Dr. F. Otto Sierich, whose collection of folk-tales I expect[23] with a high degree of interest. A man in Manu'a[24] was married to two wives and had no issue. He went to Savaii, married there a third, and was more fortunate. When his wife was near her time he remembered he was in a strange island, like a poor man; and when his child was born he must be shamed for lack of gifts. It was in vain his wife dissuaded him. He returned to his father in Manu'a seeking help; and with what he could get he set off in the night to re-embark. Now his wives heard of his coming; they were incensed he did not stay to visit them; and on the beach, by his canoe, intercepted and slew him. Now the third wife lay asleep in Savaii; her babe was born and slept by her side; and she was awakened by the spirit of her husband. 'Get up,' he said, 'my father is sick in Manu'a and we must go to visit him.' 'It is well,' said she;

'take you the child, while I carry its mats.' 'I cannot carry the child,' said the spirit; 'I am too cold from the sea.' When they were got on board the canoe the wife smelt carrion. 'How is this?' she said. 'What have you in the canoe that I should smell carrion?' 'It is nothing in the canoe,' said the spirit. 'It is the land-wind blowing down the mountains, where some beast lies dead.' It appears it was still night when they reached Manu'a – the swiftest passage on record – and as they entered the reef the bale-fires[25] burned in the village. Again she asked him to carry the child; but now he need no more dissemble. 'I cannot carry your child,' said he, 'for I am dead, and the fires you see are burning for my funeral.'

The curious may learn in Dr. Sierich's book the unexpected sequel of the tale.[26] Here is enough for my purpose. Though the man was but new dead, the ghost was already putrefied, as though putrefaction were the mark and of the essence of a spirit. The vigil on the Paumotuan grave does not extend beyond two weeks, and they told me this period was thought to coincide with that of the resolution of the body. The ghost always marked with decay – the danger seemingly ending with the process of dissolution – here is tempting matter for the theorist. But it will not do. The lady of the flowers had been long dead, and her spirit was still supposed to bear the brand of perishability. The Resident had been more than a fortnight buried, and his vampire was still supposed to go the rounds.

Of the lost state of the dead, from the lurid Mangaian[27] legend, in which infernal deities hocus and destroy the souls of all, to the various submarine and aerial limbos where the dead feast, float idle, or resume the occupations of their life on earth, it would be wearisome to tell. One story I give, for it is singular in itself, is well known in Tahiti, and has this of interest, that it is post-Christian, dating indeed from but a few years back. A princess of the reigning house died; was transported to the neighbouring isle of Raiatea; fell there under the empire of a spirit who condemned her to climb coco-palms all day and bring him the nuts; was found after some time in this miserable servitude by a second spirit, one of her own house; and by him, upon her lamentations, reconveyed to Tahiti, where she found her body still waked, but already swollen with the approaches of corruption. It is a lively point in the tale that, on the sight of this dishonoured tabernacle, the princess prayed she might continue to be numbered with the dead. But it seems it was too late, her spirit was replaced by the least dignified of entrances, and her startled family beheld the body move. The seemingly purgatorial labours, the helpful kindred spirit, and the horror of the princess at the sight of her tainted body, are all points to be remarked.

The truth is, the tales are not necessarily consistent in themselves; and they are further darkened for the stranger by an ambiguity of language. Ghosts, vampires, spirits, and gods are all confounded. And yet I seem to perceive that (with exceptions) those whom we would count gods were less maleficent. Permanent spirits haunt and do murder in corners of Samoa; but those legitimate gods of Upolu and Savaii, whose wars and cricketings of late convulsed society, I did not gather to be dreaded, or not with a like fear. The spirit of Anaa that ate souls is certainly a fearsome inmate; but the high gods, even of the archipelago, seem helpful. Mahinui – from whom our convict-catechist had been named – the spirit of the sea, like a Proteus[28] endowed with endless avatars,[29] came to the assistance of the shipwrecked and carried them ashore in the guise of a ray fish. The same divinity bore priests from isle to isle about the archipelago, and by his aid, within the century, persons have been seen to fly. The tutelar deity of each isle is likewise helpful, and by a particular form of wedge-shaped cloud on the horizon announces the coming of a ship.

To one who conceives of these atolls, so narrow, so barren, so beset with sea, here would seem a superfluity of ghostly denizens. And yet there are more. In the various brackish pools and ponds, beautiful women with long red hair are seen to rise and bathe; only (timid as mice) on the first sound of feet upon the coral they dive again for ever. They are known to be healthy and harmless living people, dwellers of an underworld; and the same fancy is current in Tahiti, where also they have the hair red. *Tetea* is the Tahitian name; the Paumotuan, *mokurea*.

PART III

THE GILBERTS

BUTARITARI

At Honolulu we had said farewell to the *Casco* and to Captain Otis, and our next adventure was made in changed conditions. Passage was taken for myself, my wife, Mr. Osbourne, and my China boy, Ah Fu,[1] on a pigmy trading schooner, the *Equator*, Captain Dennis Reid;[2] and on a certain bright June day in 1889, adorned in the Hawaiian fashion with the garlands of departure, we drew out of port and bore with a fair wind for Micronesia.

The whole extent of the South Seas is desert of ships; more especially that part where we were now to sail. No post runs in these islands; communication is by accident; where you may have designed to go is one thing, where you shall be able to arrive another. It was my hope, for instance, to have reached the Carolines, and returned to the light of day by way of Manila and the China ports; and it was in Samoa that we were destined to re-appear and be once more refreshed with the sight of mountains. Since the sunset faded from the peaks of Oahu[3] six months had intervened, and we had seen no spot of earth so high as an ordinary cottage. Our path had been still on the flat sea, our dwellings upon unerected coral, our diet from the pickle-tub or out of tins; I had learned to welcome shark's flesh for a variety; and a mountain, an onion, an Irish potato or a beef-steak, had been long lost to sense and dear to aspiration.

The two chief places of our stay, Butaritari and Apemama, lie near the line; the latter within thirty miles. Both enjoy a superb ocean climate, days of blinding sun and bracing wind, nights of a heavenly brightness. Both are somewhat wider than Fakarava, measuring perhaps (at the widest) a quarter of a mile from beach to beach. In both, a coarse kind of taro thrives; its culture is a chief business of the natives, and the consequent mounds and ditches make miniature scenery and amuse the eye. In all else they show the customary features of an atoll: the low horizon, the expanse of the lagoon, the sedge-like rim of palm-tops, the sameness and smallness of the land, the hugely superior size and interest of sea and sky. Life on such islands is in many points like life on shipboard. The atoll, like the ship, is soon taken for granted; and the islanders, like the ship's crew, become soon the centre of attention. The isles are populous, independent, seats of kinglets, recently civilised, little visited. In the last decade many changes have crept in; women no longer go unclothed till marriage; the widow no longer sleeps at night and goes abroad by day with the skull of her dead husband; and, fire-arms being introduced, the spear and the shark-tooth sword are sold for curiosities. Ten years ago all these things and practices were to be seen in use; yet ten years more, and the old society will have entirely vanished. We came in a happy moment to see its institutions still erect and (in Apemama) scarce decayed.

Populous and independent – warrens of men, ruled over with some rustic pomp – such was the first and still the recurring impression of these tiny lands. As we stood across the lagoon for the town of Butaritari, a stretch of the low shore was seen to be crowded with the brown roofs of houses; those of the palace and king's summer parlour (which are of corrugated iron) glittered near one end conspicuously bright; the royal colours flew hard by on a tall flagstaff; in front, on an artificial islet, the gaol played the part of a martello.⁴ Even upon this first and distant view, the place had scarce the air of what it truly was, a village; rather of that which it was also, a petty metropolis, a city rustic and yet royal.

The lagoon is shoal. The tide being out, we waded for some quarter of a mile in tepid shallows, and stepped ashore at last into a flagrant stagnancy of sun and heat. The lee side of a line island after noon is indeed a breathless place; on the ocean beach the trade will be still blowing, boisterous and cool; out in the lagoon it will be blowing also, speeding the canoes; but the screen of bush completely intercepts it from the shore, and sleep and silence and companies of mosquitoes brood upon the towns.

We may thus be said to have taken Butaritari by surprise. A few inhabitants were still abroad in the north end, at which we landed. As we advanced, we were soon done with encounter, and seemed to explore a city of the dead. Only, between the posts of open houses, we could see the townsfolk stretched in the siesta, sometimes a family together veiled in a mosquito net, sometimes a single sleeper on a platform like a corpse on a bier.

The houses were of all dimensions, from those of toys to those of churches. Some might hold a battalion, some were so minute they could scarce receive a pair of lovers; only in the playroom, when the toys are mingled, do we meet such incongruities of scale. Many were open sheds; some took the form of roofed stages; others were walled and the walls pierced with little windows. A few were perched on piles in the lagoon; the rest stood at random on a green, through which the roadway made a ribbon of sand, or along the embankments of a sheet of water like a shallow dock. One and all were the creatures of a single tree; palm-tree wood and palm-tree leaf their materials; no nail had been driven, no hammer sounded, in their building, and they were held together by lashings of palm-tree sinnet.[5]

In the midst of the thoroughfare, the church stands like an island, a lofty and dim house with rows of windows; a rich tracery of framing sustains the roof; and through the door at either end the street shows in a vista. The proportions of the place, in such surroundings, and built of such materials, appeared august; and we threaded the nave with a sentiment befitting visitors in a cathedral. Benches run along either side. In the midst, on a crazy dais, two chairs stand ready for the king and queen when they shall choose to worship; over their heads a hoop, apparently from a hogshead, depends by a strip of red cotton; and the hoop (which hangs askew) is dressed with streamers of the same material, red and white.

This was our first advertisement of the royal dignity, and presently we stood before its seat and centre. The palace is built of imported wood upon a European plan; the roof of corrugated iron, the yard enclosed with walls, the gate surmounted by a sort of lych-house.[6] It cannot be called spacious; a labourer in the States is sometimes more commodiously lodged; but when we had the chance to see it within, we found it was enriched (beyond all island expectation) with coloured advertisements and cuts from the illustrated papers. Even before the gate some of the treasures of the crown stand public: a bell of a good magnitude, two pieces of cannon, and a single shell. The bell cannot be rung nor the guns fired; they are curiosities, proofs of wealth, a part of the parade of the royalty, and stand to be admired like statues in a square. A straight gut of water like a canal runs almost to the palace door; the containing quay-walls excellently built of coral; over against the mouth, by what seems an effect of landscape art, the martello-like islet of the gaol breaks the lagoon. Vassal chiefs with tribute, neighbour monarchs come a-roving, might here sail in, view with surprise these extensive public works, and be awed by these mouths of silent cannon. It was impossible to see the place and not to fancy it designed for pageantry. But the elaborate theatre then stood empty; the royal house deserted, its doors and windows gaping; the whole quarter of the town immersed in silence. On the opposite bank of the canal, on a roofed stage, an ancient gentleman slept publicly, sole visible inhabitant; and beyond on the lagoon a canoe spread a striped lateen,[7] the sole thing moving.

The canal is formed on the south by a pier or causeway with a parapet. At the far end the parapet stops, and the quay expands into an oblong peninsula in the lagoon, the breathing-place and summer parlour of the king. The midst is occupied by an open house or permanent marquee – called here a *maniapa*, or, as the word is now pronounced, a *maniap'* – at the lowest estimation forty feet by sixty. The iron roof, lofty but exceedingly low-browed, so that a woman must stoop to enter, is supported externally on pillars of coral, within by a frame of wood. The floor is of broken coral, divided in aisles by the uprights of the frame; the house far enough from shore to catch the breeze, which enters freely and disperses the mosquitoes; and under the low eaves the sun is seen to glitter and the waves to dance on the lagoon.

It was now some while since we had met any but slumberers; and when we had wandered down the pier and stumbled at last into this bright shed, we were surprised to find it occupied by a society of wakeful people, some twenty souls in all, the court and guardsmen of Butaritari. The court ladies were busy making mats; the guardsmen yawned and sprawled. Half a dozen rifles lay in a rack and a cutlass was leaned against a pillar: the armoury of these drowsy musketeers. At the far end, a little closed house of wood displayed some tinsel[8] curtains, and proved, upon examination, to be a privy on the European model. In front of this, upon some mats, lolled Tebureimoa, the king; behind him, on the panels of the house, two crossed rifles represented fasces.[9] He wore pyjamas which sorrowfully misbecame his bulk; his nose was hooked and cruel, his body overcome with sodden corpulence, his eye timorous and dull; he seemed at once oppressed with drowsiness and held awake by apprehension: a pepper rajah muddled with opium, and listening for the march of a Dutch army, looks perhaps not otherwise. We were to grow better acquainted, and first and last I had the same impression; he seemed always drowsy, yet always to hearken and start; and, whether from remorse or fear, there is no doubt he seeks a refuge in the abuse of drugs.

The rajah displayed no sign of interest in our coming. But the queen, who sat beside him in a purple sacque,[10] was more accessible; and there was present an interpreter so willing that his volubility became at last the cause of our departure. He had greeted us upon our entrance:– 'That is the honourable King, and I am his interpreter,' he had said, with more stateliness than truth. For he held no appointment in the court, seemed extremely ill-acquainted with the island language, and was present, like ourselves, upon a visit of civility. Mr. Williams[11] was his name: an American darkey, runaway ship's cook, and bar-keeper at the Land We Live In tavern, Butaritari. I never knew a man who had more words in his command or less truth to communicate; neither the gloom of the monarch, nor my own efforts to be distant, could in the least abash him; and when the scene closed, the darkey was left talking.[12]

The town still slumbered, or had but just begun to turn and stretch itself; it was still plunged in heat and silence. So much the more vivid was the impression that we carried away of the house upon the islet, the Micronesian Saul wakeful amid his guards, and his unmelodious David,[13] Mr. Williams, chattering through the drowsy hours.

CHAPTER II

THE FOUR BROTHERS

The kingdom of Tebureimoa includes two islands, Great and Little Makin; some two thousand subjects pay him tribute, and two semi-independent chieftains do him qualified homage. The importance of the office is measured by the man; he may be a nobody, he may be absolute; and both extremes have been exemplified within the memory of residents.[1]

On the death of king Tetimararoa, Tebureimoa's father, Nakaeia,[2] the eldest son, succeeded. He was a fellow of huge physical strength, masterful, violent, with a certain barbaric thrift and some intelligence of men and business. Alone in his islands, it was he who dealt and profited; he was the planter and the merchant; and his subjects toiled for his behoof in servitude. When they wrought long and well their taskmaster declared a holiday, and supplied and shared a general debauch. The scale of his providing was at times magnificent; six hundred dollars' worth of gin and brandy was set forth at once; the narrow land resounded with the noise of revelry; and it was a common thing to see the subjects (staggering themselves) parade their drunken sovereign on the forehatch of a wrecked vessel, king and commons howling and singing as they went. At a word from Nakaeia's mouth the revel ended; Makin became once more an isle of slaves and of teetotalers; and on the morrow all the population must be on the roads or in the taro-patches toiling under his bloodshot eye.

The fear of Nakaeia filled the land. No regularity of justice was affected; there was no trial, there were no officers of the law; it seems there was but one penalty, the capital; and daylight assault and midnight murder were the forms of process. The king himself would play the executioner; and his blows were dealt by stealth, and with the help and countenance of none but his own wives. These were his oarswomen; one that caught a crab, he slew incontinently with the tiller; thus disciplined, they pulled him by night to the scene of his vengeance, which he would then execute alone and return well-pleased with his connubial crew. The inmates of the harem held a station hard for us to conceive. Beasts of draught, and driven by the fear of death, they were yet implicitly trusted with their sovereign's life; they were still wives and queens, and it was supposed that no man should behold their faces. They killed by the sight like basilisks;[3] a chance view of one of those boatwomen was a crime to be wiped out with blood. In the days of Nakaeia the palace was beset with some tall coco-palms which commanded the enclosure. It chanced one evening, while Nakaeia sat below at supper with his wives, that the owner of the grove was in a tree-top drawing palm-tree wine; it chanced that he looked down, and the king at the same moment looking up, their eyes encountered. Instant flight preserved the involuntary criminal. But during the remainder of that reign he must lurk and be hid by friends in remote parts of the isle; Nakaeia hunted him without remission, although still in vain; and the palms, accessories to the fact, were ruthlessly cut down. Such was the ideal of wifely purity in an isle where nubile virgins went naked as in paradise. And yet scandal found its way into Nakaeia's well-guarded harem. He was at that time the owner of a schooner, which he used for a pleasure-house, lodging on board as she lay anchored; and thither one day he summoned a new wife. She was one that had been sealed to him; that is to say (I presume), that he was married to her sister, for the husband of an elder sister has the call of the cadets. She would be arrayed for the occasion; she would come scented, garlanded, decked with fine mats and family jewels, for marriage, as her friends supposed; for death, as she well knew. 'Tell me the man's name, and I will spare you,' said Nakaeia. But the girl was staunch; she held her peace, saved her lover; and the queens strangled her between the masts.

Nakaeia was feared; it does not appear that he was hated. Deeds that smell to us of murder wore to his subjects the reverend face of justice; his orgies made him popular; natives to this day recall with respect the firmness of his government; and even the whites, whom he long opposed and kept at arm's-length, give him the name (in the canonical South Sea phrase) of 'a perfect gentleman when sober.'

When he came to lie, without issue, on the bed of death, he summoned his next brother, Nanteitei, made him a discourse on royal policy, and warned him he was too weak to reign. The warning was taken to heart, and for some while the government moved on the model of Nakaeia's. Nanteitei dispensed with guards, and walked abroad alone with a revolver in a leather mail-bag. To conceal his weakness he affected a rude silence; you might talk to him all day; advice, reproof, appeal, and menace alike remained unanswered. The number of his wives was seventeen, many of them heiresses; for the royal house is poor, and marriage was in these days a chief means of buttressing the throne. Nakaeia kept his harem busy for himself; Nanteitei hired it out to others. In his days, for instance, Messrs. Wightman⁴ built a pier with a verandah at the north end of the town. The masonry was the work of the seventeen queens, who toiled and waded there like fisher lasses; but the man who was to do the roofing durst not begin till they had finished, lest by chance he should look down and see them.

It was perhaps the last appearance of the harem gang. For some time already Hawaiian missionaries had been seated at Butaritari – Maka and Kanoa,⁵ two brave childlike men. Nakaeia would none of their doctrine; he was perhaps jealous of their presence; being human, he had some affection for their persons. In the house, before the eyes of Kanoa, he slew with his own hand three sailors of Oahu, crouching on their backs to knife them, and menacing the missionary if he interfered; yet he not only spared him at the moment, but recalled him afterwards (when he had fled) with some expressions of respect. Nanteitei, the weaker man, fell more completely under the spell. Maka, a light-hearted, lovable, yet in his own trade very rigorous man – gained and improved an influence on the king which soon grew paramount. Nanteitei, with the royal house, was publicly converted; and, with a severity which liberal missionaries disavow, the harem was at once reduced. It was a compendious act. The throne was thus impoverished, its influence shaken, the queens' relatives mortified, and sixteen chief women (some of great possessions) cast in a body on the market. I have been shipmates with a Hawaiian sailor who was successively married to two of these *impromptu* widows, and successively divorced by both for misconduct. That two great and rich ladies (for both of these were rich) should have married 'a man from another island' marks the dissolution of society. The laws besides were wholly remodelled, not always for the better. I love Maka as a man; as a legislator he has two defects: weak in the punishment of crime, stern to repress innocent pleasures.

War and revolution are the common successors of reform; yet Nanteitei died (of an overdose of chloroform), in quiet possession of the throne, and it was in the reign of the third brother, Nabakatokia, a man brave in body and feeble of character, that the storm burst. The rule of the high chiefs and notables seems to have always underlain and perhaps alternated with monarchy. The Old Men (as they were called) have a right to sit with the king in the Speak House and debate: and the king's chief superiority is a form of closure – 'The Speaking is over.' After the long monocracy of Nakaeia and the changes of Nanteitei, the Old Men were doubtless grown impatient of obscurity, and they were beyond question jealous of the influence of Maka. Calumny, or rather caricature, was called in use; a spoken cartoon ran round society; Maka was reported to have said in church that the king was the first man in the island and himself the second; and, stung by the supposed affront, the chiefs broke into rebellion and armed gatherings. In the space of one forenoon the throne of Nakaeia was humbled in the dust. The king sat in the *maniap'* before the palace gate expecting his recruits; Maka by his side, both anxious men; and meanwhile, in the door of a house at the north entry of the town, a chief had taken post and diverted the succours as they came. They came singly or in groups, each with his gun or pistol slung about his neck. 'Where are you going?' asked the chief. 'The king called us,' they would reply. 'Here is your place. Sit down,' returned the chief. With incredible disloyalty, all obeyed; and sufficient force being thus got together from both sides, Nabakatokia was summoned and surrendered. About this period, in almost every part of the group, the kings were murdered; and on Tapituea, the skeleton of the last hangs to this day in the chief Speak House of the isle, a menace to ambition. Nabakatokia was more fortunate; his life and the royal style were spared to him, but he was stripped of power. The Old Men enjoyed a festival of public speaking; the laws were continually changed, never enforced; the commons had an opportunity to regret the merits of

Nakaeia; and the king, denied the resource of rich marriages and the service of a troop of wives, fell not only in disconsideration but in debt.

He died some months before my arrival in the islands, and no one regretted him; rather all looked hopefully to his successor. This was by repute the hero of the family. Alone of the four brothers, he had issue, a grown son, Natiata, and a daughter three years old; it was to him, in the hour of the revolution, that Nabakatokia turned too late for help; and in earlier days he had been the right hand of the vigorous Nakaeia. Nantemat', 'Mr. Corpse', was his appalling nickname, and he had earned it well. Again and again, at the command of Nakaeia, he had surrounded houses in the dead of night, cut down the mosquito bars and butchered families. Here was the hand of iron; here was Nakaeia *redux*.[6] He came, summoned from the tributary rule of Little Makin: he was installed, he proved a puppet and a trembler, the unwieldy shuttlecock of orators; and the reader has seen the remains of him in his summer parlour under the name of Tebureimoa.

The change in the man's character was much commented on in the island, and variously explained by opium and Christianity. To my eyes, there seemed no change at all, rather an extreme consistency. Mr. Corpse was afraid of his brother: King Tebureimoa is afraid of the Old Men. Terror of the first nerved him for deeds of desperation; fear of the second disables him for the least act of government. He played his part of bravo in the past, following the line of least resistance, butchering others in his own defence: to-day, grown elderly and heavy, a convert, a reader of the Bible, perhaps a penitent, conscious at least of accumulated hatreds, and his memory charged with images of violence and blood, he capitulates to the Old Men, fuddles himself with opium, and sits among his guards in dreadful expectation. The same cowardice that put into his hand the knife of the assassin deprives him of the sceptre of a king.

A tale that I was told, a trifling incident that fell in my observation, depict him in his two capacities. A chief in Little Makin asked, in an hour of lightness, 'Who is Kaeia?' A bird carried the saying; and Nakaeia placed the matter in the hands of a committee of three. Mr. Corpse was chairman; the second commissioner died before my arrival;

the third was yet alive and green, and presented so venerable an appearance that we gave him the name of Abou ben Adhem.[7] Mr. Corpse was troubled with a scruple; the man from Little Makin was his adopted brother; in such a case it was not very delicate to appear at all, to strike the blow (which it seems was otherwise expected of him) would be worse than awkward. 'I will strike the blow,' said the venerable Abou; and Mr. Corpse (surely with a sigh) accepted the compromise. The quarry was decoyed into the bush; he was set to carrying a log; and while his arms were raised Abou ripped up his belly at a blow. Justice being thus done, the commission, in a childish horror, turned to flee. But their victim recalled them to his side. 'You need not run away now,' he said. 'You have done this thing to me. Stay.' He was some twenty minutes dying, and his murderers sat with him the while: a scene for Shakespeare. All the stages of a violent death, the blood, the failing voice, the decomposing features, the changed hue, are thus present in the memory of Mr. Corpse; and since he studied them in the brother he betrayed, he has some reason to reflect on the possibilities of treachery. I was never more sure of anything than the tragic quality of the king's thoughts; and yet I had but the one sight of him at unawares. I had once an errand for his ear. It was once more the hour of the siesta; but there were loiterers abroad, and these directed us to a closed house on the bank of the canal where Tebureimoa lay unguarded. We entered without ceremony, being in some haste. He lay on the floor upon a bed of mats, reading in his Gilbert Island Bible with compunction. On our sudden entrance the unwieldy man reared himself half-sitting so that the Bible rolled on the floor, stared on us a moment with blank eyes, and, having recognised his visitors, sank again upon the mats. So Eglon looked on Ehud.[8]

The justice of facts is strange, and strangely just: Nakaeia, the author of these deeds, died at peace discoursing on the craft of kings; his tool suffers daily death for his enforced complicity. Not the nature, but the congruity of men's deeds and circumstances damn and save them; and Tebureimoa from the first has been incongruously placed. At home, in a quiet bystreet of a village, the man had been a worthy carpenter, and, even bedevilled as he is, he shows some private virtues.

He has no lands, only the use of such as are impignorate[9] for fines; he cannot enrich himself in the old way by marriages; thrift is the chief pillar of his future, and he knows and uses it. Eleven foreign traders pay him a patent of a hundred dollars, some two thousand subjects pay capitation at the rate of a dollar for a man, half a dollar for a woman, and a shilling for a child: allowing for the exchange, perhaps a total of three hundred pounds a year. He had been some nine months on the throne: had bought his wife a silk dress and hat, figure unknown, and himself a uniform at three hundred dollars; had sent his brother's photograph to be enlarged in San Francisco at two hundred and fifty dollars; had greatly reduced that brother's legacy of debt; and had still sovereigns in his pocket. An affectionate brother, a good economist; he was besides a handy carpenter, and cobbled occasionally on the woodwork of the palace. It is not wonderful that Mr. Corpse has virtues; that Tebureimoa should have a diversion filled me with surprise.

CHAPTER III

AROUND OUR HOUSE

When we left the palace we were still but seafarers ashore; and within the hour we had installed our goods in one of the six foreign houses of Butaritari, namely, that usually occupied by Maka, the Hawaiian missionary. Two San Francisco firms are here established, Messrs. Crawford and Messrs. Wightman Brothers; the first hard by the palace of the mid town, the second at the north entry; each with a store and bar-room. Our house was in the Wightman compound, betwixt the store and bar, within a fenced enclosure. Across the road a few native houses nestled in the margin of the bush, and the green wall of palms rose solid, shutting out the breeze. A little sandy cove of the lagoon ran in behind, sheltered by a verandah pier, the labour of queens' hands. Here, when the tide was high, sailed boats lay to be loaded; when the tide was low, the boats took ground some half a mile away, and an endless series of natives descended the pier stair, tailed across the sand in strings and clusters, waded to the waist with the bags of copra,[1] and loitered backward to renew their charge. The mystery of the copra trade tormented me, as I sat and watched the profits drip on the stair and the sands.

In front, from shortly after four in the morning until nine at night, the folk of the town streamed by us intermittingly along the road: families going up the island to make copra on their lands; women bound for the bush to gather flowers against the evening toilet; and, twice a day, the toddy-cutters,[2] each with his knife and shell. In the first grey of the morning, and again late in the afternoon, these would straggle past about their tree-top business, strike off here and there into the bush, and vanish from the face of earth. At about the same hour, if the tide be low in the lagoon, you are likely to be bound yourself across the island for a bath, and may enter close at their heels alleys of the palm wood. Right in front, although the sun is not yet risen, the east is already lighted with preparatory fires, and the huge accumulations of the trade-wind cloud glow with and heliograph[3] the coming day. The breeze is in your face; overhead in the tops of the palms, its playthings, it maintains a lively bustle; look where you will, above or below, there is no human presence, only the earth and shaken forest. And right overhead the song of an invisible singer breaks from the thick leaves; from farther on a second tree-top answers; and beyond again, in the bosom of the woods, a still more distant minstrel perches and sways and sings. So, all round the isle, the toddy-cutters sit on high, and are rocked by the trade, and have a view far to seaward, where they keep watch for sails, and like huge birds utter their songs in the morning. They sing with a certain lustiness and Bacchic[4] glee; the volume of sound and the articulate melody fall unexpected from the treetop, whence we anticipate the chattering of fowls. And yet in a sense these songs also are but chatter; the words are ancient, obsolete, and sacred; few comprehend them, perhaps no one perfectly; but it was understood the cutters 'prayed to have good toddy, and sang of their old wars.' The prayer is at least answered; and when the foaming shell is brought to your door, you have a beverage well 'worthy of a grace.'[5] All forenoon you may return and taste; it only sparkles, and sharpens, and grows to be a new drink, not less delicious; but with the progress of the day the fermentation quickens and grows acid; in twelve hours it will be yeast for bread, in two days more a devilish intoxicant, the counsellor of crime.

The men are of a marked Arabian cast of features, often bearded and mustached, often gaily dressed, some with bracelets and anklets, all stalking hidalgo-like,[6] and accepting salutations with a haughty lip. The hair (with the dandies of either sex) is worn turban-wise in a frizzled bush; and like the daggers of the Japanese, a pointed stick (used for a comb) is thrust gallantly among the curls. The women from this bush of hair look forth enticingly: the race cannot be compared with the Tahitian for female beauty; I doubt even if the average be high; but some of the prettiest girls, and one of the handsomest women I ever saw, were Gilbertines. Butaritari, being the commercial centre of the group, is Europeanised; the coloured sacque or the white shift are common wear, the latter for the evening; the trade hat, loaded with flowers, fruit, and ribbons, is unfortunately not unknown; and the characteristic female dress of the Gilberts no longer universal. The *ridi* is its name: a cutty[7] petticoat or fringe of the smoked fibre of cocoa-nut leaf, not unlike tarry string; the lower edge not reaching the mid-thigh, the upper adjusted so low upon the haunches that it seems to cling by accident. A sneeze, you think, and the lady must surely be left destitute. 'The perilous, hairbreadth *ridi*' was our word for it; and in the conflict that rages over women's dress it has the misfortune to please neither side, the prudish condemning it as insufficient, the more frivolous finding it unlovely in itself. Yet if a pretty Gilbertine would look her best, that must be her costume. In that, and naked otherwise, she moves with an incomparable liberty and grace and life, that marks the poetry of Micronesia. Bundle her in a gown, the charm is fled, and she wriggles like an Englishwoman.

Towards dusk the passers-by became more gorgeous. The men broke out in all the colours of the rainbow – or at least of the trade-room, – and both men and women began to be adorned and scented with new flowers. A small white blossom is the favourite, sometimes sown singly in a woman's hair like little stars, now composed in a thick wreath. With the night, the crowd sometimes thickened in the road, and the padding and brushing of bare feet became continuous; the

promenades mostly grave, the silence only interrupted by some giggling
and scampering of girls; even the children quiet. At nine, bed-time
struck on a bell from the cathedral, and the life of the town ceased.
At four the next morning the signal is repeated in the darkness, and
the innocent prisoners set free; but for seven hours all must lie – I was
about to say within doors, of a place where doors, and even walls, are
an exception – housed, at least, under their airy roofs and clustered in
the tents of the mosquito-nets. Suppose a necessary errand to occur,
suppose it imperative to send abroad, the messenger must then go
openly, advertising himself to the police with a huge brand[8] of cocoa-nut,
which flares from house to house like a moving bonfire. Only the police
themselves go darkling, and grope in the night for misdemeanants. I
used to hate their treacherous presence; their captain in particular, a
crafty old man in white, lurked nightly about my premises till I could
have found it in my heart to beat him. But the rogue was privileged.

Not one of the eleven resident traders came to town, no captain
cast anchor in the lagoon, but we saw him ere the hour was out. This
was owing to our position between the store and the bar – the Sans
Souci, as the last was called. Mr. Rick was not only Messrs. Wightman's
manager, but consular agent for the States; Mrs. Rick[9] was the only
white woman on the island, and one of the only two in the archipelago;
their house besides, with its cool verandahs, its bookshelves, its comfortable furniture, could not be rivalled nearer than Jaluit[10] or Honolulu.
Every one called in consequence, save such as might be prosecuting
a South Sea quarrel, hingeing on the price of copra and the odd cent,
or perhaps a difference about poultry. Even these, if they did not
appear upon the north, would be presently visible to the southward,
the Sans Souci drawing them as with cords. In an island with a total
population of twelve white persons, one of the two drinking-shops
might seem superfluous; but every bullet has its billet, and the double
accommodation of Butaritari is found in practice highly convenient
by the captains and the crews of ships: the Land We Live In being
tacitly resigned to the forecastle,[11] the Sans Souci tacitly reserved for
the afterguard.[12] So aristocratic were my habits, so commanding was
my fear of Mr. Williams, that I have never visited the first; but in the
other, which was the club or rather the casino of the island, I regularly

passed my evenings.[13] It was small, but neatly fitted, and at night (when the lamp was lit) sparkled with glass and glowed with coloured pictures like a theatre at Christmas. The pictures were advertisements, the glass coarse enough, the carpentry amateur; but the effect, in that incongruous isle, was of unbridled luxury and inestimable expense. Here songs were sung, tales told, tricks performed, games played. The Ricks, ourselves, Norwegian Tom the bar-keeper, a captain or two from the ships, and perhaps three or four traders come down the island in their boats or by the road on foot, made up the usual company. The traders, all bred to the sea, take a humorous pride in their new business; 'South Sea Merchants' is the title they prefer. 'We are all sailors here' – 'Merchants, if you please' – '*South Sea* Merchants,' – was a piece of conversation endlessly repeated, that never seemed to lose in savour. We found them at all times simple, genial, gay, gallant, and obliging; and, across some interval of time, recall with pleasure the traders of Butaritari. There was one black sheep[14] indeed. I tell of him here where we lived, against my rule; for in this case I have no measure to preserve, and the man is typical of a class of ruffians that once disgraced the whole field of the South Seas, and still linger in the rarely visited isles of Micronesia. He had the name on the beach of 'a perfect gentleman when sober,' but I never saw him otherwise than drunk. The few shocking and savage traits of the Micronesian he has singled out with the skill of a collector, and planted in the soil of his original baseness. He has been accused and acquitted of a treacherous murder; and has since boastfully owned it, which inclines me to suppose him innocent. His daughter is defaced by his erroneous cruelty, for it was his wife he had intended to disfigure, and, in the darkness of the night and the frenzy of coco-brandy, fastened on the wrong victim. The wife has since fled and harbours in the bush with natives; and the husband still demands from deaf ears her forcible restoration. The best of his business is to make natives drink, and then advance the money for the fine upon a lucrative mortgage. 'Respect for whites' is the man's word: 'What is the matter with this island is the want of respect for whites.' On his way to Butaritari, while I was there, he spied his wife in the bush with certain natives and made a dash to capture her; whereupon one of her companions drew a knife, and the husband retreated: 'Do you call that proper respect for whites?' he cried. At an early stage of the acquaintance we proved our respect for his kind of white by forbidding him our enclosure under pain of death. Thenceforth he lingered often in the neighbourhood with I knew not what sense of envy or design of mischief; his white, handsome face (which I beheld with loathing) looked in upon us at all hours across the fence; and once, from a safe distance, he avenged himself by shouting a recondite island insult,[15] to us quite inoffensive, on his English lips incredibly incongruous.

Our enclosure, round which this composite of degradations wandered, was of some extent. In one corner was a trellis with a long table of rough boards. Here the Fourth of July[16] feast had been held not long before with memorable consequences, yet to be set forth; here we took our meals; here entertained to a dinner the king and notables of Makin. In the midst was the house, with a verandah front and back, and three rooms within. In the verandah we slung our man-of-war hammocks,[17] worked there by day, and slept at night. Within were beds, chairs, a round table, a fine hanging lamp, and portraits of the royal family of Hawaii. Queen Victoria proves nothing; Kalakaua and Mrs. Bishop[18] are diagnostic; and the truth is we were the stealthy tenants of the parsonage. On the day of our arrival Maka was away; faithless trustees unlocked his doors; and the dear rigorous man, the sworn foe of liquor and tobacco, returned to find his verandah littered with cigarettes and his parlour horrible with bottles. He made but one condition – on the round table, which he used in the celebration of the sacraments, he begged us to refrain from setting liquor; in all else he bowed to the accomplished fact, refused rent, retired across the way into a native house, and, plying in his boat, beat the remotest quarters of the isle for provender. He found us pigs – I could not fancy where – no other pigs were visible; he brought us fowls and taro; when we gave our feast to the monarch and gentry, it was he who supplied the wherewithal, he who superintended the cooking, he who asked grace at table, and when the king's health was proposed, he also started the cheering with an English hip-hip-hip. There was never a more fortunate conception; the heart of the fatted king exulted in his bosom at the sound.

Take him for all in all, I have never known a more engaging creature than this parson of Butaritari: his mirth, his kindness, his noble, friendly feelings, brimmed from the man in speech and gesture. He loved to exaggerate, to act and overact the momentary part, to exercise his lungs and muscles, and to speak and laugh with his whole body. He had the morning cheerfulness of birds and healthy children; and his humour was infectious. We were next neighbours and met daily, yet our salutations lasted minutes at a stretch – shaking hands, slapping shoulders, capering like a pair of Merry-Andrews,[19] laughing to split our sides upon some pleasantry that would scarce raise a titter in an infant-school. It might be five in the morning, the toddy-cutters just gone by, the road empty, the shade of the island lying far on the lagoon: and the ebullition[20] cheered me for the day.

Yet I always suspected Maka of a secret melancholy; these jubilant extremes could scarce be constantly maintained. He was besides long, and lean, and lined, and corded,[21] and a trifle grizzled; and his Sabbath countenance was even saturnine. On that day we made a procession to the church, or (as I must always call it) the cathedral: Maka (a blot on the hot landscape) in tall hat, black frock-coat, black trousers; under his arm the hymn-book and the Bible; in his face, a reverent gravity:– beside him Mary his wife, a quiet, wise, and handsome elderly lady, seriously attired: – myself following with singular and moving thoughts. Long before, to the sound of bells and streams and birds, through a green Lothian[22] glen, I had accompanied Sunday by Sunday a minister[23] in whose house I lodged; and the likeness, and the difference, and the series of years and deaths, profoundly touched me. In the great, dusky, palm-tree cathedral the congregation rarely numbered thirty: the men on one side, the women on the other, myself posted (for a privilege) amongst the women, and the small missionary contingent gathered close around the platform, we were lost in that round vault. The lessons were read antiphonally, the flock was catechised, a blind youth repeated weekly a long string of psalms, hymns were sung – I never heard worse singing, – and the sermon followed. To say I understood nothing were untrue; there were points that I learned to expect with certainty; the name of Honolulu, that of Kalakaua, the word Cap'n-man-o'-wa', the word ship, and a description of a storm at sea, infallibly occurred; and I was not seldom rewarded with the name of my own Sovereign in the bargain. The rest was but sound to the ears, silence for the mind: a plain expanse of tedium, rendered unbearable by heat, a hard chair, and the sight through the wide doors of the more happy heathen on the green. Sleep breathed on my joints and eyelids, sleep hummed in my ears; it reigned in the dim cathedral. The congregation stirred and stretched; they moaned, they groaned aloud; they yawned upon a singing note, as you may sometimes hear a dog when he has reached the tragic bitterest of boredom. In vain the preacher thumped the table; in vain he singled and addressed by name particular hearers. I was myself perhaps a more effective excitant; and at least to one old gentleman the spectacle of my successful struggles against sleep – and I hope they were successful – cheered the flight of time. He, when he was not catching flies or playing tricks upon his neighbours, gloated with a fixed, truculent eye upon the stages of my agony; and once, when the service was drawing towards a close, he winked at me across the church.

I write of the service with a smile; yet I was always there – always with respect for Maka, always with admiration for his deep seriousness, his burning energy, the fire of his roused eye, the sincere and various accents of his voice. To see him weekly flogging a dead horse and blowing a cold fire was a lesson in fortitude and constancy. It may be a question whether if the mission were fully supported, and he was set free from business avocations, more might not result; I think otherwise myself; I think not neglect but rigour has reduced his flock, that rigour which has once provoked a revolution, and which to-day, in a man so lively and engaging, amazes the beholder. No song, no dance, no tobacco, no liquor, no alleviative of life – only toil and church-going; so says a voice from his face; and the face is the face of the Polynesian Esau, but the voice is the voice of a Jacob[24] from a different world. And a Polynesian at the best makes a singular mission-ary in the Gilberts, coming from a country recklessly unchaste to one conspicuously strict; from a race hag-ridden with bogies to one comparatively bold against the terrors of the dark. The thought was stamped one morning in my mind, when I chanced to be abroad by moonlight, and saw all the town lightless, but the lamp faithfully burning by the missionary's bed. It requires no law, no fire, and no scouting police, to withhold Maka and his countrymen from wandering in the night unlighted.

CHAPTER IV

A TALE OF A *TAPU*

On the morrow of our arrival (Sunday, 14th July 1889) our photographers were early stirring. Once more we traversed a silent town; many were yet abed and asleep; some sat drowsily in their open houses; there was no sound of intercourse or business. In that hour before the shadows, the quarter of the palace and canal seemed like a landing-place in the *Arabian Nights* or from the classic poets; here were the fit destination of some 'faery frigot,'[1] here some adventurous prince might step ashore among new characters and incidents; and the island prison, where it floated on the luminous face of the lagoon, might have passed for the repository of the Grail.[2] In such a scene, and at such an hour, the impression received was not so much of foreign travel – rather of past ages; it seemed not so much degrees of latitude that we had crossed, as centuries of time that we had re-ascended; leaving, by the same steps, home and to-day. A few children followed us, mostly nude, all silent; in the clear, weedy waters of the canal some silent damsels waded, baring their brown thighs; and to one of the *maniap*'s before the palace gate we were attracted by a low but stirring hum of speech.

The oval shed was full of men sitting cross-legged. The king was there in striped pyjamas, his rear protected by four guards with Winchesters, his air and bearing marked by unwonted spirit and decision; tumblers and black bottles went the round; and the talk, throughout loud, was general and animated. I was inclined at first to view this scene with suspicion. But the hour appeared unsuitable for a carouse; drink was besides forbidden equally by the law of the land and the canons of the church; and while I was yet hesitating, the king's rigorous attitude disposed of my last doubt. We had come, thinking to photograph him surrounded by his guards, and at the first word of the design his piety revolted. We were reminded of the day – the Sabbath, in which thou shalt take no photographs – and returned with a flea in our ear, bearing the rejected camera.

At church, a little later, I was struck to find the throne unoccupied. So nice a Sabbatarian might have found the means to be present; perhaps my doubts revived; and before I got home they were transformed to certainties. Tom, the bar-keeper of the Sans Souci, was in conversation with two emissaries from the court. The 'keen,' they said, wanted 'din,' failing which 'perandi.'³ No 'din,' was Tom's reply, and no 'perandi'; but 'pira' if they pleased. It seems they had no use for beer, and departed sorrowing.

'Why, what is the meaning of all this?' I asked. 'Is the island on the spree?'

Such was the fact. On the 4th of July a feast had been made, and the king, at the suggestion of the whites, had raised the *tapu* against liquor. There is a proverb about horses; it scarce applies to the superior animal, of whom it may be rather said, that any one can start him drinking, not any twenty can prevail on him to stop. The *tapu*, raised ten days before, was not yet re-imposed; for ten days the town had been passing the bottle or lying (as we had seen it the afternoon before) in hoggish sleep; and the king, moved by the Old Men and his own appetites, continued to maintain the liberty, to squander his savings on liquor, and to join in and lead the debauch. The whites were the authors of this crisis; it was upon their own proposal that the freedom had been granted at the first; and for a while, in the interests of trade, they were doubtless pleased it should continue. That pleasure had now sometime ceased; the bout had been prolonged (it was conceded) unduly; and it now began to be a question how it might conclude. Hence Tom's refusal. Yet that refusal was avowedly only for the moment, and it was avowedly unavailing; the king's foragers, denied by Tom at the Sans Souci, would be supplied at the Land We Live In by the gobbling Mr. Williams.

The degree of the peril was not easy to measure at the time, and I am inclined to think now it was easy to exaggerate. Yet the conduct of drunkards even at home is always matter for anxiety; and at home our populations are not armed from the highest to the lowest with revolvers and repeating rifles, neither do we go on a debauch by the whole townful – and I might rather say, by the whole polity – king, magistrates, police, and army joining in one common scene of drunkenness. It must be thought besides that we were here in barbarous islands, rarely visited, lately and partly civilised. First and last, a really considerable number of whites have perished in the Gilberts, chiefly through their own misconduct; and the natives have displayed in at least one instance a disposition to conceal an accident under a butchery, and leave nothing but dumb bones. This last was the chief consideration against a sudden closing of the bars; the bar-keepers stood in the immediate breach and dealt direct with madmen; too surly a refusal might at any moment precipitate a blow, and the blow might prove the signal for a massacre.

Monday, 15th. – At the same hour we returned to the same *maniap'*. Kümmel[4] (of all drinks) was served in tumblers; in the midst sat the crown prince, a fatted youth, surrounded by fresh bottles and busily plying the corkscrew; and king, chief, and commons showed the loose mouth, the uncertain joints, and the blurred and animated eye of the early drinker. It was plain we were impatiently expected; the king retired with alacrity to dress, the guards were despatched after their uniforms; and we were left to await the issue of these preparations with a shedful of tipsy natives. The orgie had proceeded further than on Sunday. The day promised to be of great heat; it was already sultry, the courtiers were already fuddled; and still the kümmel continued to go round, and the crown prince to play butler. Flemish freedom followed upon Flemish excess;[5] and a funny dog, a handsome fellow, gaily dressed, and with a full turban of frizzed hair, delighted the company with a humorous courtship of a lady in a manner not to be described. It was our diversion, in this time of waiting, to observe the gathering of the guards. They have European arms, European uniforms, and (to their sorrow) European shoes. We saw one warrior (like Mars) in the article of being armed; two men and a stalwart woman were scarce strong enough to boot him; and after a single appearance on parade the army is crippled for a week.

At last, the gates under the lych-house opened; the army issued, one behind another, with guns and epaulettes; the colours stooped under the gateway; majesty followed in his uniform bedizened with gold lace; majesty's wife came next in a hat and feathers, and an ample trained silk gown; the royal imps succeeded; there stood the pageantry of Makin marshalled on its chosen theatre. Dickens might have told how serious they were; how tipsy; how the king melted and streamed under his cocked hat; how he took station by the larger of his two cannons – austere, majestic, but not truly vertical; how the troops huddled, and were straightened out, and clubbed again; how they and their firelocks raked at various inclinations like the masts of ships; and how an amateur photographer reviewed, arrayed, and adjusted them, to see his dispositions change before he reached the camera.

The business was funny to see; I do not know that it is graceful to laugh at; and our report of these transactions was received on our return with the shaking of grave heads.

The day had begun ill; eleven hours divided us from sunset; and at any moment, on the most trifling chance, the trouble might begin. The Wightman compound was in a military sense untenable, commanded on three sides by houses and thick bush; the town was computed to contain over a thousand stand of excellent new arms; and retreat to the ships, in the case of an alert, was a recourse not to be thought of. Our talk that morning must have closely reproduced the talk in English garrisons before the Sepoy mutiny;[6] the sturdy doubt that any mischief was in prospect, the sure belief that (should any come) there was nothing left but to go down fighting, the half amused, half anxious attitude of mind in which we were awaiting fresh developments.

The kümmel soon ran out; we were scarce returned before the king had followed us in quest of more. Mr. Corpse was now divested of his more awful attitude, the lawless bulk of him again encased in striped pyjamas; a guardsman brought up the rear with his rifle at the trail; and his majesty was further accompanied by a Rarotongan[7] whalerman and the playful courtier with the turban of frizzed hair. There was never a more lively deputation. The whalerman was gapingly, tearfully tipsy; the courtier walked on air; the king himself was even sportive. Seated in a chair in the Ricks' sitting-room, he bore the brunt of our prayers and menaces unmoved. He was even rated, plied with historic instances, threatened with the men-of-war, ordered to restore the *tapu* on the spot – and nothing in the least affected him. It should be done to-morrow, he said; to-day it was beyond his power, to-day he durst not. 'Is that royal?' cried indignant Mr. Rick. No, it was not royal; had the king been of a royal character we should ourselves have held a different language; and royal or not, he had the best of the dispute. The terms indeed were hardly equal; for the king was the only man who could restore the *tapu*, but the Ricks were not the only people who sold drink. He had but to hold his ground on the first question, and they were sure to weaken on the second. A little struggle they still made for the fashion's sake; and then one exceedingly tipsy deputation departed, greatly rejoicing, a case of brandy wheeling beside them in a barrow. The Rarotongan (whom I had never seen before) wrung me by the hand like a man bound on a far voyage. 'My dear frien'!' he cried, 'good-bye, my dear frien'!' – tears of kümmel standing in his eyes; the king lurched as he went, the courtier ambled, – a strange party of intoxicated children to be intrusted with that barrowful of madness.

You could never say the town was quiet; all morning there was a ferment in the air, an aimless movement and congregation of natives in the street. But it was not before half-past one that a sudden hubbub of voices called us from the house, to find the whole white colony already gathered on the spot as by concerted signal. The Sans Souci was overrun with rabble, the stair and verandah thronged. From all these throats an inarticulate babbling cry went up incessantly; it sounded like the bleating of young lambs, but angrier. In the road his royal highness (whom I had seen so lately in the part of butler) stood crying upon Tom; on the top step, tossed in the hurly-burly, Tom was shouting to the prince. Yet a while the pack swayed about the bar, vociferous. Then came a brutal impulse; the mob reeled, and returned and was rejected; the stair showed a stream of heads; and there shot into view, through the disbanding ranks, three men violently dragging in their midst a fourth. By his hair and his hands, his head forced as low as his knees, his face concealed, he was wrenched from the verandah and whisked along the road into the village, howling as he disappeared. Had his face been raised, we should have seen it bloodied, and the blood was not his own. The courtier with the turban of frizzed hair had paid the costs of this disturbance with the lower part of one ear.

So the brawl passed with no other casualty than might seem comic to the inhumane. Yet we looked round on serious faces and – a fact that spoke volumes – Tom was putting up the shutters on the bar. Custom might go elsewhither, Mr. Williams might profit as he pleased, but Tom had had enough of bar-keeping for that day. Indeed the event had hung on a hair. A man had sought to draw a revolver – on what quarrel I could never learn, and perhaps he himself could not have told; one shot, when the room was so crowded, could scarce have failed to take effect; where many were armed and all tipsy, it could scarce have failed to draw others; and the woman who spied the weapon and the man who seized it may very well have saved the white community.

The mob insensibly melted from the scene; and for the rest of the day our neighbourhood was left in peace and a good deal in solitude. But the tranquillity was only local; 'din' and 'perandi'[8] still flowed in other quarters; and we had one more sight of Gilbert Island violence. In the church, where we had wandered photographing, we were startled by a sudden piercing outcry. The scene, looking forth from the doors of that great hall of shadow, was unforgettable. The palms, the quaint and scattered houses, the flag of the island streaming from its tall staff, glowed with intolerable sunshine. In the midst two women rolled fighting on the grass. The combatants were the more easy to be distinguished, because the one was stripped to the *ridi* and the other wore a *holoku* (sacque) of some lively colour. The first was uppermost, her teeth locked in her adversary's face, shaking her like a dog; the other impotently fought and scratched. So for a moment we saw them wallow and grapple there like vermin; then the mob closed and shut them in.

It was a serious question that night if we should sleep ashore. But we were travellers, folk that had come far in quest of the adventurous; on the first sign of an adventure it would have been a singular inconsistency to have withdrawn; and we sent on board instead for our revolvers. Mindful of Taahauku, Mr. Rick, Mr. Osbourne, and Mrs. Stevenson[9] held an assault of arms on the public highway, and fired at bottles to the admiration of the natives. Captain Reid of the *Equator* stayed on shore with us to be at hand in case of trouble, and we retired to bed at the accustomed hour, agreeably excited by the day's events. The night was exquisite, the silence enchanting; yet as I lay in my hammock looking on the strong moonshine and the quiescent palms, one ugly picture haunted me of the two women, the naked and the clad, locked in that hostile embrace. The harm done was probably not much, yet I could have looked on death and massacre with less revolt. The return to these primeval weapons, the vision of man's beastliness, of his ferality, shocked in me a deeper sense than that with which we count the cost of battles. There are elements in our state and history which it is a pleasure to forget, which it is perhaps the better wisdom not to dwell on. Crime, pestilence, and death are in the day's work; the imagination readily accepts them. It instinctively rejects, on the contrary, whatever shall call up the image of our race upon its lowest terms, as the partner of beasts, beastly itself, dwelling pell-mell and hugger-mugger, hairy man with hairy woman, in the caves of old. And yet to be just to barbarous islanders we must not forget the slums and dens of our cities: I must not forget that I have passed dinnerward through Soho, and seen that which cured me of my dinner.

CHAPTER V

A TALE OF A *TAPU* — CONTINUED

Tuesday, July 16. – It rained in the night, sudden and loud, in Gilbert Island fashion. Before the day, the crowing of a cock aroused me and I wandered in the compound and along the street. The squall was blown by, the moon shone with incomparable lustre, the air lay dead as in a room, and yet all the isle sounded as under a strong shower, the eaves thickly pattering, the lofty palms dripping at larger intervals and with a louder note. In this bold nocturnal light the interior of the houses lay inscrutable, one lump of blackness, save when the moon glinted under the roof, and made a belt of silver, and drew the slanting shadows of the pillars on the floor. Nowhere in all the town was any lamp or ember; not a creature stirred; I thought I was alone to be awake; but the police were faithful to their duty; secretly vigilant, keeping account of time; and a little later, the watchman struck slowly and repeatedly on the cathedral bell; four o'clock, the warning signal.[1] It seemed strange that, in a town resigned to drunkenness and tumult, curfew and réveillé should still be sounded and still obeyed.

The day came, and brought little change. The place still lay silent; the people slept, the town slept. Even the few who were awake, mostly women and children, held their peace and kept within under the strong shadow of the thatch, where you must stop and peer to see them. Through the deserted streets, and past the sleeping houses, a deputation took its way at an early hour to the palace; the king was suddenly awakened, and must listen (probably with a headache) to unpalatable truths. Mrs. Rick, being a sufficient mistress of that difficult tongue, was spokeswoman; she explained to the sick monarch that I was an intimate personal friend of Queen Victoria's; that immediately on my return I should make her a report upon Butaritari; and that if my house should have been again invaded by natives, a man-of-war would be despatched to make reprisals. It was scarce the fact – rather a just and necessary parable of the fact, corrected for latitude; and it certainly told upon the king. He was much affected; he had conceived the notion (he said) that I was a man of some importance, but not dreamed it was as bad as this; and the missionary house was *tapu*'d under a fine of fifty dollars.

So much was announced on the return of the deputation; not any more; and I gathered subsequently that much more had passed. The protection gained was welcome. It had been the most annoying and not the least alarming feature of the day before, that our house was periodically filled with tipsy natives, twenty or thirty at a time, begging drink, fingering our goods, hard to be dislodged,[2] awkward to quarrel with. Queen Victoria's friend (who was soon promoted to be her son) was free from these intrusions. Not only my house, but my neighbourhood as well, was left in peace; even on our walks abroad we were guarded and prepared for; and, like great persons visiting a hospital, saw only the fair side. For the matter of a week we were thus suffered to go out and in and live in a fool's paradise, supposing the king to have kept his word, the *tapu* to be revived and the island once more sober.

Tuesday, July 23. – We dined under a bare trellis erected for the Fourth of July; and here we used to linger by lamplight over coffee and tobacco. In that climate evening approaches without sensible chill; the wind dies out before sunset; heaven glows a while and fades, and darkens into the blueness of the tropical night; swiftly and insensibly the shadows thicken, the stars multiply their number; you look around you and the day is gone. It was then that we would see our Chinaman draw near across the compound in a lurching sphere of light, divided by his shadows; and with the coming of the lamp the night closed about the table. The faces of the company, the spars of the trellis, stood out suddenly bright on a ground of blue and silver, faintly designed with palm-tops and the peaked roofs of houses. Here and there the gloss upon a leaf, or the fracture of a stone, returned an isolated sparkle. All else had vanished. We hung there, illuminated like a galaxy of stars *in vacuo*;[3] we sat, manifest and blind, amid the general ambush of the darkness; and the islanders, passing with light footfalls and low voices in the sand of the road, lingered to observe us, unseen.

On Tuesday the dusk had fallen, the lamp had just been brought, when a missile struck the table with a rattling smack and rebounded past my ear. Three inches to one side and this page had never been written; for the thing travelled like a cannon ball. It was supposed at the time to be a nut, though even at the time I thought it seemed a small one and fell strangely.

Wednesday, July 24. – The dusk had fallen once more, and the lamp been just brought out, when the same business was repeated. And again the missile whistled past my ear. One nut I had been willing to accept; a second, I rejected utterly. A cocoa-nut does not come slinging along on a windless evening, making an angle of about fifteen degrees with the horizon; cocoa-nuts do not fall on successive nights at the same hour and spot; in both cases, besides, a specific moment seemed to have been chosen, that when the lamp was just carried out, a specific person threatened, and that the head of the family. I may have been right or wrong, but I believed I was the mark of some intimidation; believed the missile was a stone, aimed not to hit, but to frighten.

No idea makes a man more angry. I ran into the road, where the natives were as usual promenading in the dark; Maka joined me with a lantern; and I ran from one to another, glared in quite innocent faces, put useless questions, and proffered idle threats. Thence I carried my wrath (which was worthy the son of any queen in history) to the Ricks. They heard me with depression, assured me this trick of throwing a stone into a family dinner was not new; that it meant mischief, and was of a piece with the alarming disposition of the natives. And then the truth, so long concealed from us, came out. The king had broken his promise, he had defied the deputation; the *tapu* was still dormant, the Land We Live In still selling drink, and that quarter of the town disturbed and menaced by perpetual broils. But there was worse ahead: a feast was now preparing for the birthday of the little princess; and the tributary chiefs of Kuma and Little Makin were expected daily. Strong in a following of numerous and somewhat savage clansmen, each of these was believed, like a Douglas of old,[4] to be of doubtful loyalty. Kuma (a little pot-bellied fellow) never visited the palace, never entered the town, but sat on the beach on a mat, his gun across his knees, parading his mistrust and scorn; Karaiti of Makin, although he was more bold, was not supposed to be more friendly; and not only were these vassals jealous of the throne, but the followers on either side shared in the animosity. Brawls had already taken place; blows had passed which might at any moment be repaid in blood. Some of the strangers were already here and already drinking; if the debauch continued after the bulk of them had come, a collision, perhaps a revolution, was to be expected.

The sale of drink is in this group a measure of the jealousy of traders; one begins, the others are constrained to follow; and to him who has the most gin, and sells it the most recklessly, the lion's share of copra is assured. It is felt by all to be an extreme expedient, neither safe, decent, nor dignified. A trader on Tarawa,[5] heated by an eager rivalry, brought many cases of gin. He told me he sat afterwards day and night in his house till it was finished, not daring to arrest the sale, not venturing to go forth, the bush all round him filled with howling drunkards. At night, above all, when he was afraid to sleep, and heard shots and voices about him in the darkness, his remorse was black.

'My God!' he reflected, 'if I was to lose my life on such a wretched business!' Often and often, in the story of the Gilberts, this scene has been repeated; and the remorseful trader sat beside his lamp, longing for the day, listening with agony for the sound of murder, registering resolutions for the future. For the business is easy to begin, but hazardous to stop. The natives are in their way a just and law-abiding people, mindful of their debts, docile to the voice of their own institutions; when the *tapu* is re-enforced they will cease drinking; but the white who seeks to antedate the movement by refusing liquor does so at his peril.

Hence, in some degree, the anxiety and helplessness of Mr. Rick. He and Tom, alarmed by the rabblement of the Sans Souci, had stopped the sale; they had done so without danger, because the Land We Live In still continued selling; it was claimed, besides, that they had been the first to begin. What step could be taken? Could Mr. Rick visit Mr. Muller (with whom he was not on terms) and address him thus: 'I was getting ahead of you, now you are getting ahead of me, and I ask you to forgo your profit. I got my place closed in safety, thanks to your continuing; but now I think you have continued long enough. I begin to be alarmed; and because I am afraid I ask you to confront a certain danger'? It was not to be thought of. Something else had to be found; and there was one person at one end of the town who was at least not interested in copra. There was little else to be said in favour of myself as an ambassador. I had arrived in the Wightman schooner, I was living in the Wightman compound, I was the daily associate of the Wightman coterie. It was egregious enough that I should now intrude unasked in the private affairs of Crawford's agent, and press upon him the sacrifice of his interests and the venture of his life. But bad as I might be, there was none better; since the affair of the stone I was, besides, sharp-set to be doing, the idea of a delicate interview attracted me, and I thought it policy to show myself abroad.

The night was very dark. There was service in the church, and the building glimmered through all its crevices like a dim Kirk Allowa'.[6] I saw few other lights, but was indistinctly aware of many people stirring in the darkness, and a hum and sputter of low talk that sounded stealthy. I believe (in the old phrase) my beard was sometimes on my shoulder[7] as I went. Muller's was but partly lighted, and quite silent, and the gate was fastened. I could by no means manage to undo the latch. No wonder, since I found it afterwards to be four or five feet long – a fortification in itself. As I still fumbled, a dog came on the inside and snuffed suspiciously at my hands, so that I was reduced to calling 'House ahoy!' Mr. Muller came down and put his chin across the paling in the dark. 'Who is that?' said he, like one who has no mind to welcome strangers.

'My name is Stevenson,' said I.

'O, Mr. Stevens! I didn't know you. Come inside.'

We stepped into the dark store, when I leaned upon the counter and he against the wall. All the light came from the sleeping-room, where I saw his family being put to bed; it struck full in my face, but Mr. Muller stood in shadow. No doubt he expected what was coming, and sought the advantage of position; but for a man who wished to persuade and had nothing to conceal, mine was the preferable.

'Look here,' I began, 'I hear you are selling to the natives.'

'Others have done that before me,' he returned pointedly.

'No doubt,' said I, 'and I have nothing to do with the past, but the future. I want you to promise you will handle these spirits carefully.'

'Now what is your motive in this?' he asked, and then, with a sneer, 'Are you afraid of your life?'

'That is nothing to the purpose,' I replied. 'I know, and you know, these spirits ought not to be sold at all.'

'Tom and Mr. Rick have sold them before.'

'I have nothing to do with Tom and Mr. Rick. All I know is I have heard them both refuse.'

'No, I suppose you have nothing to do with them. Then you are just afraid of your life.'

'Come now,' I cried, being perhaps a little stung, 'you know in your heart I am asking a reasonable thing. I don't ask you to lose your profit – though I would prefer to see no spirits brought here, as you would –'

'I don't say I wouldn't. I didn't begin this,' he interjected.

'No, I don't suppose you did,' said I. 'And I don't ask you to lose; I ask you to give me your word, man to man, that you will make no native drunk.'

Up to now Mr. Muller had maintained an attitude very trying to my temper; but he had maintained it with difficulty, his sentiment being all upon my side; and here he changed ground for the worse. 'It isn't me that sells,' said he.

'No, it's that nigger,' I agreed. 'But he's yours to buy and sell; you have your hand on the nape of his neck; and I ask you – I have my wife here – to use the authority you have.'

He hastily returned to his old ward. 'I don't deny I could if I wanted,' said he. 'But there's no danger, the natives are all quiet. You're just afraid of your life.'

I do not like to be called a coward, even by implication; and here I lost my temper and propounded an untimely ultimatum. 'You had better put it plain,' I cried. 'Do you mean to refuse me what I ask?'

'I don't want either to refuse it or grant it,' he replied.

'You'll find you have to do the one thing or the other, and right now!' I cried, and then, striking into a happier vein, 'Come,' said I, 'you're a better sort than that. I see what's wrong with you – you think I came from the opposite camp. I see the sort of man you are, and you know that what I ask is right.'

Again he changed ground. 'If the natives get any drink, it isn't safe to stop them,' he objected.

'I'll be answerable for the bar,' I said. 'We are three men and four revolvers; we'll come at a word, and hold the place against the village.'

'You don't know what you're talking about; it's too dangerous!' he cried.

'Look here,' said I, 'I don't mind much about losing that life you talk so much of; but I mean to lose it the way I want to, and that is, putting a stop to all this beastliness.'

He talked a while about his duty to the firm; I minded not at all, I was secure of victory. He was but waiting to capitulate, and looked about for any potent[8] to relieve the strain. In the gush of light from the bedroom door I spied a cigar-holder on the desk. 'That is well coloured,' said I.

'Will you take a cigar?' said he.

I took it and held it up unlighted. 'Now,' said I, 'you promise me.'

'I promise you you won't have any trouble from natives that have drunk at my place,' he replied.

'That is all I ask,' said I, and showed it was not by immediately offering to try his stock.

So far as it was anyway critical our interview here ended. Mr. Muller had thenceforth ceased to regard me as an emissary from his rivals, dropped his defensive attitude, and spoke as he believed. I could make out that he would already, had he dared, have stopped the sale himself. Not quite daring, it may be imagined how he resented the idea of interference from those who had (by his own statement) first led him on, then deserted him in the breach, and now (sitting themselves in safety) egged him on to a new peril, which was all gain to them, all loss to him. I asked him what he thought of the danger from the feast.

'I think worse of it than any of you,' he answered. 'They were shooting around here last night, and I heard the balls too. I said to myself, "That's bad." What gets me is why you should be making this row up at your end. I should be the first to go.'

It was a thoughtless wonder. The consolation of being second is not great; the fact, not the order of going – there was our concern.

Scott talks moderately of looking forward to a time of fighting 'with a feeling that resembled pleasure.' The resemblance seems rather an identity. In modern life, contact is ended; man grows impatient of endless manoeuvres; and to approach the fact, to find ourselves where we can push our advantage home, and stand a fair risk, and see at last what we are made of, stirs the blood. It was so at least with all my family, who bubbled with delight at the approach of trouble; and we sat deep into the night like a pack of schoolboys, preparing the revolvers and arranging plans against the morrow. It promised certainly to be a busy and eventful day. The Old Men were to be summoned to confront me on the question of the *tapu*; Muller might call us at any moment to garrison his bar; and suppose Muller to fail, we decided in a family council to take that matter into our own hands, the Land We Live In at the pistol's mouth, and make the polysyllabic Williams dance to a new tune. As I recall our humour, I think it would have gone hard with the mulatto.

Wednesday, July 24.[9] – It was as well, and yet it was disappointing that these thunder-clouds rolled off in silence. Whether the Old Men recoiled from an interview with Queen Victoria's son, whether Muller had secretly intervened, or whether the step flowed naturally from the fears of the king and the nearness of the feast, the *tapu* was early that morning re-enforced; not a day too soon, from the manner the boats began to arrive thickly, and the town was filled with the big rowdy vassals of Karaiti.

The effect lingered for some time on the minds of the traders; it was with the approval of all present that I helped to draw up a petition to the United States, praying for a law against the liquor trade in the Gilberts; and it was at this request that I added, under my own name, a brief testimony of what had passed; – useless pains; since the whole reposes, probably unread and possibly unopened, in a pigeon-hole at Washington.[10]

Sunday, July 28. – This day we had the afterpiece of the debauch. The king and queen, in European clothes, and followed by armed guards, attended church for the first time, and sat perched aloft in a precarious dignity under the barrel-hoop. Before sermon his majesty clambered from the dais, stood lopsidedly upon the gravel floor, and in a few words abjured drinking. The queen followed suit with a yet briefer allocution. All the men in church were next addressed in turn; each held up his right hand, and the affair was over – throne and church were reconciled.

CHAPTER VI

THE FIVE DAYS' FESTIVAL

Thursday, July 25. – The street was this day much enlivened by the presence of the men from Little Makin; they average taller than Butaritarians, and, being on a holiday, went wreathed with yellow leaves and gorgeous in vivid colours. They are said to be more savage, and to be proud of the distinction. Indeed, it seemed to us they swaggered in the town, like plaided Highlanders upon the streets of Inverness, conscious of barbaric virtues.

In the afternoon the summer parlour was observed to be packed with people; others standing outside and stooping to peer under the eaves, like children at home about a circus. It was the Makin company, rehearsing for the day of competition. Karaiti sat in the front row close to the singers, where we were summoned (I suppose in honour of Queen Victoria) to join him. A strong breathless heat reigned under the iron roof, and the air was heavy with the scent of wreaths. The singers, with fine mats about their loins, cocoa-nut feathers set in rings upon their fingers, and their heads crowned with yellow leaves, sat on the floor by companies. A varying number of soloists stood up for different songs; and these bore the chief part in the music. But the full force of the companies, even when not singing, contributed continuously to the effect, and marked the ictus of the measure,[1] mimicking, grimacing, casting up their heads and eyes, fluttering the feathers on their fingers, clapping hands, or beating (loud as a kettle-drum) on the left breast; the time was exquisite, the music barbarous, but full of conscious art. I noted some devices constantly employed. A sudden change would be introduced (I think of key) with no break of the measure, but emphasised by a sudden dramatic heightening of the voice and a swinging, general gesticulation. The voices of the soloists would begin far apart in a rude discord, and gradually draw together to a unison; which, when they had reached, they were joined and drowned by the full chorus. The ordinary, hurried, barking, unmelodious movement of the voices would at times be broken and glorified by a psalm-like strain of melody, often well constructed, or seeming so by contrast. There was much variety of measure, and towards the end of each piece, when the fun became fast and furious, a recourse to this figure –

$$\frac{2}{4} \; | \; \flat \; \flat \; \flat \; | \; \flat \; \flat \; \flat \; | \; \flat \; \flat \; \flat \; |$$

It is difficult to conceive what fire and devilry they get into these hammering finales; all go together, voices, hands, eyes, leaves, and fluttering finger-rings; the chorus swings to the eye, the song throbs on the ear; the faces are convulsed with enthusiasm and effort.

Presently the troop stood up in a body, the drums forming a half-circle for the soloists, who were sometimes five or even more in number. The songs that followed were highly dramatic; though I had none to give me any explanation, I would at times make out some shadowy but decisive outline of a plot; and I was continually reminded of certain quarrelsome concerted scenes in grand operas at home; just so the single voices issue from and fall again into the general volume; just so do the performers separate and crowd together, brandish the raised hand, and roll the eye to heaven – or the gallery. Already this is beyond the Thespian model;[2] the art of this people is already past the embryo; song, dance, drums, quartette and solo – it is the drama full developed although still in miniature. Of all so-called dancing in the South Seas, that which I saw in Butaritari stands easily the first. The *hula*, as it may be viewed by the speedy globe-trotter in Honolulu, is surely the most dull of man's inventions, and the spectator yawns under its length as at a college lecture or a parliamentary debate. But the Gilbert Island dance leads on the mind; it thrills, rouses, subjugates; it has the essence of all art, an unexplored imminent significance. Where so many are engaged, and where all must make (at a given moment) the same swift, elaborate, and often arbitrary movement, the toil of rehearsal is of course extreme. But they begin as children. A child and a man may often be seen together in a *maniap'*: the man sings and gesticulates, the child stands before him with streaming tears and tremulously copies him in act and sound; it is the Gilbert Island artist learning (as all artists must) his art in sorrow.

I may seem to praise too much; here is a passage from my wife's diary, which proves that I was not alone in being moved, and completes the picture: – 'The conductor gave the cue, and all the dancers, waving their arms, swaying their bodies, and clapping their breasts in perfect time, opened with an introductory. The performers remained seated, except two, and once three, and twice a single soloist. These stood in the group, making a slight movement with the feet and rhythmical quiver of the body as they sang. There was a pause after the introductory, and then the real business of the opera – for it was no less – began; an opera where every singer was an accomplished actor. The leading man, in an impassioned ecstasy which possessed him from head to foot, seemed transfigured; once it was as though a strong wind had swept over the stage – their arms, their feathered fingers thrilling with an emotion that shook my nerves as well: heads and bodies followed like a field of grain before a gust. My blood came hot and cold, tears pricked my eyes, my head whirled, I felt an almost irresistible impulse to join the dancers. One drama, I think, I very nearly understood. A fierce and savage old man took the solo part. He sang of the birth of a prince, and how he was tenderly rocked in his mother's arms; of his boyhood, when he excelled his fellows in swimming, climbing, and all athletic sports; of his youth, when he went out to sea with his boat and fished; of his manhood, when he married a wife who cradled a son of his own in her arms. Then came the alarm of war, and a great battle, of which for a time the issue was doubtful; but the hero conquered, as he always does, and with a tremendous burst of the victors the piece closed. There were also comic pieces, which caused great amusement. During one, an old man behind me clutched me by the arm, shook his finger in my face with a roguish smile, and said something with a chuckle, which I took to be the equivalent of "O, you women, you women; it is true of you all!" I fear it was not complimentary. At no time was there the least sign of the ugly indecency of the eastern islands.[3] All was poetry pure and simple. The music itself was as complex as our own, though constructed on an entirely different basis; once or twice I was startled by a bit of something very like the best English sacred music, but it was only for an instant. At last there was a longer pause, and this time the dancers were all on their feet. As the drama went on the interest grew. The performers appealed to each other, to the audience, to the heaven above; they took counsel with each other, the conspirators drew together in a knot; it was just an opera, the drums coming in at proper intervals, the tenor, baritone, and bass all where they should be – except that the voices were all of the same calibre. A woman once sang from the back row with a very fine contralto voice spoilt by being made artificially nasal; I notice all the women affect that unpleasantness. At one time a boy of angelic beauty was the soloist; and at another, a child of six or eight, doubtless an infant phenomenon being trained, was placed in the centre. The little fellow was desperately frightened and embarrassed at first, but towards the close warmed up to his work and showed much dramatic talent. The changing expressions on the faces of the dancers were so speaking, that it seemed a great stupidity not to understand them.'

Our neighbour at this performance, Karaiti, somewhat favours his Butaritarian majesty in shape and feature, being like him portly, bearded, and Oriental. In character he seems the reverse: alert, smiling, jovial, jocular, industrious. At home in his own island, he labours himself like a slave, and makes his people labour like a slave-driver. He takes an interest in ideas. George the trader[4] told him about flying-machines. 'Is that true, George?' he asked. 'It is in the papers,' replied George. 'Well,' said Karaiti, 'if that man can do it with machinery, I can do it without'; and he designed and made a pair of wings, strapped them on his shoulders, went to the end of a pier, launched himself into space, and fell bulkily into the sea. His wives fished him out, for his wings hindered him in swimming. 'George,' said he, pausing as he went up to change, 'George, you lie.' He had eight wives, for his small realm still follows ancient customs; but he showed embarrassment when this was mentioned to my wife. 'Tell her I have only brought one here,' he said anxiously. Altogether the Black Douglas[5] pleased us much; and as we heard fresh details of the king's uneasiness, and saw for ourselves that all the weapons in the summer parlour had been hid, we watched with the more admiration the cause of all this anxiety rolling on his big legs, with his big smiling face, apparently unarmed, and certainly unattended, through the hostile town. The Red Douglas,[6] pot-bellied Kuma, having perhaps heard word of the debauch, remained upon his fief; his vassals thus came uncommanded to the feast, and swelled the following of Karaiti.

Friday, July 26. – At night in the dark, the singers of Makin paraded in the road before our house and sang the song of the princess. 'This is the day; she was born to-day; Nei Kamaunaue was born to-day – a beautiful princess, Queen of Butaritari.' So I was told it went in endless iteration. The song was of course out of season, and the performance only a rehearsal. But it was a serenade besides; a delicate attention to ourselves from our new friend, Karaiti.

Saturday, July 27. – We had announced a performance of the magic lantern to-night in church; and this brought the king to visit us. In honour of the Black Douglas (I suppose) his usual two guardsmen were now increased to four; and the squad made an outlandish figure as they straggled after him, in straw hats, kilts and jackets. Three carried their arms reversed, the butts over their shoulders, the muzzles menacing the king's plump back; the fourth had passed his weapon behind his neck, and held it there with arms extended like a backboard. The visit was extraordinarily long. The king, no longer galvanised with gin, said and did nothing. He sat collapsed in a chair and let a cigar go out. It was hot, it was sleepy, it was cruel dull; there was no resource but to spy in the countenance of Tebureimoa for some remaining trait of Mr. Corpse the butcher. His hawk nose, crudely depressed and flattened at the point, did truly seem to us to smell of midnight murder. When he took his leave, Maka bade me observe him going down the stair (or rather ladder) from the verandah. 'Old man,' said Maka. 'Yes,' said I, 'and yet I suppose not old man.' 'Young man,' returned Maka, 'perhaps fo'ty.' And I have heard since he is most likely younger.

While the magic lantern was showing, I skulked without in the dark. The voice of Maka, excitedly explaining the Scripture slides,[7] seemed to fill not the church only, but the neighbourhood. All else was silent. Presently a distant sound of singing arose and approached; and a procession drew near along the road, the hot clean smell of the men and women striking in my face delightfully. At the corner, arrested by the voice of Maka and the lightening and darkening of the church, they paused. They had no mind to go nearer, that was plain. They were Makin people, I believe, probably staunch heathens, contemners of the missionary and his works. Of a sudden, however, a man broke from their company, took to his heels, and fled into the church; next moment three had followed him; the next it was a covey of near upon a score, all pelting for their lives. So the little band of the heathen paused irresolute at the corner, and melted before the attractions of a magic lantern, like a glacier in spring. The more staunch vainly taunted the deserters; these fled in a guilty silence, but still fled; and when at length the leader found the wit or the authority to get his troop in motion and revive the singing, it was with much diminished forces that they passed musically on up the dark road.

Meanwhile inside the luminous pictures brightened and faded. I stood for some while unobserved in the rear of the spectators, when I could hear just in front of me a pair of lovers following the show with interest, the male playing the part of interpreter and (like Adam) mingling caresses with his lecture.[8] The wild animals, a tiger in particular, and that old school-treat favourite, the sleeper and the mouse, were hailed with joy; but the chief marvel and delight was in the gospel series. Maka, in the opinion of his aggrieved wife, did not properly rise to the occasion. 'What is the matter with the man? Why can't he talk?' she cried. The matter with the man, I think, was the greatness of the opportunity; he reeled under his good fortune; and whether he did ill or well, the exposure of these pious 'phantoms' did as a matter of fact silence in all that part of the island the voice of the scoffer. 'Why then,' the word went round, 'why then, the Bible is true!' And on our return afterwards[9] we were told the impression was yet lively, and those who had seen might be heard telling those who had not, 'O yes, it is all true; these things all happened, we have seen the pictures.' The argument is not so childish as it seems; for I doubt if these islanders are acquainted with any other mode of representation but photography; so that the picture of an event (on the old melodrama principle that 'the camera cannot lie, Joseph,') would appear strong proof of its occurrence. The fact amused us the more because our slides were some of them ludicrously silly, and one (Christ before Pilate) was received with shouts of merriment, in which even Maka was constrained to join.

Sunday, July 28. – Karaiti came to ask for a repetition of the 'phantoms' – this was the accepted word – and, having received a promise, turned and left my humble roof without the shadow of a salutation. I felt it impolite to have the least appearance of pocketing a slight; the times had been too difficult, and were still too doubtful; and Queen Victoria's son was bound to maintain the honour of his house. Karaiti was accordingly summoned that evening to the Ricks, where Mrs. Rick fell foul of him in words, and Queen Victoria's son assailed him with indignant looks. I was the ass with the lion's skin;[10] I could not roar in the language of the Gilbert Islands; but I could stare. Karaiti declared he had meant no offence; apologised in a sound, hearty, gentlemanly manner; and became at once at his ease. He had in a dagger to examine, and announced he would come to price it on the morrow, to-day being Sunday; this nicety in a heathen with eight wives surprised me. The dagger was 'good for killing fish,' he said roguishly; and was supposed to have his eye upon fish upon two legs. It is at least odd that in Eastern Polynesia fish was the accepted euphemism for the human sacrifice. Asked as to the population of his island, Karaiti called out to his vassals who sat waiting him outside the door, and they put it at four hundred and fifty; but (added Karaiti jovially) there will soon be plenty more, for all the women are in the family way. Long before we separated I had quite forgotten his offence. He, however, still bore it in mind; and with a very courteous inspiration returned early on the next day, paid us a long visit, and punctiliously said farewell when he departed.

Monday, July 29. – The great day came round at last. In the first hours the night was startled by the sound of clapping hands and the chant of Nei Kamaunaue; its melancholy, slow, and somewhat menacing measures broken at intervals by a formidable shout. The little morsel of humanity thus celebrated in the dark hours was observed at midday playing on the green entirely naked, and equally unobserved and unconcerned.

The summer parlour on its artificial islet, relieved against the shimmering lagoon, and shimmering itself with sun and tinned iron, was all day crowded about by eager men and women. Within, it was boxed full of islanders, of any age and size, and in every degree of nudity and finery. So close we squatted, that at one time I had a mighty handsome woman on my knees, two little naked urchins having their feet against my back. There might be a dame in full attire of *holoku*[11] and hat and flowers; and her next neighbour might the next moment strip some little rag of a shift from her fat shoulders and come out a monument of flesh, painted rather than covered by the hairbreadth *ridi*. Little ladies who thought themselves too great to appear undraped upon so high a festival were seen to pause outside in the broad sunshine, their miniature *ridi*s in their hand; a moment more and they were full-dressed and entered the concert-room.

At either end stood up to sing, or sat down to rest, the alternate companies of singers; Kuma and Little Makin on the north, Butaritari and its conjunct hamlets to the south; both groups conspicuous in barbaric bravery. In the midst, between these rival camps of troubadours, a bench was placed; and here the king and queen throned it, some two or three feet above the crowded audience on the floor – Tebureimoa as usual in his striped pyjamas with a satchel strapped across one shoulder, doubtless (in the island fashion) to contain his pistols; the queen in a purple *holoku*, her abundant hair let down, a fan in her hand. The bench was turned facing to the strangers, a piece of well-considered civility; and when it was the turn of Butaritari to sing, the pair must twist round on the bench, lean their elbows on the rail, and turn to us the spectacle of their broad backs. The royal couple occasionally solaced themselves with a clay pipe; and the pomp of state was further heightened by the rifles of a picket of the guard.

With this kingly countenance, and ourselves squatted on the ground, we heard several songs from one side or the other. Then royalty and its guards withdrew, and Queen Victoria's son and daughter-in-law were summoned by acclamation to the vacant throne. Our pride was perhaps a little modified when we were joined on our high places by a certain thriftless loafer of a white;[12] and yet I was glad too, for the man had a smattering of native, and could give me some idea of the subject of the songs. One was patriotic, and dared Tembinok' of Apemama, the terror of the group, to an invasion. One mimed the planting of taro and the harvest-home. Some were historical, and commemorated kings and the illustrious chances of their time, such as a bout of drinking or a war. One, at least, was a drama of domestic interest, excellently played by the troop from Makin. It told the story of a man who has lost his wife, at first bewails her loss, then seeks another: the earlier strains (or acts) are played exclusively by men; but towards the end a woman appears, who has just lost her husband; and I suppose the pair console each other, for the finale seemed of happy omen. Of some of the songs my informant told me briefly they were 'like about the *weemen*'; this I could have guessed myself. Each side (I should have said) was strengthened by one or two women. They were all soloists, did not very often join in the performance, but stood disengaged at the back part of the stage, and looked (in *ridi*, necklace, and dressed hair) for all the world like European ballet-dancers. When the song was anyway broad these ladies came particularly to the front; and it was singular to see that, after each entry, the *première danseuse* pretended to be overcome by shame, as though led on beyond what she had meant, and her male assistants made a feint of driving her away like one who had disgraced herself. Similar affectations accompany certain truly obscene dances of Samoa, where they are very well in place. Here it was different. The words, perhaps, in this free-spoken world, were gross enough to make a carter blush; and the most suggestive feature was this feint of shame. For such parts the women showed some disposition; they were pert, they were neat, they were acrobatic, they were at times really amusing, and some of them were pretty. But this is not the artist's field; there is the whole width of heaven between such capering and ogling, and the strange rhythmic gestures, and strange, rapturous, frenzied faces with which the best of the male dancers held us spellbound through a Gilbert Island ballet.

Almost from the first it was apparent that the people of the city were defeated. I might have thought them even good, only I had the other troop before my eyes to correct my standard, and remind me continually of 'the little more, and how much it is.' Perceiving themselves worsted, the choir of Butaritari grew confused, blundered, and broke down; amid this hubbub of unfamiliar intervals I should not myself have recognised the slip, but the audience were quick to catch it, and to jeer. To crown all, the Makin company began a dance of truly superlative merit. I know not what it was about, I was too much absorbed to ask. In one act a part of the chorus, squealing in some strange falsetto, produced very much the effect of our orchestra; in another, the dancers, leaping like jumping-jacks, with arms extended, passed through and through each other's ranks with extraordinary speed, neatness, and humour. A more laughable effect I never saw; in any European theatre it would have brought the house down, and the island audience roared with laughter and applause. This filled up the measure for the rival company, and they forgot themselves and decency. After each act or figure of the ballet, the performers pause a moment standing, and the next is introduced by the clapping of hands in triplets. Not until the end of the whole ballet do they sit down, which is the signal for the rivals to stand up. But now all rules were to be broken. During the interval following on this great applause, the company of Butaritari leaped suddenly to their feet and most unhandsomely began a performance of their own. It was strange to see the men of Makin staring; I have seen a tenor in Europe stare with the same blank dignity into a hissing theatre; but presently, to my surprise, they sobered down, gave up the unsung remainder of their ballet, resumed their seats, and suffered their ungallant adversaries to go on and finish. Nothing would suffice. Again, at the first interval, Butaritari unhandsomely cut in; Makin, irritated in turn, followed the example; and the two companies of dancers remained permanently standing, continuously clapping hands, and regularly cutting across each other at each pause. I expected blows to begin with any moment; and our position in the midst was highly unstrategical. But the Makin people had a better thought; and upon a fresh interruption turned and trooped out of the house. We followed them, first because these were the artists, second because they were guests and had been scurvily ill-used. A large population of our neighbours did the same, so that the causeway was filled from end to end by the procession of deserters; and the Butaritari choir was left to sing for its own pleasure in an empty house, having gained the point and lost the audience. It was surely fortunate that there was no one drunk; but, drunk or sober, where else would a scene so irritating have concluded without blows?

The last stage and glory of this auspicious day was of our own providing – the second and positively the last appearance of the phantoms. All round the church, groups sat outside, in the night, where they could see nothing; perhaps ashamed to enter, certainly finding some shadowy pleasure in the mere proximity. Within, about one-half of the great shed was densely packed with people. In the midst, on the royal dais, the lantern luminously smoked; chance rays of light struck out the earnest countenance of our Chinaman grinding the hand-organ; a fainter glimmer showed off the rafters and their shadows in the hollow of the roof; the pictures shone and vanished on the screen; and as each appeared, there would run a hush, a whisper, a strong shuddering rustle, and a chorus of small cries among the crowd. There sat by me the mate of a wrecked schooner.[13] 'They would think this a strange sight in Europe or the States,' said he, 'going on in a building like this, all tied with bits of string.'

CHAPTER VII

HUSBAND AND WIFE

The trader accustomed to the manners of Eastern Polynesia has a lesson to learn among the Gilberts. The *ridi* is but a spare attire; as late as thirty years back the women went naked until marriage; within ten years the custom lingered; and these facts, above all when heard in description, conveyed a very false idea of the manners of the group. A very intelligent missionary described it (in its former state) as a 'Paradise of naked women' for the resident whites. It was at least a platonic Paradise, where Lothario[1] ventured at his peril. Since 1860, fourteen whites have perished on a single island, all for the same cause, all found where they had no business, and speared by some indignant father of a family; the figure was given me by one of their contemporaries who had been more prudent and survived. The strange persistence of these fourteen martyrs might seem to point to monomania or a series of romantic passions; gin is the more likely key. The poor buzzards sat alone in their houses by an open case; they drank; their brain was fired; they stumbled towards the nearest houses on chance; and the dart went through their liver. In place of a Paradise the trader found an archipelago of fierce husbands and of virtuous women. 'Of course if you wish to make love to them, it's the same as anywhere else,' observed a trader[2] innocently; but he and his companions rarely so choose.

The trader must be credited with a virtue: he often makes a kind and loyal husband. Some of the worst beachcombers in the Pacific, some of the last of the old school, have fallen in my path, and some of them were admirable to their native wives, and one made a despairing widower. The position of a trader's wife in the Gilberts is, besides, unusually enviable. She shares the immunities of her husband. Curfew in Butaritari sounds for her in vain. Long after the bell is rung and the great island ladies are confined for the night to their own roof, this chartered libertine may scamper and giggle through the deserted streets or go down to bathe in the dark. The resources of the store are at her hand; she goes arrayed like a queen, and feasts delicately every day upon tinned meats. And she who was perhaps of no regard or station among natives sits with captains, and is entertained on board of schooners. Five of these privileged dames were some time our neighbours. Four were handsome skittish lasses, gamesome like children, and like children liable to fits of pouting. They wore dresses by day, but there was a tendency after dark to strip these lendings and to career and squall about the compound in the aboriginal *ridi*. Games of cards were continually played, with shells for counters; their course was much marred by cheating; and the end of a round (above all if a man was of the party) resolved itself into a scrimmage for the counters. The fifth was a matron. It was a picture to see her sail to church on a Sunday, a parasol in hand, a nursemaid following, and the baby buried in a trade hat and armed with a patent feeding-bottle. The service was enlivened by her continual supervision and correction of the maid. It was impossible not to fancy the baby was a doll, and the church some European playroom. All these women were legitimately married. It is true that the certificate of one, when she proudly showed it, proved to run thus, that she was 'married for one night,'[3] and her gracious partner was at liberty to 'send her to hell' the next morning; but she was none the wiser or the worse for the dastardly trick. Another, I heard, was married on a work of mine in a pirated edition; it answered the purpose as well as a hall Bible.[4] Notwithstanding all these allurements of social distinction, rare food and raiment, a comparative vacation from toil, and legitimate marriage contracted on a pirated edition, the trader must sometimes seek long before he can be mated. While I was in the group one had been eight months on the quest, and he was still a bachelor.

Within strictly native society the old laws and practices were harsh, but not without a certain stamp of high-mindedness. Stealthy adultery was punished with death; open elopement was properly considered virtue in comparison, and compounded for a fine in land. The male adulterer alone seems to have been punished. It is correct manners for a jealous man to hang himself; a jealous woman has a different remedy – she bites her rival. Ten or twenty years ago it was a capital offence to raise a woman's *ridi*; to this day it is still punished with a heavy fine; and the garment itself is still symbolically sacred. Suppose a piece of land to be disputed in Butaritari, the claimant who shall first hang a *ridi* on the *tapu*-post has gained his cause, since no one can remove or touch it but himself.

The *ridi* was the badge not of the woman but the wife, the mark not of her sex but of her station. It was the collar on the slave's neck, the brand on merchandise. The adulterous woman seems to have been spared; were the husband offended, it would be a poor consolation to send his draught cattle to the shambles. Karaiti, to this day, calls his eight wives 'his horses,' some trader having explained to him the employment of these animals on farms; and Nanteitei hired out his wives to do mason-work. Husbands, at least when of high rank, had the power of life and death; even whites seem to have possessed it; and their wives, when they had transgressed beyond forgiveness, made haste to pronounce the formula of deprecation – *i kana kim*.[5] This form of words had so much virtue that a condemned criminal, repeating it on a particular day to the king who had condemned him, must be instantly released. It is an offer of abasement, and, strangely enough, the reverse – the imitation – is a common vulgar insult in Great Britain to this day.[6] I give a scene between a trader[7] and his Gilbert Island wife, as it was told me by the husband, now one of the oldest residents, but then a freshman in the group.

'Go and light a fire,' said the trader, 'and when I have brought this oil I will cook some fish.'

The woman grunted at him, island fashion.

'I am not a pig that you should grunt at me,' said he.

'I know you are not a pig,' said the woman, 'neither am I your slave.'

'To be sure you are not my slave, and if you do not care to stop with me, you had better go home to your people,' said he. 'But in the meantime go and light the fire; and when I have brought this oil I will cook some fish.'

She went as if to obey; and presently when the trader looked she had built a fire so big that the cook-house was catching in flames.

'*I kana kim!*' she cried, as she saw him coming; but he recked not, and hit her with a cooking-pot. The leg pierced her skull, blood spouted, it was thought she was a dead woman, and the natives surrounded the house in a menacing expectation. Another white[8] was present, a man of older experience. 'You will have us both killed if you go on like this,' he cried. 'She had said *i kana kim!*' If she had not said *i kana kim* he might have struck her with a caldron. It was not the blow that made the crime, but the disregard of an accepted formula.

Polygamy, the particular sacredness of wives, their semi-servile state, their seclusion in kings' harems, even their privilege of biting, all would seem to indicate a Mohammedan society and the opinion of the soullessness of woman. And not so in the least. It is a mere appearance. After you have studied these extremes in one house, you may go to the next and find all reversed, the woman the mistress, the man only the first of her thralls. The authority is not with the husband as such, nor the wife as such. It resides in the chief or the chief-woman; in him or her who has inherited the lands of the clan, and stands to the clansman in the place of parent, exacting their service, answerable for their fines. There is but the one source of power and the one ground of dignity – rank. The king married a chief-woman; she became his menial, and must work with her hands on Messrs. Wightman's pier. The king divorced her; she regained at once her former state and power. She married the Hawaiian sailor, and behold the man is her flunkey and can be shown the door at pleasure. Nay, and such low-born lords are even corrected physically, and, like grown but dutiful children, must endure the discipline.

We were intimate in one such household, that of Nei Takauti and Nan Tok';[9] I put the lady first of necessity. During our week of fool's paradise, Mrs. Stevenson had gone alone to the sea-side of the island after shells. I am very sure the proceeding was unsafe; and she soon perceived a man and woman watching her.[10] Do what she would, her guardians held her steadily in view; and when the afternoon began to fall, and they thought she had stayed long enough, took her in charge, and by signs and broken English ordered her home. On the way the lady drew from her earring-hole a clay pipe, the husband lighted it, and it was handed to my unfortunate wife, who knew not how to refuse the incommodious favour; and when they were all come to our house, the pair sat down beside her on the floor, and improved the occasion with prayer. From that day they were our family friends; bringing thrice a day the beautiful island garlands of white flowers, visiting us any evening, and frequently carrying us down to their own *maniap'* in return, the woman leading Mrs. Stevenson by the hand like one child with another.

Nan Tok', the husband, was young, extremely handsome, of the most approved good humour, and suffering in his precarious station from suppressed high spirits. Nei Takauti, the wife, was getting old; her grown son by a former marriage had just hanged himself before his mother's eyes in despair at a well-merited rebuke. Perhaps she had never been beautiful, but her face was full of character, her eye of sombre fire. She was a high chief-woman, but by a strange exception for a person of her rank, was small, spare, and sinewy, with lean small hands and corded neck. Her full dress of an evening was invariably a white chemise – and for adornment, green leaves (or sometimes white blossoms) stuck in her hair and thrust through her huge earring-holes. The husband on the contrary changed to view like a kaleidoscope. Whatever pretty thing my wife might have given to Nei Takauti – a string of beads, a ribbon, a piece of bright fabric – appeared the next evening on the person of Nan Tok'. It was plain he was a clothes-horse; that he wore livery; that, in a word, he was his wife's wife. They reversed the parts indeed, down to the least particular; it was the husband who showed himself the ministering angel in the hour of pain, while the wife displayed the apathy and heartlessness of the proverbial man.

When Nei Takauti had a headache Nan Tok' was full of attention and concern. When the husband had a cold and a racking toothache the wife heeded not, except to jeer. It is always the woman's part to fill and light the pipe; Nei Takauti handed hers in silence to the wedded page; but she carried it herself, as though the page were not entirely trusted. Thus she kept the money, but it was he who ran the errands, anxiously sedulous. A cloud on her face dimmed instantly his beaming looks; on an early visit to their *maniap'* my wife saw he had cause to be wary. Nan Tok' had a friend with him, a giddy young thing, of his own age and sex; and they had worked themselves into that stage of jocularity when consequences are too often disregarded. Nei Takauti mentioned her own name. Instantly Nan Tok' held up two fingers, his friend did likewise, both in an ecstasy of slyness. It was plain the lady had two names; and from the nature of their merriment, and the wrath that gathered on her brow, there must be something ticklish in the second. The husband pronounced it; a well-directed cocoa-nut from the hand of his wife caught him on the side of the head, and the voices and the mirth of these indiscreet young gentlemen ceased for the day.

The people of Eastern Polynesia are never at a loss; their etiquette is absolute and plenary; in every circumstance it tells them what to do and how to do it. The Gilbertines are seemingly more free, and pay for their freedom (like ourselves) in frequent perplexity. This was often the case with the topsy-turvy couple. We had once supplied them during a visit with a pipe and tobacco; and when they had smoked and were about to leave, they found themselves confronted with a problem: should they take or leave what remained of the tobacco. The piece of plug was taken up, it was laid down again, it was handed back and forth, and argued over, till the wife began to look haggard and the husband elderly. They ended by taking it, and I wager were not yet clear of the compound before they were sure they had decided wrong. Another time they had been given each a liberal cup of coffee, and Nan Tok' with difficulty and disaffection made an end of his. Nei Takauti had taken some, she had no mind for more, plainly conceived it would be a breach of manners to set down the cup unfinished, and ordered her wedded retainer to dispose of what was left. 'I have swallowed all I can, I cannot swallow more, it is a physical impossibility,' he seemed to say; and his stern officer reiterated her commands with secret imperative signals. Luckless dog! but in mere humanity we came to the rescue and removed the cup.

I cannot but smile over this funny household; yet I remember the good souls with affection and respect. Their attention to ourselves was surprising. The garlands are much esteemed, the blossoms must be sought far and wide; and though they had many retainers to call to their aid, we often saw themselves passing afield after the blossoms, and the wife engaged with her own hands in putting them together. It was no want of heart, only that disregard so incident to husbands, that made Nei Takauti despise the sufferings of Nan Tok'. When my wife was unwell she proved a diligent and kindly nurse; and the pair, to the extreme embarrassment of the sufferer, became fixtures in the sick-room. This rugged, capable, imperious old dame, with the wild eyes, had deep and tender qualities: her pride in her young husband it seemed that she dissembled, fearing possibly to spoil him; and when she spoke of her dead son there came something tragic in her face. But I seemed to trace in the Gilbertines a virility of sense and sentiment which distinguishes them (like their harsh and uncouth language) from their brother islanders in the east.

PART IV

THE GILBERTS — APEMAMA

THE KING OF APEMAMA: THE ROYAL TRADER

There is one great personage in the Gilberts: Tembinok' of Apemama: solely conspicuous, the hero of song, the butt of gossip. Through the rest of the group the kings are slain or fallen in tutelage: Tembinok' alone remains, the last tyrant, the last erect vestige of a dead society. The white man is everywhere else, building his houses, drinking his gin, getting in and out of trouble with the weak native governments. There is only one white on Apemama,[1] and he on sufferance, living far from court, and hearkening and watching his conduct like a mouse in a cat's ear. Through all the other islands a stream of native visitors comes and goes, travelling by families, spending years on the grand tour. Apemama alone is left upon one side, the tourist dreading to risk himself within the clutch of Tembinok'. And fear of the same Gorgon[2] follows and troubles them at home. Maiana once paid him tribute; he once fell upon and seized Nonuti:[3] first steps to the empire of the archipelago. A British warship[4] coming on the scene, the conqueror was driven to disgorge, his career checked in the outset, his dear-bought armoury sunk in his own lagoon. But the impression had been made; periodical fear of him still shakes the islands; rumour depicts him mustering his canoes for a fresh onfall; rumour can name his destination; and Tembinok' figures in the patriotic war-songs of the Gilberts like Napoleon in those of our grandfathers.

We were at sea, bound from Mariki to Nonuti and Tapituea,[5] when the wind came suddenly fair for Apemama. The course was at once changed; all hands were turned-to to clean ship, the decks holy-stoned, the cabin washed, the trade-room overhauled. In all our cruising we never saw the *Equator* so smart as she was made for Tembinok'. Nor was Captain Reid alone in these coquetries; for, another schooner chancing to arrive during my stay in Apemama, I found that she also was dandified for the occasion. And the two cases stand alone in my experience of South Sea traders.

We had on board a family of native tourists, from the grandsire to the babe in arms, trying (against an extraordinary series of ill-luck) to regain their native island of Peru.[6] Five times already they had paid their fare and taken ship; five times they had been disappointed, dropped penniless upon strange islands, or carried back to Butaritari, whence they sailed. This last attempt had been no better-starred; their provisions were exhausted. Peru was beyond hope, and they had cheerfully made up their minds to a fresh stage of exile in Tapituea or Nonuti. With this slant of wind their random destination became once more changed; and like the Calendar's pilot, when the 'black mountains'[7] hove in view, they changed colour and beat upon their breasts. Their camp, which was on deck in the ship's waist, resounded with complaint. They would be set to work, they must become slaves, escape was hopeless, they must live and toil and die in Apemama, in the tyrant's den. With this sort of talk they so greatly terrified their children, that one (a big hulking boy) must at last be torn screaming from the schooner's side. And their fears were wholly groundless. I have little doubt they were not suffered to be idle; but I can vouch for it that they were kindly and generously used. For, the matter of a year later, I was once more shipmate with these inconsistent wanderers on board the *Janet Nicoll*.[8] Their fare was paid by Tembinok'; they who had gone ashore from the *Equator* destitute, reappeared upon the *Janet* with new clothes, laden with mats and presents, and bringing with them a magazine of food, on which they lived like fighting-cocks throughout the voyage; I saw them at length repatriated, and I must say they showed more concern on quitting Apemama than delight at reaching home.

We entered by the north passage (Sunday, September 1st),[9] dodging among shoals. It was a day of fierce equatorial sunshine; but the breeze was strong and chill; and the mate, who conned the schooner from the cross-trees, returned shivering to the deck. The lagoon was thick with many-tinted wavelets; a continuous roaring of the outer sea overhung the anchorage; and the long, hollow crescent of palm ruffled and sparkled in the wind. Opposite our berth the beach was seen to be surmounted for some distance by a terrace of white coral, seven or eight feet high and crowned in turn by the scattered and incongruous buildings of the palace. The village adjoins on the south, a cluster of high-roofed *maniap*'s. And village and palace seemed deserted.

We were scarce yet moored, however, before distant and busy figures appeared upon the beach, a boat was launched, and a crew pulled out to us bringing the king's ladder. Tembinok' had once an accident; has feared ever since to intrust his person to the rotten chandlery[10] of South Sea traders; and devised in consequence a frame of wood, which is brought on board a ship as soon as she appears, and remains lashed to her side until she leave. The boat's crew, having applied this engine, returned at once to shore. They might not come on board; neither might we land, or not without danger of offence; the king giving pratique[11] in person. An interval followed, during which dinner was delayed for the great man; the prelude of the ladder, giving us some notion of his weighty body and sensible, ingenious character, had highly whetted our curiosity; and it was with something like excitement that we saw the beach and terrace suddenly blacken with attendant vassals, the king and party embark, the boat (a man-of-war gig) come flying towards us dead before the wind, and the royal coxswain lay us cleverly aboard, mount the ladder with a jealous diffidence, and descend heavily on deck.

Not long ago he was overgrown with fat, obscured to view, and a burthen to himself. Captains visiting the island advised him to walk; and though it broke the habits of a life and the traditions of his rank, he practised the remedy with benefit. His corpulence is now portable; you would call him lusty rather than fat; but his gait is still dull, stumbling, and elephantine. He neither stops nor hastens, but goes about his business with an implacable deliberation. We could never see him and not be struck with his extraordinary natural means for the theatre:[12] a beaked profile like Dante's in the mask,[13] a mane of long black hair, the eye brilliant, imperious, and inquiring: for certain parts, and to one who could have used it, the face was a fortune. His voice matched it well, being shrill, powerful, and uncanny, with a note like a sea-bird's. Where there are no fashions, none to set them, few to follow them if they were set, and none to criticise, he dresses – as Sir Charles Grandison[14] lived – 'to his own heart.' Now he wears a woman's frock, now a naval uniform; now (and more usually) figures in a masquerade costume of his own design: trousers and a singular jacket with shirt tails, the cut and fit wonderful for island workmanship, the material always handsome, sometimes green velvet, sometimes cardinal red silk. This masquerade becomes him admirably. In the woman's frock he looks ominous and weird beyond belief. I see him now come pacing towards me in the cruel sun, solitary, a figure out of Hoffmann.[15]

A visit on board ship, such as that at which we now assisted, makes a chief part and by far the chief diversion of the life of Tembinok'. He is not only the sole ruler, he is the sole merchant of his triple kingdom, Apemama, Aranuka, and Kuria,[16] well-planted islands. The taro goes to the chiefs, who divide as they please among their immediate adherents; but certain fish, turtles – which abound in Kuria, – and the whole produce of the coco-palm, belong exclusively to Tembinok'. 'A' cobra berong me,' observed his majesty with a wave of his hand; and he counts and sells it by the houseful. 'You got copra, king?' I have heard a trader ask. 'I got two, three outches,'[17] his majesty replied: 'I think three.' Hence the commercial importance of Apemama, the trade of three islands being centred there in a single hand; hence it is that so many whites have tried in vain to gain or to preserve a footing; hence ships are adorned, cooks have special orders, and captains array themselves in smiles, to greet the king. If he be pleased with his welcome and the fare he may pass days on board, and every day, and sometimes every hour, will be of profit to the ship. He oscillates between the cabin, where he is entertained with strange meats, and the traderoom, where he enjoys the pleasures of shopping on a scale to match his person. A few obsequious attendants squat by the house door, awaiting his least signal. In the boat, which has been suffered to drop astern, one or two of his wives lie covered from the sun under mats, tossed by the short sea of the lagoon, and enduring agonies of heat and tedium. This severity is now and then relaxed and the wives allowed on board. Three or four were thus favoured on the day of our arrival: substantial ladies airily attired in *ridi*s. Each had a share of copra, her *peculium*,[18] to dispose of for herself. The display in the traderoom – hats, ribbons, dresses, scents, tins of salmon – the pride of the eye and the lust of the flesh – tempted them in vain. They had but the one idea – tobacco, the island currency, tantamount to minted gold; returned to shore with it, burthened but rejoicing; and late into the night, on the royal terrace, were to be seen counting the sticks by lamplight in the open air.

The king is no such economist. He is greedy of things new and foreign. House after house, chest after chest, in the palace precinct, is already crammed with clocks, musical boxes, blue spectacles, umbrellas, knitted waistcoats, bolts of stuff, tools, rifles, fowling-pieces, medicines, European foods, sewing-machines, and, what is more extra-ordinary, stoves: all that ever caught his eye, tickled his appetite, pleased him for its use, or puzzled him with its apparent inutility. And still his lust is unabated. He is possessed by the seven devils of the collector. He hears a thing spoken of, and a shadow comes on his face. 'I think I no got him,' he will say; and the treasures he has seem worthless in comparison. If a ship be bound for Apemama, the merchant racks his brain to hit upon some novelty. This he leaves carelessly in the main cabin or partly conceals in his own berth, so that the king shall spy it for himself. 'How much you want?' inquires Tembinok', passing and pointing. 'No, king; that too dear,' returns the trader. 'I think I like him,' says the king. This was a bowl of gold-fish. On another occasion it was scented soap. 'No, king; that cost too much,' said the trader; 'too good for a Kanaka.' 'How much you got? I take him all,' replied his majesty, and became the lord of seventeen boxes at two dollars a cake. Or again, the merchant feigns the article is not for sale, is private property, an heirloom or a gift; and the trick infallibly succeeds. Thwart the king and you hold him. His autocratic nature rears at the affront of opposition. He accepts it for a challenge; sets his teeth like a hunter going at a fence; and with no mark of emotion, scarce even of interest, stolidly piles up the price. Thus, for our sins, he took a fancy to my wife's dressing-bag, a thing entirely useless to the man, and sadly battered by years of service. Early one forenoon he came to our house, sat down, and abruptly offered to purchase it. I told him I sold nothing, and the bag at any rate was a present from a friend; but he was acquainted with these pretexts from of old, and knew what they were worth and how to meet them. Adopting what I believe is called 'the object method,' he drew out a bag of English gold, sovereigns and half-sovereigns, and began to lay them one by one in silence on the table; at each fresh piece reading our faces with a look. In vain I continued to protest I was no trader; he deigned not to reply. There must have been twenty pounds on the table, he was still going on, and irritation had begun to mingle with our embarrassment, when a happy idea came to our delivery. Since his majesty thought so much of the bag, we said, we must beg him to accept it as a present. It was the most surprising turn in Tembinok's experience. He perceived too late that his persistence was unmannerly; hung his head a while in silence: then, lifting up a sheepish countenance, 'I 'shamed,' said the tyrant. It was the first and the last time we heard him own to a flaw in his behaviour. Half an hour after he sent us a camphorwood chest, worth only a few dollars – but then heaven knows what Tembinok' had paid for it.

Cunning by nature, and versed for forty years in the government of men, it must not be supposed that he is cheated blindly, or has resigned himself without resistance to be the milch-cow of the passing trader. His efforts have been even heroic. Like Nakaeia of Makin, he has owned schooners. More fortunate than Nakaeia, he has found captains. Ships of his have sailed as far as to the colonies. He has trafficked direct, in his own bottoms, with New Zealand. And even so, even there, the world-enveloping dishonesty of the white man prevented him; his profit melted, his ship returned in debt, the money for the insurance was embezzled, and when the *Coronet* came to be lost, he was astonished to find he had lost all. At this he dropped his weapons; owned he might as hopefully wrestle with the winds of heaven; and like an experienced sheep, submitted his fleece thenceforward to the shearers. He is the last man in the world to waste anger on the incurable; accepts it with cynical composure; asks no more in those he deals with than a certain decency of moderation: drives as good a bargain as he can; and when he considers he is more than usually swindled, writes it in his memory against the merchant's name. He once ran over to me a list of captains and supercargoes[19] with whom he had done business, classing them under three heads: 'He cheat a litty' – 'He cheat plenty' – and 'I think he cheat too much.' For the first two classes he expressed perfect toleration; sometimes, but not always, for the third. I was present when a certain merchant[20] was turned about his business, and was the means (having a considerable influence ever since the bag) of patching up the dispute. Even on the day of our arrival there was like to have been a hitch with Captain Reid: the ground of which is perhaps worth recital. Among goods exported specially for Tembinok' there is a beverage known (and labelled) as Hennessy's brandy. It is neither Hennessy, nor even brandy; is about the colour of sherry, but is not sherry; tastes of kirsch, and yet neither is it kirsch. The king, at least, has grown used to this amazing brand, and rather prides himself upon the taste; and any substitution is a double offence, being at once to cheat him and to cast a doubt upon his palate. A similar weakness is to be observed in all connoisseurs. Now the last case sold by the *Equator* was found to contain a different and I would fondly fancy a superior distillation; and the conversation opened very black for Captain Reid. But Tembinok' is a moderate man. He was reminded and admitted that all men were liable to error, even himself; accepted the principle that a fault handsomely acknowledged should be condoned; and wound the matter up with this proposal: 'Tuppoti[21] I mi'take, you 'peakee me. Tuppoti you mi'take, I 'peakee you. Mo' betta.'

After dinner and supper in the cabin, a glass or two of 'Hennetti' – the genuine article this time, with the kirsch bouquet, – and five hours' lounging on the traderoom counter, royalty embarked for home. Three tacks grounded the boat before the palace; the wives were carried ashore on the backs of vassals; Tembinok' stepped on a railed platform like a steamer's gangway, and was borne shoulder-high through the shallows, up the beach, and by an inclined plane, paved with pebbles, to the glaring terrace where he dwells.

CHAPTER II

THE KING OF APEMAMA: FOUNDATION OF EQUATOR TOWN

Our first sight of Tembinok' was a matter of concern, almost alarm, to my whole party. We had a favour to seek; we must approach in the proper courtly attitude of a suitor; and must either please him or

fail in the main purpose of our voyage. It was our wish to land and
live in Apemama, and see more near at hand the odd character of
the man and the odd (or rather ancient) condition of his island. In all
other isles of the South Seas a white man may land with his chest,
and set up house for a lifetime, if he choose, and if he have the money
or the trade; no hindrance is conceivable. But Apemama is a close
island, lying there in the sea with closed doors; the king himself, like
a vigilant officer, ready at the wicket to scrutinise and reject intrenching
visitors. Hence the attraction of our enterprise; not merely because it
was a little difficult, but because this social quarantine, a curiosity in
itself, has been the preservative of others.

Tembinok', like most tyrants, is a conservative; like many conserva-
tives, he eagerly welcomes new ideas, and, except in the field of politics,
leans to practical reform. When the missionaries came, professing a
knowledge of the truth, he readily received them; attended their
worship, acquired the accomplishment of public prayer, and made
himself a student at their feet. It is thus – it is by the cultivation of
similar passing chances – that he has learned to read, to write, to
cipher, and to speak his queer, personal English, so different from
ordinary 'Beach de Mar,'[1] so much more obscure, expressive, and
condensed. His education attended to, he found time to become critical
of the new inmates. Like Nakaeia of Makin, he is an admirer of silence
in the island; broods over it like a great ear; has spies who report daily;
and had rather his subjects sang than talked. The service, and in
particular the sermon, were thus sure to become offences: 'Here, in
my island, *I* 'peak,' he once observed to me. 'My chieps no 'peak –
do what I talk.' He looked at the missionary, and what did he see?
'See Kanaka 'peak in a big outch!' he cried, with a strong ring of
sarcasm. Yet he endured the subversive spectacle, and might even
have continued to endure it, had not a fresh point arisen. He looked
again, to employ his own figure; and the Kanaka was no longer
speaking, he was doing worse – he was building a copra-house. The
king was touched in his chief interests; revenue and prerogative were
threatened. He considered besides (and some think with him) that
trade is incompatible with the missionary claims. 'Tuppoti mitionary
think "good man": very good. Tuppoti he think "cobra": no good. I

send him away ship.' Such was his abrupt history of the evangelist in Apemama.

Similar deportations are common: 'I send him away ship' is the epitaph of not a few, his majesty paying the exile's fare to the next place of call. For instance, being passionately fond of European food, he has several times added to his household a white cook, and one after another these have been deported. They, on their side, swear they were not paid their wages; he, on his, that they robbed and swindled him beyond endurance: both perhaps justly. A more important case was that of an agent, despatched (as I heard the story) by a firm of merchants to worm his way into the king's good graces, become, if possible, premier, and handle the copra in the interest of his employers. He obtained authority to land, practised his fascinations, was patiently listened to by Tembinok', supposed himself on the highway to success; and behold! when the next ship touched at Apemama, the would-be premier was flung into a boat – had on board – his fare paid, and so good-bye. But it is needless to multiply examples; the proof of the pudding is in the eating. When we came to Apemama, of so many white men who have scrambled for a place in that rich market, one remained – a silent, sober, solitary, niggardly recluse, of whom the king remarks, 'I think he good; he no 'peak.'

I was warned at the outset we might very well fail in our design; yet never dreamed of what proved to be the fact, that we should be left four-and-twenty hours in suspense and come within an ace of ultimate rejection. Captain Reid had primed himself; no sooner was the king on board, and the Hennetti question amicably settled, than he proceeded to express my request and give an abstract of my claims and virtues. The gammon[2] about Queen Victoria's son might do for Butaritari; it was out of the question here; and I now figured as 'one of the Old Men of England,' a person of deep knowledge, come expressly to visit Tembinok's dominion, and eager to report upon it to the no less eager Queen Victoria. The king made no shadow of an answer, and presently began upon a different subject. We might have thought he had not heard, or not understood; only that we found ourselves the subject of a constant study. As we sat at meals, he took us in series and fixed upon each, for near a minute at a time, the same hard and thoughtful stare. As he thus looked he seemed to forget himself, the subject and the company, and to become absorbed in the process of his thought; the look was wholly impersonal: I have seen the same in the eyes of portrait-painters. The counts upon which whites have been deported are mainly four: cheating Tembinok', meddling overmuch with copra, which is the source of his wealth and one of the sinews of his power, ' 'peaking', and political intrigue. I felt guiltless upon all; but how to show it? I would not have taken copra in a gift: how to express that quality by my dinner-table bearing? The rest of the party shared my innocence and my embarrassment. They shared also in my mortification when after two whole meal-times and the odd moments of an afternoon devoted to this reconnoitring, Tembinok' took his leave in silence. Next morning, the same undisguised study, the same silence, was resumed; and the second day had come to its maturity before I was informed abruptly that I had stood the ordeal. 'I look your eye. You good man. You no lie,' said the king: a doubtful compliment to a writer of romance. Later he explained he did not quite judge by the eye only, but the mouth as well. 'Tuppoti I see man,' he explained. 'I no tavvy good man, bad man. I look eye, look mouth. Then I tavvy. Look *eye*, look mouth,' he repeated. And indeed in our case the mouth had the most to do with it, and it was by our talk that we gained admission to the island; the king promising himself (and I believe really amassing) a vast amount of useful knowledge ere we left.

The terms of our admission were as follows: We were to choose a site, and the king should there build us a town. His people should work for us, but the king only was to give them orders. One of his cooks should come daily to help mine, and to learn of him. In case our stores ran out, he would supply us, and be repaid on the return of the *Equator*. On the other hand, he was to come to meals with us when so inclined; when he stayed at home, a dish was to be sent him from our table; and I solemnly engaged to give his subjects no liquor or money (both of which they are forbidden to possess) and no tobacco, which they were to receive only from the royal hand. I think I remember to have protested against the stringency of this last article; at least, it was relaxed and when a man worked for me I was allowed to give him a pipe of tobacco on the premises, but none to take away.

The site of Equator Town – we named our city for the schooner – was soon chosen. The immediate shores of the lagoon are windy and blinding; Tembinok' himself is glad to grope blue-spectacled on his terrace; and we fled the neighbourhood of the red *conjunctiva*, the suppurating eyeball, and the beggar who pursues and beseeches the passing foreigner for eyewash. Behind the town the country is diversified; here open, sandy, uneven, and dotted with dwarfish palms; here cut up with taro trenches, deep and shallow, and, according to the growth of the plants, presenting now the appearance of a sandy tannery, now of an alleyed and green garden. A path leads towards the sea, mounting abruptly to the main level of the island – twenty or even thirty feet, although Findlay[3] gives five; and just hard by the top of the rise, where the coco-palms begin to be well grown, we found a grove of pandanus, and a piece of soil pleasantly covered with green underbush. A well was not far off under a rustic well-house; nearer still, in a sandy cup of the land, a pond where we might wash our clothes. The place was out of the wind, out of the sun, and out of sight of the village. It was shown to the king, and the town promised for the morrow.

The morrow came. Mr. Osbourne landed,[4] found nothing done, and carried his complaint to Tembinok'. He heard it, rose, called for a Winchester, stepped without the royal palisade, and fired two shots in the air. A shot in the air is the first Apemama warning; it has the force of a proclamation in more loquacious countries; and his majesty remarked agreeably that it would make his labourers 'mo' bright.' In less than thirty minutes, accordingly, the men had mustered, the work was begun, and we were told that we might bring our baggage when we pleased.

It was two in the afternoon ere the first boat was beached, and the long procession of chests and crates and sacks began to straggle through the sandy desert towards Equator Town. The grove of pandanus was practically a thing of the past. Fire smouldered and smoke rose in the green underbush. In a wide circuit the axes were still crashing. Those very advantages for which the place was chosen, it had been the king's first idea to abolish; and in the midst of this devastation there stood already a good-sized *maniap'* and a small closed house. A mat was spread near by for Tembinok'; here he sat superintending, in cardinal red, a pith helmet on his head, a meerschaum pipe in his mouth, a wife stretched at his back with custody of the matches and tobacco. Twenty or thirty feet in front of him the bulk of the workers squatted on the ground; some of the bush here survived; and in this the commons sat nearly to their shoulders, and presented only an arc of brown faces, black heads, and attentive eyes fixed on his majesty. Long pauses reigned, during which the subjects stared and the king smoked. Then Tembinok' would raise his voice and speak shrilly and briefly. There was never a response in words; but if the speech were jesting, there came by way of answer discreet, obsequious laughter – such laughter as we hear in schoolrooms; and if it were practical, the sudden uprising and departure of the squad. Twice they so disappeared, and returned with further elements of the city: a second house and a second *maniap'*. It was singular to spy, far off through the coco stems, the silent oncoming of the *maniap'*, at first (it seemed) swimming spontaneously in the air – but on a nearer view betraying under the eaves many score of moving naked legs. In all the affair servile obedience was no less remarkable than servile deliberation. The gang had here mustered by the note of a deadly weapon; the man who looked on was the unquestioned master of their lives; and except for civility, they bestirred themselves like so many American hotel clerks. The spectator was aware of an unobtrusive yet invincible inertia, at which the skipper of a trading dandy[5] might have torn his hair.

Yet the work was accomplished. By dusk, when his majesty withdrew, the town was founded and complete, a new and ruder Amphion[6] having called it from nothing with three cracks of a rifle. And the next morning the same conjuror obliged us with a further miracle: a mystic rampart fencing us, so that the path which ran by our doors became suddenly impassable, the inhabitants who had business across the isle must fetch a wide circuit, and we sat in the midst in a transparent privacy, seeing, seen, but unapproachable, like bees in a glass hive. The outward and visible sign of this glamour was no more than a few ragged coco-leaf garlands round the stems of the outlying palms; but its significance reposed on the tremendous sanction of the *tapu* and the guns of Tembinok'.

We made our first meal that night in the improvised city, where we were to stay two months, and which – so soon as we had done with it – was to vanish in a day as it appeared, its elements returning whence they came, the *tapu* raised, the traffic on the path resumed, the sun and the moon peering in vain between the palm-trees for the bygone work, the wind blowing over an empty site. Yet the place,[7] which is now only an episode in some memories, seemed to have been built, and to be destined to endure, for years. It was a busy hamlet. One of the *maniap*'s we made our dining-room, one the kitchen. The houses we reserved for sleeping. They were on the admirable Apemama plan: out and away the best house in the South Seas; standing some three feet above the ground on posts; the sides of woven flaps, which can be raised to admit light and air, or lowered to shut out the wind and the rain: airy, healthy, clean, and watertight. We had a hen of a remarkable kind: almost unique in my experience, being a hen that occasionally laid eggs. Not far off, Mrs. Stevenson tended a garden of salad and shalots. The salad was devoured by the hen – which was her bane. The shalots were served out a leaf at a time, and welcomed and relished like peaches. Toddy and green cocoa-nuts were brought us daily. We once had a present of fish from the king, and once of a turtle. Sometimes we shot so-called plover along on the shore, sometimes wild chicken in the bush. The rest of our diet was from tins.

Our occupations were very various. While some of the party would be away sketching,[8] Mr. Osbourne and I hammered away at a novel.[9] We read Gibbon and Carlyle[10] aloud; we blew on flageolets,[11] we strummed on guitars; we took photographs by the light of the sun, the moon, and flash-powder; sometimes we played cards. Pot-hunting engaged a part of our leisure. I have myself passed afternoons in the exciting but innocuous pursuit of winged animals with a revolver; and it was fortunate there were better shots of the party, and fortunate the king could lend us a more suitable weapon, in the form of an excellent fowling-piece, or our spare diet had been sparer still.

Night was the time to see our city, after the moon was up, after the lamps were lighted, and so long as the fire sparkled in the cook-house. We suffered from a plague of flies and mosquitoes, comparable to that of Egypt;[12] our dinner-table (lent, like all our furniture, by the king) must be enclosed in a tent of netting, our citadel and refuge; and this became all luminous, and bulged and beaconed under the eaves, like the globe of some monstrous lamp under the margin of its shade. Our cabins, the sides being propped at a variety of inclinations, spelled out strange, angular patterns of brightness. In his roofed and open kitchen, Ah Fu was to be seen by lamp and firelight, dabbling among pots. Over all, there fell in the season an extraordinary splendour of mellow moonshine. The sand sparkled as with the dust of diamonds; the stars had vanished. At intervals, a dusky night-bird, slow and low flying, passed in the colonnade of the tree stems and uttered a hoarse croaking cry.

CHAPTER III

THE KING OF APEMAMA: THE PALACE OF MANY WOMEN

The palace, or rather the ground which it includes, is several acres in extent. A terrace encloses it toward the lagoon; on the side of the land, a palisade with several gates. These are scarce intended for defence; a man, if he were strong, might easily pluck down the palisade; he need not be specially active to leap from the beach upon the terrace. There is no parade of guards, soldiers, or weapons; the armoury is under lock and key; and the only sentinels are certain inconspicuous old women lurking day and night before the gates. By day, these crones were often engaged in boiling syrup or the like household occupation; by night, they lay ambushed in the shadow or crouched along the palisade, filling the office of eunuchs to this harem, sole guards upon a tyrant life.

Female wardens made a fit outpost for this palace of many women. Of the number of the king's wives I have no guess; and but a loose idea of their function. He himself displayed embarrassment when they were referred to as his wives, called them himself 'my pamily,' and explained they were his 'cutcheons' – cousins. We distinguished four of the crowd: the king's mother; his sister, a grave, trenchant woman, with much of her brother's intelligence; the queen proper, to whom (and to whom alone) my wife was formally presented; and the favourite of the hour, a pretty, graceful girl, who sat with the king daily, and once (when he shed tears) consoled him with caresses. I am assured that even with her his relations are platonic. In the background figured a multitude of ladies, the lean, the plump, and the elephantine, some in sacque frocks, some in the hairbreadth *ridi*; high-born and low, slave and mistress; from the queen to the scullion, from the favourite to the scraggy sentries at the palisade. Not all of these of course are of 'my pamily,' – many are mere attendants; yet a surprising number shared the responsibility of the king's trust. These were key-bearers, treasurers, wardens of the armoury, the napery, and the stores. Each knew and did her part to admiration. Should anything be required – a particular gun, perhaps, or a particular bolt of stuff, – the right queen was summoned; she came bringing the right chest, opened it in the king's presence, and displayed her charge in perfect preservation – the gun cleaned and oiled, the goods duly folded. Without delay or haste, and with the minimum of speech, the whole great establishment turned on wheels like a machine. Nowhere have I seen order more complete and pervasive. And yet I was always reminded of Norse tales of trolls and ogres who kept their hearts buried in the ground for the mere safety, and must confide the secret to their wives. For these weapons are the life of Tembinok'. He does not aim at popularity; but drives and braves his subjects, with a simplicity of domination which it is impossible not to admire, hard not to sympathise with. Should one out of so many prove faithless, should the armoury be secretly unlocked, should the crones have dozed by the palisade and the weapons find their way unseen into the village, revolution would be nearly certain, death the most probable result, and the spirit of the tyrant of Apemama flit to rejoin his predecessors of Mariki and Tapituea. Yet those whom he so trusts are all women, and all rivals.

There is indeed a ministry and staff of males: cook, steward, carpenter, and supercargoes: the hierarchy of a schooner. The spies, 'his majesty's daily papers,' as we called them, come every morning to report, and go again. The cook and steward are concerned with the table only. The supercargoes, whose business it is to keep tally of the copra at three pounds a month and a percentage, are rarely in the palace; and two at least are in the other islands. The carpenter, indeed, shrewd and jolly old Rubam – query, Reuben? – promoted on my last visit[1] to the greater dignity of governor, is daily present, altering, extending, embellishing, pursuing the endless series of the king's inventions; and his majesty will sometimes pass an afternoon watching and talking with Rubam at his work. But the males are still outsiders; none seems to be armed, none is intrusted with a key; by dusk they are all usually departed from the palace; and the weight of the monarchy and of the monarch's life reposes unshared on the women.

Here is a household unlike, indeed, to one of ours; more unlike still to the Oriental harem: that of an elderly childless man, his days menaced, dwelling alone amid a bevy of women of all ages, ranks, and relationships, – the mother, the sister, the cousin, the legitimate wife, the concubine, the favourite, the eldest born, and she of yesterday; he, in their midst, the only master, the only male, the sole dispenser of honours, clothes, and luxuries, the sole mark of multitudinous ambitions and desires. I doubt if you could find a man in Europe so bold as to attempt this piece of tact and government. And seemingly Tembinok' himself had trouble in the beginning. I hear of him shooting at a wife for some levity on board a schooner. Another, on some more serious offence, he slew outright; he exposed her body in an open box, and (to make the warning more memorable) suffered it to putrefy before the palace gate. Doubtless his growing years have come to his assistance; for upon so large a scale it is more easy to play the father than the husband. And to-day, at least to the eye of a stranger, all seems to go smoothly, and the wives to be proud of their trust, proud of their rank, and proud of their cunning lord.

I conceived they made rather a hero of the man. A popular master in a girls' school might, perhaps, offer a figure of his preponderating station. But then the master does not eat, sleep, live, and wash his dirty linen in the midst of his admirers; he escapes, he has a room of his own, he leads a private life; if he has nothing else, he has the holidays, and the more unhappy Tembinok' is always on the stage and on the stretch.

In all my coming and going, I never heard him speak harshly or express the least displeasure. An extreme, rather heavy, benignity – the benignity of one sure to be obeyed – marked his demeanour; so that I was at times reminded of Samuel Richardson[2] in his circle of admiring women. The wives spoke up and seemed to volunteer opinions, like our wives at home – or, say, like doting but respectable aunts. Altogether, I conclude that he rules his seraglio[3] much more by art than terror; and those who give a different account (and who have none of them enjoyed my opportunities of observation) perhaps failed to distinguish between degrees of rank, between 'my pamily' and the hangers-on, laundresses, and prostitutes.

A notable feature is the evening game of cards; when lamps are set forth upon the terrace, and 'I and my pamily' play for tobacco by the hour. It is highly characteristic of Tembinok' that he must invent a game for himself; highly characteristic of his worshipping household that they should swear by the absurd invention. It is founded on poker, played with the honours out of many packs, and inconceivably dreary. But I have a passion for all games, studied it, and am supposed to be the only white who ever fairly grasped its principle: a fact for which the wives (with whom I was not otherwise popular) admired me with acclamation. It was impossible to be deceived; this was a genuine feeling: they were proud of their private game, had been cut to the quick by the want of interest shown in it by others, and expanded under the flattery of my attention. Tembinok' puts up a double stake, and receives in return two hands to choose from: a shallow artifice which the wives (in all these years) have not yet fathomed. He himself, when talking with me privately, made not the least secret that he was secure of winning; and it was thus he explained his recent liberality on board the *Equator*. He let the wives buy their own tobacco, which pleased them at the moment. He won it back at cards, which made him once more, and without fresh expense, that which he ought to be, – the sole fount of all indulgences. And he summed the matter up in that phrase with which he almost always concludes any account of his policy: 'Mo' betta.'

The palace compound is laid with broken coral, excruciating to the eyes and the bare feet, but exquisitely raked and weeded. A score or more of buildings lie in a sort of street along the palisade and scattered on the margin of the terrace; dwelling-houses for the wives and the attendants, storehouses for the king's curios and treasures, spacious *maniap's* for feast or council, some on pillars of wood, some on piers of masonry. One was still in hand, a new invention, the king's latest born: a European frame-house built for coolness inside a lofty *maniap'*: its roof planked like a ship's deck to be a raised, shady, and yet private promenade. It was here the king spent hours with Rubam; here I would sometimes join them; the place had a most singular appearance; and I must say I was greatly taken with the fancy, and joined with relish in the counsels of the architects.

Suppose we had business with his majesty by day: we strolled over the sand and by the dwarfish palms, exchanged a '*Kŏnamaori*' with the crone on duty, and entered the compound. The wide sheet of coral glared before us deserted; all having stowed themselves in dark canvas from the excess of room. I have gone to and fro in that labyrinth of a place, seeking the king; and the only breathing creature I could find was when I peered under the eaves of a *maniap'*, and saw the brawny body of one of the wives stretched on the floor, a naked Amazon[4] plunged in noiseless slumber. If it were still the hour of the 'morning papers' the quest would be more easy, the half-dozen obsequious, sly dogs squatting on the ground outside a house, crammed as far as possible in its narrow shadow, and turning to the king a row of leering faces. Tembinok' would be within, the flaps of the cabin raised, the trade blowing through, hearing their report. Like journalists nearer home, when the day's news were scanty, these would make the more of it in words; and I have known one to fill up a barren morning with an imaginary conversation of two dogs. Sometimes the king deigns to laugh, sometimes to question or jest with them, his voice sounding shrilly from the cabin. By his side he may have the heir-apparent, Paul, his nephew and adopted son, six years old, stark naked, and a model of young human beauty. And there will always be the favourite and perhaps two other wives awake; four more lying supine under mats and whelmed in slumber. Or perhaps we came later, fell on a more private hour, and found Tembinok' retired in the house with the favourite, an earthenware spittoon, a leaden inkpot, and a commercial ledger. In the last, lying on his belly, he writes from day to day the uneventful history of his reign; and when thus employed he betrayed a touch of fretfulness on interruption with which I was well able to sympathise. The royal annalist once read me a page or so, translating as he went; but the passage being genealogical, and the author boggling extremely in his version, I own I have been sometimes better entertained. Nor does he confine himself to prose, but touches the lyre too, in his leisure moments, and passes for the chief bard of his kingdom, as he is its sole public character, leading architect, and only merchant. His competence, however, does not reach to music; and his verses, when they are ready, are taught to a professional musician, who sets them and instructs the chorus. Asked what his songs were about, Tembinok' replied, 'Sweethearts and trees and the sea. Not all the same true, all the same lie.' For a condensed view of lyrical poetry (except that he seems to have forgot the stars and flowers) this would be hard to mend. These multifarious occupations bespeak (in a native and an absolute prince) unusual activity of mind.

The palace court at noon is a spot to be remembered with awe, the visitor scrambling there, on the loose stones, through a splendid nightmare of light and heat; but the sweep of the wind delivers it from flies and mosquitoes; and with the set of sun it became heavenly. I remember it best on moonless nights. The air was like a bath of milk. Countless shining stars were overhead, the lagoon paved with them. Herds of wives squatted by companies on the gravel, softly chatting. Tembinok' would doff his jacket, and sit bare and silent, perhaps meditating songs; the favourite usually by him, silent also. Meanwhile in the midst of the court, the palace lanterns were being lit and marshalled in rank upon the ground – six or eight square yards of them; a sight that gave one strange ideas of the number of 'my pamily': such a sight as may be seen about dusk in a corner of some great terminus at home. Presently these fared off into all corners of the precinct, lighting the last labours of the day, lighting one after another to their rest that prodigious company of women. A few lingered in the middle of the court for the card-party, and saw the honours shuffled and dealt, and Tembinok' deliberating between his two hands, and the queens losing their tobacco. Then these also were scattered and extinguished; and their place was taken by a great bonfire, the night-light of the palace. When this was no more, smaller fires burned likewise at the gates. These were tended by the crones, unseen, unsleeping – not always unheard. Should any approach in the dark hours, a guarded alert made the circuit of the palisade; each sentry signalled her neighbour with a stone; the rattle of falling pebbles passed and died away; and the wardens of Tembinok' crouched in their places silent as before.

CHAPTER IV

THE KING OF APEMANA: EQUATOR TOWN AND THE PALACE

Five persons were detailed to wait upon us. Uncle Parker,[1] who brought us toddy and green nuts, was an elderly, almost an old man, with the spirits, the industry, and the morals of a boy of ten. His face was ancient, droll, and diabolical, the skin stretched over taut sinews, like a sail on the guide-rope; and he smiled with every muscle of his head. His nuts must be counted every day, or he would deceive us in the tale; they must be daily examined, or some would prove to be unhusked; nothing but the king's name, and scarcely that, would hold him to his duty. After his toils were over he was given a pipe, matches, and tobacco, and sat on the floor in the *maniap'* to smoke. He would not seem to move from his position, and yet every day, when the things fell to be returned, the plug had disappeared; he had found the means to conceal it in the roof, whence he could radiantly produce it on the morrow. Although this piece of legerdemain was performed regularly before three or four pairs of eyes, we could never catch him in the fact; although we searched after he was gone, we could never find the tobacco. Such were the diversions of Uncle Parker, a man nearing sixty. But he was punished according unto his deeds: Mrs. Stevenson took a fancy to paint him, and the sufferings of the sitter were beyond description.

Three lasses came from the palace to do our washing and racket with Ah Fu. They were of the lowest class, hangers-on kept for the convenience of merchant skippers, probably low-born, perhaps out-islanders, with little refinement whether of manner or appearance, but likely and jolly enough wenches in their way. We called one Guttersnipe,[2] for you may find her image in the slums of any city: the same lean, dark-eyed, eager, vulgar face, the same sudden, hoarse guffaws, the same forward and yet anxious manner, as with a tail of an eye on the policeman: only the policeman here was a live king, and his truncheon a rifle. I doubt if you could find anywhere out of the islands, or often there, the parallel of Fatty, a mountain of a girl, who must have weighed near as many stones as she counted summers, could have given a good account of a life-guardsman, had the face of a baby, and applied her vast mechanical forces almost exclusively to play. But they were all three of the same merry spirit. Our washing was conducted in a game of romps; and they fled and pursued, and splashed, and pelted, and rolled each other in the sand, and kept up a continuous noise of cries and laughter like holiday children. Indeed, and however strange their own function in that austere establishment, were they not escaped for the day from the largest and strictest Ladies' School in the South Seas?

Our fifth attendant was no less a person than the royal cook. He was strikingly handsome both in face and body, lazy as a slave, and insolent as a butcher's boy. He slept and smoked on our premises in various graceful attitudes; but so far from helping Ah Fu, he was not at the pains to watch him. It may be said of him that he came to learn, and remained to teach; and his lessons were at times difficult to stomach. For example, he was sent to fill a bucket from the well. About half-way he found my wife watering her onions, changed buckets with her, and leaving her the empty, returned to the kitchen with the full. On another occasion he was given a dish of dumplings for the king, was told they must be eaten hot, and that he should carry them as fast as possible. The wretch set off at the rate of about a mile in the hour, head in air, toes turned out. My patience, after a month of trial, failed me at the sight. I pursued, caught him by his two big shoulders, and thrusting him before me, ran with him down the hill, over the sands, and through the applauding village, to the Speak House, where the king was then holding a pow-wow. He had the impudence to pretend he was internally injured by my violence, and to profess serious apprehensions for his life.

All this we endured; for the ways of Tembinok' are summary, and I was not yet ripe to take a hand in the man's death. But in the meanwhile, here was my unfortunate China boy slaving for the pair, and presently he fell sick. I was now in the position of Cimourdain, Lantenac, and indeed all the characters in *Quatre-Vingt-Treize*:[3] to continue to spare the guilty, I must sacrifice the innocent. I took the usual course and tried to save both, with the usual consequence of failure. Well rehearsed, I went down to the palace, found the king alone, and obliged him with a vast amount of rigmarole. The cook was too old to learn: I feared he was not making progress; how if we had a boy instead? – boys were more teachable. It was all in vain; the king pierced through my disguises to the root of the fact; saw that the cook had desperately misbehaved; and sat a while glooming. 'I think he tavvy too much,' he said at last, with grim concision; and immediately turned the talk to other subjects. The same day another high officer, the steward, appeared in the cook's place, and, I am bound to say, proved civil and industrious.

As soon as I left, it seems the king called for a Winchester and strolled outside the palisade, awaiting the defaulter. That day Tembinok' wore the woman's frock; as like as not, his make-up was completed by a pith helmet and blue spectacles. Conceive the glaring stretch of sandhills, the dwarf palms with their noonday shadows, the line of the palisade, the crone sentries (each by a small clear fire) cooking syrup on their posts – and this chimaera waiting with his deadly engine. To him, enter at last the cook, strolling down the sandhill from Equator Town, listless, vain and graceful; with no thought of alarm. As soon as he was well within range, the travestied monarch fired the six shots over his head, at his feet, and on either hand of him: the second Apemama warning, startling in itself, fatal in significance, for the next time his majesty will aim to hit. I am told the king is a crack shot; that when he aims to kill, the grave may be got ready; and when he aims to miss, misses by so near a margin that the culprit tastes six times the bitterness of death. The effect upon the cook I had an opportunity of seeing for myself. My wife and I were returning from the sea-side of the island, when we spied one coming to meet us at a very quick, disordered pace, between a walk and a run. As we drew nearer we saw it was the cook, beside himself with some emotion, his usual warm, mulatto colour declined into a bluish pallor. He passed us without word or gesture, staring on us with the face of a Satan, and plunged on across the wood for the unpeopled quarter of the island and the long, desert beach, where he might rage to and fro unseen, and froth out the vials of his wrath, fear, and humiliation. Doubtless in the curses that he there uttered to the bursting surf and the tropic birds, the name of the *kaupoi* – the rich man – was frequently repeated. I had made him the laughing-stock of the village in the affair of the king's dumplings; I had brought him by my machinations into disgrace and the immediate jeopardy of his days; last, and perhaps bitterest, he had found me there by the way to spy upon him in the hour of his disorder.

Time passed, and we saw no more of him. The season of the full moon came round, when a man thinks shame to lie sleeping; and I continued until late – perhaps till twelve or one in the morning – to walk on the bright sand and in the tossing shadow of the palms. I played, as I wandered, on a flageolet, which occupied much of my attention; the fans overhead rattled in the wind with a metallic chatter; and a bare foot falls at any rate almost noiseless on that shifting soil. Yet when I got back to Equator Town, where all the lights were out, and my wife (who was still awake, and had been looking forth) asked me who it was that followed me, I thought she spoke in jest. 'Not at all,' she said. 'I saw him twice as you passed, walking close at your heels. He only left you at the corner of the *maniap*'; he must be still behind the cook-house.' Thither I ran – like a fool, without any weapon – and came face to face with the cook. He was within my *tapu*-line, which was death in itself; he could have no business there at such an hour but either to steal or to kill; guilt made him timorous; and he turned and fled before me in the night in silence. As he went I kicked him in that place where honour lies, and he gave tongue faintly like an injured mouse. At the moment I daresay he supposed it was a deadly instrument that touched him.

What had the man been after? I have found my music better qualified to scatter than to collect an audience. Amateur as I was, I could not suppose him interested in my reading of the 'Carnival of Venice,' or that he would deny himself his natural rest to follow my variations on 'The Ploughboy.'[4] And whatever his design, it was impossible I should suffer him to prowl by night among the houses. A word to the king, and the man were not, his case being far beyond pardon. But it is one thing to kill a man yourself; quite another to bear tales behind his back and have him shot by a third party; and I determined to deal with the fellow in some method of my own. I told Ah Fu the story, and bade him fetch me the cook whenever he should find him. I had supposed this would be a matter of difficulty; and far from that, he came of his own accord: an act really of desperation, since his life hung by my silence, and the best he could hope for was to be forgotten. Yet he came with an assured countenance, volunteered no apology or explanation, complained of injuries received, and pretended he was unable to sit down. I suppose I am the weakest man God made; I had kicked him in the least vulnerable part of his big carcase; my foot was bare, and I had not even hurt my foot. Ah Fu could not control his merriment. On my side, knowing what must be the nature of his apprehensions, I found in so much impudence a kind of gallantry, and secretly admired the man. I told him I should say nothing of his night's adventure to the king; that I should still allow him, when he had an errand, to come within my *tapu*-line by day; but if ever I found him there after the set of the sun I would shoot him on the spot; and to the proof showed him a revolver. He must have been incredibly relieved; but he showed no sign of it, took himself off with his usual dandy nonchalance, and was scarce seen by us again.

These five, then, with the substitution of the steward for the cook, came and went, and were our only visitors. The circle of the *tapu* held at arm's-length the inhabitants of the village. As for 'my pamily,' they dwelt like nuns in their enclosure; only once have I met one of them abroad, and she was the king's sister, and the place in which I found her (the island infirmary) was very likely privileged. There remains only the king to be accounted for. He would come strolling over, always alone, a little before a meal-time, take a chair, and talk and eat with us like an old family friend. Gilbertine etiquette appears defective on the point of leave-taking. It may be remembered we had trouble in the matter with Karaiti; and there was something childish and disconcerting in Tembinok's abrupt 'I want go home now,' accompanied by a kind of ducking rise, and followed by an unadorned retreat. It was the only blot upon his manners, which were otherwise plain, decent, sensible, and dignified. He never stayed long nor drank much, and copied our behaviour where he perceived it to differ from his own. Very early in the day, for instance, he ceased eating with his knife. It was plain he was determined in all things to wring profit from our visit, and chiefly upon etiquette. The quality of his white visitors puzzled and concerned him; he would bring up name after name, and ask if its bearer were a 'big chiep,' or even a 'chiep' at all – which, as some were my excellent good friends, and none were actually born in the purple, became at times embarrassing. He was struck to learn that our classes were distinguishable by their speech, and that certain words (for instance) were *tapu* on the quarter-deck of a man-of-war; and he begged in consequence that we should watch and correct him on the point. We were able to assure him that he was beyond correction. His vocabulary is apt and ample to an extraordinary degree. God knows where he collected it, but by some instinct or some accident he has avoided all profane or gross expressions. 'Obliged,' 'stabbed,' 'gnaw,' 'lodge,' 'power,' 'company,' 'slender,' 'smooth,' and 'wonderful,' are a few of the unexpected words that enrich his dialect. Perhaps what pleased him most was to hear about saluting the quarter-deck of a man-of-war. In his gratitude for this hint he became fulsome. 'Schooner cap'n no tell me,' he cried; 'I think no tavvy! You tavvy too much; tavvy 'teama', tavvy man-a-wa'. I think you tavvy everything.' Yet he gravelled me often enough with his perpetual questions; and the false Mr. Barlow stood frequently exposed before the royal Sandford.[5] I remember once in particular. We were showing the magic-lantern; a slide of Windsor Castle was put in, and I told him there was the 'outch' of Victoreea. 'How many pathom he high?' he asked, and I was dumb before him. It was the builder, the indefatigable architect of palaces, that spoke; collector though he was, he did not collect useless information; and all his questions had a purpose. After etiquette, government, law, the police, money, and medicine were his chief interests – things vitally important to himself as a king and the father of his people. It was my part not only to supply new information, but to correct the old. 'My patha he tell me,' or 'White man he tell me,' would be his constant beginning; 'You think he lie?' Sometimes I thought he did. Tembinok' once brought me a difficulty of this kind, which I was long of comprehending. A schooner captain had told him of Captain Cook;[6] the king was much interested in the story; and turned for more information – not to Mr. Stephen's Dictionary,[7] not to the *Britannica*, but to the Bible in the Gilbert Island version (which consists chiefly of the New Testament and the Psalms). Here he sought long and earnestly; Paul he found, and Festus, and Alexander[8] the coppersmith: no word of Cook. The inference was obvious: the explorer was a myth. So hard it is, even for a man of great natural parts like Tembinok', to grasp the ideas of a new society and culture.

CHAPTER V

KING AND COMMONS

We saw but little of the commons of the isle. At first we met them at the well, where they washed their linen and we drew water for the table. The combination was distasteful; and, having a tyrant at command, we applied to the king and had the place enclosed in our *tapu*. It was one of the few favours which Tembinok' visibly boggled about granting, and it may be conceived how little popular it made the strangers. Many villagers passed us daily going afield; but they fetched a wide circuit round our *tapu*, and seemed to avert their looks. At times we went ourselves into the village – a strange place. Dutch by its canals, Oriental by the height and steepness of the roofs, which looked at dusk like temples; but we were rarely called into a house: no welcome, no friendship, was offered us; and of home life we had but the one view: the waking of a corpse, a frigid, painful scene: the widow holding on her lap the cold, bluish body of her husband, and now partaking of the refreshments which made the round of the company, now weeping and kissing the pale mouth. ('I fear you feel this affliction deeply,' said the Scottish minister. 'Eh, sir, and that I do!' replied the widow. 'I've been greetin' a' nicht; an' noo I'm just gaun to sup this bit parritch,[1] and then I'll begin an' greet again.') In our walks abroad I have always supposed the islanders avoided us, perhaps from distaste, perhaps by order; and those whom we met we took generally by surprise. The surface of the isle is diversified with palm groves, thickets, and romantic dingles four feet deep, relics of old taro plantation; and it is thus possible to stumble unawares on folk resting or hiding from their work. About pistol-shot from our township there lay a pond in the bottom of a jungle; here the maids of the isle came to bathe, and were several times alarmed by our intrusion. Not for them are the bright cold rivers of Tahiti or Upolu,[2] not for them to splash and laugh in the hour of the dusk with a villageful of gay companions; but to steal here solitary, to crouch in a place like a cow-wallow, and wash (if that can be called washing) in lukewarm mud, brown as their own skins. Other, but still rare, encounters occur to my memory. I was several times arrested by a tender sound in the bush of voices talking, soft as flutes and with quiet intonations. Hope told a flattering tale; I put aside the leaves; and behold! in place of the expected dryads,[3] a pair of all too solid ladies squatting over a clay pipe in the ungraceful *ridi*. The beauty of the voice and the eye was all that remained to these vast dames; but that of the voice was indeed exquisite. It is strange I should have never heard a more winning sound of speech, yet the dialect should be one remarkable for violent, ugly, and outlandish vocables; so that Tembinok' himself declared it made him weary, and professed to find repose in talking English.

The state of this folk, of whom I saw so little, I can merely guess at. The king himself explains the situation with some art. 'No; I no pay them,' he once said. 'I give them tobacco. They work for me *all the same brothers*.' It is true there was a brother once in Arden![4] But we prefer the shorter word. They bear every servile mark, – levity like a child's, incurable idleness, incurious content. The insolence of the cook was a trait of his own; not so his levity, which he shared with the innocent Uncle Parker. With equal unconcern both gambolled under the shadow of the gallows, and took liberties with death that might have surprised a careless student of man's nature. I wrote of Parker that he behaved like a boy of ten: what was he else, being a slave of sixty? He had passed all his years in school, fed, clad, thought for, commanded; and had grown familiar and coquetted with the fear of punishment. By terror you may drive men long, but not far. Here, in Apemama, they work at the constant and the instant peril of their lives; and are plunged in a kind of lethargy of laziness. It is common to see one go afield in his stiff mat ungirt, so that he walks elbows-in like a trussed fowl; and whatsoever his right hand findeth to do, the other must be off duty holding on his clothes. It is common to see two men carrying between them on a pole a single bucket of water. To make two bites of a cherry is good enough: to make two burthens of a soldier's kit, for a distance of perhaps half a furlong, passes measure. Woman, being the less childish animal, is less relaxed by servile conditions. Even in the king's absence, even when they were alone, I have seen Apemama women work with constancy. But the outside to be hoped for in a man is that he may attack his task in little languid fits, and lounge between-whiles. So I have seen a painter, with his pipe going, and a friend by the studio fireside. You might suppose the race to lack civility, even vitality, until you saw them in the dance. Night after night, and sometimes day after day, they rolled out their choruses in the great Speak House – solemn andantes and adagios,[5] led by the clapped hand, and delivered with an energy that shook the roof. The time was not so slow, though it was slow for the islands; but I have chosen rather to indicate the effect upon the hearer. Their music had a church-like character from near at hand, and seemed to European ears more regular than the run of island music. Twice I have heard a discord regularly solved. From farther off, heard at Equator Town for instance, the measures rose and fell and crepitated like the barking of hounds in a distant kennel.

The slaves are certainly not overworked – children of ten do more without fatigue – and the Apemama labourers have holidays, when the singing begins early in the afternoon. The diet is hard; copra and a sweetmeat of pounded pandanus are the only dishes I observed outside the palace; but there seems no defect in quantity, and the king shares with them his turtles. Three came in a boat from Kuria during our stay; one was kept for the palace, one sent to us, one presented to the village. It is the habit of the islanders to cook the turtle in its carapace; we had been promised the shells, and we asked a *tapu* on this foolish practice. The face of Tembinok' darkened and he answered nothing. Hesitation in the question of the well I could understand, for water is scarce on a low island; that he should refuse to interfere upon a point of cookery was more than I had dreamed of; and I gathered (rightly or wrongly) that he was scrupulous of touching in the least degree the private life and habits of his slaves. So that even here, in full despotism, public opinion has weight; even here, in the midst of slavery, freedom has a corner.

Orderly, sober, and innocent, life flows in the isle from day to day as in a model plantation under a model planter. It is impossible to doubt the beneficence of that stern rule. A curious politeness, a soft and gracious manner, something effeminate and courtly, distinguishes the islanders of Apemama; it is talked of by all the traders, it was felt even by residents so little beloved as ourselves, and noticeable even in the cook, and even in that scoundrel's hours of insolence. The king, with his manly and plain bearing, stood out alone; you might say he was the only Gilbert Islander in Apemama. Violence, so common in Butaritari, seems unknown. So are theft and drunkenness. I am assured the experiment has been made of leaving sovereigns on the beach before the village: they lay there untouched. In all our time on the island I was but once asked for drink. This was by a mighty plausible fellow, wearing European clothes and speaking excellent English – Tamaiti his name, or, as the whites have now corrupted it, 'Tom White': one of the king's supercargoes at three pounds a month and a percentage, a medical man besides, and in his private hours a wizard. He found me one day in the outskirts of the village, in a secluded place, hot and private, where the taro-pits are deep and the plants high. Here he buttonholed me, and, looking about him like a conspirator, inquired if I had gin.

I told him I had. He remarked that gin was forbidden, lauded the prohibition a while, and then went on to explain that he was a doctor, or 'dogstar' as he pronounced the word, that gin was necessary to him for his medical infusions, that he was quite out of it, and that he would be obliged to me for some in a bottle. I told him I had passed the king my word on landing; but since his case was so exceptional, I would go down to the palace at once, and had no doubt that Tembinok' would set me free. Tom White was immediately overwhelmed with embarrassment and terror, besought me in the most moving terms not to betray him, and fled my neighbourhood. He had none of the cook's valour; it was weeks before he dared to meet my eye; and then only by the order of the king and on particular business.

The more I viewed and admired this triumph of firm rule, the more I was haunted and troubled by a problem, the problem (perhaps) of to-morrow for ourselves. Here was a people protected from all serious misfortune, relieved of all serious anxieties, and deprived of what we call our liberty. Did they like it? and what was their sentiment toward the ruler? The first question I could not of course ask, nor perhaps the natives answer. Even the second was delicate; yet at last, and under charming and strange circumstances, I found my opportunity to put it and a man to reply. It was near the full of the moon, with a delicious breeze; the isle was bright as day – to sleep would have been sacrilege; and I walked in the bush, playing my pipe. It must have been the sound of what I am pleased to call my music that attracted in my direction another wanderer of the night. This was a young man attired in a fine mat, and with a garland on his hair, for he was new come from dancing and singing in the public hall; and his body, his face, and his eyes, were all of an enchanting beauty. Every here and there in the Gilberts youths are to be found of this absurd perfection; I have seen five of us pass half an hour in admiration of a boy at Mariki; and Te Kop (my friend in the fine mat and garland) I had already several times remarked, and long ago set down as the loveliest animal in Apemama. The philtre of admiration must be very strong, or these natives specially susceptible to its effects, for I have scarce ever admired a person in the islands but what he has sought my particular acquaintance. So it was with Te Kop. He led me to the ocean side; and for an hour or two we sat smoking and talking on the resplendent sand and under the ineffable brightness of the moon. My friend showed himself very sensible of the beauty and amenity of the hour. 'Good night! Good wind!' he kept exclaiming, and as he said the words he seemed to hug myself. I had long before invented such reiterated expressions of delight for a character (Felipe, in the story of 'Olalla')[6] intended to be partly bestial. But there was nothing bestial in Te Kop; only a childish pleasure in the moment. He was no less pleased with his companion, or was good enough to say so; honoured me, before he left, by calling me Te Kop; apostrophised me as 'My name!' with an intonation exquisitely tender, laying his hand at the same time swiftly on my knee; and after we had risen, and our paths began to separate in the bush, twice cried to me with a sort of gentle ecstasy, 'I like you too much!' From the beginning he had made no secret of his terror of the king; would not sit down nor speak above a whisper till he had put the whole breadth of the isle between himself and his monarch, then harmlessly asleep; and even there, even within a stone-cast of the outer sea, our talk covered by the sound of the surf and the rattle of the wind among the palms, continued to speak guardedly, softening his silver voice (which rang loud enough in the chorus) and looking about him like a man in fear of spies. The strange thing is that I should have beheld him no more. In any other island in the whole South Seas, if I had advanced half as far with any native, he would have been at my door next morning, bringing and expecting gifts. But Te Kop vanished in the bush for ever. My house, of course, was unapproachable; but he knew where to find me on the ocean beach, where I went daily. I was the *kaupoi*, the rich man; my tobacco and trade were known to be endless: he was sure of a present. I am at a loss how to explain his behaviour, unless it be supposed that he recalled with terror and regret a passage in our interview. Here it is:

'The king, he good man?' I asked.

'Suppose he like you, he good man,' replied Te Kop: 'no like, no good.'

That is one way of putting it, of course. Te Kop himself was probably no favourite, for he scarce appealed to my judgment as a type of industry. And there must be many others whom the king (to adhere to the formula) does not like. Do these unfortunates like the king? Or is not rather the repulsion mutual? and the conscientious Tembinok', like the conscientious Braxfield[7] before him, and many other conscientious rulers and judges before either, surrounded by a considerable body of 'grumbletonians'?[8] Take the cook, for instance, when he passed us by, blue with rage and terror. He was very wroth with me; I think by all the old principles of human nature he was not very well pleased with his sovereign. It was the rich man he sought to waylay:

I think it must have been by the turn of a hair that it was not the king he waylaid instead. And the king gives, or seems to give, plenty of opportunities; day and night he goes abroad alone, whether armed or not I can but guess; and the taro-patches, where his business must so often carry him, seem designed for assassination. The case of the cook was heavy indeed to my conscience. I did not like to kill my enemy at second-hand; but had I a right to conceal from the king, who had trusted me, the dangerous secret character of his attendant? And suppose the king should fall, what would be the fate of the king's friends? It was our opinion at the time that we should pay dear for the closing of the well; that our breath was in the king's nostrils; that if the king should by any chance be bludgeoned in a taro-patch, the philosophical and musical inhabitants of Equator Town might lay aside their pleasant instruments, and betake themselves to what defence they had, with a very dim prospect of success. These speculations were forced upon us by an incident which I am ashamed to betray. The schooner *J. L. Tiernan* (since capsized at sea,[9] with the loss of eleven lives) put in to Apemama in a good hour for us, who had near exhausted our supplies. The king, after his habit, spent day after day on board; the gin proved unhappily to his taste; he brought a store of it ashore with him; and for some time the sole tyrant of the isle was half-seas-over. He was not drunk – the man is not a drunkard, he has always stores of liquor at hand, which he uses with moderation, – but he was muzzy, dull, and confused. He came one day to lunch with us, and while the cloth was being laid fell asleep in his chair. His confusion, when he awoke and found he had been detected, was equalled by our uneasiness. When he was gone we sat and spoke of his peril, which we thought to be in some degree our own; of how easily the man might be surprised in such a state by 'grumbletonians'; of the strange scenes that would follow – the royal treasures and stores at the mercy of the rabble, the palace overrun, the garrison of women turned adrift. And as we talked we were startled by a gun-shot and a sudden, barbaric outcry. I believe we all changed colour; but it was only the king firing at a dog and the chorus striking up in the Speak House. A day or two later I learned the king was very sick; went down, diagnosed the case; and took at once the highest medical degree by the exhibition of bicarbonate of soda. Within the hour Richard was himself again;[10] and I found him at the unfinished house, enjoying the double pleasure of directing Rubam and making a dinner off cocoa-nut dumplings, and all eagerness to have the formula of this new sort of 'pain-killer' – for 'pain-killer' in the islands is the generic name of medicine. So ended the king's modest spree and our anxiety.

On the face of things, I ought to say, loyalty appeared unshaken. When the schooner at last returned for us, after much experience of baffling winds, she brought a rumour that Tebureimoa had declared war on Apemama. Tembinok' became a new man; his face radiant; his attitude, as I saw him preside over a council of chiefs in one of the palace *maniap*'s, eager as a boy's; his voice sounding abroad, shrill and jubilant, over half the compound. War is what he wants, and here was his chance. The English captain, when he flung his arms in the lagoon, had forbidden him (except in one case) all military adventures in the future: here was the case arrived. All morning the council sat; men were drilled, arms were bought, the sound of firing disturbed the afternoon; the king devised and communicated to me his plan of campaign, which was highly elaborate and ingenious, but perhaps a trifle fine-spun for the rough and random vicissitudes of war. And in all this bustle the temper of the people appeared excellent, an unwonted animation in every face, and even Uncle Parker burning with military zeal.

Of course it was a false alarm. Tebureimoa had other fish to fry. The ambassador who accompanied us on our return to Butaritari[11] found him retired to a small island on the reef, in a huff with the Old Men, a tiff with the traders, and more fear of insurrection at home than appetite for wars abroad. The plenipotentiary had been placed under my protection; and we solemnly saluted when we met. He proved an excellent fisherman, and caught bonito over the ship's side. He pulled a good oar, and made himself useful for a whole fiery afternoon, towing the becalmed *Equator* off Mariki.[12] He went to his post and did no good. He returned home again, having done no harm. *O si sic omnes!*[13]

CHAPTER VI

THE KING OF APEMAMA: DEVIL-WORK

The ocean beach of Apemama was our daily resort. The coast is broken by shallow bays. The reef is detached, elevated, and includes a lagoon about knee-deep, the unrestful spending-basin of the surf. The beach is now of fine sand, now of broken coral. The trend of the coast being convex, scarce a quarter of a mile of it is to be seen at once; the land being so low, the horizon appears within a stone-cast; and the narrow prospect enhances the sense of privacy. Man avoids the place – even his footprints are uncommon; but a great number of birds hover and pipe there fishing, and leave crooked tracks upon the sand. Apart from these, the only sound (and I was going to say the only society) is that of the breakers on the reef.

On each projection of the coast, the bank of coral clinkers immediately above the beach has been levelled, and a pillar built, perhaps breast-high. These are not sepulchral; all the dead being buried on the inhabited side of the island, close to men's houses, and (what is worse) to their wells. I was told they were to protect the isle against inroads from the sea – divine or diabolical martellos, probably sacred to Taburik, God of Thunder.

The bay immediately opposite Equator Town, which we call Fu Bay, in honour of our cook, was thus fortified on either horn. It was well sheltered by the reef, the enclosed water clear and tranquil, the enclosing beach curved like a horseshoe, and both steep and broad. The path debouched about the midst of the re-entrant angle, the woods stopping some distance inland. In front, between the fringe of the wood and the crown of the beach, there had been designed a regular figure, like the court for some new variety of tennis, with borders of round stones imbedded, and pointed at the angles with low posts, likewise of stone. This was the king's Pray Place. When he prayed, what he prayed for, and to whom he addressed his supplications, I could never learn. The ground was *tapu*.

In the angle, by the mouth of the path, stood a deserted *maniap'*.

Near by there had been a house before our coming, which was now transported and figured for the moment in Equator Town. It had been, and it would be again when we departed, the residence of the guardian and wizard of the spot – Tamaiti. Here, in this lone place, within sound of the sea, he had his dwelling and uncanny duties. I cannot call to mind another case of a man living on the ocean side of any open atoll; and Tamaiti must have had strong nerves, the greater confidence in his own spells, or, what I believe to be the truth, an enviable scepticism. Whether Tamaiti had any guardianship of the Pray Place I never heard. But his own particular chapel stood farther back in the fringe of the wood. It was a tree of respectable growth. Around it there was drawn a circle of stones like those that enclosed the Pray Place; in front, facing towards the sea, a stone of a much greater size, and somewhat hollowed, like a piscina,[1] stood close against the trunk; in front of that again a conical pile of gravel. In the hollow of what I have called the piscina (though it proved to be a magic seat) lay an offering of green cocoa-nuts; and when you looked up you found the boughs of the tree to be laden with strange fruit: palm branches elaborately plaited, and beautiful models of canoes, finished and rigged to the least detail. The whole had the appearance of a midsummer and sylvan Christmas-tree *al fresco*.[2] Yet we were already well enough acquainted in the Gilberts to recognise it, at the first sight, for a piece of wizardry, or, as they say in the group, of Devil-work.

The plaited palms were what we recognised. We had seen them before on Apaiang,[3] the most christianised of all these islands; where excellent Mr. Bingham[4] lived and laboured and has left golden memories; whence all the education in the northern Gilberts traces its descent; and where we were boarded by little native Sunday-school misses in clean frocks, with demure faces, and singing hymns as to the manner born.

Our experience of Devil-work at Apaiang[5] had been as follows:– It chanced we were benighted at the house of Captain Tierney. My wife and I lodged with a Chinaman some half a mile away; and thither Captain Reid and a native boy escorted us by torchlight. On the way the torch went out, and we took shelter in a small and lonely Christian chapel to rekindle it. Stuck in the rafters of the chapel was a branch of knotted palm. 'What is that?' I asked. 'O, that's Devil-work,' said the Captain. 'And what is Devil-work?' I inquired. 'If you like, I'll show you some when we get to Johnnie's,' he replied. 'Johnnie's' was a quaint little house upon the crest of the beach, raised some three feet on posts, approached by stairs; part walled, part trellised. Trophies of advertisement-photographs were hung up within for decoration. There was a table and a recess-bed, in which Mrs. Stevenson slept; while I camped on the matted floor with Johnnie, Mrs. Johnnie, her sister, and the devil's own regiment of cockroaches. Hither was summoned an old witch, who looked the part to horror. The lamp was set on the floor; the crone squatted on the threshold, a green palm-branch in her hand, the light striking full on her aged features and picking out behind her, from the black night, timorous faces of spectators. Our sorceress began with a chanted incantation; it was in the old tongue, for which I had no interpreter; but ever and again there ran among the crowd outside that laugh which every traveller in the islands learns so soon to recognise, – the laugh of terror. Doubtless these half-Christian folk were shocked, these half-heathen folk alarmed. Chench or Taburik thus invoked, we put our questions; the witch knotted the leaves, here a leaf and there a leaf, plainly on some arithmetical system; studied the result with great apparent contention of mind; and gave the answers. Sidney Colvin[6] was in robust health and gone a journey; and we should have a fair wind upon the morrow: that was the result of our consultation, for which we paid a dollar. The next day dawned cloudless and breathless; but I think Captain Reid placed a secret reliance on the sibyl, for the schooner was got ready for sea. By eight the lagoon was flawed with long cat's-paws, and the palms tossed and rustled; before ten we were clear of the passage and skimming under all plain sail, with bubbling scuppers. So we had the breeze, which was well worth a dollar in itself; but the bulletin about my friend in England proved, some six months later, when I got my mail, to have been groundless. Perhaps London lies beyond the horizon of the island gods.

Tembinok', in his first dealings, showed himself sternly averse from superstition: and had not the *Equator* delayed, we might have left the island and still supposed him an agnostic. It chanced one day, however, that he came to our *maniap'*, and found Mrs. Stevenson in the midst of a game of patience. She explained the game as well as she was able, and wound up jocularly by telling him this was her devil-work, and if she won, the *Equator* would arrive next day. Tembinok' must have drawn a long breath; we were not so high-and-dry after all; he need no longer dissemble, and he plunged at once into confessions. He made devil-work every day, he told us, to know if ships were coming in; and thereafter brought us regular reports of the results. It was surprising how regularly he was wrong; but he had always an explanation ready. There had been some schooner in the offing out of view; but either she was not bound for Apemama, or had changed her course, or lay becalmed. I used to regard the king with veneration as he thus publicly deceived himself. I saw behind him all the fathers of the Church, all the philosophers and men of science of the past; before him, all those that are to come; himself in the midst; the whole visionary series bowed over the same task of welding incongruities. To the end Tembinok' spoke reluctantly of the island gods and their worship, and I learned but little. Taburik is the god of thunder, and deals in wind and weather. A while since there were wizards who could call him down in the form of lightning. 'My patha he tell me he see: you think he lie?' Tienti – pronounced something like 'Chench,' and identified by his majesty with the devil – sends and removes bodily sickness. He is whistled for in the Paumotuan manner, and is said to appear; but the king has never seen him. The doctors treat disease by the aid of Chench: eclectic Tembinok' at the same time administering 'pain-killer' from his medicine-chest, so as to give the sufferer both chances. 'I think mo' betta,' observed his majesty, with more than his usual self-approval. Apparently the gods are not jealous, and placidly enjoy both shrine and priest in common. On Tamaiti's medicine-tree, for instance, the model canoes are hung up *ex voto*[7] for a prosperous voyage, and must therefore be dedicate to Taburik, god of the weather; but the stone in front is the place of sick folk come to pacify Chench.

It chanced, by great good luck, that even as we spoke of these affairs, I found myself threatened with a cold. I do not suppose I was ever glad of a cold before, or shall ever be again; but the opportunity to see the sorcerers at work was priceless, and I called in the faculty of

Apemama. They came in a body, all in their Sunday's best and hung with wreaths and shells, the insignia of the devil-worker. Tamaiti I knew already: Terutak' I saw for the first time – a tall, lank, raw-boned, serious North-Sea fisherman turned brown; and there was a third in their company whose name I never heard, and who played to Tamaiti the part of *famulus*.[8] Tamaiti took me in hand first, and led me, conversing agreeably, to the shores of Fu Bay. The *famulus* climbed a tree for some green cocoa-nuts. Tamaiti himself disappeared a while in the bush and returned with coco tinder, dry leaves, and a spray of waxberry. I was placed on the stone, with my back to the tree and my face to windward; between me and the gravel-heap one of the green nuts was set; and then Tamaiti (having previously bared his feet, for he had come in canvas shoes, which tortured him) joined me within the magic circle, hollowed out the top of the gravel-heap, built his fire in the bottom, and applied a match: it was one of Bryant and May's. The flame was slow to catch, and the irreverent sorcerer filled in the time with talk of foreign places – of London, and 'companies,' and how much money they had; of San Francisco, and the nefarious fogs, 'all the same smoke,' which had been so nearly the occasion of his death. I tried vainly to lead him to the matter in hand. 'Everybody make medicine,' he said lightly. And when I asked him if he were himself a good practitioner – 'No savvy,' he replied, more lightly still. At length the leaves burst in a flame, which he continued to feed; a thick, light smoke blew in my face, and the flames streamed against and scorched my clothes. He in the meanwhile addressed, or affected to address, the evil spirit, his lips moving fast, but without sound; at the same time he waved in the air and twice struck me on the breast with his green spray. So soon as the leaves were consumed the ashes were buried, the green spray was imbedded in the gravel, and the ceremony was at an end.

A reader of the *Arabian Nights* felt quite at home. Here was the suffumigation;[9] here was the muttering wizard; here was the desert place to which Aladdin was decoyed by the false uncle. But they manage these things better in fiction. The effect was marred by the levity of the magician, entertaining his patient with small talk like an affable dentist, and by the incongruous presence of Mr. Osbourne with a camera. As for my cold, it was neither better nor worse.

I was now handed over to Terutak', the leading practitioner or medical baronet of Apemama. His place is on the lagoon side of the island, hard by the palace. A rail of light wood, some two feet high, encloses an oblong piece of gravel like the king's Pray Place; in the midst is a green tree; below, a stone table bears a pair of boxes covered with a fine mat; and in front of these an offering of food, a cocoa-nut, a piece of taro or a fish, is placed daily. On two sides the enclosure is lined with *maniap*'s; and one of our party,[10] who had been there to sketch, had remarked a daily concourse of people and an extraordinary number of sick children; for this is in fact the infirmary of Apemama. The doctor and myself entered the sacred place alone; the boxes and the mat were displaced; and I was enthroned in their stead upon the stone, facing once more to the east. For a while the sorcerer remained unseen behind me, making passes in the air with a branch of palm. Then he struck lightly on the brim of my straw hat; and this blow he continued to repeat at intervals, sometimes brushing instead my arm and shoulder. I have had people try to mesmerise me a dozen times, and never with the least result. But at the first tap – on a quarter no more vital than my hat-brim, and from nothing more virtuous than a switch of palm wielded by a man I could not even see – sleep rushed upon me like an armed man. My sinews fainted, my eyes closed, my brain hummed, with drowsiness. I resisted – at first instinctively, then with a certain flurry of despair, in the end successfully; if that were indeed success which enabled me to scramble to my feet, to stumble home somnambulous, to cast myself at once upon my bed, and sink at once into a dreamless stupor. When I awoke my cold was gone. So I leave a matter that I do not understand.

Meanwhile my appetite for curiosities (not usually very keen) had been strangely whetted by the sacred boxes. They were of pandanus wood, oblong in shape, with an effect of pillaring along the sides like straw work, lightly fringed with hair or fibre and standing on four legs. The outside was neat as a toy; the inside a mystery I was resolved to penetrate. But there was a lion in the path. I might not approach Terutak', since I had promised to buy nothing in the island; I dared not have recourse to the king, for I had already received from him more gifts than I knew how to repay. In this dilemma (the schooner being at last returned) we hit on a device. Captain Reid came forward in my stead, professed an unbridled passion for the boxes, and asked and obtained leave to bargain for them with the wizard. That same afternoon the captain and I made haste to the infirmary, entered the enclosure, raised the mat, and had begun to examine the boxes at our leisure, when Terutak's wife bounced out of one of the nigh houses, fell upon us, swept up the treasures, and was gone. There was never a more absolute surprise. She came, she took, she vanished, we had not a guess whither; and we remained, with foolish looks and laughter, on the empty field. Such was the fit prologue of our memorable bargaining.

Presently Terutak' came, bringing Tamaiti along with him, both smiling; and we four squatted without the rail. In the three *maniap*'s of the infirmary a certain audience was gathered: the family of a sick child under treatment, the king's sister playing cards, a pretty girl, who swore I was the image of her father; in all perhaps a score. Terutak's wife had returned (even as she had vanished) unseen, and now sat, breathless and watchful, by her husband's side. Perhaps some rumour of our quest had gone abroad, or perhaps we had given the alert by our unseemly freedom: certain, at least, that in the faces of all present expectation and alarm were mingled.

Captain Reid announced, without preface or disguise, that I was come to purchase; Terutak', with sudden gravity, refused to sell. He was pressed; he persisted. It was explained we only wanted one: no matter, two were necessary for the healing of the sick. He was rallied, he was reasoned with: in vain. He sat there, serious and still, and refused. All this was only a preliminary skirmish; hitherto no sum of money had been mentioned; but now the captain brought his great guns to bear. He named a pound, then two, then three. Out of the *maniap*'s one person after another came to join the group, some with mere excitement, others with consternation in their faces. The pretty girl crept to my side; it was then that – surely with the most artless flattery – she informed me of my likeness to her father. Tamaiti the infidel sat with hanging head and every mark of dejection. Terutak' streamed with sweat, his eye was glazed, his face wore a painful rictus, his chest heaved like that of one spent with running. The man must have been by nature covetous; and I doubt if ever I saw moral agony more tragically displayed. His wife by his side passionately encouraged his resistance.

And now came the charge of the old guard. The captain, making a skip, named the surprising figure of five pounds. At the word the *maniap*'s were emptied. The king's sister flung down her cards and came to the front to listen, a cloud on her brow. The pretty girl beat her breast and cried with wearisome iteration that if the box were hers I should have it. Terutak's wife was beside herself with pious fear, her face discomposed, her voice (which scarce ceased from warning and encouragement) shrill as a whistle. Even Terutak' lost that image-like immobility which he had hitherto maintained. He rocked on his mat, threw up his closed knees alternately, and struck himself on the breast after the manner of dancers. But he came gold out of the furnace; and with what voice was left him continued to reject the bribe.

And now came a timely interjection. 'Money will not heal the sick,' observed the king's sister sententiously; and as soon as I heard the remark translated my eyes were unsealed, and I began to blush for my employment. Here was a sick child, and I sought, in the view of its parents, to remove the medicine-box. Here was the priest of a religion, and I (a heathen millionaire) was corrupting him to sacrilege. Here was a greedy man, torn in twain betwixt greed and conscience; and I sat by and relished, and lustfully renewed his torments. *Ave, Caesar!*[11] Smothered in a corner, dormant but not dead, we have all the one touch of nature: an infant passion for the sand and blood of the arena. So I brought to an end my first and last experience of the joys of the millionaire, and departed amid silent awe. Nowhere else can I expect to stir the depths of human nature by an offer of five pounds; nowhere else, even at the expense of millions, could I hope to see the evil of riches stand so legibly exposed. Of all the bystanders, none but the king's sister retained any memory of the gravity and danger of the thing in hand. Their eyes glowed, the girl beat her breast, in senseless animal excitement. Nothing was offered them; they stood neither to gain nor to lose; at the mere name and wind of these great sums Satan possessed them.

From this singular interview I went straight to the palace; found the king; confessed what I had been doing; begged him, in my name, to compliment Terutak' on his virtue, and to have a similar box made for me against the return of the schooner. Tembinok', Rubam, and one of the Daily Papers – him we used to call 'the Facetiae[12] Column' – laboured for a while of some idea, which was at last intelligibly delivered. They feared I thought the box would cure me; whereas, without the wizard, it was useless; and when I was threatened with another cold I should do better to rely on 'pain-killer'. I explained I merely wished to keep it in my 'outch' as a thing made in Apemama; and these honest men were much relieved.

Late the same evening, my wife, crossing the isle to windward, was aware of singing in the bush. Nothing is more common in that hour and place than the jubilant carol of the toddy-cutter, swinging high overhead, beholding below him the narrow ribbon of the isle, the surrounding field of ocean, and the fires of the sunset. But this was of a graver character, and seemed to proceed from the ground-level. Advancing a little in the thicket, Mrs. Stevenson saw a clear space, a fine mat spread in the midst, and on the mat a wreath of white flowers and one of the devil-work boxes. A woman – whom we guess to have been Mrs. Terutak' – sat in front, now drooping over the box like a mother over a cradle, now lifting her face and directing her song to heaven. A passing toddy-cutter told my wife that she was praying. Probably she did not so much pray as deprecate; and perhaps even the ceremony was one of disenchantment. For the box was already doomed; it was to pass from its green medicine-tree, reverend precinct, and devout attendants; to be handled by the profane; to cross three seas; to come to land under the foolscap of St. Paul's; to be domesticated within hail of Lillie Bridge;[13] there to be dusted by the British house-maid, and to take perhaps the roar of London for the voice of the outer sea along the reef. Before even we had finished dinner Chench had begun his journey, and one of the newspapers had already placed the box upon my table as the gift of Tembinok'.

I made haste to the palace, thanked the king, but offered to restore the box, for I could not bear that the sick of the island should be made to suffer. I was amazed by his reply. Terutak', it appeared, had still three or four in reserve against an accident; and his reluctance, and the dread painted at first on every face, was not in the least occasioned by the prospect of medical destitution, but by the immediate divinity of Chench. How much more did I respect the king's command, which had been able to extort in a moment and for nothing a sacrilegious favour that I had in vain solicited with millions! But now I had a difficult task in front of me; it was not in my view that Terutak' should suffer by his virtue; and I must persuade the king to share my opinion, to let me enrich one of his subjects, and (what was yet more delicate) to pay for my present. Nothing shows the king in a more becoming light than the fact that I succeeded. He demurred at the principle; he exclaimed, when he heard it, at the sum. 'Plenty money!' cried he, with contemptuous displeasure. But his resistance was never serious; and when he had blown off his ill-humour – 'A'right,' said he. 'You give him. Mo' betta.'

Armed with this permission, I made straight for the infirmary. The night was now come, cool, dark, and starry. On a mat, hard by a clear fire of wood and coco-shell, Terutak' lay beside his wife. Both were smiling; the agony was over, the king's command had reconciled (I must suppose) their agitating scruples; and I was bidden to sit by them and share the circulating pipe. I was a little moved myself when I placed five gold sovereigns in the wizard's hand; but there was no sign of emotion in Terutak' as he returned them, pointed to the palace, and named Tembinok'. It was a changed scene when I had managed to explain. Terutak', long, dour Scots fisherman as he was, expressed his satisfaction within bounds; but the wife beamed; and there was an old gentleman present – her father, I suppose – who seemed nigh translated. His eyes stood out of his head; '*Kaupoi, kaupoi* – rich, rich!' ran on his lips like a refrain; and he could not meet my eye but what he gurgled into foolish laughter.

I might now go home, leaving that fire-lit family party gloating over their new millions, and consider my strange day. I had tried and rewarded the virtue of Terutak'. I had played the millionaire, had behaved abominably, and then in some degree repaired my thoughtlessness. And now I had my box, and could open it and look within. It contained a miniature sleeping-mat and a white shell. Tamaiti, interrogated next day as to the shell, explained it was not exactly Chench, but a cell, or body, which he would at times inhabit. Asked why there was a sleeping-mat, he retorted indignantly, 'Why have you mats?' And this was the sceptical Tamaiti! But island scepticism is never deeper than the lips.

CHAPTER VII

THE KING OF APEMAMA

Thus all things on the island, even the priests of the gods, obey the word of Tembinok'. He can give and take, and slay, and allay the scruples of the conscientious, and do all things (apparently) but interfere in the cookery of a turtle. 'I got power' is his favourite word; it interlards his conversation; the thought haunts him and is ever fresh; and when he has asked and meditates of foreign countries, he looks up with a smile and reminds you, '*I* got *power.*' Nor is his delight only in the possession, but in the exercise. He rejoices in the crooked and violent paths of kingship like a strong man to run a race, or like an artist in his art. To feel, to use his power, to embellish his island and the picture of the island life after a private ideal, to milk the island vigorously, to extend his singular museum – these employ delightfully the sum of his abilities. I never saw a man more patently in the right trade.

It would be natural to suppose this monarchy inherited intact through generations. And so far from that, it is a thing of yesterday. I was already a boy at school while Apemama was yet republican, ruled by a noisy council of Old Men, and torn with incurable feuds. And Tembinok' is no Bourbon;[1] rather the son of a Napoleon. Of course he is well-born. No man need aspire high in the isles of the Pacific unless his pedigree be long and in the upper regions mythical. And our king counts cousinship with most of the high families in the archipelago, and traces his descent to a shark and a heroic woman. Directed by an oracle, she swam beyond sight of land to meet her revolting paramour, and received at sea the seed of a predestined family. 'I think lie,' is the king's emphatic commentary; yet he is proud of the legend. From this illustrious beginning the fortunes of the race must have declined; and Teñkoruti, the grandfather of Tembinok',[2] was the chief of a village at the north end of the island. Kuria and Aranuka were yet independent; Apemama itself the arena of devastating feuds. Through this perturbed period of history the figure of Teñkoruti stalks memorable. In war he was swift and bloody; several towns fell to his spear, and the inhabitants were butchered to a man. In civil life his arrogance was unheard of. When the council of Old Men was summoned, he went to the Speak House, delivered his mind, and left without waiting to be answered. Wisdom had spoken: let others opine according to their folly. He was feared and hated, and this was his pleasure. He was no poet; he cared not for arts or knowledge. 'My gran'patha one thing savvy, savvy pight,' observed the king. In some lull of their own disputes the Old Men of Apemama adventured on the conquest of Kuria and Aranuka; and this unlicked Caius Marcius[3] was elected general of the united troops. Success attended him; the islands were reduced, and Teñkoruti returned to his own government, glorious and detested. He died about 1860, in the seventieth year of his age and the full odour of unpopularity. He was tall and lean, says his grandson, looked extremely old, and 'walked all the same young man.' The same observer gave me a significant detail. The survivors of that rough epoch were all defaced with spearmarks; there was none on the body of this skilful fighter. 'I see old man, no got a spear,' said the king.

Teñkoruti left two sons, Tembaitake and Tembinatake. Tembaitake, our king's father, was short, middling stout, a poet, a good genealogist, and something of a fighter; it seems he took himself seriously, and was perhaps scarce conscious that he was in all things the creature and nursling of his brother. There was no shadow of dispute between the pair: the greater man filled with alacrity and content the second place; held the breach in war, and all the portfolios in the time of peace; and, when his brother rated him, listened in silence, looking on the ground. Like Teñkoruti, he was tall and lean and a swift walker – a rare trait in the islands. He possessed every accomplishment. He knew sorcery, he was the best genealogist of his day, he was a poet, he could dance and make canoes and armour;

and the famous mast of Apemama, which ran one joint higher than the mainmast of a full-rigged ship, was of his conception and design. But these were avocations, and the man's trade was war. 'When my uncle go make wa', he laugh,' said Tembinok'. He forbade the use of field fortification, that protractor of native hostilities; his men must fight in the open, and win or be beaten out of hand; his own activity inspired his followers; and the swiftness of his blows beat down, in one lifetime, the resistance of three islands. He made his brother sovereign, he left his nephew absolute. 'My uncle make all smooth,' said Tembinok'. 'I mo' king than my patha: I got power,' he said, with formidable relish.

Such is the portrait of the uncle drawn by the nephew. I can set beside it another by a different artist, who has often – I may say always – delighted me with his romantic taste in narrative, but not always – and I may say not often – persuaded me of his exactitude. I have already denied myself the use of so much excellent matter from the same source, that I begin to think it time to reward good resolution; and his account of Tembinatake agrees so well with the king's, that it may very well be (what I hope it is) the record of a fact, and not (what I suspect) the pleasing exercise of an imagination more than sailorly. A.,[4] for so I had perhaps better call him, was walking up the island after dusk, when he came on a lighted village of some size, was directed to the chief's house, and asked leave to rest and smoke a pipe. 'You will sit down, and smoke a pipe, and wash, and eat, and sleep,' replied the chief, 'and to-morrow you will go again.' Food was brought, prayers were held (for this was in the brief day of Christianity), and the chief himself prayed with eloquence and seeming sincerity. All evening A. sat and admired the man by the firelight. He was six feet high, lean, with the appearance of many years, and an extraordinary air of breeding and command. 'He looked like a man who would kill you laughing,' said A., in singular echo of one of the king's expressions. And again: 'I had been reading the Musketeer books, and he reminded me of Aramis.'[5] Such is the portrait of Tembinatake, drawn by an expert romancer.

We had heard many tales of 'my patha'; never a word of my uncle till two days before we left. As the time approached for our departure

Tembinok' became greatly changed; a softer, a more melancholy, and, in particular, a more confidential man appeared in his stead. To my wife he contrived laboriously to explain that though he knew he must lose his father in the course of nature, he had not minded nor realised it till the moment came; and that now he was to lose us he repeated the experience. We showed fireworks one evening on the terrace. It was a heavy business; the sense of separation was in all our minds, and the talk languished. The king was specially affected, sat disconsolate on his mat, and often sighed. Of a sudden one of the wives stepped forth from a cluster, came and kissed him in silence, and silently went again. It was just such a caress as we might give to a disconsolate child, and the king received it with a child's simplicity. Presently after we said good-night and withdrew; but Tembinok' detained Mr. Osbourne,[6] patting the mat by his side and saying: 'Sit down. I feel bad. I like talk.' Osbourne sat down by him. 'You like some beer?' said he; and one of the wives produced a bottle. The king did not partake, but sat sighing and smoking a meerschaum pipe. 'I very sorry you go,' he said at last. 'Miss Stlevens he good man, woman he good man, boy he good man; all good man. Woman he smart all the same man. My woman' (glancing towards his wives) 'he good woman, no very smart. I think Miss Stlevens he big chiep all the same cap'n man-o'-wa'. I think Miss Stlevens he rich man all the same me. All go schoona. I very sorry. My patha he go, my uncle he go, my cutcheons he go, Miss Stlevens he go: all go. You no see king cry before. King all the same man: feel bad, he cry. I very sorry.'

In the morning it was the common topic in the village that the king had wept. To me he said: 'Last night I no can 'peak: too much here,' laying his hand upon his bosom. 'Now you go away all the same my pamily. My brothers, my uncle go away. All the same.' This was said with a dejection almost passionate. And it was the first time I had heard him name his uncle, or indeed employ the word. The same day he sent me a present of two corselets, made in the island fashion of plaited fibre, heavy and strong. One had been worn by Teñkoruti, one by Tembaitake; and the gift being gratefully received, he sent me, on the return of his messengers, a third[7] – that of Tembinatake. My curiosity was roused; I begged for information as to the three wearers;

and the king entered with gusto into the details already given. Here was a strange thing, that he should have talked so much of his family, and not once mentioned that relative of whom he was plainly the most proud. Nay, more: he had hitherto boasted of his father; thenceforth he had little to say of him; and the qualities for which he had praised him in the past were now attributed where they were due, — to the uncle. A confusion might be natural enough among islanders, who call all the sons of their grandfather by the common name of father. But this was not the case with Tembinok'. Now the ice was broken the word uncle was perpetually in his mouth; he who had been so ready to confound was now careful to distinguish; and the father sank gradually into a self-complacent ordinary man, while the uncle rose to his true stature as the hero and founder of the race.

The more I heard and the more I considered, the more this mystery of Tembinok's behaviour puzzled and attracted me. And the explanation, when it came, was one to strike the imagination of a dramatist. Tembinok' had two brothers. One, detected in private trading, was banished, then forgiven, lives to this day in the island, and is the father of the heir-apparent, Paul. The other fell beyond forgiveness. I have heard it was a love-affair with one of the king's wives, and the thing is highly possible in that romantic archipelago. War was attempted to be levied; but Tembinok' was too swift for the rebels, and the guilty brother escaped in a canoe. He did not go alone. Tembinatake had a hand in the rebellion, and the man who had gained a kingdom for a weakling brother was banished by that brother's son. The fugitives came to shore in other islands, but Tembinok' remains to this day ignorant of their fate.

So far history. And now a moment for conjecture. Tembinok' confused habitually, not only the attributes and merits of his father and his uncle, but their diverse personal appearance. Before he had even spoken, or thought to speak, of Tembinatake, he had told me often of a tall, lean father, skilled in war, and his own schoolmaster in genealogy and island arts. How if both were fathers, one natural, one adoptive? How if the heir of Tembaitake, like the heir of Tembinok' himself, were not a son, but an adopted nephew? How if the founder of the monarchy, while he worked for his brother, worked at the same time for the child of his loins? How if on the death of Tembaitake, the two stronger natures, father and son, king and kingmaker, clashed, and Tembinok', when he drove out his uncle, drove out the author of his days? Here is at least a tragedy four-square.

The king took us on board in his own gig, dressed for the occasion in the naval uniform. He had little to say, he refused refreshments, shook us briefly by the hand, and went ashore again. That night the palm-tops of Apemama had dipped behind the sea, and the schooner sailed solitary under the stars.

NOTES

I am particularly indebted in these Notes to: Margaret Stevenson, *From Saranac to the Marquesas and Beyond, being Letters written by Mrs. M. I. Stevenson during 1887–8, to her sister, Jane Whyte Balfour*, ed. M. C. Balfour (London, 1903); Fanny Stevenson, *The Cruise of the 'Janet Nichol' Among the South Sea Islands: A Diary by Mrs. Robert Louis Stevenson* (London, 1915); R. L. Stevenson and Fanny Stevenson, *Our Samoan Adventure: with a Three-year Diary by Mrs. Stevenson now published for the first time*, ed. Charles Neider (London, 1956); Patrick O'Reilly and Raoul Teissier, *Tahitiens: répertoire bio-bibliographique de la Polynésie française* and *Supplément* (Paris, 1962 and 1966); R. L. Stevenson, *The Letters of Robert Louis Stevenson*, ed. Bradford A. Booth and Ernest Mehew (New Haven & London, 1994–5); R. L. Stevenson's unpublished journals of the *Casco* and *Equator* voyages (Huntington Library, San Marino); and Lloyd Osbourne's Diary for 1889 (Beinecke Library, Yale University, New Haven).

PART I: THE MARQUESAS

CHAPTER I: AN ISLAND LANDFALL

1. *Lord Tennyson's hero*: The narrator of Tennyson's 'Locksley Hall' (1842), who prefers Europe to an exotic escape: 'Better fifty years of Europe than a cycle of Cathay'.
2. *Rob Roy or Barbarossa*: 'Red Robert', the Scottish freebooter, Robert Macgregor; 'Redbeard', the Holy Roman Emperor, Frederick I.
3. *the sad Tahitian proverb*: Invented by Herman Melville (adapting an authentic Tahitian saying) in *Omoo: A Narrative of Adventures in the South Seas* (1847).
4. *Vivien*: Enchantress of Arthurian romance.

5. *the Directory*: Alexander G. Findlay, *A Directory for the Navigation of the South Pacific Ocean*. Stevenson had the fifth edition (London, 1884).

6. *Gaius or Papinian*: Distinguished Roman jurists.

7. *blood-boltered*: Clotted or clogged with blood.

CHAPTER II: MAKING FRIENDS

1. *'Beach-la-Mar'*: The lingua franca of the Pacific (its name derived from the Portuguese 'bicho do mar', sea-slug), called 'Beach de Mar' by Stevenson in Part IV, Ch. II.

2. *Majuro . . . Jaluit*: Islands in the Marshall Islands, visited by Stevenson in the *Janet Nicoll*, 19–26 June 1890.

3. *a gendarme who had taught school in Rapa-iti*: Probably the 'sergeant of gendarmerie' Stevenson met at Atuona, Hiva Oa (Part I, Ch. XIV), who had taught on Rapa-iti (Rapa, in the Austral Islands).

4. *Mr. Benjamin Hird*: The Aberdonian supercargo on the *Janet Nicoll* and one of those on board to whom Stevenson dedicated *Island Nights' Entertainments* (1893).

5. *'Janet Nicoll'*: The steamer in which Stevenson sailed the Pacific, 11 April to 26 July 1890.

6. *Noumea*: Capital of the French colony of New Caledonia where Stevenson stayed, 26 July to 2 August 1890.

7. *Cook*: James Cook (1728–79), the Pacific voyager.

8. *Captain Speedy*: Member of the British military expedition to Abyssinia of 1868.

9. *Mr. Andrew Lang*: (1844–1912) London-based Scottish scholar, writer, translator of Homer and friend of Stevenson.

10. *long-pig*: An English translation of a supposed cannibal term for human flesh.

11. *Kanaka*: ('Man' in Hawaiian) a Pacific islander.

12. *Lovat and Struan*: 18th-century Scottish Jacobite chiefs.

13. *Michael Scott*: (c. 1175–c. 1230) Scottish scholar and astrologer with a reputation as a wizard.

14. *Lord Derwentwater*: James Radcliffe, 3rd Earl of Derwentwater, English Jacobite, beheaded in 1716.

15. *the second-sight*: Power of seeing as present things distant in time or space.

16. *the Water Kelpie*: In Scottish folklore a malignant water-spirit taking the form of a horse.

17. *the legend of Rahero*: a Tahitian legend Stevenson heard at Tautira, Tahiti, and made into his ballad 'The Song of Rahéro', published in *Ballads* (1891).

18. *the Cluny Macphersons . . . the Appin Stewarts*: The Macphersons of Cluny and the Stewarts of Appin, Argyle, were involved in Jacobite affairs in the 18th century.

19. *the Tevas*: Distinguished Tahitian dynasty, to which Stevenson allied himself by exchanging names with his Tahitian host, Teriitera (or Ori a Ori).

20. *from the blue bed to the brown*: Alluding to the opening of Goldsmith's *The Vicar of Wakefield* (1766), which describes the tranquil life of the vicar and his wife: 'all our adventures were by the fire-side, and all our migrations from the blue bed to the brown'.

21. *the flying city of Laputa*: In Swift's *Gulliver's Travels* (1726).

22. *Captain Otis*: A. H. Otis, captain of the *Casco*.

CHAPTER III: THE MAROON

1. *the Hawaiian poet*: Unidentified.

2. *'Que le jour me dure'*: Song with words and music by Jean-Jacques Rousseau (1712–78).

3. *purao*: *Hibiscus tiliaceus*, the beach hibiscus.

4. *maya*: 'Illusion', a term of Hindu philosophy.

5. *Mrs. Stevenson and the ship's cook*: Fanny Stevenson and the *Casco*'s original cook, Antone Cousina.

6. *den*: A narrow valley.

7. *the cook (whose conscience was not clear)*: He had not paid for favours received from a Marquesan lady.

8. *Sandwich Islands*: Former name of the Hawaiian Islands.

9. *Molokai*: The leper colony of the Hawaiian Islands, visited by Stevenson in May 1889 and the subject of South Sea Letters not collected in *In the South Seas* (1896).

10. *popoi*: Cooked and mashed breadfruit.

CHAPTER IV: DEATH

1. *Bishop Dordillon*: Mgr René Ildefonse Dordillon (1808–88), Catholic missionary, arrived Taiohae, Nukuhiva, in 1846 and died there.

2. *Tai-o-hae*: Capital of the Marquesas, on the island of Nukuhiva (see Part I, Ch. VIII).

3. *Stanislao Moanatini*: (Otherwise Stanislaos, or Stanislaus) adopted son and heir of Temoana, the Taiohae chief promoted to 'king' by the Europeans (see Part I, Ch. IX).

4. *Herman Melville*: (1819–91) American author whose first work, *Typee: A Peep at Polynesian Life* (1846), is based on his four weeks at Nukuhiva in 1842.

5. *Charles Warren Stoddard*: (1843–1909) American South Sea traveller and author of *South-Sea Idyls* (1873) who met Stevenson in San Francisco in late 1879 or 1880 and introduced him to Melville's South Sea works.

6. *mummy-apple*: The fruit of the mammee tree.

7. *Mr. Osbourne*: Lloyd Osbourne (1868–1947), Stevenson's stepson.

8. *tapu*: 'Taboo' is the usual English spelling of the Polynesian word.

9. *I heard*: From Père Orens at Hiva Oa.

10. *eva*: Probably the plant *Ceodes brunoniana*.

11. *Queen Vaekehu*: (1823?–1901) Wife of the chief Temoana of Taiohae, Nukuhiva, promoted to 'queen' by the Europeans.

12. *erimatua*: As Stevenson says, the word does not appear in Tahitian dictionaries.

13. *M. Nouveau*: Pierre Nouveau (1854–1904), one of two gendarmes Stevenson met at Atuona, Hiva Oa (see Part I, Ch. XIV), not 'the sergeant' who 'had taught school in Rapa-iti' (Part I, Chs XIV, II) but 'the younger gendarme', according to Stevenson's MS journal.

14. *Penrhyn*: (Or Tongareva) one of the Cook Islands, visited by Stevenson in the *Janet Nicoll*, 9–10 May 1890.

15. *Cato*: Marcus Porcius Cato, the Elder (234–149 BC), a stern moralist.

16. *Dr. Codrington*: Stevenson is quoting (though not exactly) from *The Melanesian Languages* (1885), by the missionary and anthropologist R. H. Codrington.

CHAPTER V: DEPOPULATION

1. *Mr. Darwin's theory of coral islands*: Charles Darwin (1809–82) formed his theory about the formation of coral islands during his voyage in the *Beagle*.

2. *'Happy is the man that has his quiver full of them'*: Psalms, 127:5.

3. *I shall have to tell in another place . . . how a child in Manihiki*: Reflecting Stevenson's (unfulfilled) intention of publishing an account of occurrences 6–7 May 1890 at Manihiki in the Cook Islands, which were later described by Fanny Stevenson in *The Cruise of the 'Janet Nichol'*, 46ff.

4. *the Tahitian brotherhood of Oro*: A Tahitian society described in the journals kept by Joseph Banks and James Cook during the voyage of the *Endeavour* (1768–71), rewritten and edited in John Hawkesworth's *Account of the Voyages* (1773).

5. *Mangareva*: In the Tuamotu (formerly Paumotu) Islands.

6. *pamphlet by the Rev. S. E. Bishop: 'Why are the Hawaiians Dying Out?'*: A paper read by S. E. Bishop (1827–1909) to the Honolulu Social Science Association in November 1888 and discussed by Stevenson in a letter to Bishop (*Letters*, VI, 308–9).

7. *Tartuffe*: The hypocritical prude in Molière's *Le Tartuffe* (1664).

8. *lotos islands*: With reference to the lotos fruit in the *Odyssey* which makes those who eat it forget their homes and wish to remain for ever in Lotos-land.

9. *mairedupalais*: 'Mayor of the palace', or *major domus*, the title of the prime ministers of the Frankish kings.

10. *the Hawaiian account of Cook*: The account of Hawaii in James Cook and James King, *A Voyage to the Pacific Ocean* (1784).

11. *Krusenstern's . . . description of a Russian man-of-war at the Marquesas*: In A. J. Krusenstern, *Voyage Round the World* (1813).

12. *the story of the discovery of Tutuila, when the . . . women . . . prostituted themselves . . . to the French*: See the account of the Samoan island of Tutuila in J.-F. de Galaup de La Pérouse, *Voyage de La Pérouse autour du monde* (1797).

13. *Mr. Lawes, the missionary of Savage Island, told me*: When Stevenson visited the mission station on Savage Island (or Niue), an island between the Cook Islands and the Tonga Islands, in the *Janet Nicoll*, 28 April 1890.

14. *a Lascar*: An East Indian sailor.

15. *Ratcliffe Highway*: Location of squalid brothels catering for sailors in 18th- and 19th-century London.

CHAPTER VI: CHIEFS AND *TAPUS*

1. *the return and the wars of the French*: The French took possession of Nukuhiva in 1842, but evacuated their troops from Taiohae in December 1849, only to return them a few months later in 1850 when local wars broke out.

2. *Nestor*: An elder statesman among the Greeks in the *Iliad*.

3. *Father Siméon Delmas*: Jean-Baptiste Delmas (1862–1939), missionary and author of a history of the Catholic mission in the Marquesas.

4. *the peeled wand before a Highland inn*: Forbidding entry (see, for example, Ch. 28 of Scott's *Roy Roy* (1817)).

5. *tuhuka*: 'Which seems to mean priest, wizard, tattooer, practiser of any art, or, in a word, esoteric person', according to Stevenson in Part I, Ch. XIII, a definition consistent with that in Dordillon's *Grammaire et dictionnaire de la langue des Iles Marquises* (Paris, 1931–2): 'savant, artiste', etc.

6. *Ah Fu*: The Chinese cook taken aboard the *Casco* at Taiohae, who served Stevenson and family at Waikiki and on the *Equator* voyage.

7. *Dr. Campbell's 'Poenamo'*: J. L. Campbell, *Poenamo: Sketches of the Early Days of New Zealand* (1881). Stevenson had a presentation copy.

CHAPTER VII: HATIHEU

1. *Majuro*: Island in the Marshall Islands, visited by Stevenson in the *Janet Nicoll*, 20–24 June 1890.

2. *Pierre Loti*: Pseudonym of Julien Viaud (1850–1923), French naval officer and author of novels set in exotic locations, notably *Le Mariage de Loti* (1880), set in Tahiti and (partly) Nukuhiva.

3. *taluses*: Slopes of shattered rock.

4. *Brother Michel*: Eutrope Blanc (1832–99), a carpenter by trade, came to the Marquesas in 1863, constructed various buildings for the Catholic mission, and died at Atuona, Hiva Oa.

5. *Dr. Paul, of the West Kirk*: John Paul (1795–1873), minister of St Cuthbert's, Edinburgh.

6. *relievo*: A work in relief.

7. *la Dominique*: The Marquesan island Alvaro de Mendaña sailed past on a Sunday in 1595 and called Dominica, better known as Hiva Oa.

8. *I wrote in my journal I could not believe it*: He wrote: 'Père Michel is reported to have said that he would prefer death to the building of another church; now that I have examined his work, I believe he still dreams at night of more ambitious enterprises.'

9. *Augurs*: Officials in ancient Rome who sought knowledge of the future by observing the behaviour of birds and other indications.

CHAPTER VIII: THE PORT OF ENTRY

1. *The port . . . white falls*: The opening of this chapter is echoed in the opening paragraph of Stevenson and Osbourne's *The Wrecker* (1892), which begins at Taiohae.

2. *the shrewd Scot*: A Mr Cuthill, according to Margaret Stevenson, Stevenson's mother.

3. *cotton gin-mill*: Factory for separating seeds from fibre of cotton.

4. *tuhukas*: See note 5 to Part I, Ch. VI.

5. *loved not wisely, but too well*: Alluding to Othello's description of himself as 'one that lov'd not wisely but too well' (Shakespeare, *Othello*, V.ii.343).

6. *elephantiasis*: A disease chiefly of the tropics, resulting in the swelling of the legs and scrotum.

7. *Raiatea*: One of the Leeward Islands group within the Society Islands.

8. *A trader, who did not sell opium*: Identified in the MS journal as Regler, the trader at Anaho, Nukuhiva.

9. *Captain Hart*: John Hart (1838–1900), London-born American trader and planter who bought land on Hiva Oa (see Part I, Ch. XII).

10. *Government at Papeete*: The Marquesas were governed from Papeete, the capital of Tahiti.

11. *nostrum*: Pet remedy or scheme.

CHAPTER IX: THE HOUSE OF TEMOANA

1. *At least twice they have seized the archipelago, at least once deserted it*: The French took possession of the Marquesas in 1842, but evacuated all personnel from Vaitahu, Tahuata, in 1847, and from Taiohae, Nukuhiva, in 1849. They returned to Taiohae in 1850 to establish a penal colony, and remained in occupation when the penal colony was transferred to New Caledonia in 1853.

2. *Temoana*: (1821?–63) Chief of Taiohae.

3. *shampooed*: Massaged.

4. *the Comédie-Française*: The French national theatre, founded in the 17th century.

5. *'Marquis de Villemer'*: Novel by George Sand (Aurore Dupin), published in 1861, dramatized 1864.

6. *her leg was one of the sights of Tai-o-hae*: According to Herman Melville, who was aboard the US frigate *United States* when Vaekehu came aboard at Taiohae in October 1843 (see the first chapter of *Typee: A Peep at Polynesian Life*).

7. *whether . . . she might not regret and aspire after the barbarous and stirring past*: The narrator of Loti's *Le Mariage de Loti* wonders similarly: 'Regrette-t-elle son indépendance et la sauvagerie qui s'en va . . . ?'

8. *ganger*: Foreman of a gang of workmen.

9. *the story of Gordon*: Charles George Gordon (1833–85), British military hero killed at Khartoum.

10. *the Indian Mutiny*: The rebellion of Indian soldiers in the service of the British East India Company, which developed into an Anglo-Indian war of 1857–8.

11. *Spottiswoode*: When his Indian soldiers were to be disarmed, some of them having mutinied, Lieutenant-Colonel Spottiswoode felt the dishonour to his regiment so keenly that he killed himself.

12. *Sir Hugh Rose*: Sent to India in 1857, Sir Hugh Rose (1801–85) regained control of central India.

CHAPTER X: A PORTRAIT AND A STORY

1. *the time of the French exodus*: The French left Taiohae in December 1849 and returned a few months later in 1850.

2. *Mrs. Fisher, of Hatiheu*: Gertrude Maud Fisher (1859–1923), wife of a trader at Hatiheu, Nukuhiva, widowed 1892 and subsequently store-keeper at Taiohae.

3. *nostrum*: (Here) a special device or pet scheme of political or social reform.

4. *one of these native missionaries*: According to a note (probably by Sidney Colvin) in the 1896 edition of *In the South Seas*, 'The reference is to Maka, the Hawaiian missionary, at Butaritari in the Gilberts' (see Part III, Chs II, III).

5. *Nathan*: Biblical prophet who rebuked King David for adultery and murder (see II Samuel 12:1–14).

6. *Kauwealoha*: Samuel Kauwealoha, Hawaiian Protestant missionary, stationed on Ua Pou in the Marquesas from 1864 until his death in 1909.

7. *Kekela*: James Kekela, Hawaiian Protestant missionary, stationed on Hiva Oa in the Marquesas until his return to Honolulu in 1890.

8. *Mr. Whalon*: Jonathan Whalon, of the New England whaler *Congress*.

9. *ipsissima verba*: Very words.

CHAPTER XI: LONG-PIG – A CANNIBAL HIGH PLACE

1. *Mrs. Stevenson, senior*: In a letter to Colvin of January 1891, Fanny protested at these words ('that truly dreadful "Mrs Stevenson senior"') in *The South Seas* (1890) (*The Letters of Robert Louis Stevenson*, VII, 80). In his copy of *The South Seas* Colvin underlined the objectionable phrase and wrote 'my mother' in the margin (see the page reproduced in the catalogue of the *George Barr McCutcheon Sale*, 15 April, No. 639, American Art Association (New York, 1925)).

2. *Tautira*: Village in Tahiti where Stevenson stayed, 28 October to 25 December 1888.

3. *'dread foundations'*: Alluding to Wordsworth's line 'And Love her towers of dread foundation laid' ('Miscellaneous Sonnets', XLIV).

4. *to eat a man's flesh after he is dead is far less hateful than to oppress him whilst he lives*: Echoing Montaigne: 'Je pense qu'il y a plus de barbarie à manger un homme vivant qu'à le manger mort, à deschirer par tourmens et par geénes un corps encore plein de sentiment, ... que de le rostir et manger après qu'il est trespassé' ('Des cannibales', *Essais* (1580)).

5. *Theseus*: Hero of Greek legend who destroyed various monsters and brigands on his way to Athens.

6. *marae*: Correctly glossed by Stevenson in Part II, Ch. VI, as 'old Tahitian temple'.

7. *Melanesia*: One of the three main divisions of the Pacific islands, designating those with black-skinned inhabitants (from the Greek μέλας, black, + νῆοος, island).

8. *Micronesia*: One of the three main divisions of the Pacific islands, designating several groups of small islands in the western part of the North Pacific (from the Greek μικρός, small, + νῆοος, island).

9. *the Marshalls*: The Marshall Islands (Micronesia), visited by Stevenson in the *Janet Nicoll*, June 1890.

10. *the Gilbert zone*: The part of the Pacific containing the Gilbert Islands, now the Republic of Kiribati (Micronesia), visited by Stevenson in the *Equator*, July–November 1889 (see Parts III and IV), and again in the *Janet Nicoll*, June and July 1890.

11. *Dr. Turner*: George Turner, Protestant missionary who ran the Samoan Missionary Seminary at Malua, Upolu, and wrote *Nineteen Years in Polynesia* (1861).

12. *Malua*: On the north-west coast of the Samoan island of Upolu, visited by Stevenson when he addressed the Samoan students at the Seminary in January 1890.

13. *Onoatoa*: (Or Onotoa) one of the Gilbert Islands.

14. *Bougainville*: Louis Antoine de Bougainville (1729–1811), French Pacific voyager.

15. *carneying*: Cajoling, wheedling.

16. *one authority*: Probably Father Siméon Delmas.

CHAPTER XII: THE STORY OF A PLANTATION

1. *'Better fifty years of Europe . . .'*: The 'verdict of Lord Tennyson's hero' referred to in the second paragraph of *In the South Seas* (Part I, Ch. I).

2. *the American War*: The American Civil War, 1861–5.

3. *the late French war*: Perhaps referring to the French invasion of Hiva Oa which restored colonial order in 1880.

4. *tapa*: Cloth made by Polynesians from the bark of the Paper Mulberry.

5. *one of the Godeffroys*: An agent of the Hamburg firm of J. C. Godeffroy and Son, founded in 1877 and the largest of the early Pacific commercial organizations.

6. *chassepots*: Breech-loading rifles used by the French army between 1866 and 1874.

7. *kava*: A narcotic drink prepared from the masticated root and stem of the *Piper methysticum*.

8. *the survivor*: John Hart, who lived until 1900, Bishop Dordillon having died in 1888.

9. *Molokai*: The Hawaiian leper colony on the island of Molokai.

10. *Ile Masse*: The island of Eiao, in the north of the Marquesas.

CHAPTER XIII: CHARACTERS

1. *Captain Dewar*: James Cumming Dewar (1857–1908) had been at Menton on the French Riviera when Stevenson was there, November–December 1873 (see *Letters*, I, 366).

2. *Cape Flattery*: On the north-west coast of Washington, US.

3. *Rudel*: Jaufré Rudel, 12th-century troubadour, known for songs celebrating distant love ('amor de lonh').

4. *Celia's arbour*: Alluding to the lyric by Thomas Moore, 'By Celia's arbour all the night', set to music by Mendelssohn. An arrangement for flageolet was listed in the sales catalogue of Stevenson's books and papers.

5. *scuttle-butt*: A cask with a hole in it, for drinking-water on ships.

6. *Penelope*: In Homer's *Odyssey* she weaves a shroud by day which she unravels by night so that the work remains unfinished.

7. *Hercules*: Hero of Greek myth whose exploits included twelve labours.

CHAPTER XIV: IN A CANNIBAL VALLEY

1. *flamboyant*: A tropical tree, *Poiciana regia*, with flame-coloured flowers, its name the same in English as in French.

2. *fe'efe'e*: Elephantiasis.

3. *Father Orens*: Jean-Marie Fréchou (1811–95), Catholic missionary who came to the Marquesas in 1843 and died at Atuona, Hiva Oa, after fifty-two years in the islands.

4. *brummagem*: Something showy, sham, worthless (made in Birmingham).

5. *goyle*: A channel.

CHAPTER XV: THE TWO CHIEFS OF ATUONA

1. *when Ori and I 'made brothers'*: When staying at the Tahitian village of Tautira in November–December 1888, Stevenson exchanged names and became 'brothers' with the subchief, Teriitera (1838–1916), also known as Ori a Ori.

2. *animus affiliandi*: Desire to become adopted.

3. *One evening Captain Otis and Mr. Osbourne were on shore in the village*: An account of this evening by Captain Otis is reported in Arthur Johnstone, *Recollections of Robert Louis Stevenson in the Pacific* (1905), 30–34.

4. *Prester John*: A fabulous Christian king reputed in medieval times to rule over an empire in Asia or, alternatively, Africa.

5. *Assaracus*: A Trojan prince, great-grandfather of Aeneas.

6. *M. Grévy*: Jules Grévy, President of France, 1879–87.

7. *Jacob and Esau*: Jacob bought the birthright from his brother, Esau, and then obtained the paternal blessing intended for Esau (see Genesis 25, 27).

PART II: THE PAUMOTUS

CHAPTER I: THE DANGEROUS ARCHIPELAGO – ATOLLS AT A DISTANCE

1. *the atoll; a thing of problematic origin and history, the reputed creature of an insect apparently unidentified*: The atoll's origins are still debated but it is now known to be the creature of the coral polyp.

2. *instances*: Solicitations, entreaties.

3. *The mate*: Georges Henri Goltz (1826–1912), father of 'Mrs. Fisher of Hatiheu' (Part I, Ch. X), was engaged at Taiohae as pilot and was dignified, according to Stevenson's mother, but 'too fond of talking' and drinking, so dismissed at Tahiti (Margaret Stevenson, *From Saranac to the Marquesas*, 139).

4. *'nihil astra praeter/ Vidit et undas'*: 'Saw nothing but stars and waves' (Horace, *Odes*, III.xxvii).

5. *'such stuff as dreams are made on'*: Shakespeare, *The Tempest*, IV.i.156–7.

6. *Roggewein*: Jacob Roggeveen crossed the Pacific in 1722 in command of a Dutch exploring expedition.

7. *Mr. Narii Salmon*: (1856–1906) Ship's captain, brother of Moetia and Tati (the Princess Moe and Chief Tati of Papara encountered by Stevenson in Tahiti).

8. *Emerson's verses*: 'And the lone seaman all the night/ Sails, astonished, amid stars' (Emerson, 'Initial, Daemonic, and Celestial Love', *Poems* (1847)).

CHAPTER II: FAKARAVA: AN ATOLL AT HAND

1. *the coral . . . and the fish*: The passage has similarities with the description of the *Farallone*'s arrival at the atoll in Stevenson and Osbourne's *The Ebb Tide* (1894), 123.

2. *Oceanus*: (Ocean) sea-god of Greek myth, and river encircling the Earth.

3. *Anaa*: Like Fakarava, an island in the north-western Tuamotus (or Paumotus).

4. *abattis*: Defensive rampart made of felled trees.

5. *stumbling among taro as I went*: Alluding to the line 'Stumbling on melons, as I pass' in 'The Garden' by Andrew Marvell (1621–78).

6. *solum*: Ground, soil.

7. *M. Cuzent*: Gilbert Cuzent, author of various studies of the flora of the French Pacific colonies.

8. *Apemama*: (Or Abemama) the island in the Gilbert Islands where Stevenson stayed, September–October 1889 (see Part IV).

9. *Funafuti and Arorai*: Funafuti is one of the Ellice Islands and Arorai (or Arorae) one of the Gilbert Islands. For Stevenson's encounters with coral on those islands, on 27 May and 9 June 1890, see *The Cruise of the 'Janet Nichol'*, 94, 112–14, and Fanny Stevenson to Sidney Colvin, January 1891, *The Letters of Robert Louis Stevenson*, VII, 79–80.

CHAPTER III: A HOUSE TO LET IN A LOW ISLAND

1. *Mr. Donat*: François Donat-Rimarau, half French, half Tahitian, briefly interviewed in Maryland Allen, 'South Sea Memories of R.L.S.', *The Bookman*, XLIII, March – August 1916, 591–603.

2. *the Governor in Papeete*: Like the Marquesas, the Tuamotus were governed from Papeete, Tahiti.

3. *dominie*: Schoolmaster, teacher.

4. *Wilkie*: David Wilkie (1785–1841), Scottish painter known for his genre pictures. The print on Fakarava, according to Stevenson's mother, was 'David Wilkie's "Village School" ' (*From Saranac to the Marquesas*, 149).

5. *Mulready*: William Mulready (1786–1863), Irish painter known for his genre pictures.

6. *'Le brigade du Général Lepasset brûlant son drapeau devant Metz'*: An incident in the Franco-Prussian war, 1870–71.

7. *precentor*: Leader of singing in church.

8. *Cincinnatus*: Legendary Roman hero of 5th century B C who was called from his plough in a military crisis, quickly defeated the enemy and returned to his plough.

9. *to shift*: To change clothing.

CHAPTER IV: TRAITS AND SECTS IN THE PAUMOTUS

1. *a pamphlet (I will not give the author's name)*: Perhaps Clary Wilmot, *Notice sur l'archipel des îles Tuamotu* (Papeete, 1888), which Stevenson mentions in the *Black and White* version of the 'Paumotus' part of *In the South Seas*.

2. *sirens*: Female creatures of Greek myth whose fatally enticing song lured passing voyagers.

3. *congeners*: Of the same kind or nature (the peoples of the Tuamotus and the Marquesas were Polynesians).

4. *they*: The children.

5. *they*: The children.

6. *jealously*: Carefully.

7. *jealously*: Suspiciously.

8. *Mr. Wilmot*: Clary Wilmot (1835–1903), master mariner whose *Notice sur l'archipel des îles Tuamotu* (Papeete, 1888) Stevenson mentions in the *Black and White* version of 'The Paumotus'.

9. *an orthodox fellow-countryman*: Presumably the Duncan Cameron mentioned later in this chapter.

10. *Tiree*: An island in the Hebrides.

11. *Joseph Smith . . . Brigham Young*: After the murder in 1884 of their founder, Joseph Smith, the Mormons moved under Brigham Young to Salt Lake, Utah.

12. *the Cameronians and the United Presbyterians*: Factions of the Protestant Church in Scotland.

13. *the Pharisees*: Jewish sect at the time of Christ which stressed ritual purity and strict adherence to religious laws.

14. *the Holy Willies*: Religious hypocrites, after the narrator of Burns's poem 'Holy Willie's Prayer' (1799).

15. *My informant*: Donat-Rimarau.

16. *Taiarapu*: The Taiarapu peninsula, Tahiti. (Tautira, where Stevenson stayed, November–December 1888, was on the north coast of Taiarapu.)

17. *an eye-witness, Tasmanian born*: Named in the M S journal as Captain Smith.

18. *Makatea*: An island in the Tuamotus.

19. *'The Heaving of the Lead'*: Song by William Shield (1748–1829) to words by W. Pearce.

CHAPTER V: A PAUMOTUAN FUNERAL

1. *that chapter in Job*: Job 14.

2. *I wrote at the time in my diary*: He wrote in his MS journal: 'Mr Donat called it a jest; it seemed to me somewhat in the nature of a terrified conjuration [etc.]'.

CHAPTER VI: GRAVEYARD STORIES

1. *my own doorstep in Upolu*: At Vailima on the Samoan island of Upolu, where Stevenson was reworking his journal into South Sea Letters for newspaper and periodical publication.

2. *Lafaele . . . afraid of 'spilits in the bush'*: The incident is mentioned in Fanny's diary entry for 23 October 1890, in *Our Samoan Adventure*, 57, and by Stevenson to Colvin, 2 [or 3] November 1890, *Letters*, VII, 24.

3. *The gods of Upolu and Savaii . . . are at war*: The account of the wars of the spirits of the Samoan islands of Upolu and Savaii was given to Stevenson and Fanny by Henry Simele, a minor chief from Savaii (see Fanny's diary, 7 October 1890, *Our Samoan Adventure*, 39–40).

4. *these reports have certainly significance*: As portents of war in Samoa (see Fanny's diary, 7 October 1890, *Our Samoan Adventure*, 40).

5. *a village, the name of which I do not mean to tell*: Probably Tautira, Tahiti, where Stevenson stayed, November–December 1888.

6. *a latitudinarian*: One with liberal views in religious matters.

7. *Herbert Spencer*: (1820–1903) English philosopher and social scientist.

8. *a man with a genius for such narrations*: François Donat-Rimarau, whose ghost stories told on the verandah of the rented house on Fakarava contributed to the atmosphere of Stevenson's story 'The Isle of Voices', collected in *Island Nights' Entertainments* (1893).

9. *Katiu*: An island in the Tuamotus.

10. *Christian in the Valley of the Shadow*: Bunyan's hero in the Valley of the Shadow of Death in *The Pilgrim's Progress* (1678, 1684).

11. *Haraiki*: An island in the Tuamotus.

12. *My authority*: Probably Donat-Rimarau, who was half Tahitian.

13. *Rua-a-mariterangi is again my authority*: At second hand, via 'My informant' (see note 15 below), probably Donat-Rimarau.

14. *Taenga*: An island in the Tuamotus.

15. *My informant*: Probably Donat-Rimarau.

16. *Penrhyn*: (Or Tongareva) in the northern Cook Islands, visited by Stevenson in the *Janet Nicoll*, 9–10 May 1890.

17. *a certain chief*: The story of this chief's reburial (told to Stevenson by Ben Hird, supercargo of the *Janet Nicoll*) is repeated by Fanny in *The Cruise of the 'Janet Nichol'*, 65, and the chief is briefly mentioned in a South Sea Letter not collected in *In the South Seas*, 'A Pearl Island: Penrhyn', reprinted in *Miscellanea, Works*, Vailima Edition, XXVI (1923), 427–35.

18. *Rarotongan*: From the island of Rarotonga in the southern Cook Islands.

19. *the late war*: In 1888–9 between Chiefs Tamasese and Mataafa (for an account, see Stevenson's *A Footnote to History* (1892)).

20. *The present king*: Referring probably to Malietoa Laupepa rather than to his rival, Mataafa Iosefo, and perhaps to 'some interesting talk with him [Laupepa] about Samoan superstitions' (Stevenson to Colvin, 2 [or 3] November 1890, *Letters*, VII, 20).

21. *the Carolines*: The Caroline Islands in the Western Pacific.

22. *A man*: Probably Donat-Rimarau.

23. *Dr. F. Otto Sierich, whose collection of folk-tales I expect*: Dr Sierich's collection of folk-tales, 'Samoanische Märchen', was published in instalments in *Internationales Archiv für Ethnographie*, XIII–XVII (1900–1904).

24. *Manu'a*: The Manua Islands form a group in the Samoan Islands.

25. *bale-fires*: Funeral fires.

26. *the unexpected sequel of the tale*: The dead man comes back to life (see 'Die Kahnfahrt eines Gespenstes', *Internationales Archiv für Ethnographie*, XVI (1903), 88–90).

27. *Mangaian*: From the island of Mangaia, in the southern Cook Islands.

28. *Proteus*: In Greek legend a sea-god who could assume many different shapes.

29. *avatars*: Incarnations, manifestations.

PART III: THE GILBERTS

CHAPTER I: BUTARITARI

1. *Mr. Osbourne, and my China boy, Ah Fu*: In the *Auckland Star* instalments of the two parts of 'The Gilberts' (published September 1891 to January 1892, before the break between Stevenson's family and his stepdaughter's husband, Joe Strong, in June–July 1892), Joe Strong's name appeared here, between Lloyd Osbourne's and Ah Fu's, and at five other places from which it has also been cut in *In the South Seas* by Stevenson or Colvin.

2. *Captain Dennis Reid*: A Scotsman in his twenties who habitually wore a Tam o' Shanter.

3. *Oahu*: The Hawaiian island on which Honolulu is situated.

4. *martello*: A circular fort for coastal defence.

5. *sinnet*: Braid or cord made by pleating strands of rope, grass, etc.

6. *lych-house*: A 'lych-house' is a mortuary, but the context implies the roofing part of a 'lych-gate', a roofed churchyard gate.

7. *lateen*: A triangular sail.

8. *tinsel*: Gaudy, tawdry.

9. *fasces*: The bundle of rods borne before an ancient Roman magistrate, consequently a symbol of authority.

10. *sacque*: A loose-fitting dress; in the MS journal a 'holuku' (or *holoku*), the voluminous 'Mother Hubbard' introduced to the Pacific by the missionaries.

11. *Mr. Williams*: L. B. Williams, who had deserted from an American ship, 21 October 1888.

12. *talking*: The mate of the *Equator* remarked that Williams 'could pay out more cable without coming to anchor than any man in the Islands' (quoted in Thomson Murray MacCallum, *Adrift in the South Seas, including Adventures with Robert Louis Stevenson* (Los Angeles, 1934), 251).

13. *Saul . . . and . . . David*: The biblical king of Israel and the minstrel whose playing soothed the troubled king (see I Samuel 16:14–23).

CHAPTER II: THE FOUR BROTHERS

1. *the memory of residents*: In the *Auckland Star* of 19 September 1891 the final paragraph of this chapter, 'The Four Brothers', reads: 'This chapter of history I have collected from the lips of eye-witnesses and actors; from Maka himself, from Mr Benson, an old resident, and from a fair helper, Mrs Adolph Rick'. (Maka was a Hawaiian missionary, Mrs Adolf Rick the wife of the manager of Wightman Brothers' Butaritari tradestore.)

2. *king Tetimararoa . . . Nakaeia*: High Chief Te Itimaroroa was succeeded in July 1852 by his son, Kaiea, aged fourteen.

3. *basilisks*: Mythical serpents which could kill with a glance.

4. *Messrs. Wightman*: Wightman Brothers, San Francisco traders, owners of the *Equator*.

5. *Maka and Kanoa*: Protestant missionaries, they appear with their wives in a photograph published in Fanny Stevenson's *The Cruise of the 'Janet Nichol'*. Maka worked on Butaritari from 1865 until 1894, when he returned to Hawaii, dying on Oahu in 1907; Kanoa came to Abaiang in the Gilberts with the American missionary Hiram Bingham in 1857.

6. *redux*: Brought back, returned.

7. *Abou ben Adhem*: After the character in the poem 'Abou Ben Adhem' by Leigh Hunt (1784–1859).

8. *Eglon . . . Ehud*: The biblical king of Moab and his assassin (see Judges 3:12–30).

9. *impignorate*: Pledged, pawned.

CHAPTER III: AROUND OUR HOUSE

1. *copra*: The dried kernel of the coconut, yielding coconut oil.

2. *toddy-cutters*: Those drawing sap for fermentation as toddy, palm-tree wine.

3. *heliograph*: Signal by reflecting the sun's rays.

4. *Bacchic*: Pertaining to Bacchus, the Roman god of wine.

5. *well 'worthy of a grace'*: Alluding to the line in Burns's 'To a Haggis': 'Weel are you wordy o' a grace'.

6. *hidalgo*: Spanish nobleman of the lowest rank.

7. *cutty*: Short.

8. *brand*: Torch.

9. *Mr. Rick . . . Mrs. Rick*: Adolf Rick, born in Prussia *c.* 1846, naturalized US citizen, Wightman Brothers' manager at Butaritari from 1880 to 1891, when he joined the rival firm of Crawford and Company; Mrs Rick, German American.

10. *Jaluit*: Island in the Marshall Islands, visited by Stevenson in the *Janet Nicoll*, 19 and 26 June 1890.

11. *the forecastle*: The crew.

12. *the afterguard*: The officers.

13. *I regularly passed my evenings*: A photograph of Stevenson in the Sans Souci was published in Frank McLynn, *Robert Louis Stevenson: A Biography* (1993).

14. *one black sheep*: Possibly the 'beachcomber named Enry' mentioned in Lloyd's diary entry for 6 August 1889, but more probably 'that most degraded of beachcombers, Arthur Wise', recalled in Fanny's diary entry for 6 October 1890 (*Our Samoan Adventure*, 35).

15. *a recondite island insult*: If the 'black sheep' (see previous note) is Arthur Wise, this probably refers to the occasion recalled in Fanny's diary entry for 6 October 1890, when Wise, 'wishing to insult us, called out as we sat at table, "Do you know who that is you have got dining with you? *That man doesn't belong to this island!*" ' (*Our Samoan Adventure*, 35).

16. *the Fourth of July*: American Independence Day.

17. *man-of-war hammocks*: Made for Stevenson at Honolulu by the sailors of HMS *Cormorant*.

18. *Kalakaua and Mrs. Bishop*: David Kalakaua (1836–91), Stevenson's friend, the penultimate monarch of Hawaii, and Chiefess Bernice Pauahi Bishop, member of the Hawaiian royal family and wife of the American, C. R. Bishop.

19. *Merry-Andrews*: Buffoons.

20. *ebullition*: Outburst, effervescence.

21. *corded*: Ribbed with raised lines like cords.

22. *Lothian*: Region of south-east Scotland containing Edinburgh.

23. *a minister*: Probably Stevenson's maternal grandfather, Lewis Balfour (1777–1860), minister at Colinton, near Edinburgh.

24. *Esau . . . Jacob*: Sons of the patriarch Isaac, who was deceived when blind and dying by Jacob (supplanter), who disguised himself with goatskins as his elder brother Esau (hairy), so that Isaac said: 'The voice is Jacob's voice, but the hands are the hands of Esau' (Genesis 27:22).

CHAPTER IV: A TALE OF A *TAPU*

1. *'faery frigot'*: Enchanted boat, probably after the 'fairy frigate' in Scott's *Lady of the Lake* (1810), I.xxiv.

2. *the Grail*: In medieval legend and romance, the platter (or cup) used by Christ at the Last Supper.

3. *'din' . . . 'perandi'*: Gin . . . brandy.

4. *Kümmel*: A German liqueur flavoured with cumin.

5. *Flemish freedom . . . Flemish excess*: With reference to the Flemings' reputation for intoxication, as in 'this Flemish drunkard' (Shakespeare, *The Merry Wives of Windsor*, II.i.23).

6. *the Sepoy mutiny*: The Indian Mutiny of 1857–8.

7. *Rarotongan*: From Rarotonga in the Cook Islands.

8. *'din' and 'perandi'*: Stevenson here implies that imported European spirits are to blame for the fight between two women that he goes on to describe, but in his MS journal he says he was told the women 'have been drinking sour toddy', as Fanny also reports in her account of the same (or a similar) incident in *The Cruise of the Janet Nichol*.

9. *Mr. Rick, Mr. Osbourne, and Mrs. Stevenson*: And 'Mr Strong', according to the *Auckland Star* of 24 October 1891.

CHAPTER V: A TALE OF A *TAPU* – CONTINUED

1. *the warning signal*: Indicating the end of the curfew: 'the signal that the natives might go abroad' (MS journal).

2. *hard to be dislodged*: Contradicted (unusually) by the MS journal: 'We had never the least trouble in sending them about their business'.

3. *in vacuo*: In empty space.

4. *a Douglas of old*: A member of the Scottish noble family of Douglas, powerful and politically active in the 13th to 16th centuries.

5. *A trader on Tarawa*: The trader on the island of Tarawa in the Gilbert Islands is identified in the MS journal as a 'Mr Leonard'.

6. *Kirk Allowa'*: The church in Alloway, Scotland, where Tam sees mysterious lights and is frightened by warlocks and witches in Burns's poem 'Tam o' Shanter' (1791).

7. *my beard was sometimes on my shoulder*: 'With the beard on the shoulder', watchful, wary, is quoted as a Spanish proverb in Scott's *Peveril of the Peak* (1822), I, 156.

8. *potent*: Crutch, support.

9. *Wednesday, July 24*: Perhaps in error for 'Thursday, July 25', but the narrative of 'A Tale of a *Tapu*' and the chronology of the journal are in tension at this point.

10. *a brief testimony . . . in a pigeon-hole at Washington*: Rick's petition and a copy of Stevenson's brief testimony are reprinted from the US National Archives in Washington in H. E. Maude, 'Two Letters of Robert Louis Stevenson', *Journal of Pacific History*, II (1967), 184–6. Stevenson's holograph MS is published in *Letters*, VI, 326–7.

CHAPTER VI: THE FIVE DAYS' FESTIVAL

1. *the ictus of the measure*: The accented beat of the bar.

2. *the Thespian model*: The 6th-century BC poet Thespis was credited by Aristotle with transforming choral performance into drama.

3. *the eastern islands*: Of the Pacific.

4. *George the trader*: Identified in the MS journal as 'Rick's man'.

5. *the Black Douglas*: The Black Douglas and the Red Douglas were two branches of the Scottish family of Douglas referred to in the previous chapter (see Part III, Ch. V, note 4).

6. *the Red Douglas*: See previous note.

7. *Scripture slides*: At Honolulu the missionary Francis Damon had lent

Stevenson a set of slides (for the magic lantern) depicting the life of Christ.

8. *(like Adam) mingling caresses with his lecture*: In Milton's *Paradise Lost* (1667).

9. *our return afterwards*: The *Equator* revisited Butaritari, 30 October to 4 November 1889.

10. *the ass with the lion's skin*: Alluding to the fable of an ass that disguised itself in a lion's skin but was given away by its braying.

11. *holoku*: The loose-fitting 'Mother Hubbard' dress introduced by the missionaries.

12. *a certain thriftless loafer of a white*: Identified in the MS journal as 'Joe'.

13. *the mate of a wrecked schooner*: Identified in the MS journal as 'Dick Tomlinson'.

CHAPTER VII: HUSBAND AND WIFE

1. *Lothario*: A seducer, after the character of that name in Nicholas Rowe's play *The Fair Penitent* (1703).

2. *a trader*: Identified in the MS journal as 'Mr Leonard'.

3. *'married for one night'*: The factual basis for the marriage certificate in Stevenson's story 'The Beach of Falesá' which read 'for one night' in Stevenson's manuscript but 'for one week' when it was published in *Island Nights' Entertainments* (1893).

4. *a hall Bible*: A large family Bible.

5. *i kana kim*: Translated in the MS journal as 'je mange le cul à'.

6. *a common vulgar insult in Great Britain to this day*: Kiss my arse?

7. *a trader*: Identified in the MS journal as 'Mr Benson'.

8. *Another white*: Identified in the MS journal only as 'a Scotchman'.

9. *Nei Takauti and Nan Tok'*: Photographs of the couple were published by Fanny in *The Cruise of the 'Janet Nichol'*. Nei Takauti appears on the cover of this Penguin Classics edition.

10. *she soon perceived a man and woman watching her*: Fanny gives an account of her encounter with Nei Takauti and Nan Tok' in *The Cruise of the 'Janet Nichol'*.

PART IV: THE GILBERTS − APEMAMA

CHAPTER I: THE KING OF APEMAMA: THE ROYAL TRADER

1. *only one white on Apemama*: Stevenson calls him 'a silent, sober, solitary, niggardly recluse' in Part IV, Ch. II, and Fanny calls him 'Johnny, an inoffensive, dying "poor white"', but Arthur Grimble, who succeeded him in 1917 as British District Officer on Abemama, knew him as George McGhee Murdoch. Tem Binoka's cousin told Grimble that Murdoch, a consumptive Scot, had been instrumental in persuading Tem Binoka to grant Stevenson permission to stay on Abemama. (Fanny Stevenson, *The Cruise of the 'Janet Nichol'*, 125, and see Arthur Grimble, *A Pattern of Islands* (London, 1952), 177.)

2. *Gorgon*: Terrible monster of Greek myth.

3. *Maiana . . . Nonuti*: Islands neighbouring Abemama.

4. *A British warship*: HMS *Dart* investigated and checked Binoka's colonial adventure.

5. *Mariki . . . Nonuti . . . Tapituea*: Islands in the Gilberts north-west and south-east of Abemama.

6. *Peru*: (Or Beru) island in the Gilberts south-east of Abemama.

7. *the Calendar's pilot . . . the 'black mountains'*: In the story in the *Arabian Nights' Entertainments* of the third calender (a 'calender' – the usual spelling – is a mendicant dervish), the pilot of the calender's ship is distraught at the prospect of a 'black mountain' with an irresistible magnetic force.

8. *a year later . . . on board the 'Janet Nicoll'*: Fanny gives an account of the Beru itinerants, encountered again in July 1890, in *The Cruise of the 'Janet Nichol'*.

9. *Sunday, September 1st*: According to Lloyd's diary, the *Equator* 'Made the island of Apamama at 9.30 in the morning' of Friday 30 August and he 'Slept ashore' on Saturday 31 August.

10. *chandlery*: Goods sold by a specialist retailer, in this case a ship-chandler.

11. *pratique*: Permission to a ship to trade or deal with a port.

12. *his extraordinary natural means for the theatre*: A photograph was published in Alexandra Lapierre, *Fanny Stevenson: entre passion et liberté* (Paris, 1993).

13. *Dante's in the mask*: The mask of Dante Alighieri in the Palazzo Vecchio, Florence.

14. *Sir Charles Grandison*: The hero of Samuel Richardson's novel *Sir Charles Grandison* (1754).

15. *a figure out of Hoffmann*: A character from the fantastic tales of the German Romantic author, Ernst Hoffmann (1776–1822).

16. *Aranuka . . . Kuria*: Satellite islands of Abemama.

17. *outches*: Houses.

18. *peculium*: Private property.

19. *supercargoes*: Ships' officers responsible for cargo and commercial transactions.

20. *a certain merchant*: Harry Henderson of the firm that had chartered the *Janet Nicoll*, if Stevenson is referring to the incident described by Fanny in *The Cruise of the 'Janet Nichol'*, 129–38.

21. *Tuppoti*: Suppose.

CHAPTER II: THE KING OF APEMAMA: FOUNDATION OF
EQUATOR TOWN

1. *'Beach de Mar'*: The Pacific lingua franca called 'Beach-la-Mar' in Part I, Ch. II.

2. *gammon*: Humbug.

3. *Findlay*: Alexander G. Findlay, *A Directory for the Navigation of the North Pacific Ocean* (London, 1886).

4. *Mr. Osbourne landed*: In the *Auckland Star* of 19 December 1891, 'Mr Strong' also landed.

5. *dandy*: A sloop or cutter with a jigger-mast abaft.

6. *Amphion*: The music of his lyre, according to Greek myth, drew the stones of the walls of Thebes into place.

7. *the place*: There is a photograph of Equator Town in *The Cruise of the Janet Nichol'*.

8. *some of the party would be away sketching*: The *Auckland Star* instalment of 19 December 1891 reads instead: 'Mr Strong would be away sketching'.

9. *a novel*: Stevenson and Osbourne's *The Wrecker* (1892). Lloyd's diary entry for 22 September 1889 records that ' "The Wrecker" makes substantial daily progress'.

10. *Gibbon and Carlyle*: According to Margaret Stevenson's diary, they 'began to read aloud Gibbon's *Decline and Fall*' (*The History of the Decline and Fall of the Roman Empire* (1776–88)) on 5 July 1888, while sailing to the Marquesas in the *Casco* ('Notes about Robert Louis Stevenson from his Mother's Diary', *Miscellanea, Works*, Vailima Edition, XXVI (1923), 362). Lloyd's diary specifies 'Carlyle's French Revolution' (*The French Revolution: A History* (1837)) in his entry for 22 September 1889.

11. *flageolets*: Small wind instruments of the flute family.

12. *plague . . . of Egypt*: The plague of flies described in Exodus 8:21–4.

CHAPTER III: THE KING OF APEMAMA: THE PALACE OF
MANY WOMEN

1. *Rubam . . . promoted on my last visit*: Otherwise Roboam, whose new status at the time of the *Janet Nicoll* visit – and aspiration to escape Abemama – are recorded by Fanny in *The Cruise of the Janet Nichol'*.

2. *Samuel Richardson*: The novelist Samuel Richardson (1689–1761) was at the centre of a circle of admiring young ladies.

3. *seraglio*: Harem.

4. *Amazon*: One of a tribe of warlike women of Greek myth.

CHAPTER IV: THE KING OF APEMAMA: EQUATOR TOWN AND THE PALACE

1. *Uncle Parker*: Encountered again on the *Janet Nicoll* voyage (see *The Cruise of the 'Janet Nichol'*, 140, 165).

2. *Guttersnipe*: Encountered again on the *Janet Nicoll* voyage (see *The Cruise of the 'Janet Nichol'*, 164).

3. *Quatre-Vingt-Treize*: Novel by Victor Hugo, published 1874, about the Royalist risings after the French Revolution, with many ironies of the kind Stevenson mentions.

4. *'Carnival of Venice'* . . . *'The Ploughboy'*: An Italian tune arranged and popularized by Paganini (1782–1840); an Irish and English folk-song, popularized in a version with music by William Shield (1748–1829) and words by John O'Keeffe (1747–1833).

5. *Mr. Barlow* . . . *Sandford*: The tutor and a pupil in Thomas Day's didactic children's book, *The History of Sandford and Merton* (1783–9).

6. *Captain Cook*: James Cook (1728–79), the Pacific voyager.

7. *Mr. Stephen's Dictionary*: Leslie Stephen (1832–1904), editor 1882–91 of *The Dictionary of National Biography*.

8. *Paul* . . . *Festus* . . . *Alexander*: Paul, the apostle; Festus, the procurator of Judaea who heard Paul's case; Alexander, a coppersmith mentioned by Paul (see Acts 25; II Timothy 4:14).

CHAPTER V: KING AND COMMONS

1. *greetin'* . . . *parritch*: Crying . . . porridge.

2. *Upolu*: The Samoan island on which Stevenson lived and died.

3. *dryads*: Wood-nymphs of Greek myth.

4. *there was a brother once in Arden*: In Shakespeare's *As You Like It* (*c.* 1599) a usurper rules in place of the rightful duke, his brother, who lives in the forest of Arden.

5. *andantes and adagios*: Pieces of music in moderately slow and slow tempi.

6. *'Olalla'*: Stevenson's story was first published in 1885 and subsequently collected in *The Merry Men* (1887).

7. *Braxfield*: Robert Macqueen, Lord Braxfield (1722–99), eminent Scottish judge on whom Stevenson based the character of Adam Weir, Lord Hermiston, in his unfinished novel *Weir of Hermiston* (1896).

8. *'grumbletonians'*: Members of the 'country' party in English politics after 1689, supposedly motivated by personal ambition.

9. *capsized at sea*: Fanny gives an account derived from a survivor in *The Cruise of the Janet Nichol'*.

10. *Richard was himself again*: Alluding to King Richard's words, 'Richard's himself again', in Colly Cibber's adaptation (1700) of Shakespeare's *Richard III*.

11. *our return to Butaritari*: After collecting Stevenson's party from Abemama, the *Equator* returned to Butaritari, anchoring there 30 October 1889.

12. *the becalmed 'Equator' off Mariki*: On the return voyage from Abemama to Butaritari, the *Equator* was becalmed off the island of Mariki (or Marakei) on 27 October 1889.

13. *O si sic omnes!*: O that all were thus.

CHAPTER VI: THE KING OF APEMAMA: DEVIL-WORK

1. *piscina*: A stone church basin.

2. *al fresco*: In the open air.

3. *Apaiang*: (Or Abaiang) island in the Gilbert Islands where the *Equator* spent 21–5 August 1889, on the passage between Butaritari and Abemama.

4. *Mr. Bingham*: Hiram Bingham (1831–1908), American Protestant missionary in charge of the station established at Abaiang in 1857.

5. *Our experience of Devil-work at Apaiang*: Stevenson gives another description of this experience at Abaiang on 24 August 1889 in a letter written to Sidney Colvin from Abemama (see *Letters*, VI, 329–30).

6. *Sidney Colvin*: (1845–1927) friend, mentor and editor of Stevenson, and Keeper of the Department of Prints and Drawings at the British Museum, 1884–1912.

7. *ex voto*: Because of a vow.

8. *famulus*: An attendant, particularly on a scholar or magician.

9. *suffumigation*: Fumigation from below.

10. *one of our party*: In the *Auckland Star* of 10 October 1891, 'Mr Strong'.

11. *Ave, Caesar!*: 'Ave Caesar, morituri te salutant', 'Hail Caesar, those who are about to die salute you' (the gladiators' address to the Emperor when they entered the arena).

12. *Facetiae*: Witticisms.

13. *Lillie Bridge*: Near the home of Andrew Lang, to whom the box was sent.

CHAPTER VII: THE KING OF APEMAMA

1. *Bourbon*: A member of the old royal family of France.

2. *Teñkoruti, the grandfather of Tembinok'*: The succession of the High Chiefs of Abemama is as follows: Teng Karotu retired in the 1840s and was succeeded by his son Ten Tawaia, who was succeeded *c.* 1850 by his son (or half-brother), Tem Baiteke, who retired in 1878 and was succeeded by his son, Tem Binoka (see H. E. Maude, 'Baiteke and Binoka of Abemama', in J. W. Davidson and Deryck Scarr, ed., *Pacific Island Portraits* (1976), 201–24).

3. *Caius Marcius*: Coriolanus (5th century BC), legendary Roman (and Shakespearian) military hero.

4. *A.*: Identified in the MS journal as 'Captain Reid of the Equator'.

5. *Aramis*: One of the dashing heroes of *Les Trois Mousquetaires* (1844) by Alexandre Dumas.

6. *Mr. Osbourne*: Actually Joe Strong, as in the MS journal and the *Auckland Star* of 17 October 1891, which reads ' "Sit down, Stlong" '. The ' "boy he good man" ' Tem Binoka mentions is Lloyd Osbourne.

7. *two corselets . . . a third*: The three corselets were sold in 1914 by Belle Strong, Stevenson's stepdaughter, and are illustrated in the sales catalogue.

EMENDATIONS

The following is a complete list of the substantive emendations made to the text of the Edinburgh Edition of *In the South Seas* (1896) for the present edition. The sources of emendations are indicated as follows: MS = Stevenson's MS journals of his cruises in the *Casco* and the *Equator* (HM 2412, Huntington Library, San Marino, California); BW = *Black and White*; AS = *Auckland Star*.

PENGUIN TEXT	EDINBURGH EDITION
6 20th of July (MS)	28th of July
40 Siméon Delmas (MS)	Siméon Delmar
41, 50, 88, 90, 91 *tuhuka* (MS)	Tahuku
63 Mrs. Fisher (MS)	Miss Fisher
67 Tha' (MS)	Ma'
70 to eat a man's flesh (MS, BW)	to cut a man's flesh
82 a piece of *tapa* (MS)	a piece of tapu
109 for either Takaroa or Takapoto (MS, BW)	for either Takaroa
111 He had had enough of night (MS)	He had enough of night
114 the reef carried an islet (MS, BW)	the reef carried an inlet
115 We landed and walked long. (BW)	[omitted]
124 fol-de-rol (BW)	tol-de-rol
158 lay in a rack (MS)	lay on a rock
161 between the masts (MS, AS)	between the mats
176 under the lych-house (MS, AS)	under the king's house
185 not to be sold (MS, AS)	not to be used
188 and make the polysyllabic Williams (AS)	and with the polysyllabic Williams,

PENGUIN TEXT	EDINBURGH EDITION
188 barrel-hoop (AS)	barrel-hoops
193 Kamaunaue (MS, AS)	Kamaunave
194 these fled (MS, AS)	three fled
195 Kamaunaue (MS, AS)	Kamaunava
196 mimed (MS, AS)	mixed
201 hall Bible (AS)	Hall Bible
203 our week (AS)	one week
219 Fire smouldered (MS)	Fire surrounded
240 *J. L. Tiernan* (MS)	*H. L. Haseltine*
253 conquest of Kuria and Aranuka (MS)	conquest of Apemama

Visit Penguin on the Internet
and browse at your leisure

- preview sample extracts of our forthcoming books
- read about your favourite authors
- investigate over 10,000 titles
- enter one of our literary quizzes
- win some fantastic prizes in our competitions
- e-mail us with your comments and book reviews
- instantly order any Penguin book

and masses more!

'To be recommended without reservation ... a rich and rewarding on-line experience' – Internet Magazine

www.penguin.co.uk

READ MORE IN PENGUIN

In every corner of the world, on every subject under the sun, Penguin represents quality and variety – the very best in publishing today.

For complete information about books available from Penguin – including Puffins, Penguin Classics and Arkana – and how to order them, write to us at the appropriate address below. Please note that for copyright reasons the selection of books varies from country to country.

In the United Kingdom: Please write to *Dept. EP, Penguin Books Ltd, Bath Road, Harmondsworth, West Drayton, Middlesex UB7 ODA*

In the United States: Please write to *Consumer Sales, Penguin Putnam Inc., P.O. Box 999, Dept. 17109, Bergenfield, New Jersey 07621-0120*. VISA and MasterCard holders call 1-800-253-6476 to order Penguin titles

In Canada: Please write to *Penguin Books Canada Ltd, 10 Alcorn Avenue, Suite 300, Toronto, Ontario M4V 3B2*

In Australia: Please write to *Penguin Books Australia Ltd, P.O. Box 257, Ringwood, Victoria 3134*

In New Zealand: Please write to *Penguin Books (NZ) Ltd, Private Bag 102902, North Shore Mail Centre, Auckland 10*

In India: Please write to *Penguin Books India Pvt Ltd, 210 Chiranjiv Tower, 43 Nehru Place, New Delhi 110 019*

In the Netherlands: Please write to *Penguin Books Netherlands bv, Postbus 3507, NL-1001 AH Amsterdam*

In Germany: Please write to *Penguin Books Deutschland GmbH, Metzlerstrasse 26, 60594 Frankfurt am Main*

In Spain: Please write to *Penguin Books S. A., Bravo Murillo 19, 1° B, 28015 Madrid*

In Italy: Please write to *Penguin Italia s.r.l., Via Benedetto Croce 2, 20094 Corsico, Milano*

In France: Please write to *Penguin France, Le Carré Wilson, 62 rue Benjamin Baillaud, 31500 Toulouse*

In Japan: Please write to *Penguin Books Japan Ltd, Kaneko Building, 2-3-25 Koraku, Bunkyo-Ku, Tokyo 112*

In South Africa: Please write to *Penguin Books South Africa (Pty) Ltd, Private Bag X14, Parkview, 2122 Johannesburg*

READ MORE IN PENGUIN

A CHOICE OF CLASSICS

Francis Bacon	**The Essays**
Aphra Behn	**Love-Letters between a Nobleman and His Sister**
	Oroonoko, The Rover and Other Works
George Berkeley	**Principles of Human Knowledge/Three Dialogues between Hylas and Philonous**
James Boswell	**The Life of Samuel Johnson**
Sir Thomas Browne	**The Major Works**
John Bunyan	**The Pilgrim's Progress**
Edmund Burke	**Reflections on the Revolution in France**
Frances Burney	**Evelina**
Margaret Cavendish	**The Blazing World and Other Writings**
William Cobbett	**Rural Rides**
William Congreve	**Comedies**
Thomas de Quincey	**Confessions of an English Opium Eater**
	Recollections of the Lakes and the Lake Poets
Daniel Defoe	**A Journal of the Plague Year**
	Moll Flanders
	Robinson Crusoe
	Roxana
	A Tour Through the Whole Island of Great Britain
Henry Fielding	**Amelia**
	Jonathan Wild
	Joseph Andrews
	The Journal of a Voyage to Lisbon
	Tom Jones
John Gay	**The Beggar's Opera**
Oliver Goldsmith	**The Vicar of Wakefield**
Lady Gregory	**Selected Writings**

A CHOICE OF CLASSICS

William Hazlitt	**Selected Writings**
George Herbert	**The Complete English Poems**
Thomas Hobbes	**Leviathan**
Samuel Johnson/	
James Boswell	**A Journey to the Western Islands of Scotland** and **The Journal of a Tour of the Hebrides**
Charles Lamb	**Selected Prose**
George Meredith	**The Egoist**
Thomas Middleton	**Five Plays**
John Milton	**Paradise Lost**
Samuel Richardson	**Clarissa**
	Pamela
Earl of Rochester	**Complete Works**
Richard Brinsley	
Sheridan	**The School for Scandal and Other Plays**
Sir Philip Sidney	**Selected Poems**
Christopher Smart	**Selected Poems**
Adam Smith	**The Wealth of Nations (Books I–III)**
Tobias Smollett	**The Adventures of Ferdinand Count Fathom**
	Humphrey Clinker
	Roderick Random
Laurence Sterne	**The Life and Opinions of Tristram Shandy**
	A Sentimental Journey Through France and Italy
Jonathan Swift	**Gulliver's Travels**
	Selected Poems
Thomas Traherne	**Selected Poems and Prose**
Henry Vaughan	**Complete Poems**

READ MORE IN PENGUIN

A CHOICE OF CLASSICS

Matthew Arnold	**Selected Prose**
Jane Austen	**Emma**
	Lady Susan/The Watsons/Sanditon
	Mansfield Park
	Northanger Abbey
	Persuasion
	Pride and Prejudice
	Sense and Sensibility
William Barnes	**Selected Poems**
Anne Brontë	**Agnes Grey**
	The Tenant of Wildfell Hall
Charlotte Brontë	**Jane Eyre**
	Shirley
	Villette
Emily Brontë	**Wuthering Heights**
Samuel Butler	**Erewhon**
	The Way of All Flesh
Lord Byron	**Selected Poems**
Thomas Carlyle	**Selected Writings**
Arthur Hugh Clough	**Selected Poems**
Wilkie Collins	**Armadale**
	The Moonstone
	No Name
	The Woman in White
Charles Darwin	**The Origin of Species**
	Voyage of the *Beagle*
Benjamin Disraeli	**Sybil**
George Eliot	**Adam Bede**
	Daniel Deronda
	Felix Holt
	Middlemarch
	The Mill on the Floss
	Romola
	Scenes of Clerical Life
	Silas Marner

READ MORE IN PENGUIN

A CHOICE OF CLASSICS

Charles Dickens	**American Notes for General Circulation**
	Barnaby Rudge
	Bleak House
	The Christmas Books (in two volumes)
	David Copperfield
	Dombey and Son
	Great Expectations
	Hard Times
	Little Dorrit
	Martin Chuzzlewit
	The Mystery of Edwin Drood
	Nicholas Nickleby
	The Old Curiosity Shop
	Oliver Twist
	Our Mutual Friend
	The Pickwick Papers
	Selected Short Fiction
	A Tale of Two Cities
Elizabeth Gaskell	**Cranford/Cousin Phillis**
	The Life of Charlotte Brontë
	Mary Barton
	North and South
	Ruth
	Sylvia's Lovers
	Wives and Daughters
Edward Gibbon	**The Decline and Fall of the Roman Empire** (in three volumes)
George Gissing	**New Grub Street**
	The Odd Women
William Godwin	**Caleb Williams**

READ MORE IN PENGUIN

A CHOICE OF CLASSICS

Thomas Hardy	**Desperate Remedies**
	The Distracted Preacher and Other Tales
	Far from the Madding Crowd
	Jude the Obscure
	The Hand of Ethelberta
	A Laodicean
	The Mayor of Casterbridge
	A Pair of Blue Eyes
	The Return of the Native
	Selected Poems
	Tess of the d'Urbervilles
	The Trumpet-Major
	Two on a Tower
	Under the Greenwood Tree
	The Well-Beloved
	The Woodlanders
Lord Macaulay	**The History of England**
Henry Mayhew	**London Labour and the London Poor**
John Stuart Mill	**The Autobiography**
	On Liberty
William Morris	**News from Nowhere** and **Other Writings**
John Henry Newman	**Apologia Pro Vita Sua**
Robert Owen	**A New View of Society and Other Writings**
Walter Pater	**Marius the Epicurean**
John Ruskin	**Unto This Last and Other Writings**
Walter Scott	**Ivanhoe**
	Heart of Mid-Lothian
	Old Mortality
	Rob Roy
	Waverley

READ MORE IN PENGUIN

A CHOICE OF CLASSICS

Robert Louis Stevenson	**Kidnapped**
	Dr Jekyll and Mr Hyde and Other Stories
	The Master of Ballantrae
	Weir of Hermiston
William Makepeace Thackeray	**The History of Henry Esmond**
	The History of Pendennis
	The Newcomes
	Vanity Fair
Anthony Trollope	**An Autobiography**
	Barchester Towers
	Can You Forgive Her?
	The Duke's Children
	The Eustace Diamonds
	Framley Parsonage
	He Knew He Was Right
	The Last Chronicle of Barset
	Phineas Finn
	The Prime Minister
	Rachel Ray
	The Small House at Allington
	The Warden
	The Way We Live Now
Oscar Wilde	**Complete Short Fiction**
	De Profundis and Other Writings
	The Picture of Dorian Gray
Mary Wollstonecraft	**A Vindication of the Rights of Woman**
	Mary and **Maria** (includes Mary Shelley's **Matilda**)
Dorothy and William Wordsworth	**Home at Grasmere**